CHRIST AND
HIS BENEFITS

ARLAND J. HULTGREN

CHRIST AND HIS BENEFITS

Christology and Redemption in the New Testament

FORTRESS PRESS   **PHILADELPHIA**

Library of Congress Cataloging-in-Publication Data

Hultgren, Arland J.
  Christ and His benefits.

  Includes indexes.
  1. Jesus Christ—History of doctrines—Early church, ca. 30-600. 2. Jesus Christ—Person and offices—Biblical teaching. 3. Salvation—Biblical teaching. 4. Bible. N.T.—Theology. I. Title.
  BT198.H84 1987   232'.3'09015   86–45917
  ISBN 0–8006–0861–5

2657J86 Printed in the United States of America 1–861

To my mother
Ina L. Hultgren
and in memory of my father
Arnold E. Hultgren

Contents

Contents

Preface

HOWEVER ELSE IT may be described, Christianity is a religion of redemption. Its foundational documents, the books of the New Testament, portray Jesus of Nazareth in his role as the Christ primarily as a redemptive figure. The ways they do that constitute the subject of this book.

The portrayal of Jesus as a redemptive figure is certainly a major, if not the central, theme of the entire New Testament. Therefore it is strange that it has not been given attention in contemporary scholarship. There are probably several reasons for this neglect, but whatever these might be, it seems that an attempt should be made to fill the void. The subject is of crucial importance for the study of New Testament theology, for systematic theology, and for teaching and proclamation in the church.

The book was written during a sabbatical at the University of Cambridge in England during the 1984–85 academic year. Cheerful and grateful appreciation is extended to persons and institutions involved in making that time of research and writing possible. Thanks are extended particularly to the president and board of directors of Luther Northwestern Theological Seminary for granting the sabbatical and to Lutheran Brotherhood for providing funding through its seminary faculty sabbatical support program. Thanks are also extended to various institutions in Cambridge. I was granted access there to use the vast resources of the University Library and the libraries of the Divinity School and Westfield House. For the privileges and courtesies extended to me, I am grateful indeed.

It is a pleasure to extend thanks to some specific persons. I am indebted especially to Professor Reginald H. Fuller for valuable and substantive comments on the work, which prompted improvements in the final draft.

I also wish to thank John A. Hollar at Fortress Press for his suggestions and editing of the entire work. Thanks are due to two colleagues at Luther Northwestern Theological Seminary. Professor David L. Tiede read the entire manuscript and provided comments which proved to be helpful in strengthening the work here and there. Professor Lee E. Snook has listened to much of what I have to say in this book, since he and I have taught a course together on christology. I have learned from his observations as well as his own lectures on christology from the point of view of a systematic theologian. The encouragement that all of these persons have extended has been gratifying.

Long before my formal education, it was my parents who led me to an awareness of Christ and his benefits. They did so in the only way that would have worked in my case: with grace, without narrowness, and within a home and congregation that encouraged growth. The book is dedicated to my mother and to the fond memory of my father.

Luther Northwestern Theological Seminary   ARLAND J. HULTGREN
St. Paul, Minnesota

Abbreviations

ANCIENT SOURCES

Pseudepigrapha
Pss. of Sol.   Psalms of Solomon
Sib. Or.   Sibylline Oracles
T. Judah   Testament of Judah
T. Levi   Testament of Levi
T. Reuben   Testament of Reuben
T. Solomon   Testament of Solomon
Philo
Conf. ling.   *On the Confusion of Tongues (De Confusione Linguarum)*
De aetern. mundi   *On the Eternity of the World (De Aeternitate Mundi)*
Mut. nom.   *On the Change of Names (De Mutatione Nominum)*
Rer. div. her.   *Who Is the Heir (Quis Rerum Divinarum Heres)*

JOURNALS, REFERENCE WORKS, AND SERIALS

AB   Anchor Bible
ACNT   Augsburg Commentary on the New Testament
AGSU   Arbeiten zur Geschichte des Spätjudentums und Urchristentums
AnBib   Analecta Biblica
ASNU   Acta Seminarii Neotestamentici Upsaliensis

BAGD	W. Bauer, W.F. Arndt, and F.W. Gingrich, *A Greek-English Lexicon of the New Testament and Other Early Christian Literature*, 2d ed., rev. F.W. Gingrich and F.W. Danker (Chicago: Univ. of Chicago Press, 1979)
BDF	F. Blass, A. Debrunner, and R.W. Funk, *A Greek Grammar of the New Testament and Other Early Christian Literature* (Chicago: Univ. of Chicago Press, 1961)
BETL	Bibliotheca Ephemeridum Theologicarum Lovaniensium
BEvT	Beiträge zur evangelischen Theologie
BTS	Biblisch-theologische Studien
BZNW	Beihefte zur Zeitschrift für die neutestamentliche Wissenschaft
CBQ	*Catholic Biblical Quarterly*
CGTC	Cambridge Greek Testament Commentary
EBib	Études Bibliques
EKKNT	Evangelisch-katholischer Kommentar zum Neuen Testament
EvT	*Evangelische Theologie*
ExpTim	*Expository Times*
FBBS	Facet Books, Biblical Series
FRLANT	Forschungen zur Religion und Literatur des Alten und Neuen Testaments
HNT	Handbuch zum Neuen Testament
HNTC	Harper's New Testament Commentary
HTKNT	Herders theologischer Kommentar zum Neuen Testament
ICC	International Critical Commentary
Int	*Interpretation*
JB	Jerusalem Bible
JBL	*Journal of Biblical Literature*
JSNTSup	Journal for the Study of the New Testament Supplement Series
JTC	*Journal for Theology and the Church*
JTS	*Journal of Theological Studies*
KJV	King James Version
LCC	Library of Christian Classics
LCL	Loeb Classical Library
LXX	The Septuagint

MeyerK	Kritisch-exegetischer Kommentar über das Neue Testament ("Meyer Kommentar")
MNTC	Moffatt New Testament Commentary
NAB	New American Bible
NCB	New Century Bible
NEB	New English Bible
NICNT	New International Commentary on the New Testament
NIGTC	New International Greek Testament Commentary
NIV	New International Version
NovT	*Novum Testamentum*
NovTSup	Novum Testamentum, Supplements
NTAbh	Neutestamentliche Abhandlungen
NTD	Das Neue Testament Deutsch
NTS	*New Testament Studies*
NTTS	New Testament Tools and Studies
OTP	*The Old Testament Pseudepigrapha*, ed. James H. Charlesworth, 2 vols. (Garden City, N.Y.: Doubleday, 1983–84)
PC	Proclamation Commentaries
RNT	Regensburger Neues Testament
RSV	Revised Standard Version
SANT	Studien zum Alten und Neuen Testament
SBLDS	Society of Biblical Literature Dissertation Series
SBLMS	Society of Biblical Literature Monograph Series
SBLSBS	Society of Biblical Literature Sources for Biblical Study
SBLSPS	Society of Biblical Literature Seminar Papers Series
SBLTT	Society of Biblical Literature Texts and Translations
SBT	Studies in Biblical Theology
SHR	Studies in the History of Religion
SNT	Studien zum Neuen Testament
SNTSMS	Society for New Testament Studies Monograph Series
ST	*Studia Theologica*
Str-B	H. Strack and P. Billerbeck, *Kommentar zum Neuen Testament aus Talmud und Midrasch,* 6 vols. (Munich: C.H. Beck'sche, 1922–61)
SUNT	Studien zur Umwelt des Neuen Testaments
TB	Babylonian Talmud (Talmud Bavli)
TBC	Torch Bible Commentaries

TDNT	*Theological Dictionary of the New Testament,* ed. G. Kittel and G. Friedrich, 10 vols. (Grand Rapids: Wm. B. Eerdmans, 1964–76)
TEV	Today's English Version
THKNT	Theologischer Handkommentar zum Neuen Testament
TLZ	*Theologische Literaturzeitung*
TNTC	Tyndale New Testament Commentary
TRu	*Theologische Rundschau*
TS	*Theological Studies*
TU	Texte und Untersuchungen
WMANT	Wissenschaftliche Monographien zum Alten und Neuen Testament
WUNT	Wissenschaftliche Untersuchungen zum Neuen Testament
ZNW	*Zeitschrift für die neutestamentliche Wissenschaft*
ZTK	*Zeitschrift für Theologie und Kirche*

PART ONE

CHRISTOLOGY, REDEMPTION, AND REDEMPTIVE CHRISTOLOGY

1

To Know Christ and His Benefits

IN HIS *Loci Communes* of 1521, Philipp Melanchthon wrote his well-known statement: "This is to know Christ, [namely,] to know his benefits."[1] In the same paragraph he goes on to say, over against the scholastic theologians, that knowing Christ is not a matter of perceiving "his natures and the mode of his incarnation." Nor is knowing Christ achieved by an acquaintance with the historical or earthly Jesus. One can know Christ only in light of his redemptive work: "Unless one knows why Christ took upon himself human flesh and was crucified, what advantage would accrue from having learned his life's history?"

Melanchthon's aim was to cut through the speculative christology of the Christian tradition—yet without dispensing with it—in order to get at the soteriological meaning of Christ that was so essential to the Reformation. Reformation theology and proclamation emphasized the "for us," the *pro nobis,* character of the incarnation, death, and resurrection of Christ. Jesus Christ is to be understood as God's saving gift to humanity. Christology, as discourse about Christ, cannot be limited to ontology but must penetrate into the soteriological, or redemptive, work of Christ, for it is on the basis of the work of Christ—his "benefits"—that we know who he is (his person).

The study of the christology, or better, the christologies, of the New Testament in the present era has been a vigorous enterprise. Attention has been focused on three areas in particular: (1) the christological titles (Christ, Lord, Son of God, Son of Man, etc.); (2) the origins and developments of christology from the earliest times into the second century; and (3) the christologies of various New Testament writers (Paul, Mark, Hebrews, etc.). Yet relatively little has been done to investigate the christologies of the New Testament in conjunction with their redemptive

3

significance. That is in many respects surprising, for it is generally recognized that Christianity from its beginning is a "religion of redemption"
and that the christologies of the New Testament are expressions by
which—to a large degree, even if not solely—early Christians spoke of
how saving benefits have come into the world through Jesus Christ. In
consequence of his advent, life, death, and resurrection, there are saving
benefits for humanity which are not otherwise available. And it is in
consequence of speaking of these saving benefits that, in turn, the origins
and development of christology are given impetus. Christology can hardly
be thought to have developed in a speculative vacuum simply for its own
sake, going through an evolutionary process starting in the early part of
the New Testament era and extending to the Council of Chalcedon (A.D.
451). It developed rather through a process of seeking to explicate the
fullness of who Christ is in light of the benefits which he has secured
for humanity. What he has done, his function or work, gives rise to
questions of his person (ontological christology).

AIM OF THIS STUDY

The aim of this study is to investigate patterns of thought in the New
Testament concerning christology and redemption. Two basic questions
guide the discussion: How do the New Testament writers portray Christ
in his redemptive role? And what are the benefits which he brings and
which would not otherwise be available to humanity?

The fusion of questions regarding christology and redemption is appropriate and even necessary if one is to speak of either in the study of
the New Testament. Christological titles everywhere in the New Testament, christological formulations in creedal statements, and the christological portraits provided by the evangelists communicate that in Jesus
Christ the hopes and promises of divine salvation have been confirmed.
Christology is of course related to various themes in the New Testament,
including theology (the doctrine of God in the narrow sense), creation,
revelation, redemption, pneumatology, ecclesiology, the sacraments, eschatology, and so forth. It is a "nexus doctrine." But christology is not
related to all of these everywhere in the New Testament. For example,
the Gospel of Mark does not relate christology to creation; the Pastoral
Epistles allude to Baptism (Titus 3:5), but not to the Eucharist; and
Hebrews speaks of Christ in relationship to the Spirit in his own self-
offering (9:14), but it does not have a developed pneumatology in regard
to the Christian community. But christology and redemption are always
intertwined.[2] Without the connection, there would have been no interest
in either.

The major portion of this investigation is devoted to the ways in which the New Testament writers express christology and redemption, and a typology is proposed in chapter 4 concerning them. In its specifically christological aspects, this typology departs radically from prior approaches to the study of New Testament christology, and it is therefore necessary to state at the outset where this study can be located within the study of New Testament christology in general.

1. First, while the next two chapters deal with the question of how a redemptive significance came to be attached to Jesus, the major interest is directed toward christology and redemption in the actual books of the New Testament, considered in their historical contexts. In recent years some of the most engaging and instructive work in New Testament studies has been directed toward the christologies of the early communities which antedate the canonical texts. These include research into the christologies expressed in the so-called Q material,[3] early creeds and hymns,[4] pre-Pauline Christianity (that to which Paul was directly indebted),[5] early Hellenistic Jewish Christianity apart from Paul,[6] and so-called Jewish Christianity (which continued to observe ritual law and circumcision) from the Aramaic-speaking community in Jerusalem to the Ebionites of the second century.[7] It will be necessary to come to terms with research in these areas at the point at which investigators have drawn conclusions about how a redemptive significance came to be attached to Jesus (see chapters 2 and 3). But once that has been done, our focus will shift immediately to the books of the New Testament themselves. This means that a thoroughgoing historical approach, which would seek to construct a theory of how traditions developed along the various streams from the earliest times on into the books of the New Testament and even into the second century, is being set aside. But it is also a fruitful enterprise, and certainly a less conjectural one, to dispense with such an attempt and to investigate the New Testament books themselves in order to discern the emphases of their writers as they construe christology and redemption.

2. A second way to locate the approach taken here within contemporary study of New Testament christology is to indicate that the typology used in discussing christology and redemption in the writings of the New Testament does not conform to, nor does it depend upon, recent constructions of "patterns" in christology. These constructions have been expressed in two main ways. One way has been to speak of "understanding the *structure* of the New Testament christology as a whole, a way of seeing the *pattern* of its development."[8] This was the approach of John Knox, who traced the "pattern" of development from an original "adoptionism" through "kenoticism" and on to "incarnationalism."[9] The other main way has been to speak of christological patterns to be found in

major strata of the tradition: early Palestinian Christianity, Hellenistic Jewish Christianity, and Hellenistic gentile Christianity. This was the approach of Reginald H. Fuller.[10] Departing from these approaches to christological patterns in favor of another does not imply that these approaches are thereby judged to be inadequate. The departure simply follows from a shift in focus. The approaches of Knox and Fuller deal largely (but not exclusively) with developments prior to the writing of the canonical documents, tracing stages of development. The types (or patterns) discussed in this study (part 2) have to do with (1) christology *and* redemption as well as (2) their expression at the level of actual texts in the New Testament.

3. This study also falls outside that area of study which has received the greatest amount of attention, namely, research concerning the christological titles.[11] The titles used by the various writers will have to be recorded in the investigations, and the impact of contemporary title research will have to be given its due where appropriate. But in a study which seeks to hold christology and redemption together in unity the range of title usage and the statistics concerning them can be considered as only one ingredient. The various christological titles yield only aspects of the christologies of the New Testament era, not the christologies themselves.[12] Nor can christologies be labeled by titles, as though each title gives expression to a distinct christology over against others. Moreover, it is quite possible that the early communities did not attach as much importance to titles as the scholarship itself suggests. Barnabas Lindars, for example, has called into question the view that a primitive "Son of man christology" ever existed as a dominating christology in any community.[13] The titles, it must be said, belong to the living language of the communities in their proclamation, worship, and mission.[14] None of the writers of the New Testament books adopted a single title as the normative prism by which to view all others or to define the meaning of Jesus.[15] Further, in a study of christology and redemption it is necessary to give attention to how the writers portray Jesus as a redemptive figure beyond their use of titles: in narrative (as in the case of the Gospels), through sustained treatment of his work (as often in the Epistles), by the incorporation of creedal, confessional, and hymnic materials, and in exhortations which point the way to how one should live on the basis of what Christ (or God in Christ) has done. The matter has been put crisply by H. R. Balz: "title christology cannot grasp the totality of New Testament soteriology."[16]

4. Finally, this study does not concern itself explicitly with the question with which many are preoccupied today, particularly but not exclusively in British scholarship and debate, namely, the question of how one can

speak of Christ as God incarnate, or as the preexistent Son of God who has become incarnate, in light of the New Testament.[17] At one point, however, we cannot avoid engaging such studies, and that is where it will be asserted in our discussion that various writers affirm the preexistence of Christ. One of the most significant books in this field is James D. G. Dunn's *Christology in the Making,* which concludes that it is only in the Fourth Gospel that one can speak of "a full blown conception of Christ's personal pre-existence and a clear doctrine of incarnation."[18] In this judgment—when all the elements of the statement are included—Dunn is undoubtedly correct. And he is also correct, in our view, to conclude that "the most immediate antecedent to the doctrine of the incarnation" can be found in wisdom christology.[19] But it seems that he is too rigid in denying a concept of preexistence in places where, on the basis of a broader definition, it most obviously occurs. For example, he concludes that Paul did not think in terms of Christ's preexistence,[20] and he does so after careful work with all the major texts which appear to commend it (e.g., Rom. 8:3; 1 Cor. 8:6; 15:47; 2 Cor. 8:9; Gal. 4:4; and Phil. 2:6–11). But the problem is with Dunn's use of the term preexistence. Preexistence, for him, appears to signify the existence of a personal being who is with God, but distinct from God, prior to an incarnation.[21] That is strikingly Johannine in formulation, however, and if that is what the concept must mean, the result is that, of course, it will be found only in the Johannine literature. But the concept need not be so narrowly defined. As Dunn himself grants, the concept of preexistence is related to, and dependent upon, wisdom traditions in the Old Testament and intertestamental Judaism.[22] But in his analysis of such material he sees only two possibilities: Wisdom had to be understood either as "a divine being . . . independent of Yahweh" or as "a personification, . . . a way of speaking about God himself."[23] The first is rejected, as it should be, and the second is accepted. But a third view is possible, and that is to recognize that Wisdom came to be considered not only a personification of God's activities but also, without becoming a second divine being, an agent of God in creation and revelation (Prov. 8:1–21; Wisd. of Sol. 7:22–24; 8:3–4; 9:2)[24]—and even in redemption: "she brought [the people of Israel] over the Red Sea, and led them through the deep waters; but she drowned their enemies" (Wisd. of Sol. 10:18–19). To speak in such ways about Wisdom is not to speak in the same manner as those biblical writers who could say, for example, that the arm or hand of God has done a mighty deed (as in Ps. 98:1, "His right hand and his holy arm have gotten him victory"). We are at a stage removed from anthropomorphic expressions used in reference to God, so that Wisdom is a divine agent—without becoming an independent divine being, however subtle that may appear.

7

And on that basis, even if Paul and other writers of the New Testament do not develop the concept as fully as the Fourth Gospel does, they could speak of Christ as preexistent, signifying that the origins and redemptive work of Christ are located in the being of God himself, so that one can confess that Christ is the one sent by God for a redemptive purpose.[25] This implies a concept of preexistence, even if it does not measure up to criteria derived from the Gospel of John.

The investigation of christology and redemption—Christ and his benefits—at the level of the New Testament writings has to proceed on a course that has not been charted previously. How to proceed is itself a major problem. To go from the literary works of one author to another, by following either the sequence of the canon or the probable historical sequence of the writers, would not be salutary, for the results would be either a collage of impressions (especially if we were to follow the sequence of the canon) or an impression of historical, straight-line developments (following the probably historical sequence), and that would be a false impression, as subsequent chapters will show (particularly chapter 9). The procedure followed here is to gather the various writings under four major types of expression, which are identified in chapter 4. The types are rather broadly conceived, allowing for the particular emphases of the various writers within them to be heard.

Whether the typology is successful may itself be an issue. But the intent of the study is to expose and explore the ways in which christology and redemption are given expression throughout the New Testament. The rise of the Christian movement and the production of its writings can only be accounted for because there were persons who claimed and proclaimed that certain benefits follow for humanity, or even the whole cosmos, in consequence of the life, death, and resurrection of Jesus of Nazareth, and that these benefits would not exist otherwise. It is difficult to imagine that anyone would have become or remained a participant in the Christian movement, or in any of its communities, unless such a person saw a door opened into a new world as a consequence of the "Christ event." Certain benefits were seen to come exclusively from Christ, and to discern the ways in which these were conceived is to approach the vital impulses which gave rise to Christianity and sustained it throughout the New Testament era.

"REDEMPTION" AND "REDEMPTIVE CHRISTOLOGY" AS CATEGORIES

What language can one use to speak of the work of Christ in general and of Christ and his work as a unity? The terms should be applicable throughout the New Testament, and they should be terse, a kind of shorthand. The terms adopted here are "redemption" and "redemptive christology," and both call for comment.

The term "redemption" is familiar, and that commends its use, but it is not actually used universally in the New Testament to speak of the work of Christ. The two Greek nouns usually translated as "redemption" are *lytrōsis* and the compound *apolytrōsis,* and they actually appear only twelve times in soteriological contexts in the New Testament.[26] Two other nouns, usually translated as "ransom," are closely related *(lytron* and *antilytron),* and these are used on only three occasions.[27] Surprisingly, the term "redeemer" *(lytrōtēs)* is never used as a designation for Jesus;[28] it appears only once in the New Testament (Acts 7:35) in the speech of Stephen, and there it is applied to Moses, not Jesus. A review of verbs expressing the concept of redemption ("to redeem") fares no better. There are three verbs which can be translated "to redeem" *(lytrousthai, exagorazesthai,* and *hryesthai),* and these appear in soteriological contexts a total of thirteen times.[29] In terms of which authors use redemptive language specifically and which do not, the picture that emerges is this: it is used by Matthew, Mark, and Luke among the Gospels. It is used by the apostle Paul, who is taken in this study to be the author of seven letters for certain (Romans, 1 and 2 Corinthians, Galatians, Philippians, 1 Thessalonians, and Philemon); along with other interpreters, we shall consider the other letters of the Pauline corpus (2 Thessalonians, Colossians, Ephesians, 1 and 2 Timothy, and Titus) to be deutero-Pauline.[30] All of the deutero-Paulines, except 2 Thessalonians, use the terminology. In addition, it is found in Hebrews and 1 Peter. It is noticeably absent in all of the Johannine writings (the Gospel of John, 1, 2, and 3 John, and Revelation), nor does it appear in James, 2 Peter, and Jude.

The language of the New Testament concerning the work of Christ ranges far beyond the specifically "redemptive" terminology. It includes the nouns "salvation," "justification," and "reconciliation" and the corresponding verbs "to save," "to justify," and "to reconcile," as well as the phrases "to enter the kingdom" and "to have eternal life." In fact, the most commonly used terms are those which have to do with "salvation"— either using the noun *(sōtēria)* or the verb "to save" *(sōzō).* An examination of a concordance shows that every writer uses one or the other except the authors of Colossians and the Epistles of John (who can be distinguished from the author of the Fourth Gospel and Revelation).[31]

The fact of the matter is that a variety of terms is used by the various New Testament writers to speak of the work of Christ. No one term does justice to the variety. But a choice has to be made in spite of the risks. One could speak of christology and soteriology, for example, instead of christology and redemption. This would have the benefit of giving the Gospel of John its due in particular. But in the final analysis it would not be a gain. The concept of salvation has a more "subjective" nuance to it, signifying healing, well-being, peace, and eternal security which come to the believer in consequence of faith, whereas the concept of redemption has a more "objective" nuance, signifying the action of God or Christ for humanity which makes salvation possible. Since our interest in this study is fastened on the ways the writers speak of the beneficial consequences of Christ—what has now changed for the human situation—the term "redemption" is used throughout. Where nuances exist in the writings making "salvation" the appropriate term, these will have to be brought to light. It should be stressed then that the term "redemption" is used rather broadly in our study as a convenient shorthand to speak of the work of God in Christ, or Christ's work itself.

The other term used in the study is "redemptive christology." This term carries risks as well. Above all, it is a neologism, combining a qualifying adjective with the general term "christology." Yet it is not unusual to apply adjectives in this way. In the study of the christology of the New Testament (especially in light of developments after it) it has long been customary to speak, for example, of "functional christology" and "ontological christology."[32] Since our aim is to explore the ways the New Testament writers have portrayed Christ in terms of his redemptive significance for the world, the term coined here seems appropriate, even if it is new. An obvious problem with it is that, since it is new, it is impossible to show how our own views of "redemptive christology" would differ from those of other interpreters. We have to step out into unexplored territory; this course involves challenge and perhaps promise.

2

The Search for the Origins of Redemptive Christology in the Future Role of Christ

IT WILL BECOME clear in later chapters that all of the writers of the New Testament books consider the cross or the cross and resurrection of Jesus to have redemptive significance, even if they differ in how that is so. But it cannot be assumed that such an estimate existed from the very beginning of the Christian movement. Rudolf Bultmann, for example, has maintained that the earliest Christian community did not attach redemptive significance to the death and resurrection of Jesus. According to him, the early church shared the futuristic orientation of Jesus who proclaimed (1) the coming of the kingdom of God and, in Bultmann's view (which is not universally shared today), (2) the advent of the Son of Man as a messianic figure of the future. The resurrection of Jesus meant "no more than proof of the exaltation of the Crucified to Son of Man."[1] And "Jesus' importance as Messiah–Son-of-Man lies not at all," for the earliest community, "in what he did in the past, but entirely in what is expected of him in the future."[2] When the early church proclaimed Jesus as the Messiah, it proclaimed him *as the coming Messiah, in other words as Son of Man*. Not his *return* as Messiah, but his *coming* as Messiah was expected."[3] The proclamation of the cross or the cross and resurrection as the decisive event in redemption can be traced to an early time too, but not to the very beginnings of the Christian movement.[4] At the outset the cross and resurrection could be considered no more than a prelude to *the* redemptive event—which was considered to be in the future.

In recent years there have been three areas of study which have furthered this point of view. In each case interpreters have claimed that evidence exists in the New Testament that early Christians considered redemption as a gift of the future and that it would come with the advent of the Messiah, Lord, or Son of Man; the death or death and resurrection of Jesus was not yet considered to be redemptive. These areas of study include investigations into (1) a segment of the preaching of Peter in Acts, (2) the *maranatha* formula, and (3) the Q material. The last is particularly important, for it would provide evidence that the futuristic outlook persisted even beyond the earliest period of Christianity, since the Q material (in the view of those who subscribe to its existence in written form) would have been composed and used after the composition of creedal formulas (e.g., the pre-Pauline formula in 1 Cor. 15:3–7) which speak of the death or death and resurrection of Christ as redemptive, and its form of proclamation would have coexisted throughout the time of the Pauline mission. In terms of procedure, we shall first review the proposals arising out of these three areas of study, and then an assessment will be made.

THREE PROPOSALS

1. Peter's Sermon (Acts 3:12–26). It has been suggested by John A. T. Robinson that "the most primitive Christology of all" is reflected in Peter's sermon in Acts 3:12–26.[5] According to Robinson's proposal, Luke incorporated this sermon into Acts with only slight variations, the most important of these being the addition of the phrase "that his Christ should suffer" (3:18, "his" referring to God).[6] But once this Lucan "interpolation" is removed, the christological perspective is entirely future oriented. In this speech Peter speaks of Jesus as God's servant (3:13, 26) and prophet (3:22–23) who was killed by his enemies and raised by God. Then Peter goes on to say that his hearers should repent in order that the Lord "may send the Christ appointed for you, Jesus, whom heaven must receive until the time for establishing all that God spoke" through the prophets (3:19–21). According to Robinson, this speech betrays a primitive christology in which Jesus is not considered the Messiah in consequence of his resurrection, but rather as the servant of God and prophet, once killed and now vindicated, who will appear in the future as the Messiah at his coming. For now he is the "Christ-elect."[7] The present is a time of waiting for the Messiah's coming, who will be Jesus. It goes without saying that, if Robinson is correct, the death or death and resurrection of Jesus in this form of presentation would neither be "the eschatological event" nor redemptive for the earliest community.[8] The resurrection would be redemptive (as an act of deliverance) for Jesus only; as far as humanity is concerned, any redemptive work would be a future act of deliverance, the vindication of those who await his coming—the restored followers of Jesus and others who, through repentance, join them. Robinson goes on to maintain that this can be considered the most primitive christology of all by claiming that it continues the essential message of Jesus himself:

> Nothing is more natural than that the first Christology should have expressed the Gospel within the same frame of reference in which Jesus himself preached it—namely, that he had come among men as Servant of the Lord and Prophet of the end bringing the good news of God and the final call to repentance, but that all this was but in preparation for the act which would inaugurate the messianic rule of God and vindicate him as the Christ. Indeed, if we had not such a theology as that represented in Acts 3, we should almost be compelled to supply it.[9]

2. *Maranatha!* A second instance of an old tradition which may not have attached any redemptive significance to the death or death and resurrection of Jesus, but looked solely to the future as the time of redemption, is the Aramaic liturgical formula *maranatha* preserved in transliteration at 1 Cor. 16:22 and *Didache* 10.6, and in Greek translation at Rev. 22:20. There is a high degree of consensus among interpreters on at least three points concerning this formula: (1) although on linguistic grounds there are other possibilities,[10] the transliteration represents two Aramaic words *(marana tha)*, an imperative utterance meaning, "Our Lord, come!"[11]; (2) the setting for the composition and use of the formula was eucharistic worship in the Aramaic-speaking Palestinian church;[12] and (3) its function was to invoke the coming of the Lord, his parousia.[13] Where there is disagreement is whether the prayer invoked the presence of the Lord at the eucharist, as well as his coming in the parousia,[14] or whether its sole function was to call upon the Lord for his speedy coming, his parousia.[15]

It is not our purpose to try to resolve this disputed issue but to indicate that the formula has been taken as evidence for a primitive christological belief that Jesus was regarded as "the Lord who will come in the last days to bring salvation (grace, mercy) and judgment,"[16] and that the community that uttered this prayer attached no redemptive significance to the death and resurrection of Jesus. Ferdinand Hahn has claimed such, saying in connection with his study of the formula that the primitive church's outlook was oriented to the Lord's final appearing, and that the resurrection "was regarded as a pledge of the eschatological reality and office of Jesus but did not imply any conception of His exaltation and eternal presence."[17] The eucharistic celebrations in which the formula would have been used, he says, continued the outlook of the last supper as "an anticipation of the banquet of the Kingdom" and were devoid of a "retrospective glance at the death of Jesus and its meaning for salvation."[18] The "retrospective glance" was a later development within eucharistic celebrations, although "still in the Palestinian sphere," through an assimilation of the motifs of vicarious atonement, covenant, and memorial.[19]

3. *The Q Material.* The passage in Acts 3 and the *maranatha* formula provide a very small textual base. It is possible that a much larger body, the so-called Q material,[20] provides more extensive evidence of a christology which attached no redemptive significance to the death or death and resurrection of Jesus. (We shall not enter the debate whether Q existed as a source for Matthew and Luke, but address only the implications drawn from its presumed existence.)[21] Although one cannot easily define the exact contents of Q, and it cannot be proved that all of the Q material which ever existed has been incorporated into Matthew and Luke,[22] it is probable—and held by interpreters today without exception—that Q did not contain a narrative of the passion and resurrection, nor did it contain any kerygmatic summaries of them.

What to make of this is assessed in various ways. It is clear, on the basis of the material itself, that the community in which this collection of teachings of Jesus was made and used sought by it to continue Jesus' proclamation of the imminent coming of God's kingdom (Luke 10:9// Matt. 10:7; Luke 13:28–30//Matt. 8:11–12; Luke 16:16//Matt. 11:12–13; cf. Luke 7:28//Matt.11:11; Luke 12:2–3//Matt. 10:26–27). And whether Jesus proclaimed the coming of the Son of Man or not in his actual ministry (a question we shall leave aside), the Q community proclaimed that the Son of Man would come and carry out the final judgment (Luke 12:8–9//Matt. 10:32–33; cf. Luke 12:39–40, 41–46//Matt. 24:43–44, 45–51; Luke 17:22–25, 26–30//Matt. 24:26–27, 37–39). Those who belong to Jesus on earth will be confirmed for salvation by the Son of Man at his coming (Luke 12:8–9//Matt. 10:32–33; cf. Luke 10:16//Matt. 10:40; Luke 10:21–22//Matt. 11:25–27).[23] In the estimation of H. E. Tödt, the Q community, "concentrating its attention almost exclusively on Jesus' teaching, was convinced that Jesus' pointing to the coming of God's reign had not lost its meaning in the post-Easter situation, but must be proclaimed anew."[24]

Does this mean that for the Q community no redemptive significance was attached to the death or death and resurrection of Jesus—except that the resurrection would have signified divine deliverance for Jesus only? Responses to the question differ. T. W. Manson suggested that a passion narrative (and presumably a kerygmatic summary concerning the cross and resurrection) was not required for the Q materials because Q was "a book of instruction for people who [were] already Christians and [knew] the story of the Cross by heart."[25] H. E. Tödt has suggested that the Q community would indeed "have attributed a fundamental meaning to the events of the passion and resurrection" or the community "would not have been established at all." The passion and resurrection, he says, "were not what had to be preached but what had enabled them to preach."[26] On the other hand, it has been said that for this community Jesus is "the redeemer of the future,"[27] and Richard A. Edwards has concluded that the Q material (and the community which composed it) preserved a nonkerygmatic approach to the death of Jesus.

> Salvation is promised to those who respond to Jesus as the Son of Man and who are prepared for his imminent return. The death of Jesus is understood as a feature of the last days before the coming of the Kingdom when the forces of evil attempt to destroy those who speak in YHWH's name. The fate of the prophets has always been persecution, misunderstanding, and often death: as Jesus died at the hands of those who claim to be God's people, so those who follow in his steps can expect persecution. His death is highly significant, but it is not the basis for salvation. . . . There is an implicit assumption in Q that Jesus is alive and a source of inspiration, although there is no speculation about, or recounting of, the resurrection.[28]

ASSESSMENT OF THE PROPOSALS

At one time it was thought that a decisive shift took place between Jesus and Paul so that there was little continuity from the one to the other. For example, shortly after the turn of the century William Wrede wrote about the "distance between . . . Pauline doctrine and the preaching of Jesus."[29] "No one," he says, "who sets out to describe the religion which lives in the sayings and similitudes of Jesus could hit by any chance on the phrase 'religion of redemption.'"[30] But Paul's religion was obviously such; "he laid the foundation of religion in [the] acts of salvation, in the incarnation, death, and resurrection of Christ."[31] And so, he said, Paul can be regarded as "the second founder of Christianity."[32]

On the basis of the proposals above, if they are essentially correct, one would have to say that the problem of continuity between the proclamation of Jesus (in its future orientation) and the proclamation of the cross or cross and resurrection as redemptive is not simply a Jesus-and-Paul problem, but a problem within early Christianity itself. That is to say, there were persons and communities at the outset of the Christian movement who shared the futuristic perspective of Jesus and who saw no redemptive significance in his death or death and resurrection. Furthermore, the Q community provides evidence that such a perspective persisted at least into the middle of the first century, if the conventional dating of Q to the middle of that century is accepted.[33] One could go on from this point in time, moreover, into the second century. The Gospel of Thomas gives no redemptive significance whatsoever to the cross and resurrection; on the other hand, it is different from the traditions already cited, since it has no expectation of the coming of a "Christ-elect" (Acts 3), "Lord" (as in the *maranatha* expression), or the "Son of Man" (of Q).[34]

The problem of continuity is compounded by the fact that there is evidence for the proclamation of the cross or cross and resurrection as redemptive at a very early stage. The pre-Pauline, traditional formula of 1 Cor. 15:3–7 affirms that "Christ died for our sins in accordance with the scriptures" and that "he was raised on the third day in accordance with the scriptures" (15:3–4). Paul indicates that he had "received" this tradition (15:3), and it included not only the kerygma but also the list of those to whom the risen Christ appeared (15:5–6a, 7). It has been maintained by various interpreters that the formula must have been composed in the early Palestinian church.[35] Some have suggested that this would have occurred prior to Paul's visit to Jerusalem (recounted in Gal. 1:18) in A.D. 35 or 36, and that Paul received it on that occasion.[36] The suggestion cannot be proved, but Paul would most likely have received the tradition either on that occasion or else three years earlier during his visit to Damascus (referred to at Gal. 1:17), for (1) his later encounters with Jerusalem apostles at Jerusalem itself or at Antioch in A.D. 48 or 49 (recorded in Gal. 2:1–14) were not occasions on which Paul would have been disposed to receive instruction on matters of "first importance" (1 Cor. 15:3) concerning the kerygma, and (2) Paul speaks of the formula in a way that considers it to be the common apostolic tradition from the earliest times (indeed a solemn and set formula), and as though its formulation antedates his own mission.

Be that as it may, the three proposals surveyed above share the view that from the earliest times on, and even into the time of Paul and beyond, there were persons and communities which did not give a redemptive interpretation to the cross or cross and resurrection of Jesus. Helmut Koester has sketched out four different types of expressions of faith in early Christianity: (1) Jesus as Lord of the future, (2) Jesus as the divine man, (3) Jesus as Wisdom, and (4) Jesus raised from the dead.[37] It is the last which "became the central criterion of faith for the 'canonical' writers,"[38] he says, but it must be recognized that between Jesus and the canonical writers there were other expressions of faith, and at least some of these endured well into the second century.

Of these four types of expression, it is the first (Jesus as Lord of the future) which is generally regarded as the most primitive, as seen in the three proposals.[39] Redemption is future; the cross and resurrection have no redemptive significance. But what does "redemptive significance" mean? If one means an interpretation of the cross as an atoning event (as in 1 Cor. 15:3), there can be no doubt that that is lacking in the three examples cited. But the categories of atonement and redemption need not, and should not, be equated. We shall return to this point while assessing the three specific proposals and again in the conclusion to this chapter.

1. *Peter's Sermon (Acts 3:12–26).* It is questionable how far Acts 3:12–26 represents the earliest form of proclamation. It is notoriously difficult to distinguish between "tradition" and "redaction" in Acts, and this applies particularly to the speeches.[40] Even if the speeches contain traditional materials, they have hardly been untouched by Luke. Within Acts 3:12–26 there are unusual terms,[41] and that gives credence to the view that Luke has incorporated traditional material here, but most are found elsewhere in the Luke-Acts corpus. Terms which are not found elsewhere are the passive verb "to be blotted out" (*exaleiphthēnai,* 3:19), the phrase "times of refreshing" (*kairoi anapsyxeōs,* 3:20), the "times of restoration" (*chronōn apokatastaseōs,* 3:20), and the designation of the audience as "sons of the prophets and of the covenant" (3:25). However, even these cannot be excluded from the "linguistic range" of Luke. The verb "to be blotted out" is a common term in the LXX, appearing frequently in reference to the blotting out of sin,[42] and Luke is known to archaize his materials, using the language and style of the LXX to achieve it.[43] The terminology of "refreshing" (*anapsyxis*) has its antonym in a verb "to faint" (*apopsychō,* Luke 21:26), and the noun "restoration" (*apokatastasis*) has its analogue in Luke's use of the verb "to restore" (*apokathistanō,* Acts 1:6). The designation of the audience as "sons of the prophets and of the covenant" is, as always in the speeches of Acts, made fitting, since it is preceded by reference to the prophets in the previous verse (3:24) and then the covenant with Abraham immediately following it.

What is even more striking than the unusual features are precisely those which are commonly found in Luke-Acts. This is so both in terms of the structure of the speech and its terminology. Martin Dibelius has shown that essentially the same outline (with minor variations) is to be discerned in the speeches of Acts, whether by Peter or Paul, and he concluded from this that the speeches are Lucan compositions. The outline consists of the following parts (and references to points in Peter's sermon in Acts 3:12–26 are provided here):[44] after an introduction showing the situation, there is kerygma of Jesus' life, passion, and resurrection (cf. 3:13–15), an emphasis on the disciples as witnesses (3:15), evidence from the Scriptures (3:22–26), and an exhortation to repentance (3:17–20). Eduard Schweizer has refined the outline and its elements more precisely, but he too discerns that in 3:12–26 the common outline appears. In sum, he has concluded that all the speeches of Peter and Paul in Acts were composed by one and the same author, the author of Acts himself.[45]

As indicated previously, John A. T. Robinson claimed that the statement "his Christ should suffer" (3:18) is Lucan, and that is justified. But is it an interpolation? No, it is integral to the argument of the passage as a whole.[46] The call to repentance in the following verse is based on the prior claim of 3:18 that the suffering of God's Christ was foretold by the prophets. Those addressed by Peter (along with their "rulers") "acted in ignorance" (3:17) of the divine purpose. But if they would only understand the Scriptures, they would see that the crucifixion was purposed by God himself, and they would now repent that their sins might be blotted out (3:19). In the Lucan perspective, the true Israel consists of the "repentant portion of the 'empirical' Israel; they are Jews . . . to whom and for whom the promises have been fulfilled";[47] gentiles are given a share in the salvation that comes from them,[48] while the unrepentant portion of empirical Israel forfeits its membership in the people of God.[49] In sum, not only is it that the language of 3:18 (*pathein ton Christon autou*) is decidedly Lucan (cf. Luke 24:26, 46; Acts 17:3; cf. also Acts 26:23), but the reference to the suffering of God's Christ is integral to the argument of 3:17–19, and the entire section must be considered a Lucan composition.

There are other elements of the speech which appear elsewhere in Luke-Acts. These include the rare christological titles (all of them confined to speeches in Acts) of "servant" (*pais*, 3:13, 26; cf. 4:27, 30), the "Holy One" (3:14; cf. 4:27, 30), the "Righteous One" (3:14; cf. 7:52), and "Author" (*archēgos*, 3:15; cf. 5:31); the designation of Jesus as the prophet like Moses (3:22–23) and the quotation from Deut. 18:15, which reappears at Acts 7:37; the theme of "ignorance" of those who crucified Jesus (Luke 23:34; Acts 13:27); and the theme of healing in "the name" of Jesus (3:16; cf. 3:6; 4:7, 10; 16:18; 19:13).

The question remains, however, whether the passage sets forth a christology of Jesus as the "Christ-elect" and looks solely to the future for redemption. If it is the case that the reference to God's Christ as suffering (3:18) is integral to the speech, and we have argued that it is, it must be concluded that Jesus is portrayed as not only the "Christ-elect" but the Christ who has suffered, is now exalted, and is expected to return. Furthermore, the statement in 3:13 that God has "glorified" (*edoxasen*) his "servant" (*pais*) Jesus is most likely an allusion to the LXX version of Isa. 52:13, in which it is said that God's "servant" (*pais*) will be "exalted" (*hypsōthēsetai*) and "glorified" (*doxasthēsetai*).[50] This leads to the conclusion that Jesus is interpreted here to have been more than a "servant"; he is "the Servant" who has suffered through crucifixion and has been raised (glorified). Nor is Robinson correct that "the Christ is inoperative because he has not yet been sent," and that the gift of the Spirit is seen to be future—with the coming of the "Christ-elect."[51] The healing of the lame man (3:1–11) is attributed within the speech itself to faith in the risen, "glorified" Jesus (3:16; cf. 3:12–13). And the "times of refreshing from the face of the Lord" (3:19), as well as God's blessing (3:26), come in consequence of repentance and forgiveness (3:19), or along with such turning to God (3:26), in the present. They are not dependent on God's sending "the Christ appointed" (3:20) in the future, but upon present repentance.[52] They are available in the present—"these days" spoken of by the prophets (3:24). These "times of refreshing" are thus due to the gift which in Luke's view comes in consequence of repentance (Acts 2:38; 5:31–32; 10:43–44; 11:15–18; 15:7–8; cf. 7:51).

In summary, the sermon of Peter in Acts 3:12–26 is (1) so permeated with Lucan compositional features that, whatever traditions it contains, it is impossible to consider it to be a relatively untouched transcript of early proclamation; (2) it does not present a "Christ-elect" christology in its present form; (3) it does not contain a tradition which presents such a christology and which can be recovered by removing the reference to the suffering of Christ in 3:18; and (4) it cannot be used as evidence that such a christology therefore existed in the earliest proclamation of the Christian movement.

2. *Maranatha!* Is it the case that, on the basis of the *maranatha* formula, one can or ought to conclude that for the Aramaic-speaking community the resurrection of Jesus was but a "pledge" of his eschatological reality and office in the future, "but did not imply any conception of His exaltation and eternal presence"?[53] The formula obviously looks to the future coming of the Lord for the final act of redemption. Yet the sheer fact that the prayer is addressed to the "Lord" (= Jesus), beseeching *him* to come rather than invoking God the Father to send the one who is to come, indicates that the resurrection was considered more than a "pledge" of Jesus' "eschatological reality and office." An "exaltation" to lordship and an "eternal presence"—so that Jesus is now set over the creation and can hear and respond to the prayers of his own in consequence of the resurrection—is implied. In fact, that is the confessional presupposition of the prayer itself. For the primitive community, gathered for worship in the Spirit, the call upon the Lord to come would have been based on the prior conviction that the crucified Jesus had been vindicated and exalted and is now to be acclaimed and addressed as Lord.

It is at this point that a distinction of categories becomes essential. While it is true that no *atoning significance* appears to be attached to

19

the *death* of Jesus, in the sense that on the cross he bore the sins of others (and that is actually an argument from silence), that does not mean that a *redemptive significance* is lacking for the *cross and resurrection* of Jesus. The resurrection of the crucified Jesus was considered even here as more than the divine deliverance of Jesus from death or a "pledge" that he will gain an office of majesty at the time of God's sending him to inaugurate salvation and judgment. To be sure, salvation in its fullness is future, but that is so to one degree or another everywhere in the New Testament. The cross and resurrection of Jesus is presupposed in the *maranatha* formula as the turning point of the ages. Jesus is endowed already with an office of majesty in the presence of God, and the community understands itself as Spirit-filled and in union with the risen Lord to the degree that it can call upon him to come. It anticipates in its eucharistic celebrations that union in its fullness. All of this signifies that the community understands that a newness of life has been inaugurated, and that it is realized in part already within its own eucharistic fellowship; it speaks of Jesus as "our Lord" in the present and calls upon him to come speedily to bring that newness to its complete fulfillment. The cross and resurrection are therefore not totally lacking in redemptive significance. The crucified Jesus has been raised and has been given an office of majesty as "our Lord," and the community considers itself to have been delivered (or redeemed) to the extent that it conducts itself as the eschatological congregation, a people of the Lord Jesus who has entered into his glorious and eternal reign which the community expects to be made manifest to all the world speedily. The community can therefore think that through the cross and resurrection of Jesus a new world has been inaugurated, and in its own eucharistic celebrations it certifies to itself—in its confession of the Lord Jesus and through its invocation of his coming—that it belongs to him and the new world which has begun and will be brought into its fullness at his parousia.

3. *The Q Material.* As with the *maranatha* formula, the Q material has a future orientation. The Son of Man will come as the eschatological deliverer, and the present is a time of anticipation. But is it sufficient to say that, for the Q community, the death of Jesus was not thought of as "the basis for salvation" and that the community would not have given thought to the meaning of the resurrection?[54]

Within the Q material there are allusions to the passion and death of Jesus. Some of these are of a more general nature, linking the death of Jesus and his prophets with the long line of prophets who had been killed previously: the present generation will witness the shedding of the blood of God's prophets (Luke 11:49–51//Matt. 23:34–36); and Jerusalem habitually kills prophets sent to her (Luke 13:34//Matt. 23:37). Yet there

20

are other passages which allude more specifically to the crucifixion of Jesus: he is the Son of Man who has no place to lay his head; that is, he is homeless and rejected (Luke 9:58//Matt. 8:20); the story of the man (or nobleman) who went away (Luke 19:12//Matt. 25:15) and returned (Luke 19:15//Matt. 25:19) in the parable of the pounds/talents and who is addressed as "lord" (Luke 19:16, 18, 20, 25; Matt. 25:20, 22, 24) most certainly has allegorical overtones of the crucifixion and parousia;[55] and the saying that one must bear one's own "cross" and follow Jesus in order to be a disciple (Luke 14:27//Matt. 10:38) presupposes the cross of Jesus.[56]

Given these allusions to the crucifixion, it goes without saying that the Q community would have had to reflect on the question of why Jesus had been put to death and what that might mean.[57] It has been suggested that the community interpreted it solely in terms of the persecution and killing of the prophets—as to them, so to Jesus—without attaching any redemptive significance to it.[58] But the saying about bearing one's own cross and following after Jesus as a requirement for discipleship calls this into question. To be sure, the metaphor of bearing one's cross signifies primarily a life style for the members of the community.[59] But the saying recalls that Jesus himself had gone to the cross; and when the saying goes on to declare that one must "come after" the crucified Jesus in order to be his disciple, it indicates that his crucifixion was considered foundational for the community's existence. Furthermore, it was on the basis of the resurrection that Jesus was considered the Son of Man (Luke 12:40//Matt. 24:44; Luke 17:26–30//Matt. 24:37–39) at whose coming, and by whom, the final judgment would take place (Luke 12:8–9//Matt. 10:32–33). And finally, the community thought of itself, in consequence of the resurrection, as a community in which the Holy Spirit was vital in its witness and worship; to oppose the manifest activity of the Spirit is unforgivable (Luke 12:10//Matt. 12:32).[60] Such a complex of motifs concerning the cross, the exaltation of Jesus as the Son of Man, and the presence of the Spirit indicates that the Q community considered itself to be living in an era in which the redemptive activity of God has already been set in operation, calling and gathering a people of the new age— inaugurated through the death and resurrection of Jesus and the gift and activity of the Spirit—even while the community still awaited redemption's fulfillment at the parousia. The fact that the Q material does not recite the passion, death, and resurrection, nor contain kerygmatic formulas about them—but communicates only the sayings tradition of Jesus—is explainable on the grounds that Q was composed "for the need of the community itself" (rather than for missionary purposes)[61]— "for whose existence the primitive Christian kerygma was a presupposition"[62]—in order to strengthen its faith in the Son of Man, as well as the coming of the kingdom of God, and to provide for community guidance in life and exhortation.[63] In sum, the Q material does not offer evidence for a presentation of christology and redemption which looks only to the future and sees no redemptive significance in the cross and resurrection. This does not mean that the Q community had a well-considered understanding and proclamation concerning the cross and resurrection on a par with Pauline Christianity—although that cannot be excluded outright (for that would be an argument from silence). Rather, since the cross of Jesus is considered foundational for discipleship and therefore the existence of the community, since Jesus has been exalted as Son of Man, and since the Spirit is manifestly vital in the community, the death and resurrection of Jesus must have been regarded as marking the turn of the ages—from the old aeon to the age of redemption, still to be fulfilled at the parousia of the Son of Man, but already realized in part.

CONCLUSIONS

The question posed in this chapter has been whether there is evidence in the sources for forms of proclamation which antedate and then coexist with the proclamation of the cross and resurrection as redemptive, and which look solely to the future for the redemptive event. Was the proclamation of the cross and resurrection as redemptive a second stage, however early? Or could it be that there were two ways from the earliest times of treating redemptive christology—one which looked to the future and another which looked to the past (e.g., 1 Cor. 15:3–4)—and that both persisted for several years until the latter became dominant in the canonical writers, and the former became more and more relegated to a "doctrine of last things"?

For all their differences, the three proposals reviewed here seek to account for the transition from the preaching of Jesus to the preaching of the early church. That is to say, they seek to show that the essentially future orientation of Jesus was continued in the early church. But our assessment has raised questions. It has raised questions above all concerning the view that Acts 3 contains a primitive form of christology, that of a "Christ-elect," which Luke has incorporated as a fossil of tradition into his own work. That proposal simply does not hold up.

With the *maranatha* formula and the Q material a redemptive christology of the future is most clearly put forth, but our assessment has raised the question whether the usual way of categorization is appropriate. If these traditions do not explicitly proclaim the cross and resurrection—and they do not—and if they do not explicitly interpret the death of Christ as an atoning death—and again they do not—does that mean that the "backward glance" had not yet occurred in the communities to which these traditions belonged? It is still possible that, even if an atoning interpretation of the death of Jesus did not exist from the very beginning, the cross and resurrection (as a unitary event) was regarded as a turning point not only in regard to the status of Jesus—who is now "our Lord" in the one case, the exalted Son of Man in the other—but also in regard to the self-understanding and outlook of these communities. To borrow a term from Rudolf Bultmann,[64] the present era of "between-ness," the time between the resurrection and the parousia, was hardly considered by these communities merely as an era of anticipation and preparation for redemption; that is a view that comes to expression in late writings of the New Testament. Rather, in the time of "between-ness" these communities considered themselves to have entered into newness of life already. In the one case, believers confessed their belonging to the exalted Lord Jesus, whom they invoked to come speedily, and in the other case, the sense of newness was manifest both in the communal estimate of Jesus as the exalted Son of Man and its experience of the Spirit. It does not follow that wherever an interpretation of the death of Jesus as an atoning (i.e., sin-bearing) event is lacking there is no redemptive significance attached to the cross and resurrection. Atonement through the death of Jesus on the cross is a narrower category than redemption by God through the cross and resurrection. The latter means liberation or deliverance, and it is presupposed wherever a community considers itself to have entered into an era of newness of life, even if it assigns finality to the future—as the New Testament writers do in general. In regard to the communities discussed here, the cross and resurrection of Jesus as a unitary event was not regarded simply as that which qualified him to be a redemptive figure of the future; it was also regarded as the basis for the newness of life (the sense of eschatological existence) into which the communities had entered.

More needs to be said about this. And we must also deal with the questions of how and when an atoning significance was attached to the cross. These matters are taken up in the next chapter.

23

3

The Search for the Origins of Redemptive Christology in Light of the Cross and Resurrection

THE NEW TESTAMENT writers, for all their differences, present redemptive christologies which look back upon the cross or the cross and resurrection as that which makes redemption possible. But where do the origins of this view lie? At one time, prior to the rise of critical scholarship, the answer was simple: (1) Jesus provided the interpretation for his disciples during his earthly ministry, (2) just as the Gospels attest (Mark 10:45// Matt. 20:28; Mark 14:24//Matt. 26:27–28//Luke 22:20), and (3) the disciples shared this interpretation with others after the first Easter. This answer to the question is not to be dismissed out of hand, for it may in fact be correct, and it can be found today, even if presented with more subtlety, in critical scholarship. But it must be acknowledged that critical scholarship has generally not been satisfied with it in such simple form. The major reason for that is that the Gospels cannot be thought of as relaying the teachings of Jesus unaltered. The Gospels were written forty to seventy years after the death of Jesus. They are permeated with traditions and interpretations concerning the cross and resurrection, for they were written after decades of proclamation, catechesis, apologetics, and worship. That means that interpretations of the cross or the cross and resurrection attributed to Jesus in the Gospels may be interpretations given by Christian interpreters in the era running from the early 30s to the latter part of the first century A.D.

Given this situation, how can one account for the origins of a redemptive interpretation of the cross and resurrection? Do the origins lie essentially in a renewed study of the Scriptures within the earliest communities, by which new insights were gained and applied to the cross and resurrection? Do the origins lie essentially in a particular experience of the earliest disciples after the death of Jesus and his subsequent presence among them, an experience which disclosed the meaning of what had happened? Or can we trace the origins, by critical examination of the texts, back to Jesus himself? These would seem to be the most likely alternatives. And each has its proponents. Outstanding proponents for each view are, respectively, Norman Perrin, Edward Schillebeeckx, and Martin Hengel. We shall review the proposals of each.

THREE PROPOSALS

1. Norman Perrin. Perrin published several articles on the christology of the New Testament during the period 1965–71, and they have been collected together and reprinted in a single volume.[1] These essays are devoted primarily to the Son of Man concept in the New Testament and to the christology of the Gospel of Mark, but in them Perrin also takes up the questions of the origins of christology and the genesis of reflection on the redemptive significance of the cross and resurrection. In practically all that he does, Perrin's interest in the origins of the Son of Man concept shines through. Along with certain other interpreters of the New Testament,[2] he maintains that the concept of an apocalyptic Son of Man to come and to preside over the final judgment did not exist in Judaism prior to the Christian movement, that no apocalyptic Son of Man sayings can be attributed to Jesus as authentic statements, and that all of them were produced during the post-Easter era in the early church.[3] In fact, he considers all Son of Man sayings (therefore also those concerning the earthly ministry of the Son of Man and those concerning the suffering, death, and resurrection of the Son of Man) as products of early Christian theologizing.[4] It is on the basis of his proposal of how the Son of Man concept originated in the post-Easter church that Perrin gets involved in the issue of christological origins in general.

The Son of Man concept, according to Perrin, had its origins in early Christian reflection on the resurrection of Jesus in light of passages from Scripture. Perrin maintains that, just as the *pesher* method of scriptural interpretation was used at Qumran, by which the community understood and interpreted "events within its own experience and aspects of its own expectation in the light of Old Testament passages," so there was "a Christian pesher type use of the Old Testament." Furthermore, like interpreters of the Qumran community, early Christian interpreters used "considerable freedom with regard to the wording of the Old Testament passage concerned."[5] In the case of the Son of Man concept, Perrin contends it had its rise through an interpretation of the resurrection in light of Ps. 110:1 ("The Lord says to my lord: 'Sit at my right hand, till I make your enemies your footstool'") and Dan. 7:13 ("There came one like a son of man, and he came to the Ancient of Days and was presented before him").[6] The link between these two passages is made in the words of Stephen at his martyrdom in Acts 7:55–56. Perrin does not claim that the words can be attributed in their present form in Acts to the historical Stephen, but rather that the passage attests the use of the Old Testament and the linking of texts in christological interpretation, and that here Jesus, who has been exalted through his resurrection to God's right hand (allusion to Ps. 110:1), is regarded as the Son of Man (allusion to Dan. 7:13).[7] This, for Perrin, is the beginning of christology.[8] Moreover, like the resurrection, the passion and death of Jesus were interpreted by means of insights from Old Testament passages. This time Dan. 7:13 is linked with Zech. 12:10–14 ("when they look upon him whom they have pierced"), and the link is attested at Revelation 1:7.[9] At first, however, this amounted to a "passion apologetic" rather than a soteriological interpretation of the death of Jesus. The apologetic received further development, and the soteriological interpretation developed at another stage of reflection in which Isaiah 53 came into use.[10]

Perrin does not give a precise answer to the question of how soon or where the soteriological interpretation developed. In one place he hints that it may go back to Palestinian Christianity.[11] In another place, however, he writes that the soteriological tradition "is thoroughly Greek" and that it "belongs to the area of Hellenistic Christianity," but then he adds: "Not that Palestinian Christianity did not meditate ultimately upon the soteriological significance of the cross, but it came to it rather more slowly and when it did come to it, it seems to me to have come to it very largely in a Passover setting."[12] In a footnote he adds that that would not have happened as early as A.D. 31.[13]

The work of Perrin thus moves from a study of the origins of a concept, the Son of Man, to the larger question of the origins of a soteriological interpretation of the death of Jesus. Throughout his essays Perrin maintains that the various facets of interpreting Jesus as the Son of Man, his death, and his resurrection are the result of scriptural interpretation, so he speaks of "the scribes of earliest Christianity" and "Christian exegetical traditions,"[14] and he considers the interpretations to have taken place over time. But his procedure begs questions. For him the chronology of interpretive steps is: (1) the death and resurrection of Jesus had to be interpreted; (2) early Christian scribes thought that they could find the meaning in passages of the Scriptures, which are the key to the meaning of present events (*pesher* method); and (3) from certain texts they derived insights by which to interpret the cross and resurrection. But is such a chronology plausible? It is less likely that Old Testament passages were the basis for interpretation at the outset than that a fundamental understanding was the occasion and catalyst for searching the Scriptures in subsequent times and places *to demonstrate* that what had happened was "in accord with the Scriptures." There must have been some prior field of meaning attached to the death and resurrection of Jesus which provoked a search of the Scriptures to confirm that what had happened— and what it all meant—was in accord with the divine purposes, as attested in Scripture. The presupposition of a Christian scribal tradition at the beginning among those who followed one who "taught them as one who had authority, and not as the scribes" (Mark 1:22) is difficult to conceive. But, rather, the very need within the early church, already convinced of the soteriological meaning of the cross and resurrection, to confirm that what had happened was "in accord with the Scriptures," plus the heightened sense that the Scriptures speak in all their fullness to the present moment of fulfillment, would have driven the followers of Jesus and those who joined them to demonstrate their claim, using techniques of interpretation current in their day. And the results of these interpretive methods have left their mark in the New Testament writings, composed a generation and more after the rise of the earliest convictions. It is at this point—rather than at the beginnings of christological reflection—that the work of Perrin has its greatest impact and significance.[15]

2. *Edward Schillebeeckx.* In his massive study of Jesus and early christology, Schillebeeckx takes an approach far different from that of Perrin. Schillebeeckx centers his analysis on the role of early Christian experience, rather than scribal activity, in seeking to give an account of what transpired between the crucifixion of Jesus and the moment when the disciples came to believe in him as risen Lord and the one who brings salvation.[16] He works out his proposal on the basis of what he calls a "Jewish conversion model," in which a person, by "illumination," passes from "not seeing" to "seeing." In the case of the disciples this conversion took place as Jesus enlightened the disciples and thus "made himself seen." The disciples had abandoned Jesus at his crucifixion. They fell short of following after him. At "the very worst moment they left him in the lurch" and were "'of little faith'—something against which Jesus had repeatedly warned them."[17] Yet they had not forgotten Jesus' fellowship with them and his eating and drinking in fellowship with sinners. On the initiative of Peter, the disciples met together after the death of Jesus, and in "a process of repentance and conversion"[18] they had an "Easter experience," an experience of Jesus' appearing to them and offering forgiveness to those who had abandoned him. This is not to be construed simply as human insight, but as a moment of revelation from the risen Christ.

What it signifies is no model but a living reality. Understood thus, the ground of Christian belief is indubitably Jesus of Nazareth in his earthly proffer of salvation, renewed after his death, now experienced and enunciated by Peter and the Twelve. . . . The experience of having their cowardice and want of faith forgiven them, an experience further illuminated by what they were able to remember of the general tenor of Jesus' life on earth, thus became the matrix in which faith in Jesus as the risen One was brought to birth.[19]

The proposal of Schillebeeckx is well argued, captivating, and based on a thorough engagement with contemporary biblical scholarship. He has been able to bring into a creative synthesis the results of various investigations concerning the life and message of Jesus as well as the post-resurrection testimonies. But questions arise. What he has sought to do is to give an account of how the disciples would have first come to believe, and he limits his presentation to their experience of failure at the crucifixion and their subsequent overwhelming experience of forgiveness. Even if he is correct in his account, however, that means that the disciples would have experienced and then enunciated their own case—that *they* had been forgiven for a particular offense against Jesus, a personal betrayal. Those who had personally failed Jesus were themselves personally forgiven. But this does not do justice to the claim of the kerygma that Jesus gave his life as a "ransom for many" (Mark 10:45), that he "died for our sins" (1 Cor. 15:3), or that he "was put to death for our trespasses and raised for our justification" (Rom. 4:25). Schillebeeckx has not accounted for the conviction that the death and resurrection of Jesus had universal consequences—that is, for all humanity—which was fundamental for the Christian mission from the outset.

3. *Martin Hengel.* Hengel has taken an approach which in some respects resembles that of Schillebeeckx, but he goes considerably beyond it in his study of the atonement.[20] Like Schillebeeckx, but independently of him, he speaks both of the "utter failure and deep guilt" of Jesus' former disciples, who had abandoned him at the crucifixion,[21] and of the experience of salvation in the utterances of "peace" to them from the risen Lord.[22] But he goes a step further, suggesting that an answer to the question of how the death of Jesus could have been interpreted as atoning must be found in Jesus himself. Specifically he traces the interpretation back to the last supper, at which Jesus "related the broken bread to the breaking of his body" and "the wine in the cup of blessing to the pouring out of his blood through which the new eschatological covenant with God would be founded and atonement would be achieved for all." The disciples' "encounter with the risen Lord confirmed . . . this

legacy of Jesus."[23] And their eucharistic celebrations continued to recall it.

Hengel's proposal rests on two critical judgments. First, he has judged that the words of interpretation concerning the bread and the cup essentially as given in their Pauline form (1 Cor. 11:24–25) can be traced back to Jesus himself at the last supper. Second, he has judged that two sacrificial concepts (which are quite different in the Old Testament) were alluded to in the sayings of Jesus at the last supper, those of covenant sacrifice and atoning sacrifice: the pouring out of Jesus' blood would be the means by which "the new eschatological covenant with God would be founded and atonement would be achieved for all."

Each of these judgments is subject to debate. In regard to the first, it is widely held today that, indeed, the Pauline tradition provides an older tradition than any given in the Synoptic Gospels;[24] nevertheless, every eucharistic tradition in the New Testament, including Paul's, contains secondary elements which derive from liturgical practices in the early church.[25] And in regard to the second judgment, it has been said that the two concepts of vicarious expiation and covenant sacrifice in the Lord's Supper traditions have been "clamped together only at second hand."[26] But let us assume that Hengel is correct in both instances. There is still something missing in the account of how the disciples at a later time would have derived an atoning significance of the cross from the words of Jesus. The traditions of the last supper, including that of Paul (1 Cor. 11:26), have an eschatological orientation which is expressed in the synoptic accounts most clearly where Jesus speaks of his not drinking (to which Luke adds, not eating) again until the kingdom of God comes (Mark 14:25//Matt. 26:29; Luke 22:16, 18).[27] This saying is attested in two streams of tradition: that of Mark, which Matthew follows, and that of Luke, which is independent. It can be held that the eschatological expectation the saying conveys belongs to the last supper/Lord's Supper tradition from the earliest times and that it most likely goes back to Jesus himself.[28] On the basis of this pronouncement, the expectation of the disciples would be that the day of redemption and the resumption of drinking lies in the future when the kingdom of God comes. It is clear that the disciples did not attach an atoning significance to Jesus' death prior to the Easter event, which Hengel grants. The actual death of Jesus on the cross was a crushing blow to whatever conceptions they had entertained about Jesus and his role, and they all forsook him and fled. The appearances of the risen Jesus to his disciples would have established that he had been vindicated or, to adopt Hengel's term, that his "legacy" had been confirmed. But if that legacy was that through Jesus' death a new covenant and atonement were to be established, that would at least initially retain a future reference: the time of the kingdom of God when, on the basis of a new covenant and atonement, there would be a resumption of drinking. The disciples would have expected the promise, given on the night of betrayal, to be fulfilled with the coming of the kingdom.[29] Another factor had to enter into their awareness to signify for them that the death of Jesus had already established a new covenant and atonement. They had to be able to detach Jesus' promise from its future orientation so that they could consider that what had been promised of the future kingdom was a present reality, originating in his horrible death. To put it another way, they had to understand that the resurrection certified (a) not only divine deliverance of the crucified Jesus and (b) the validation of his promise, but that it also certified that (b') the promise had been fulfilled already and (a') that they too had been delivered (redeemed) in what had transpired. Moreover, they had to understand that what had transpired had universal significance beyond their own circle. All of this shows no basic disagreement with the Hengel proposal as far as it goes. The point made is simply that another factor had to enter into the experience of the disciples which would lead them to conclude that it was not only the risen Jesus who had entered into a new world, the new age, but that they had been delivered into it as well in consequence of his death and resurrection and in spite of their awareness of living in the old age, soon to pass away. The next section sketches what that additional factor would have been.

CHRIST, CROSS, AND SPIRIT

Seeking the origins of a redemptive interpretation of the cross or the cross and resurrection is a matter of historical investigation. It is difficult to judge what can count as historical in the early Christian traditions, as every interpreter knows, and therefore it is necessary to begin with data which virtually everyone would consider historical. We shall list four items. (1) The earthly Jesus, following his baptism by John, proclaimed the coming of the kingdom of God, called disciples, performed miracles of healing,[30] and declared forgiveness of sins and salvation to those considered by their contemporaries to be unworthy, thereby becoming accountable to God on behalf of others. (2) The earthly Jesus was crucified under the authority of Pontius Pilate as a messianic pretender—regardless of how Jesus might have interpreted his own role—as indicated above all by the charge and inscription "King of the Jews" (Mark 15:26; Matt. 27:37; Luke 23:38; John 19:19). This formulation could not have risen out of early Christian theologizing or apologetics, since early Christians would have hesitated to apply such a title to Jesus because of its political consequences for the Christian movement itself[31] and since it is the most fitting charge to explain the crucifixion of Jesus under Roman rule. (3) After Jesus' death on the cross, his disciples experienced his presence among them, claimed that he had been raised from the dead and had appeared to them in majestic power and glory, and attributed to him a status of majesty. We need not speculate concerning the nature of this experience. Our point is that it can be agreed that there was such an experience about which such claims were made; it is a matter of history. (4) Attending the first experience was a second. That was an experience of the presence and power of the Holy Spirit in and among them. They believed themselves to be endowed by the Spirit sent from God and mediated to them by the risen Christ (Acts 2:33; John 20:22; cf. Luke 24:49; Acts 1:8). Again, we need not speculate further on the experience, but only register the experience itself as a historical phenomenon.

There may well be other "hard data" which can be added. But these four items would not be seriously questioned in contemporary scholarship. And these four alone are sufficient to bring us to the threshold of a redemptive interpretation of the cross and resurrection. We shall go on to maintain that at the first stage of development the cross and resurrection together were considered the redemptive event, basing this conclusion on the four items listed, and that at a second stage—after further reflection—the death of Jesus came to be considered an atoning death. Such reflection would have taken into consideration the motifs of atonement present in the Old Testament. Yet even here, while the cross and resurrection were distinguished, there was never a separate concentration on either to the exclusion of the other.

The earthly life and proclamation of Jesus, his crucifixion as a messianic pretender, and the disciples' experience of him as risen and appearing to them in majesty have all been taken into account in studies of early christology and the origins of a redemptive or atoning interpretation of the cross and resurrection. But the experience of the disciples' being encountered by the Spirit and the Spirit's working in and among them is a neglected factor in the search for origins. This experience, however, was a radically transforming one, and it has importance for the origins of redemptive christology.

In the Old Testament and Jewish tradition it is affirmed again and again that the Spirit of God came upon and worked through various individuals, particularly the prophets (1 Sam. 10:10; Isa. 61:1; Ezek. 2:2–7; Mic. 3:8; etc.). In spite of the saying attributed to Moses in Num. 11:29 ("Would that all the Lord's people were prophets, that the Lord would put his spirit upon them"), the pouring out of the Spirit on the people as a whole does not occur.[32] Yet the book of the prophet Isaiah (eighth century B.C.) anticipates a day of salvation and judgment when the Spirit will be "poured out upon us from on high" (Isa. 32:15), resulting in the transformation of nature and the establishment of righteousness, peace, and trust (32:15–20). Moreover, the result of the Spirit's advent is judgment and cleansing (Isa. 4:4). Such anticipations of the Lord's pouring out of his Spirit upon all Israel are expressed also in the works of exilic and postexilic prophets. In Deutero-Isaiah of the exilic period the writer declares the word of the Lord: "I will pour my Spirit upon your descendants" (Isa. 44:3). And in the book of Ezekiel, also from the exilic era, the Lord proclaims to "the whole house of Israel" (Ezek. 37:11), "I will put my Spirit within you, and you shall live" (37:14; cf. 39:29), and along with the Spirit's coming the people will have a "new heart" (36:26; 11:19). The postexilic prophet Joel speaks of God's pouring out his Spirit "on all flesh" (Joel 2:28–29) in days to come, on "the great and terrible day of the Lord" (2:31). This outpouring will result in prophecy and visions by the sons and daughters of Israel (2:28), the redemption of the faithful of Israel (2:32), and the judgment of the nations (3:2). In all of these utterances there are common features: (1) the Spirit will be poured out upon Israel corporately; (2) this is a future expectation, taking place at some decisive day to come; and (3) the day of the Spirit's coming will be a day of salvation.

During the postexilic era, and extending into the common era, it was held in some circles that prophecy and the manifest activity of the Spirit had ceased with the last of the prophets (Haggai, Zechariah, and Malachi).[33] This view comes to its fullest expression in the rabbinic text *Tosefta Sotah* 13.3: "When the latter prophets died, that is, Haggai, Zechariah, and Malachi, then the Holy Spirit came to an end in Israel."[34] But there are earlier expressions of the same in the postexilic prophet Zechariah (13:2–6); Ps. 74:9 ("there is no longer any prophet"), which may be from the Maccabean era; and 1 Macc. 9:27 ("Thus there was great distress in Israel, such as had not been since the time that prophets ceased to appear among them"). Within the first century A.D. the same point of view is expressed by Josephus, who assigns the prophets to the era between Moses and Artaxerxes (*Against Apion* 1.8.40–41;[35] Artaxerxes succeeded Xerxes ca. 465 B.C.) and by the writer of 2 *Baruch*, who speaks of prophets as belonging to "former times and former generations" and says that "now . . . the prophets are sleeping" (85.1–3).[36]

It is neither necessary nor sound, however, to consider this outlook as normative or consistently operative for actual life in postbiblical Judaism. Evidence is abundant from Philo, Josephus, Qumran texts, and rabbinic literature that various persons were considered to have been endowed by the Spirit and the gift of prophecy.[37] This is significant for New Testament studies in connection with the assessment of Jesus in history. That he was considered to be endowed by the Spirit from the time of his baptism by John, and was therefore in some sense a "prophet" or "charismatic" figure, does not mean that he would therefore have been considered an anomaly.[38]

But what is more significant for the origins of redemptive christology is the expectation of the outpouring of the Spirit in the future. The Old Testament prophets cited expected the outpouring of the Spirit to take place in Israel's future. This future would probably be conceived in "this worldly" (historical) terms. Yet the prophets actually leave themselves open concerning the time and manner of this fulfillment. The prophecy of Joel that speaks of the outpouring of the Spirit "on all flesh" on the "great and terrible day of the Lord" points to a decisive day, a day of deliverance and salvation, and several rabbinic texts take this to mean the messianic age,[39] as does the Book of Acts (2:15–21). The gift of the Spirit is also associated in rabbinic texts with the coming of Elijah and the resurrection of the dead, so that the world to come is ushered in by the advent of the Spirit.[40] Whether the rabbinic texts can be taken as reflecting pre-Christian conceptions is debatable; what is more certain is that the text from Joel and the others cited indicate an expectation of an outpouring of the Spirit upon the people of God in a day of redemption in which humanity is transformed.[41] There are also texts from the pre-Christian era which speak of the rise of prophecy in the future (1 Macc. 4:46; 14:41; *Sib. Or.* 3.781–82)[42] and the endowment of the Messiah with the Spirit (*Pss. of Sol.* 17.37; 18.7; cf. *T. Levi* 18.7; *T. Judah* 24.2).

When we consider early Christian experience of the Spirit, we are confronted with a decisive turn of events. First, however widespread or limited the expectation was in first-century Judaism that there would be a revival of prophecy and/or an outpouring of the Spirit on the people as a whole,[43] it is clear that from the beginning of the Christian movement the presence and power of the Spirit were a matter of experience and that this expectation in Scripture and tradition was brought forth and considered to have been fulfilled. Luke portrays this experience of the presence and power of the Spirit as taking place first on Pentecost (Acts 2:1–36); the Fourth Evangelist associates it with the appearance of the resurrected Jesus to his disciples on the day of resurrection itself (John 20:22). The two accounts cannot be harmonized in terms of chronology. They have in common, however, the presupposition that the activity of the Spirit was a consequence of the Easter event.[44] Moreover, it was not a matter of the Spirit at work simply in singular prophetic figures. The Spirit was considered active among the disciples corporately. It was also considered operative in the lives of each member of the community individually. It is stated or assumed in various books of the New Testament that all Christians possess the Spirit (1 Cor. 12:13; Gal. 4:6; 1 Thess. 4:8; Heb. 6:4; 1 Pet. 1:2; 1 John 3:24; 4:13), and this is assumed to have been so from the beginning—a view which is explicit in the Gospel of John and implicit in the Epistles of Paul. Even Luke's modification, allowing for an interlude for the apostles to witness Jesus' ascension and to select Matthias, does not alter the picture significantly.

Second, this experience of the Spirit, together with the experienced appearances of the risen Jesus, signified that a new age had dawned and that the old age had passed away.[45] This experience would attest that not only had the crucified Jesus been vindicated through his resurrection, so that something decisive had happened for him, but that something decisive had happened for his disciples as well. That "something" was more than a matter of "forgiveness" of their failure in abandoning Jesus previously, but an experiential awareness of having been placed in a new era, the era of eschatological redemption. This experience of newness would be described later in terms of the believer's being a "new creation" (2 Cor. 5:17), "born anew" (1 Pet. 1:3), and "born from above" (John 3:3, 7). Besides these metaphors of new creation and rebirth, Paul speaks of the Christian as walking "in newness of life" (Rom. 6:4), receiving "life" from the Spirit (Rom. 8:11; 1 Cor. 15:45), and being justified and sanctified in the Spirit (1 Cor. 6:11); the deutero-Paulines speak of sanctification by the Spirit (2 Thess. 2:13) and being sealed by the Spirit for the day of final redemption (Eph. 4:30); and 1 Peter speaks of the readers of the letter as sanctified by the Spirit (1:2). In each of these instances where the term sanctification is used, it is not thought of as a goal to which the Christian moves; rather, the thought is that the Christian is one who has been made holy, set apart from the world, and transferred into the new age by the Spirit.

On the basis of this experience of having been placed into a new era in which the Spirit is vital among them individually and corporately, Christians from the earliest times would have understood themselves to have been delivered or redeemed from the present age, which is passing away. And it is on the basis of this certainty of redemption, a matter of experience which began with the appearances of the risen Christ, that the cross and resurrection of Jesus would have been considered *the* act of divine redemption. Although the cross could still be only a horrible, ghastly memory, and probably could not be understood at the very beginning as a redemptive event, the cross and resurrection could be so understood. At the deepest moment of despair and loss, when the disciples had fled in fear, and the innocent Jesus suffered and died, there God initiated an act of deliverance—for both Jesus and his disciples. Possessed

35

of the sense of being a people now reclaimed by God through the power of the Spirit manifest among them in both its corporate and individual aspects, and certain of Jesus' vindication through his resurrection from the dead, they could think virtually in no other terms except that God had redeemed them—not in spite of the cross, but indeed through the cross and resurrection of Jesus. The secret of the cross, "a secret and hidden wisdom of God," cannot be known, Paul was to write later, except through divine revelation through the Spirit (1 Cor. 2:7–10). Indeed, he says, "we have received . . . the Spirit which is from God, that we might understand the gifts bestowed on us by God" (1 Cor. 2:12; cf. Eph. 3:5; 1 Pet. 1:12).

Along with this experience of having actually been restored and redeemed, it would have been recognized that it was none other than the Messiah who had been crucified and raised. In spite of the fact that the Judaism of the day knew no concept of a dying and rising Messiah, as far as we know, the one who appeared to the disciples was Jesus, who had been accused and crucified as a messianic pretender. Whatever else Jesus had taught or implied concerning his own identity during his earthly ministry, he was crucified on the charge of being "King of the Jews," and it is a matter of astonishment that he implicitly accepted the charge. The Gospels, of course, do not agree in their accounts of what Jesus replied to the question whether he was King of the Jews. We simply do not know what his reply would have been—whether it was evasive (Mark 15:2; Matt. 27:11; Luke 23:3; John 18:33–38), or whether it consisted of silence on further inquiry (Mark 15:4–5; Matt. 27:12–14). But the trial proceeded on the basis of the charge, the judgment of guilty was given, the charge was inscribed on the cross, and there was no defense, no protest, on the part of Jesus, unless such was suppressed at the outset in early Christian gospel traditions. And this is not likely, for there is no apparent advantage in doing so. The implication is that Jesus accepted the verdict and went to his death under sentence of being a Messiah claimant.[46]

Here the four items of historical data listed at the outset of this section converge. The earthly Jesus—proclaimer of the kingdom, worker of miracles, and master of disciples, who already granted forgiveness and salvation in his ministry, thereby being answerable to God for the sake of others—was crucified as a messianic claimant, a charge he did not reject. His disciples, who had abandoned him at the moment of his greatest crisis, experienced (1) his presence and appearances among them as one who had been raised from death to an exalted majesty and (2) the presence and power of the Spirit among them in an era of restoration, renewal, and life—a time of salvation. They had been delivered into a new era inaugurated through the death and resurrection of the Messiah Jesus. Such a conclusion did not require scribal learning or skillful doctrinal construction. It required only a modest acquaintance with the story of the God of Israel—the God of covenant, blessing, and redemption—as revealed in the Scriptures read in the synagogue, the vivid memory of the crucifixion of Jesus as King of the Jews, and the twin experiences of the appearance of the risen Jesus to them and the presence and power of the Spirit among them. The God of Israel had raised Jesus to life, delivering him from death, and had reconstituted the disciples through his Spirit and therefore certified to them that they had been delivered into a new age. It was through the cross and resurrection, then, that redemption had taken place.

If this reconstruction is sound, it follows that redemptive christology at the outset did not distinguish between the cross and resurrection as two discrete events, depicting the cross as the atoning event and the resurrection as its certification. In fact the stress at the outset was placed on the resurrection. This is attested in early formulas of the New Testament which have been designated "adoptionistic"—in a functional, not ontological sense—in their christology. The main instances appear at Acts 2:36; 13:33; Rom. 1:3–4; Heb. 5:5; and 2 Tim. 2:8. In one of these (Acts 2:36) the crucifixion is mentioned (attributed to human cause), and in two others his death is alluded to (Rom. 1:4; 2 Tim. 2:8), but in the others there is no reference to the crucifixion at all, even though it is obviously presupposed. The accent in all five cases is on the exaltation or resurrection of Jesus. Descended from David, Jesus is "risen from the dead" (2 Tim. 2:8); God has made the crucified Jesus to be Lord and Christ (Acts 2:36); God has raised Jesus and begotten him thereby as his Son (Acts 13:33, alluding to Ps. 2:7); God has appointed Jesus as the Messiah (Heb. 5:5, alluding to Ps. 2:7 also); and God has designated Jesus as Son of God by raising him from the dead (Rom. 1:4). In each of these instances Jesus' exaltation/resurrection is front and center; there is no redemptive interpretation applied to the death of Jesus itself. These brief passages may reflect, or even represent, the earliest form of proclamation and christology.[47] It has been suggested that such formulas were developed in early (pre-Pauline) Hellenistic Jewish Christianity.[48] That may be so, but one should not think in terms of Aramaic-speaking and Greek-speaking communities as existing in sequential stages, but as contemporaneous, as attested in Acts 6:1–15, which speaks of the Hebrews (= Aramaic-speaking Christians) and Hellenists (= Greek-speaking Christians) in Jerusalem at the outset.[49] The "adoptionistic" passages appearing here and there reflect an early form of proclamation and christology which could have been common to both "Hebrews" and "Hellenists," although that cannot be proved. In any case, according to these passages the redemptive era has been inaugurated through the resurrection, and implicitly then the cross and resurrection, but the cross has not yet been interpreted as redemptive in the sense that one would say, "Christ died for our sins."

At some point, still within the earliest times, however, the crucifixion and resurrection could be distinguished as two parts of one dramatic act. Although the two parts could never be separated, the death of Jesus came to be spoken of explicitly as the atoning event, and the resurrection as the basis for Jesus' appearances, reign, and expected return. Such a distinction would have been made in consequence of interpreting each part of the drama (death and resurrection) in light of the Old Testament. The evidence for such an interpretive process—in which each part of the drama has received its own attention in light of the Old Testament—is provided in the pre-Pauline formula: (1) "Christ died for our sins in accordance with the scriptures," and (2) "he was raised on the third day in accordance with the scriptures" (1 Cor. 15:3–4). There were other ways of expressing the two parts of the drama, as in the statement of Paul, which may also have pre-Pauline origins: he (1) "was put to death for our trespasses" and (2) "raised for our justification" (Rom. 4:25). This too demonstrates that both the death and resurrection were pondered and assigned their own meanings, but they were nevertheless two parts of one drama. The "adoptionistic" formulas had conceived of the redemptive action of God as one dramatic act. Now there are two parts, but they are but two parts, or scenes, within that one dramatic act.

The results of this chapter and the previous one can now be brought together. It has been proposed that the earliest forms of redemptive christology looked solely to the future, the parousia, and assigned no redemptive significance to the cross and resurrection. That view has been challenged by a reconsideration of the texts on which it is based (chapter 2). It has also been proposed, to some extent in light of the other proposals, that the origins of a redemptive interpretation of the death and resurrection of Jesus can be found in either scriptural interpretation, the disciples' experience of forgiveness for their leaving Jesus "in the lurch" at the crucifixion, or in the teachings of Jesus himself. In this chapter it has been suggested that all of these may have been attendant factors in the development of redemptive christology. But it has been maintained that a redemptive interpretation of the cross and resurrection arose at the very outset among the disciples of Jesus who, through the experience of being confronted by the risen Jesus in majesty and the experience of the presence and power of the Spirit among them corporately and individually, considered themselves to have been transferred and set within a new world, the age of life, new birth, and new creation. They had been redeemed. The God of Israel had performed a redemptive act—indeed *the* redemptive act—through the death and resurrection of Jesus, who had been crucified as the King of Israel. The cross and resurrection was the saving event. And then among this circle of believers and others added to them, further interpretations of the cross and resurrection were developed, singly and yet together, as the Scriptures were heard, read, and then searched, and as Jesus' teaching, passion, death, and resurrection were recalled and then considered again in light of the Scriptures searched.

4

A Typology: The Four Main Types of Redemptive Christology in the New Testament

IT IS CLEAR that a redemptive interpretation of the death or death and resurrection of Jesus occurred early in the history of the Christian movement. It is found already in creedal statements prior to the writing of the New Testament books, and it comes to expression in one way or another in virtually all the books themselves at the level of their composition. A redemptive interpretation belongs to a widely shared tradition, and it must therefore be considered early and also decisive for various tributaries of the Christian tradition.

It is not our purpose to trace the history of the tradition along its various tributaries. Such a task would be worth pursuing, and it would probably be carried out best if one were to adopt essentially the method proposed by James M. Robinson and Helmut Koester,[1] in which one would place the history of a particular tradition within the context of the broader stream of traditions about Jesus as well as in the larger cultural setting. The historian would observe how that tradition was expressed in various ways, then perhaps even eclipsed by alternative traditions of equal force, and then possibly reasserted once again along its trajectory from the earliest times into the second century. But our purpose is of another kind: that is, to move directly to the documents of the New Testament itself and to map out ways in which redemptive christology came to be expressed by the various writers at the literary level. We shall use a typology which suggests that there are at least "four main types" of redemptive christology which emerge within the New Testament writings. These four types come to expression at different times, but there is no strict chronological sequence to them. Each type represents a way of expressing redemptive christology, and each is based on various factors which will be reviewed in chapter 9. Essentially the different types come to expression, however, on the basis of how the various writers reflected upon the status and role of Christ in the redemptive drama.

Before sketching the typology, it is necessary to introduce additional terminology. In connection with each type the terms "theopractic" or "christopractic" will be used. "Theopractic" signifies that, although Christ is the agent of redemption, the major actor in redemption is God; God is the one who sends the Son or reconciles the world to himself. "Christopractic" signifies that, although God is still the one who wills redemption and exerts his saving purpose in Christ, the major actor in redemption is Christ; Christ is the one who comes from above to rescue humanity and to bring humanity into a reconciled relationship to God. Obviously such terms are relative, signifying only a degree of emphasis. But that different degrees of emphasis are present can be seen to emerge in the four types. These four types will be explored more fully in chapters 5 through 8. Here it is sufficient to indicate the main features and thrust of each and to anticipate what writings belong to each type.

REDEMPTION ACCOMPLISHED
IN CHRIST

The first of the four main types of redemptive christology discernible in the New Testament preserves the theopractic character of the Old Testament and Jewish tradition most clearly. Christ is of course portrayed as the one in whom redemption is accomplished, but the accent is on what God has done in Christ for human redemption; Christ's role is more that of the obedient Son of God than of a figure who comes of his own volition from above to rescue humanity. God is active; Christ tends to be portrayed in a relatively passive role. Attention is focused largely on his death, which is understood to be a means by which sin or sins and their consequences are borne in accord with the divine purpose for the sake of humanity, and his resurrection, which is effected by God's raising him from the dead. This type of redemptive christology comes to expression in the letters of Paul and the Gospel of Mark.

REDEMPTION CONFIRMED
THROUGH CHRIST

The second main type of redemptive christology also preserves the theopractic character of the Old Testament and Jewish tradition, but in this type Christ emerges more forthrightly as integrally involved in the drama of redemption. He is portrayed here too as obedient to God, but his will and the will of God are more closely intertwined. The twin themes of promise-and-fulfillment and redemptive history are woven into the fabric of presentation. There is less emphasis on the death of Christ as redemptive, and stress is placed primarily on his authority and power to effect human redemption in his exalted state in consequence of his death and resurrection. That implies, of course, that it is only by means of his death and resurrection, and in no way otherwise, that redemption is possible. But in this type of redemptive christology the cross and resurrection essentially confirm the redemptive purpose of God expressed in his prior promises. God has confirmed these promises through the ministry, death, resurrection, and reign of Christ. This type of redemptive christology is expressed in the Gospel of Matthew and in the writings of Luke, his Gospel and the Acts of the Apostles.

REDEMPTION WON BY CHRIST

The third main type of redemptive christology marks a decisive shift. Here, without dispensing with the divine initiative, the presentation takes on a christopractic emphasis and coloring so that the action of Christ is pronounced considerably more in the drama of redemption. Christ is portrayed consistently as having had a preexistent status, as having come from above to rescue humanity, as having won redemption, and as having returned to the status he had enjoyed prior to his coming. His action of winning redemption is interpreted in a variety of ways: He offers himself as a sacrifice; he does battle with the principalities and powers or with Satan; he abolishes death; he brings humanity to God; or he reconciles all things to himself or to God. His death on the cross is taken seriously, but the emphasis falls upon his triumphant resurrection and heavenly reign, by which he obtains a new situation for humanity, a future salvation. This type of redemptive christology is expressed in Colossians, Ephesians, the Pastoral Epistles, 1 Peter, Hebrews, and Revelation.

REDEMPTION MEDIATED BY CHRIST

The fourth main type of redemptive christology is, like the third, christopractic in emphasis. Christ is the one sent from God—so the divine initiative is preserved here as well—but he is the one who actually mediates salvation. All that the Father has to give to humanity is offered by Christ to those who will receive him, and the way to receive him is to receive his word proclaimed by his witnesses. Christ is the Son of Man who has come down from above, who reveals the Father to those who will receive him as the one sent by the Father and who has returned again to his Father through his death and resurrection, resuming the glory he had before. He has voluntarily laid down his life, but he has power to take it up again. He has given his word to his disciples, and it is through the reception of his word that one receives him, and in receiving him, believing in him, a person receives eternal life. Since it is the exalted Christ who gives life to all who believe in him, it can be said that salvation is mediated from Christ to believers. This type of redemptive christology is presented in the Gospel of John and in the Epistles of John.

It will be seen by this sketch of what is to follow that the redemptive christology of most books of the New Testament will be treated. There are four books in the New Testament which do not receive treatment. James,[2] Jude, and 2 Peter[3] are not treated separately since they do not offer sufficient materials to describe a redemptive christology in them. Moreover, since 2 Thessalonians is not considered in this study to be genuinely Pauline (see the next chapter), it too is left out of the list of books given above. But, like the other three mentioned here, this book offers very little to go on. At the close of chapter 7, however, both 2 Thessalonians and 2 Peter are mentioned briefly, since they imply a conception related to the third type of redemptive christology.

PART TWO

INVESTIGATIONS OF
REDEMPTIVE CHRISTOLOGY
UNDER ITS FOUR
MAIN TYPES

5

Redemption Accomplished in Christ

THE CONSTANT FEATURES of this type of redemptive christology are that (1) the God of Israel is the one who performs the redemptive act in Christ; (2) the crucified and risen Christ is the agent or instrument of the divine act; (3) this Christ dies "on behalf of" humanity, assuming onto himself the divine judgment upon sin; and (4) his death and resurrection are the clues to his meaning as the Christ; they are the foci of christology. The *variable* features are (1) the kind of metaphors used to speak of the redemptive act and its effects and (2) whether the preexistence of Christ is affirmed. This redemptive christology is given its fullest expression in the Epistles of Paul and the Gospel of Mark.

THE LETTERS OF PAUL

The seven letters which are universally attributed to Paul (Romans, 1 and 2 Corinthians, Galatians, Philippians, 1 Thessalonians, and Philemon) contain a wealth of christological and redemptive expressions. Although on one occasion Paul speaks of Christ as "Savior" (Phil. 3:20) and on another of Christ's Davidic descent (Rom. 1:3, but does not use the title "Son of David"), generally he uses three terms:[1] "Christ" (271 times), "Lord" (*kyrios,* 168 times),[2] and "Son of God" (15 times). Occasionally the terms "Lord" and "Christ" are used in combination (41 times) as in the phrase "our Lord Jesus Christ." The alternative expressions "Christ Jesus" and "Jesus Christ" do not appear to have any significant differences in meaning.[3]

All of these terms were used prior to Paul's own use of them. Werner Kramer has investigated their use in pre-Pauline formulas embedded in Paul's letters and has concluded that they were used for different tasks.[4]

The term "Christ" tended to be used to designate the one who died "for us" and whom God raised, the one to whom faith and preaching relate. The title "Lord" tended to be used in confessional statements, particularly at worship, in which the church submitted itself to the dominion of the Lord Jesus. And "Son of God" tended to be used in formulas speaking of Jesus' "adoption" as God's Son through the resurrection and in connection with God's "giving" or "sending" his Son for a redemptive purpose.

Paul's own usage, according to Kramer, is less precise. The tendencies can still be seen to appear, but Paul uses the titles in three main fields and employs both "Christ" and "Lord" in each.[5] When he speaks of salvation, he can speak of it either as issuing forth from the death and resurrection of "Christ" or as coming from the "Lord" who has the power to give and to demand. When Paul speaks of the church, he can speak of it as the assembly of believers in "Christ" or as the assembly of those who recognize the present power of the "Lord" who governs them. And when he gives ethical instruction, he may demand action which conforms to the death of "Christ" or he may point to the authority of the "Lord." The term "Son of God" is used less, and it appears usually to state the relationship between Jesus as bearer of salvation and God. Almost without exception it is used in places where God has just been mentioned.

These are tendencies only, but Kramer's observations alert us to expect that in statements concerning redemptive christology Paul will use any of the three main christological titles, depending on (1) the context (confessional, hortatory, etc.) in which a statement is made and (2) whether he transmits a pre-Pauline formula. So, for example, he will exhort his readers: "Let every one lead the life which *the Lord* has assigned to him" (1 Cor. 7:17), but in another instance he will quote a pre-Pauline formula: "*Christ* died for our sins" (1 Cor. 15:3).

Paul's redemptive christology can be derived neither from the christological titles alone nor from statistics concerning them, but rather through observing ways in which he puts the titles to use for a variety of tasks in proclamation, exhortation, teaching, and even in sending greetings to his readers. His redemptive christology is given expression primarily in (1) his use of brief kerygmatic formulas, whether received or coined by him, (2) his hortatory treatment of various topics (e.g., baptism, conduct, etc.) in which he draws upon his understanding of the death and resurrection of Christ as a theological presupposition, and (3) his summaries of the place of Christ in the history of salvation.

1. The kerygmatic formulas consist of two kinds. The first is the *hyper*-formula, of which the basic structure is made up of (1) Christ (or another title) as subject, (2) an aorist verb (e.g., "died"/"was put to death"), and (3) the preposition *hyper* ("for," "on behalf of," or "for the sake of")[6]

followed by a genitive noun (e.g., "sins" or "the ungodly") or pronoun (e.g., "us"). The origins of this formula can be traced to pre-Pauline proclamation, as 1 Cor. 15:3 demonstrates. Yet its frequency in Paul's letters indicates that the formula became a part of the apostle's own proclamation. The passages are as follows:[7] "Christ died for the ungodly" (Rom. 5:6); "Christ died for us" (Rom. 5:8); "Christ died for our sins" (1 Cor. 15:3); "[Christ] has died for all" (2 Cor. 5:14); "[our Lord Jesus Christ] gave himself for our sins" (Gal. 1:4); "[the Son of God] gave himself for me" (Gal. 2:20); "[Christ became] a curse for us" (Gal. 3:13); and "[our Lord Jesus Christ] died for us" (1 Thess. 5:10). Closely related in structure is a saying which uses another preposition: "[Jesus our Lord] was put to death for [*dia*] our trespasses" (Rom. 4:25).

The second type of formula used is the "sending formula." The structure of this formula consists of four parts: (1) God as the subject, (2) a verb ("sent" or "gave up") in aorist tense,[8] (3) the "Son" as the direct object, and (4) a statement of purpose, which is always a redemptive one. There are three such passages in Paul's letters:[9] "For God has done what the law could not do: . . . sending his own Son in the likeness of sinful flesh and for sin, he condemned sin in the flesh" (Rom. 8:3); "He who did not spare his own Son but gave him up for us all . . ."(Rom. 8:32); and "God sent forth his Son . . . to redeem those who were under the law, so that we might receive adoption as sons" (Gal. 4:4–5).

It will be seen at once that the "sending formula" is longer and more detailed than the *hyper*-formula, and in fact the former even includes the latter in one instance (Rom. 8:32, *hyper hēmōn,* "for us"; cf. Rom. 8:3, *peri hamartias,* "for sin"). It is also clear that the "sending formula" is filled with more "Pauline" content in those instances at which the law is spoken of as incompetent to lead to salvation (Rom 8:3) or as that from under which God's Son redeems (Gal. 4:5).

Several observations can be made concerning these two formulas— both separately and together. Concerning the *hyper*-formula passages, there is a preference for using "Christ" as the subject, although the titles "Lord" and "Son of God" are used as well, or are at least the antecedents of pronouns or relative pronouns.[10] Second, the death of Christ is a past event, an event in history which is complete and sufficient as the redemptive work of God. Third, the preposition *hyper* is followed by two kinds of objects: either by "our sins" (1 Cor. 15:3; Gal. 1:4; cf. Rom. 4:25) or by terms designating humanity: "the ungodly" (Rom. 5:6), "us" (Rom. 5:8; Gal. 3:13, 1 Thess. 5:10), or "all" (2 Cor. 5:14). The one exception is "for me" (Gal. 2:20), which is required by the particular context. Although it has been suggested that the phrase "for us" is the earlier and that "for our sins" is a more developed interpretation,[11] that is impossible to substantiate and may not in fact be so. Within the Old Testament the language of atonement is parallel to the phenomenon found in Paul: Atonement can be made for sins (Exod. 32:30; Num. 29:11) or for people (Lev. 4:20; 16:30; 23:28).[12] Likewise for Paul, the death of Christ can be considered a means for the cancellation of sin and its power over humanity (Rom. 5:20–21; 6:18; 2 Cor. 5:19), and therefore it is also the means by which the weak and ungodly (Rom. 5:6, 8) are rescued.

The sending formula differs from the *hyper*-formula not only because it has a four-part structure but in other formal ways as well. First, the subject is always God, not Christ. Second, the direct object is always the "Son"; no other title is used. And finally in the two formulas which contain the verb "to send" (*pempein* in Rom. 8:3; *exapostellein* in Gal. 4:4), the redemptive significance of the sending is made explicit, and the second clause picks up terminology from the first: God sent his Son "in the likeness of sinful flesh and for sin" and then "condemned sin in the flesh" (Rom. 8:3); and God sent "his Son" in order that (*hina*) we might receive "sonship" (Gal. 4:4–5). Moreover, besides these differences in formal structure, there is a material difference in terms of christology, for the preexistence of Christ is both presupposed and asserted.[13]

What emerges from these passages in terms of redemptive christology can now be surveyed. The redemptive act accomplished in Christ is based on the divine initiative. This is more clearly stated in the sending formula passages, where God is the subject, than in those cast within the *hyper*-formula, where Christ is the subject; Paul, however, cancels out the distinction when he combines the two formulas in Rom. 8:3, 32. The redemptive work accomplished in Christ is a divine act carried out for the sake of humanity. There is no hint in any of the passages that Christ represents humanity over against God, offering a perfect sacrifice on the part of humanity to appease God. Rather, Christ is the agent of redemption on the basis of God's initiative, and he takes to himself—on God's behalf— God's own judgment against sinful humanity. This is expressed above all in the statement that God not only sent his Son but also condemned sin in the flesh, in the very likeness of which the Son has come (Rom. 8:3). He has become a "curse" for us (Gal. 3:13), thereby liberating humanity from the judgment and sentence due. God "gave him up for us all" (Rom. 8:32). The judgment and sentence have been carried out at the cross. In all of this the atoning death of Christ has an "objective" character. It happened once and for all, while humanity was weak and ungodly (Rom. 5:6, 8). It also has a "universal" character; it was "for us" and "for all." It is not said that it happened for the sake of an elect or even for those who would come to believe in the death as atoning. Instead the "objective" and "universal" character of the atoning death of Christ is what constitutes the gospel as being truly good news. The gospel is the news of what has happened, what has been accomplished, at the cross. And faith comes from hearing the preaching of Christ (Rom. 10:17).

2. In addition to these brief kerygmatic formulas, Paul articulates a redemptive christology in exhortations to his readers. Two passages are particularly prominent. In Romans 6 the apostle raises the question whether Christians should "continue in sin that grace may abound" (6:1). This query makes sense in light of the argument of the previous chapter (i.e., Romans 5) where Paul affirmed that the grace of God in Christ is mightier than the effects of sin (which leads to condemnation and death), arguing that point basically on the principle that the greater sin has been, the greater grace has been; from this one might conclude that grace can be increased by sinning. Paul's reply to his own question, an emphatic no, is substantiated by his treatment of Christian baptism as a burial (6:4), a being united with Christ in his death (6:5), crucifixion (6:6), and death (6:8, 11). So, he concludes, "you must consider yourselves dead to sin and alive to God in Christ Jesus" (6:11). Christians are to "walk in newness of life" (6:4).

Paul's treatment of baptism, however, is based on a prior interpretation of the death of Christ. This death was a death "to sin" (*tē hamartia*, a dative, 6:10), and the life that Christ has in consequence of the resurrection is one of living to God. Christians, having been baptized, are to consider themselves dead to sin and alive to God as well (6:11). The analogy breaks down at one point. The death of the Christian to sin is a metaphorical expression for no longer continuing in sin. But the death of Christ "to sin" does not have the same meaning, for Christ cannot be thought of as having lived formerly in sin. The verse therefore has a different nuance. The dative in Greek allows for the understanding that Christ's death was "for" or "in respect to" sin (a dative of respect), and this has to be its meaning. Christ has taken to himself the consequences of sin (judgment and the punishment following it) on behalf of humanity. And those who have been baptized have been delivered over to him; they now have the benefits of his redemptive death. This is the presupposition for Paul's treatment of the question of Christian existence. Already delivered from the effects of sin, made effective and certified in baptism, Christians are not to "still live in" sin (6:2), as though nothing has happened. The force of the argument is primarily exhortation, but the death of Christ is alluded to as the means by which the consequences of sin have been taken by Christ in his death. A "newness of life" is thus a possibility (6:4). Nothing is said here concerning God's granting power for the new life through the Spirit. The new life is primarily motivated, in this instance, by a new self-understanding (6:11), but that new self-

51

understanding is based on the new condition in which the Christian is found to be: freed from judgment and the sentence due in consequence of sin.

Another hortatory passage which speaks of the redemptive work of God in Christ is the Philippian Hymn (2:6–11). Paul exhorts his readers to avoid selfishness and to consider other persons and their interests more than they do their own. In Christ, he says, they have a new mind (or understanding, Phil. 2:5). And then he quotes from the hymn, which is usually regarded to be pre-Pauline, although Paul may have added one phrase ("even death on a cross," 2:8).[14] The hymn consists of two stanzas. The first (2:6–8) opens with the relative pronoun "who," referring to "Christ Jesus" in the previous verse (2:5), and therefore Christ is the subject of the clauses. Christ is the one who "emptied himself," was "born in human likeness," "humbled himself," and "became obedient unto death." Preexistence, incarnation, passion, and death are all asserted. Christ is the actor of the drama to this point, for it is not said that God sent him. But in the second stanza (2:9–11) the subject of the main clause is God. God has exalted the crucified Christ and has bestowed on him the name which is above every other, namely, "Lord" (2:9, 11). The exalted Jesus is to receive homage from all creatures—heavenly, earthly, and subterranean. This vision of Jesus as cosmic Lord looks to the eschatological future, and those who acclaim him Lord will not be simply or exclusively those who acclaim him such in the present age.[15] Acclaiming him Lord in the present is done by those persons (believers) for whom the end of the old age has come and upon whom the eschatological age has already arrived. But the acclamation will be joined by others when the new age comes upon the world in its fullness. One may ask the question whether this is "doxological hyperbole" and whether Paul would have endorsed the implications of the hymn. But the fact that he uses it and that other passages in Paul point in the same direction confirms that he did. Some of these passages will be referred to in the next section.

3. Among those passages in which Paul treats christology and redemption at relative length, two are most important. The first is at Rom. 3:21–26. Prior to this passage, Paul has argued that "all people, both Jews and Greeks, are under the power of sin" (3:9). Then at 3:21 he makes a radical transition. "But now," he says, "the righteousness of God has been manifested." The term "now" has more than a logical force; it has a temporal meaning in consequence of the atoning death and resurrection of Christ.[16] God's righteousness is, for Paul, God's power to save.[17] In both the Old Testament and intertestamental Jewish literature there are passages which expect that God's righteousness as saving power will be manifested with the coming of the Messiah or the messianic age.[18]

In Paul's understanding, even if 3:21–26 may contain elements of a pre-Pauline tradition[19] (and that is not certain),[20] it is held here that the righteousness of God has indeed been manifested, since the Christ has come. In Christ has come the redemption *(apolytrōsis)* of sinful humanity (3:24), leading to justification. Drawing upon the imagery of the Old Testament regarding the Day of Atonement (Exod. 25:17–22; 31:7; 35:12; 38:5, 7–8 [Hebrew, 37:6–9]; Lev. 16:2, 13–15; Num. 7:89) and alluding specifically to the "mercy seat" (Hebrew, *kappōreth;* LXX, *hilastērion*) as the "type," the crucified Christ is designated the "antitype" and is spoken of as the "mercy seat" *(hilastērion),* the place at which atonement is made (Rom. 3:25).[21] The structure of the statement of Romans 3:25 has features similar to the sending formula: God is the subject; an aorist verb is used ("put forth"); Christ (rather than "the Son") is the object; and the redemptive significance of the event is articulated—the crucified Christ has been put forth "as the mercy seat in his blood" (= in his death). For Paul the eschatological expectation of God's manifesting his righteousness for salvation has been fulfilled in the crucified Jesus. The mercy seat of the old cultus was the place where God was thought to be invisibly enthroned (Exod. 25:22; Lev. 16:2; Ps. 99:1) and where atonement was made by use of blood (Lev. 16:14–24). So the cross too is the sign of God's presence in the world for faith—although outwardly the sign of his complete absence—and it was the place at which atonement was made through the blood (= death) of Jesus. Again, as in other formulations, Christ in his death is portrayed as one who bears the judgment and sentence upon sin for humanity; through his death he is the means of redemption. All of this demonstrates that God is righteous (Rom. 3:25–26); he justifies by his grace as a gift (3:24).

The other passage in which Paul treats christology and redemption in a sustained presentation is Rom. 5:12–21. Paul starts by saying that sin came into the world by Adam and that death came as its consequence. He goes on to maintain, however, that justification came into the world through Christ and that life has come as its consequence. The thrust of the presentation is that, however great the effects of Adam, the effects of Christ are greater (5:15, 17). It is at the close of the section that the paralleled contrasts are worked out with precision, and they can be seen best when presented in columns. The translation is our own.

Rom. 5:18

As through one's [Adam's] trespass	so through one's [Christ's] act of righteousness
[there has been]	[there is]
for all persons	for all persons
condemnation,	justification resulting in life.[22]

53

Rom. 5:19

As through one's [Adam's]	so through one's [Christ's]
disobedience	obedience
many	many
were made	will be made
sinners,	righteous.

Adam, according to Paul, is the prototype and head of humanity in its actual character before God. Paul begins his discussion by saying that through Adam sin entered the world, and all persons have sinned ever since (5:12–14). But there is more to be said. In 5:15, 17, 18 Paul uses the term "trespass" *(paraptōma)* in regard to Adam. Etymologically the term is related to the verb "to fall" *(piptō)* and is an equivalent to "sin" (cf. 5:13 and 5:20) as a disruption of humanity's relationship to God.[23] Adam's "trespass"—his fall—has set the whole world in rebellion against God. All of humanity bears the character of Adam as the fallen one: "by one man's trespass, many died" (5:15). The sentence of death upon Adam (Gen. 3:19) has been extended to all.

But as shown by the chart of parallel expressions (5:18–19), the redemptive work of God in Christ has altered the situation. Adam's "trespass" *(paraptōma)* has been countered by Christ's "act of righteousness" *(dikaiōma)*, and Adam's "disobedience" *(parakoē)* has been superseded by Christ's "obedience" *(hypakoē)*. And while Adam's "trespass" brought "condemnation" and his "disobedience" made many (= "all," for no one would be excluded) to be "sinners," Christ's "act of righteousness" has brought "justification resulting in life" and his "obedience" causes "many" (= "all") to be made "righteous."

What is significant, and even astounding, in this passage is that justification and righteousness are said to be world embracing. Christ's act of righteousness results in "justification resulting in life for all persons" *(eis pantas anthrōpous,* 5:18). His obedience makes "many" to be "righteous" (5:19), and the term "many" refers to "all" persons.[24] The background for Paul's expression is Isa. 53:11, where it is said that "the righteous one," the Lord's Servant, will make "many" to be accounted righteous and he will bear their sins. The redemptive work of God has been accomplished in the "act of righteousness" and "obedience" of Christ who, through his own death, has taken the judgment of death and condemnation upon himself, thereby liberating humanity from this judgment. As Adam was the head of humanity in the old aeon, leading all to destruction, so Christ is the head of humanity in the new age which has dawned, leading all to justification and life. The grace of God in

Christ amounts to "much more" than the trespass of Adam and its effects (5:17). All of humanity is in view here without exceptions.[25]

Paul is perhaps best known for his setting forth his gospel of justification by faith. But less recognized is his gospel of the justification of humanity, which he sets forth in Rom. 5:12–21. Both are found in Paul, and they cohere theologically. The justification of humanity is the basis for justification by faith. That is to say, through Christ all of humanity has been justified. But that will be revealed only at the final judgment. For now it is known only through the gospel, and it becomes effective proleptically for those who hear and believe the gospel in the present; there is no condemnation for those who are in Christ (Rom. 8:1). This concept of the justification of humanity has a parallel and its confirmation where Paul uses the metaphor of reconciliation. He says that "in Christ God was reconciling the world to himself, not counting their trespasses against them" (2 Cor. 5:19). Furthermore, God has entrusted to Paul and others "the message of reconciliation." Their vocation is to appeal to all who will hear: "be reconciled to God" (2 Cor. 5:19–20). On the "divine side"—or in an "objective" way[26]—the world has been reconciled to God. But humanity does not know this except through the message of reconciliation. And those who receive the message enter into the new world of peace and reconciliation (Rom. 5:1).

This concludes our survey of the main passages in which the redemptive christology of Paul comes to expression. But prior to drawing up a summation, it is necessary to consider briefly two related themes. These have to do with words of judgment in Paul's letters and also with his apostleship and mission.

It goes without saying that Paul speaks on various occasions of eschatological peril for both the world at large and also for Christians who do not continue in fidelity to their confession. Such passages present a challenge to the redemptive christology which has been described. Concerning the world at large, Paul summons all the world to divine judgment (Rom. 1:18—2:16), and in other instances he speaks of perishing, death, and destruction for those who are outside (or opposed to) the Christian community (1 Cor. 1:18; 2 Cor. 2:16; Phil. 1:28; 3:18–19). But these instances must be weighed in light of Paul's countervailing claims spelled out in extended theological treatments concerning the salvation of Israel (Rom. 11:25–31), the justification of humanity in Christ (Rom. 5:12–21), the reconciliation of the world (2 Cor. 5:19), the final acclamation of every tongue that "Jesus Christ is Lord" (Phil. 2:10–11), and the final consummation when God will be everything to everyone (1 Cor. 15:28). Concerning those who are Christians, Paul warns them of possible peril if they become slaves of sin (Rom. 6:16, 21–23), have false security (1

Thess. 5:3), continue in immorality (1 Cor. 6:9–10; Gal. 5:21), and the like. These warnings are given for the sake of purifying the community and directing its members along the path of Christian obedience.[27] That does not mean that they are to be taken less seriously, for the threat of peril is thought by Paul to be real. But they are the penultimate word, which preaching must entail, if Paul is to expose illusion and self-deception, and if he is to remain true to his own biblical heritage and witness of both the threat and promise of God. But the final word of Paul is the gospel that there is no condemnation for those who are in Christ (Rom. 8:1), that the justified have peace with God (Rom. 5:1), and that there is nothing that can separate them from the love of God in Christ (Rom. 8:38–39).

Paul's mission as an apostle was to bear the gospel of reconciliation to the nations (Rom. 11:3; cf. Gal. 2:8–9; Rom. 15:16, 18).[28] Already in the Old Testament the eschatological vision portrays the conversion, enlightenment, and gathering of all the nations before the God of Israel.[29] Now in the end time the apostle Paul, commissioned by the risen Christ, proclaims the gospel of reconciliation of humanity to God, inaugurating the procession of the nations toward the goal of the final assembly. God has declared through his prophet that he will send his witnesses to declare his glory "among the nations" (Isa. 66:19). "And they shall bring all your brethren from all the nations as an offering to the Lord" (66:20). So Paul speaks of himself as a minister of Christ to the nations "in the priestly service of the gospel . . . so that the offering of the nations may be acceptable, sanctified by the Holy Spirit" (Rom. 15:16).[30] His converts are the "offering." They are the first of those who shall ultimately gather in worship of the God of Israel. Using cultic terminology again, Paul speaks of his converts as the "first fruits" (Rom. 16:5; 1 Cor. 16:15; cf. Rom. 11:16). In the Old Testament the offering of the first fruits (Exod. 23:16; 34:26; Num. 28:26; Deut. 26:1–11) is an act by which God is acknowledged as owner of all things; the remaining crop is sanctified and shares in the divine blessing;[31] the first fruits represent the whole.[32] In the Pauline vision, all of humanity has been reconciled to God in Christ and at the end will assemble to worship the God of Israel. The procession of the nations is being inaugurated in his own apostolic mission among the nations. God leads his apostle in triumph through and among the nations and "through us," he says, "spreads the fragrance of the knowledge of him everywhere" (2 Cor. 2:14), and "grace extends to more and more people" (2 Cor. 4:15). The eschatological expectation, set forth in the Scriptures of Israel, is being realized in the present, and will be realized fully at the parousia.

On the basis of an examination of kerygmatic formulas, hortatory passages, and texts treating christology and redemption specifically, a consistent picture emerges. God has acted decisively to redeem humanity by sending forth his Son. The death of Christ was "for" (*hyper*) humanity, and in that death God's judgment and sentence upon sin (and therefore upon humanity) have been carried out. Atonement has been made. The effects of Adam's "trespass" or fall, leading to condemnation and death for all, have been countered and surpassed by Christ's act of righteousness and obedience—and that is world embracing in its effects. The "objective" character and the "universal" scope of Christ's atoning death constitute the gospel. But that gospel is not known through human reason or wisdom (1 Cor. 1:21—2:13). It was revealed to Paul (Gal. 1:12) and must be proclaimed among the nations. When it is proclaimed and heard, it becomes a power unto salvation for those who believe (Rom. 1:16). Those who believe enter into a new world, the assembly of the new age, and justification is theirs apart from the law (Rom. 3:21–25, 28). For those who have not heard and believed, the "glorious liberty of the children of God" is still in the future (Rom. 8:21).[33] And even those who reject the gospel—and for Paul that is empirical Israel in particular—will finally be saved in the end time purely by the grace of God (Rom. 11:26).[34] Paul himself had opposed the gospel and persecuted the church (Gal. 1:13; 1 Cor. 15:9; Phil. 3:6), but God revealed his Son to him (Gal. 1:16; cf. 1 Cor. 9:1; 15:8) and commissioned him to proclaim the gospel to the nations. Therefore Paul could envision the appearance of Christ to all humanity—at his parousia—when all human defenses will give way, Christ will be acclaimed Lord by all (Phil. 2:10–11), and God will finally be "everything to everyone" (1 Cor. 15:28). Although in the present era God has consigned all persons to disobedience, so that all stand under his judgment, he has at the same time exercised his saving righteousness in Christ, and his mercy shall finally extend to all (Rom. 11:32), confirming the gospel of human redemption.

THE GOSPEL OF MARK

The Gospel of Mark uses several christological titles. The term "Christ" is clearly used by Mark himself as a designation (1:1), and it is used six other times, probably from traditions he received, for a total of seven instances.[35] The term "Son of God" may or may not be used by the evangelist at 1:1. The title is lacking in some major Greek witnesses, but it is present in others. There is an inclination among text critics today to include the phrase as genuinely belonging to the text of Mark, and so it appears in the latest edition (the twenty-sixth) of the Nestle-Aland Greek text (1979)—although in brackets—and in the RSV since 1971. Besides this disputed instance, however, the title appears seven times (sometimes, however, as simply "the Son" or "Son of the Blessed").³⁶ The title "Son of man" appears—always in sayings of Jesus himself—fourteen times.³⁷ The title "Son of David" appears three times.³⁸ And on six occasions— all in the passion narrative—Jesus either is asked by Pilate whether he is "King of the Jews" or is mocked and crucified on the charge that he had claimed to be such.³⁹

Other terms are used in reference to Jesus, but they are either not major christological titles for Mark or not christological at all. The term "lord" or "Lord" (*kyrios* can mean either) is used at 7:28 and may mean no more than a polite form of address (hence, "lord"). There are four instances, however, where the term has more definite christological associations.⁴⁰ The term "Lord" is therefore known by Mark as a christological title, but it actually does not figure prominently in his work. Other terms commonly used of Jesus, which are not christological titles, are rabbi, teacher, and prophet.⁴¹

Interpreters have debated whether any one of the major titles (Christ, Son of God, Son of Man, Son of David, or King of the Jews) is fundamental to Mark's christology, an axis around which the others are to be interpreted. Some interpreters have held that "Son of God" is the most important.⁴² Others have maintained that "Son of Man" is.⁴³

The investigation of titles and their use in Mark, however, is not sufficient for discerning the meaning of Jesus as a redemptive figure in this Gospel. A more comprehensive approach is needed. At the outset of his Gospel, Mark has written "[The] beginning [*archē*] of the gospel of Jesus Christ" (and some important Greek witnesses have the additional words "the Son of God," 1:1). What can this mean? It is not likely that Mark intends this opening line to be a title for his work.⁴⁴ Nor is it likely that he means that the Gospel begins with the ministry of John the Baptist (1:2–8) or with his ministry and the baptism and temptation of Jesus (1:2–13)—a beginning which is then completed in the ministry of Jesus subsequently.⁴⁵ When Mark uses the term "gospel" elsewhere, it refers to the good news which Jesus proclaims (1:14–15) or the good news preached by the church concerning Jesus Christ (8:35; 10:29; 13:10; 14:9).⁴⁶ The "gospel" referred to in 1:1 can therefore refer to the gospel which is being preached in the church and world of Mark's own day.⁴⁷ This gospel has a "beginning" in the story of Jesus. All of Mark 1:1— 16:8 (the entire book) is the "beginning" of the gospel.⁴⁸ Given the situation in which Mark worked, when the church knew persecution (13:9–13), apostasy (13:5–6, 21–22), lack of faith (11:22–24; cf. 6:6;

9:19), and perhaps an inadequate—or even false—understanding of the gospel,[49] and given the fact that some forty years had passed since Jesus' death and resurrection,[50] Mark sets out to portray the "beginning" of the gospel to instruct and encourage the church of his time. The gospel as kerygmatic address needs to be augmented, and perhaps even reformed, by an account of its beginnings.[51] The Gospel of Mark is then an "archaeology" of the gospel—an ordered presentation of its beginning.

Extending throughout the Gospel of Mark there are various themes, and four are particularly important for discerning the redemptive christology set forth. We can touch on each only briefly.

1. First, although Jesus is placed front and center as an actor in the drama, the gospel as Mark implicitly conceives it is the good news of what God has done in the ministry, death, and resurrection of this central figure.[52] All that takes place in the course of the drama of redemption is in accord with what must take place in the purpose and plan of God. It is necessary (*dei*) for the Son of Man to suffer, be rejected, be killed, and rise after three days (8:31).[53] The course of events takes place "as it has been written" (*kathōs* or *hōs gegraptai*) in the Scriptures of Israel: the ministry of John the Baptist (1:2; 9:13), the hypocrisy of Jesus' opponents (7:6), the suffering and contemptuous treatment of the Son of Man (9:12), his death (14:21), and Jesus' being abandoned by his disciples (14:27).[54] In the parable of the wicked tenants (12:1–11), where the owner of the vineyard represents God allegorically, it is the owner who has sent his servants (12:2–5) and his son (12:6); and even though the son was killed, Mark's account ends with a christological use of Ps. 118:22–23, which speaks of the rejected "stone" (the Son) as having been exalted (= by God, a divine passive; 12:10–11). All of these features indicate that for Mark the course of Jesus' ministry and destiny is divinely initiated, determined, and guided.[55]

2. A second theme of importance is the so-called "messianic secret" which was highlighted by William Wrede at the turn of the century[56] and which has occupied scholarly attention ever since.[57] Within Mark's Gospel, Jesus commands demons, persons healed, and the disciples not to speak of his deeds or identity (1:25, 34, 43–45; 3:12; 5:43; 7:36; 8:26, 30; 9:9). Jesus is said to speak to the crowds in parables in order that they might not comprehend his message (4:10–13), and the disciples, in spite of their receiving private instructions and revelations, comprehend neither his teaching nor who he truly is (4:13, 40–41; 6:50–52; 7:18; 8:16–21; 9:5–6). The significance of this motif within the Gospel of Mark and for our understanding of it has been debated; probably no other topic has received as much attention in Marcan studies. The interpretations run all the way from denying that it has importance for the

evangelist[58] to the view that it was the most decisive factor and presupposition for Mark's creation of the gospel genre, that is, that Mark's Gospel arose out of a situation in which the author put together traditions about Jesus already considered christological in such a way as to conform them to the kerygma of his death and resurrection.[59] On several issues it can be said that many interpreters would agree: (1) a "secret" motif does appear in Mark's Gospel; (2) whether Mark received it in his traditions in elementary form or whether he was the first to implement it, it is a Marcan emphasis; and (3) it serves to postpone a premature estimation of the person and ministry of Jesus until the cross and resurrection; then and there, and only then and there, is his meaning fully disclosed.[60]

3. A third motif in Mark, which has received less attention, is the portrayal of Jesus as a numinous figure.[61] Jesus bears authority (1:22, 27; 2:10; 11:27–33), and Mark uses a variety of verbs to express astonishment and awe on the part of the crowds and the disciples alike at Jesus' miraculous deeds and teaching. They are amazed (*existēmi*, 2:12; 5:42; 6:51; *ekthambeō*, 9:15), astonished (*ekplēssomai*, 1:22; 6:2; 7:37; 10:26; 11:18; *thambeomai*, 1:27; 10:32; *thaumazō*, 5:20), and experience fear (*phobeomai*, 4:41; 5:15, 33; 6:50; 9:32; 10:32; *tarassō*, 6:50). In consequence of the resurrection, the women at the tomb are amazed (*ekthambeō*, 16:5) and are afraid (*phobeomai*, 16:8), for trembling and astonishment (*tromos kai ekstasis*) had come upon them (16:8). Many of these notations are considered form critically to be "choric endings" of miracle stories and many belong to the essential structure of miracle stories in the traditions which Mark has received, but that is not true of all. Some of them are clearly Mark's own redactional work, appearing in summaries, introductions, or conclusions to accounts, and they have been composed by the evangelist himself (e.g., 1:22; 2:12; 4:41; 5:20; 7:37; 9:15, 32; 10:32; 16:8). Moreover, there are instances in which a command to silence does not follow miracle stories (2:1–12; 3:1–5; 4:35–41; 5:25–34; 6:30–44, 45–51; 8:1–10; 9:14–29; 10:46–52);[62] some of these end on the note of awe and astonishment (2:1–12; 4:35–41; 6:45–51; cf. 5:33); and subsequent to the exorcism in the account of the Geresene demoniac (5:1–13), Jesus actually commands the man to go and tell what the Lord has done for him (5:19). All these things, considered together, demonstrate that Mark has not become dogmatically single-minded in stamping his entire work with the messianic secret motif, but that he has an interest also in presenting Jesus as one through whom divine powers are operative and effective. Endowed by the Spirit since his baptism by John (1:9–11), Jesus' authority and wonder-working powers are from God (3:27; 11:27–33). They are signs of God's eschatological authority and rule coming into the lives of those to whom Jesus ministered

and among those who saw what was happening. Amazement is not censored but heightened by Mark, for Jesus is a numinous figure.

4. Finally, it is obviously necessary, in seeking to discern Mark's redemptive christology, to observe how he interprets Jesus' passion, death, and resurrection. The passion is anticipated in narrative at 3:6; 11:18; and 12:12–13 and in the sayings of Jesus at 2:20; 8:31; 9:31; 10:33–34, 45; and 14:24. Some of the sayings anticipate the resurrection as well.

In speaking of his death, the Jesus of Mark's Gospel says that the Son of Man has come to give his life as a "ransom for many" (*lytron anti pollōn,* 10:45) and that his death is a means by which his covenant-establishing blood is poured out "for many" (*hyper pollōn,* 14:24). The term "many" is generally regarded as a Semitism representing "all" (cf. Isa. 53:11–12).[63] Concerning the term "ransom" (*lytron,* 10:45), one should not speculate to whom the ransom in this instance is given, but consider rather the function and effect of such giving. In the Old Testament (and particularly where the LXX uses the term *lytron*) the effect of a ransom is liberation for a person previously held in bondage.[64] And the preposition "for" (*anti,* 10:45) has the meaning not of "instead of" or "in place of" many, but "for the sake of" or "on behalf of" many.[65] The innocent suffering and death of Jesus (14:56–57; 15:14) are thus portrayed as a means of liberation done for the benefit of others. And in the saying concerning the covenent-establishing aspect of this death (14:24), the words Moses spoke while pouring out blood to establish a covenant between God and his people (Exod. 24:8) are recalled. The death of Jesus is the antitype of this event by which a covenant is made for the benefit of "the many." It can only be conjectured whether the prophecy in Jer. 31:31–34 of God's establishing a "new covenant" in the age of salvation is alluded to in this instance. Paul uses the term "new covenent" (1 Cor. 11:25), as does Luke who shares the same tradition (22:20), and in these instances the allusion to Jeremiah 31 is clear. It would seem that Mark's tradition presupposes the same allusion—even though the precise terminology of a "new" covenant "has dropped out"[66]—but one cannot be absolutely certain.

Having given attention to these four aspects of the Gospel of Mark, it is possible to draw upon them to discern the redemptive christology of Mark. For Mark the "beginning of the gospel" (Mark 1:1—16:8) took place in a drama initiated and directed by God. Although Jesus is portrayed as one who bears authority and who is a numinous figure, his destiny is to suffer, die, and rise, and his meaning for Christian faith cannot be understood apart from this destiny. The giving of his life as a means of liberation for humanity (10:45) is acted out in a series of events which eclipse his numinous character. The degree to which this series of events is due to tradition which Mark had received is debatable. It has been held by many interpreters that Mark received a previously composed passion narrative,[67] but others have suggested that Mark formulated much of it himself from smaller units of tradition.[68] In any case, the Marcan narrative as we have it portrays Jesus as distressed, troubled, sorrowful, and even asking momentarily that he be spared from suffering (14:33–34, 36a), but nevertheless he submits to the Father's will (14:36b). He is accused falsely (14:56; 15:3–4), mocked (15:17–20, 29–32), and the crowds seek his death by crucifixion (15:13–14). Betrayed by Judas (14:10–11, 21, 41–46), denied by Peter (14:66–72; cf. 14:30), and abandoned by the rest of his disciples (14:50), he cries out from the cross, asking why God has forsaken him (15:34), and then he utters a loud cry and dies (15:37). The events are accompanied by darkness over the earth (15:33) and the rending of the temple curtain (15:38)—events which attest the crucifixion as the eschatological saving event with cosmic and universal significance.[69] It is, however, the pagan centurion at the cross who bears witness that Jesus truly was the Son of God (15:39). No one except this man—a man of the world, who stands where no one has pure hands, and who is implicated in the actual execution—understands both what has taken place and also the identity of the crucified one.[70] The account comes to a close with the certification to Pilate that Jesus is dead (15:44–45).

In the post-resurrection account (16:1–8) the word of the young man to the women is that the crucified Jesus has been raised (*ēgerthē*, 16:6). He directs them to go and "tell his disciples and Peter" that they will see the risen one in Galilee. Overcome by trembling and astonishment, the women flee from the tomb, "and they said nothing to anyone, for they were afraid" (16:8). Some interpreters have suggested that Mark means in this verse that after this event the women were therefore silent, failing to communicate the message given to them.[71] But that is not likely Mark's meaning. It is more likely that Mark intends to portray the women as overcome by awe at what has taken place—a *mysterium tremendum*—when he describes them as trembling, astonished, and fearful.[72] The terminology is Marcan, recalling the awe, amazement, and fear caused by numinous events previously in the gospel narrative. It is also possible that Mark sought to portray the women as single-minded in their duty to deliver the news directly to the disciples, as they had been commanded; that is, they said nothing to anyone along the way.[73]

Mark's account of the "beginning of the gospel" subordinates Jesus to the redemptive purpose of God. While it is Jesus who "gives" his life as a means of redemption, the drama unfolds in such a way that he is virtually swept along and becomes a victim of forces which crush him and lead to his death in abandonment and a sense of forsakenness. Indeed the one who came "to give" *(dounai)* his life is more frequently spoken of as one who was "given over" or "delivered" *(paradidotai,* 9:31; 10:33; 14:41; cf. 14:42), attesting that his destiny through suffering and death is according to the divine purpose.[74] Likewise, although Jesus says that the Son of Man "came" to give his life as a ransom for many (10:45), which seems at first sight to attribute an initiative to Jesus, he also speaks of himself as "sent" from God (9:37).[75] Even more pronounced are the emphases on "necessity" and the fulfillment of the Scriptures ("as it is written") in the course of events, attesting that his obedience outranks his initiative. The initiative is God's, and Jesus as Son of God completes the course set for him in obedience to the divine will and purpose. And his resurrection is by divine action, as the passive *(ēgerthē)* indicates (16:6).

As in the Epistles of Paul, so in the Gospel of Mark the redemptive work of God in Christ retains a theopractic character, and it is "objective" in character and "universal" in scope. The death of Jesus as a "ransom for many" depends in no way upon human initiative, nor is it a means by which the wrath of God is appeased; it is completely carried out by divine grace. The ransom saying (10:45)—whatever factors went into its composition in earliest Christianity—is at the Marcan level an allusion to Isaiah 53:10–11,[76] at which the Servant of the Lord dies as a means of atonement for "many." For Mark the death of Jesus is the means by which one, the crucified Christ, bears the judgment and sentence due to sin on behalf of the many, humanity as a whole, and his resurrection attests that he has been reclaimed by God. And if he has been reclaimed, God has also reclaimed humanity in him. This is the "beginning of the gospel" (1:1) which is to be proclaimed "to all nations" (13:10) or "in all the world" (14:9).

It is in light of this prior claim—that the redemptive work of God in Christ has humanity in its view—that the words of judgment in the Gospel of Mark must be understood. Whoever blasphemes against the Holy Spirit "never has forgiveness, but is guilty of an eternal sin" (3:29). A testimony is to be given against those who do not receive the emissaries of Jesus (6:11). Those who seek to save their own lives will lose them (8:35). Whoever is ashamed of the Son of Man, of such will he be ashamed (8:38). It is better to enter life maimed in order to avoid sin than to enter hell whole (9:43–47). It is difficult for a rich person to enter the kingdom of God (10:24). Such passages constitute a mixture of sayings—some gnomic, some christological, some dogmatic—from the traditions which Mark had received and incorporated into his Gospel. Some may come from Jesus, others from later stages of the tradition, but in any case they are presented by Mark as a part of the hortatory content that preaching and teaching require if the church of his day is to remain faithful to its Lord. The Christian must both give his or her own life in sacrificial service to others (8:34; 10:43–44) and bear witness to Jesus (13:9–13; cf. 8:38).

Yet Mark's Gospel does not in principle preclude from final salvation those who are outside the circle of discipleship, that is, humanity which has not heard and believed the gospel. The emphasis is upon God's act of redemption in Christ on behalf of the human family, the necessity *(dei)* of proclaiming this good news to all the nations (13:10), and the fidelity required of those who proclaim this gospel, even through persecution and death (8:35; 10:29; 13:9–13). Mark's Gospel is not itself a tract for evangelism, but is an account of the "beginning of the gospel" for those who are already Christians, in order that they might understand what has been done and what has been given to them.[77] The Christian movement, as Mark understood it, was already severed from Judaism, since it included gentiles and was no longer Torah observant;[78] thus, the saying at 12:9 (within the parable of the wicked husbandmen) that the "lord of the vineyard" (= God) will give the vineyard to "others" alludes to the existence of a church which understands itself as having assumed the place of Israel in the history of salvation.[79] Moreover, there are indications within the Gospel of Mark that the Christian movement known to the author had already taken on features of a religious belief system and institutional life,[80] and was not simply a movement "within" Judaism. This accounts for the hortatory sayings which threaten peril for Christians who might fall away. But essentially the Gospel of Mark proclaims for its community the promise of salvation based on the redemptive work of God in Christ. Moreover, this redemptive work envisions humanity in its scope, and that is why the good news of redemption is to be proclaimed to all the nations.

RETROSPECT

The oldest christological formulas are theopractic. The oldest of all may have been: "[We believe that] God raised Jesus from the dead."[81] Traces of this formula can be found in the Epistles of Paul and the sermons in Acts.[82] In these instances God is the actor, and the object of his action is "Jesus," not a christological title. The theopractic emphasis is precisely what one might expect at the outset of the Christian movement, for that would have been in keeping with its monotheistic heritage from Judaism. Further, that "Jesus" was the object of the action is what one might expect in the earliest formulations, for the earliest proclaimers would have remembered Jesus the man, not a figure bearing a christological title, as the one by whom they had been encountered "in the days of his flesh" and who had been crucified and raised.

The theopractic accent can still be heard in the redemptive christologies of Paul and Mark. Although other christological formulas are used by both—and a proliferation of christological titles has set in—both writers place their emphasis of the action of God in Christ for the redemption of the world. That does not mean that Jesus ceases to be within himself an ego capable of decision and will. When Paul speaks of Jesus, he generally does so by using christological titles,[83] and it may seem initially that Jesus as a person has lost his essentially human character and is therefore totally passive in a divine drama of redemption. But that is not actually the case. Paul speaks of Christ as one who in his earthly life acted in love (Gal. 2:20), was obedient to God (Rom. 5:19; Phil. 2:8), and gave his life for others (the *hyper*-formula). Likewise Mark portrays Jesus as a deliberating man in Gethsemane who contests the will of God ("remove this cup from me," 14:36) and yet gave his life for the benefit of others (10:45).

The theopractic character of redemptive christology in Paul and Mark does not therefore obliterate the role of the earthly Jesus in redemption. What it stresses instead is that, while Christ is front and center in the drama, the one who initiates, guides, and brings the drama to its conclusion is the God of Israel.[84] Instead of portraying Christ as a majestic redeemer figure who comes from above to rescue humanity and then— to cite an example of presentation at another time and place—abolishes death and brings life and immortality to light (2 Tim. 1:10), these writers portray him essentially as the one in whom God does the saving deed, and his own role is primarily that of obedience to the divine purpose. Jesus is the suffering Messiah, the lowly one, the crucified. And by divine appointment he bears the consequences of sin for the benefit of humanity. His resurrection is the result of God's raising him from the dead, signaling the divine verdict. Redemption has been wrought in him.

There are certain subsidiary features of this type of redemptive chris- tology that can be listed. In doing such a listing we run the danger of harmonizing Paul and Mark where we should not. But at a minimum we can list six items which belong to the redemptive christology which they share.

1. By placing the emphasis on the divine action in Christ, christology is expressed more along functional than ontological lines. Of course Paul holds to the preexistence of Christ (1 Cor. 8:6; 2 Cor. 8:9; Phil. 2:6–7) and uses the major titles to express different christological aspects. But,

as seen in our treatment, these are essentially put to service within a functional framework: God's "sending" his "Son," Jesus as "Lord" of the community, "Christ" as the one who gave himself, and so on. Mark knows nothing of a preexistence of Christ—or at least gives no hint of it—and his christology is expressed through a narrative which moves along rapidly toward its goal, a story of the obedient Son of God who travels the course of redemption determined by God.

2. The centrality of the cross to the drama of redemption is asserted boldly in this type of redemptive christology. The death of Christ is not simply the prelude to the saving work of God in him; it is not just a step along the way to an exalted life and status, from which alone the saving benefits come. The death of Christ has an atoning significance in itself, for it is the means by which sin and its consequences are borne for the benefit of others.

3. Redemption is an accomplished fact in this type of redemptive christology. In one respect that is an overstatement. The old age continues to exist, and the new comes fully into its own only at the parousia. But in another respect it is not an overstatement. The cross and resurrection, considered together, mark the end of the old and the inauguration of the new. The conditions of the old age—humanity's bondage to sin and its consequences—no longer have an abiding legacy. God has already condemned sin in Christ's sacrificial death (Paul); the life of Jesus has been given as a ransom for many, thereby liberating them (Mark). The new age has come through God's raising the crucified to life, which opens the future for humanity. The gospel attests that this is so, that it has happened.

4. This "objective" character of God's redemption of humanity in Christ entails a universality. The redemptive work of God in Christ is not for Israel alone; it has been done for the benefit of all people, that is, for Jews as Jews and for gentiles as gentiles. There is no thought that gentiles must first undergo circumcision (i.e., technically become Jews) in order to share in redemption. The God of Israel is understood to be the God of all the world, both as its creator and its redeemer. In his sacrificial death Christ assumes the burden of all persons—their sin and its consequences. The "mythos" of the redemptive christology under the first type is that all humanity under heaven is in need of redemption, and redemption has been accomplished once and for all in the death and resurrection of Jesus the Christ.

5. Since the redemptive work of God in Christ is for all people, this good news, this gospel, is to be proclaimed to the whole world, and the church becomes an integral factor in the extension of the gospel. Wherever the gospel is proclaimed and believed, the redemptive work of God

in Christ becomes realized, and people enter into a new world even while living in the old. What is in store for humanity, now set free for life in the new world to come, becomes a present reality and basis for existence. The church is the vital community in which this new existence takes on its social form. This is more obvious in Paul than in Mark, but as indicated in our survey of the Gospel of Mark, the evangelist also takes for granted a community of believers, and these persons gather for the Lord's Supper and exercise care and discipline.[85] It is in the church, for both Paul and Mark, that the gospel is proclaimed and mutual upbuilding takes place, and the church is commissioned as well to proclaim the gospel to those outside. There is continuing peril that believers will fall away, and therefore no longer live in the realm of realized redemption, so the church becomes a social context for mutual care, support, and discipline.

6. Yet the church in this redemptive christology is not envisioned as constituting the sum total of the beneficiaries of the redemptive work of God in Christ. The redemptive mythos remains universal in scope. While the church is the sign and temporal-earthly embodiment of the redemptive work of God in Christ, essentially no part of creation is left to fall beyond the horizons. Again this is more explicit in the writings of Paul than in the Gospel of Mark. Nevertheless, both writers, in spite of their warnings of peril for those who are believers already, portray Christ as having given his life for the redemption of the world, the one for the many, and the "many" is humanity as a whole. The gospel is to be proclaimed to the world on the basis of this prior claim. The mythos of the redemptive christology of the first type goes precisely in the direction of the universal scope of redemption, even though both writers who employ it make utterances which seem at first to call it into question. But such utterances of divine threat are necessary for the sake of calling upon believers to realize in their own lives what is required of those who claim to have entered into the new world of redemption already, regardless of how much that is so only in part.

The redemptive christology explored in this chapter is of course but one aspect of the Epistles of Paul and the Gospel of Mark, and it is also but one aspect of their respective christologies. Our concern, however, has been to focus on redemptive christology alone. The writings of Paul and Mark differ from one another in many respects, but they can be considered together as representing in broad outline one type of redemptive christology. This will become more clear as we go on in subsequent chapters to show additional ways in which redemptive christology is expressed by other writers.

6

Redemption Confirmed
Through Christ

OUR ATTENTION IN this chapter shifts to another way of linking christology and redemption. For all their differences, the Gospel of Matthew and the two volumes of Luke (his Gospel and the Acts of the Apostles) can be treated together under the second type of redemptive christology: redemption confirmed through Christ. For both of these writers, Jesus is the one through whom God fulfills, or confirms, his redemptive purpose, making salvation possible for humanity. Fundamentally these two writers share a single type of redemptive christology. Its features will be drawn out in detail at the end of the chapter.

THE GOSPEL OF MATTHEW

The Gospel of Matthew is generally regarded as having arisen in Syria during the last two decades of the first century.[1] It has been suggested that its rise can be understood partly in light of events following the destruction of Jerusalem (A.D. 70), particularly the gathering of leading Pharisees at Jamnia to reconstitute Judaism along essentially Pharisaic lines.[2] These leaders sought to preserve traditions, systematize them, and apply them to the new situation; this process led ultimately to the formation of the Mishnah, Talmud, and other rabbinic literature in succeeding centuries. In a similar way, the author of this Gospel[3] collected traditions about Jesus (including Mark, Q, and special Matthean traditions), ordered them in a systematic way,[4] and applied the teachings of Jesus to life and its issues in the Christian community within which he lived. The author did his work in the manner of a scribe "who brings out of his treasure what is new and what is old" (Matt. 13:52), that is, draws from his tradition the law as interpreted by Jesus. For the writer of this

Gospel, as for any person of Jewish heritage, the will of God is expressed through the law. What is disputed is the interpretation of the law.[5] From the perspective of Matthew, the will of God is expressed through the law, as interpreted by Jesus. The community which the writer seeks to instruct is Greek speaking and made up of both Jews and gentiles.[6]

Matthew makes use of all the usual christological titles and more than most New Testament writers. These include "Christ" (fourteen times),[7] "Lord" (thirty times),[8] "Son of God" (seventeen times),[9] "Son of man" (thirty-one times),[10] and "Son of David" (eight times)[11] as major titles. In addition to these, Jesus is spoken of as the "son of Abraham" (1:1), "he who is to come" (11:3, a Q saying; cf. Luke 7:19), "King of Israel" (27:42, from Mark 15:32), "King of the Jews" (four times),[12] and Emmanuel (1:23). Jesus is also called "prophet," "rabbi," and "teacher," but these terms do not appear to be titles of majesty, strictly speaking.[13]

Much of the discussion of Matthean christology has been dominated by debate over the relative importance of the titles of majesty used.[14] So various interpreters have maintained that the major, dominating title is "Son of man,"[15] "Christ,"[16] "Lord,"[17] "Son of God,"[18] or a combination of titles.[19] The debate suggests that Matthew was concerned about a particular title as that which discloses the essential nature of Jesus and in terms of which other titles are to be understood. But that is unlikely. Each of the titles just mentioned is important in its own way. The title "Son of man" is obviously important, since Matthew uses it on eleven occasions beyond the twenty instances in Mark and Q.[20] The term has the widest conceivable span of meanings, for it is as Son of Man that Jesus forgives sins, that he suffers, dies, and rises, and that he will come in glory with his angels to exercise judgment.[21] "Christ" is obviously important, since it was the most universally used title in the early church, and Matthew knows Jesus primarily as "Jesus Christ" (1:1, 18) or "the Christ" (1:16–17; 2:4; 16:16, 20). Matthew uses the title "Lord" no less than twenty-five times beyond the mere five instances in Mark (Q has none).[22] And in the case of "Son of God," it appears six times in addition to the eleven instances in Mark and Q;[23] moreover, the title is used at pivotal points—not only, as in Mark, at Jesus' baptism, transfiguration, and crucifixion (Matt. 3:17; 17:5; 27:54), but also in Peter's confession (16:16) and in the commission at the close of the Gospel (28:19). It may well be that the chief interest of Matthew is not christology at all, but rather the interpretation of the law, the ordering of the church, and eschatology.[24] In any case, the debate about titles in Matthew tends to narrow the christology which does exist within the Gospel, resulting in a title reductionism. Matthew uses and extends a rich variety of titles in the service of christology. Here as elsewhere in the New Testament it should be seen that christology is not expressed by titles alone,[25] nor can a writer's christology be defined in terms of a particular title.

When set within the question of its redemptive significance, Matthew's christology portrays Jesus as the one in whom the promises of God to Israel have been confirmed. Through him, the one who has been raised and now reigns over the entire cosmos, salvation is possible for all people. Jesus' earthly ministry is seen to fulfill the Scriptures of Israel, which Matthew seeks to document by frequent use of his so-called "formula quotations."[26] At the same time Jesus is the authoritative interpreter of the Scriptures of Israel. He does not annul the moral teachings of the law and the prophets (5:17–20) but interprets them (5:21–48),[27] and does so in light of the double commandment of love for God above all things and one's neighbor as oneself; "on these two commandments depend all the law and the prophets" (22:40). That is to say, "the whole law and the prophets can be exegetically deduced from the command to love God and the neighbor, they 'hang' exegetically on these."[28] In this way the double commandment of love is established as the key for right interpretation of the law and the prophets over against Pharisaic interpretation,[29] with which Matthew contends and which Matthew regards as evading the will of God expressed through the law (cf. 23:23). Similarly, the law and the prophets are summarized by the so-called golden rule (7:12). Jesus is able to carry on the interpretation of the law because, as the "Lord" (the title used so often in address to him by the disciples), he bears divine authority; as the "Son of God" he is in unity with the Father (11:27) who had "delivered" all things to him; and as the "Messiah" (or "Christ") he is the teacher of Israel. Moreover, Torah and Wisdom had already been identified with one another in Jewish traditions (Sir. 24:23–24; Bar. 4:1), and for Matthew Jesus incarnates Wisdom (and therefore can give expression to the law).[30] This motif is brought out at 11:28–30, which is partially dependent on Sir. 51:23–30 for its imagery. Statements uttered by *sophia* in the latter are attributed to Jesus in Matthew.

This Jesus is a redemptive figure in the Gospel of Matthew. At the outset of the Gospel it is said that the child born to Mary is to be called "Jesus," and that is so for a particular reason: "for he will save his people from their sins" (1:21). The name "Jesus" (meaning "Yahweh saves" or "Yahweh is salvation")[31] suggests to Matthew the soteriological significance of the one who bears it, and that is salvation from sins. For Matthew, the obstacle to salvation for humanity is "sins," which are an affront to God. Matthew does not think in terms of "sin" as a power of bondage over humanity, leading to death—as in Pauline theology—but rather of "sins": attitudes, words, and deeds which are seen to be offensive to the divine will in light of the law when the law is interpreted correctly. When the law is interpreted rightly, or "radicalized,"[32] all persons are found to fall short of the divine will. At this point Matthew could have in principle endorsed the Pauline view that "through the law comes knowledge of sin" (Rom. 3:20).

Since the human problem before God is "sins," the remedy is either to cover up sins, transfer them away, or to forgive them. Matthew tends to stress the last, although that is not the whole of his soteriology, as will be shown. But the importance of the forgiveness of sins for salvation in Matthew's Gospel cannot be overlooked. Within the Lord's Prayer, which Christians are to pray (6:9), there is the petition, "forgive us our debts" (6:12a), and to the saying of Jesus at the last supper about the blood of the covenant poured out for many—presumably to be recited at celebrations of the Lord's Supper in the community—Matthew adds that it is "for the forgiveness of sins" (26:28), a phrase not found in Mark's account (14:24). This means that in the primary cultic observances of the community, through use of the Lord's Prayer and the celebration of the Lord's Supper, the forgiveness of sins is both requested of God and received according to the promise of Christ. Divine forgiveness is to be mirrored by Christians in their forgiveness of others (6:12b, 14–15; 18:35). In each instance that this duty is set forth, it is presented in reference to the final judgment—God's own expected forgiveness.[33]

Although it is said that Jesus "will save his people from their sins" (1:21), the Gospel of Matthew is nevertheless not primarily soteriologically oriented. Matthew repeats the Marcan saying of Jesus that the Son of Man came "to give his life as a ransom for many" (20:28//Mark 10:45), so the death of Jesus is understood in some way to be redemptive.[34] But how that is so can only be inferred from Matthew's portrait of Jesus and his career in general; it is not made explicit. As Son of David and Messiah, Jesus appears as a royal figure throughout the course of the gospel narrative. This is no less so in the narrative of his passion, death, and post-resurrection appearances.[35] Jesus has resources of power at his disposal from the Father, and he could at any time avoid his suffering and death.[36] But he goes to the cross and his death to fulfill the divine purpose, and it is actually the resurrected Christ who bestows benefits upon his disciples. The benefits of Christ are thus in consequence of his resurrection, and his death is redemptive only in the sense that it is the necessary culmination of a life and ministry which is obedient to the Father, fulfills the Scriptures, and leads to his resurrection. This can be illustrated by reference to a few Matthean emphases in his passion, death, and post-resurrection accounts.

In Jesus' prayer in Gethsemane, the Marcan saying, "Father, all things are possible with you; remove this cup from me" (Mark 14:36), is altered by Matthew to read, "My Father, if it is possible, let this cup pass from me" (26:39); later Matthew adds, "My Father, if this cannot pass unless I drink it, your will be done" (26:42). Jesus' intimacy with the Father and his accession to the divine will are thus heightened. At his arrest in Gethsemane, the Matthean Jesus declares to his captors, "Do you think that I cannot appeal to my Father, and he will at once send me more than twelve legions of angels? But how then should the scriptures be fulfilled, that it must be so?" (26:53–54). All that is taking place is in fulfillment of the Scriptures (26:56). And in his death the Marcan statement that Jesus "breathed his last" (Mark 15:39) is replaced by the Matthean statement that Jesus "yielded up his spirit" (27:50). The Marcan statement implies simply that Jesus "expired" in the manner of anyone who dies, but Matthew's alteration has the result of making Jesus, who is a majestic and authoritative figure throughout Matthew's Gospel, even in his passion and death, die of his own accord,[37] rendering up his spirit to the Father.

The majestic and authoritative portrait is extended and completed in Matthew's post-resurrection account. The angel of the Lord announces to the women at the empty tomb that Jesus has been raised (28:6), which is said also in Mark's account (16:6), but Matthew has the additional words, "as he said," recalling the authoritative words of Jesus himself at prior moments (16:21; 17:23; 20:19). In the closing scene, which tells of the encounter of Jesus with the eleven disciples, Jesus declares that "all authority in heaven and on earth has been given" to him, and he commissions his disciples to go, make disciples, baptizing and teaching people to observe all that he has commanded; "and lo," he says, "I am with you always, to the close of the age" (28:18–20).

How, in all of this, can it be said that Jesus fulfills his purpose (1:21) and saves his people from their sins? It is not said that Jesus does this by bearing their sins, or as one "who was put to death for our trespasses" in the Pauline sense (Rom. 4:25). Rather, as the royal Son of God, Jesus gave up his life, in accord with the divine purpose, in light of the prospect of his resurrection and his assuming of all authority in heaven and on earth. God's redemptive purpose, in the Matthean perspective, is thus carried out and confirmed through the authority of the risen Christ. Christ establishes it as truly having come to pass by the authority he possesses, and it is on the basis of that authority that people are to believe that salvation is offered to them. This view is inaugurated in the post-resurrection scene. The disciples had themselves forsaken Jesus (26:56), and Peter had denied him (26:69–75), so they had in effect disqualified themselves from salvation in the future kingdom (cf. the saying at 10:33). But the risen Christ reveals himself to them, and even then in spite of the doubt of "some" (28:17),[38] he commissions them as his emissaries, which implies forgiveness.[39]

Here we begin to see the Matthean view of the benefits of Christ. Already in Judaism it was abundantly clear that God forgives sins, and that he does so freely. The Gospel of Matthew would not offer anything new if it only declared that there is forgiveness of sins and salvation in the world to come for the righteous and the penitent. But obviously for Matthew and his community there are saving benefits brought into the world by Christ. That is to say, in consequence of the life, ministry, death, and resurrection of Christ, something new and decisive has come about—which could not be so apart from him—even if it is not said that Jesus bore the sins of humanity on the cross. The fact that persons were baptized (28:19) and were willing to face persecution and abuse for the name of Christ (5:10–12; 10:23; 24:9) indicates that they found in Christ and his community, the church (16:18; 18:17), certain benefits which were not known in Jewish tradition or, in the case of gentiles, Hellenistic religious traditions. What is different and new over against the Jewish heritage is that, as Jesus granted forgiveness of sins in his earthly ministry (9:2, 6), so the forgiveness of sins is enacted "on earth" in the church. This is brought out particularly in the story of the healing of the paralytic (9:1–8). Matthew takes over the story from Mark (Mark 2:1–12) and repeats the saying of Jesus that "the Son of man has authority on earth to forgive sins" (Mark 2:10//Matt. 9:6), but he appends to the story that the crowds glorified God "who had given such authority to people" (9:8). In Jewish tradition it is taught, as indicated already, that God forgives, and does so readily. But in the case of Jesus, and also then for the church, the forgiveness of God is not simply proclaimed; it is actually exercised.[40] This is carried out in the power given to the church to "bind and loose" on earth (18:18), that is, to declare sins forgiven and to admit into fellowship, or to refrain from forgiving and even exclude persons from the community.[41] And in the community's celebration of the Lord's Supper its members consider themselves as those to whom forgiveness of sins is conveyed in the present on the basis of the authority and promise of Christ himself (26:28).

Jesus, crucified and risen, and now present with his people (1:23; 18:20; 28:20), thus opens up both a new life and a new way of life for them in the present and on into the future. Warning is given in the Gospel of Matthew to the community about possibly falling away (24:10); twice it is said explicitly that only those who endure to the end will be saved (10:22; 24:13); and those who follow must observe that which the authoritative, royal Messiah has taught (7:24–27; 28:20). There is thus the possibility that one may not stand in the final judgment when the Son of Man will judge the nations of the world (25:31–46). In fact it will then be disclosed that there are false disciples in the church, and the righteous will be saved and those who do evil will be condemned (13:36–43, 47–50; 22:11–14). Even true disciples are chided for their "little faith" (6:30; 8:26; 14:31; 16:8). There is missing in Matthew the Pauline accent that nothing "will be able to separate us from the love of God in Christ Jesus our Lord" (Rom. 8:39). Indeed "many will fall away, and betray one another, and hate one another" (24:10) and the love of most will "grow cold" (24:12). Jesus' role as the one who will save his people from their sins is that of offering forgiveness to those who enter into his community through baptism and then participate in discipleship within the community, forgiving and being forgiven, enduring persecution, and doing the will of God, which is expressed through the law as interpreted by Jesus. Salvation is still future, and it will be given to those who endure to the end, but it is realized in part through the present forgiveness of sins and the new life given through the resurrected Christ who has authority over all things and can therefore do as he wills.

Matthew does not go as far as Paul to claim that in Christ God has reconciled the world to himself (2 Cor. 5:19), nor can it be said that for Matthew the basic human need of redemption from the power of sin and its consequences (again, Pauline thought) has been accomplished. For Matthew the need of humanity before God is forgiveness of sins, which leads to life. At that point the evangelist is in agreement with Pharisaic Judaism.[42] But he goes beyond the latter in the claim that through the ministry, death, and resurrection of Jesus the redemptive purpose of God is confirmed in history, fulfilling the divine purpose. Jesus is the Messiah of Israel who interprets the law, fulfills the utterances of the prophets, and is given all authority as the resurrected Lord. His disciples and those gathered to them through their own mission constitute now the true Israel; unbelieving Israel has lost its election, and the church made up of Jews and gentiles is the "nation" (or people) to whom the kingdom is given (21:43; cf. 1:21; 8:11–12; 16:18–19).[43] For Matthew it is fellowship in this community which makes salvation possible, beginning in part in one's historical existence through the forgiveness of sins pronounced in Jesus' name, but completed at the final judgment for those who endure in fidelity and obedience. There is thus an *ordo salutis,* an order of salvation, initiated with faith, baptism, and forgiveness, but maintained through obedience to the Lord, observance of his teachings, and reception of the forgiveness of sins again and again through the Lord's Supper, and completed at the final judgment. The redemptive work of God is confirmed through Jesus and partially received in the community of dis-

75

ciples, but it is still essentially future, awaiting the day when the Son of Man exercises judgment upon all the nations. The possibility of final salvation for others besides Christians—specifically, those who do acts of mercy to the hungry, thirsty, homeless, sick, and imprisoned—is expected in the Matthean view, as expressed in the vision (or parable) of the last judgment (25:31–46),[44] while Christians who simply make of their piety a matter of words without deeds have no advantage whatsoever (7:21–23). Matthew intends that the church realize within its own membership the life of discipleship under the royal rule of the risen Christ. Christ saves them from their sins, but he does not guarantee salvation no matter what. Whoever is forgiven is to be as a sound tree which bears good fruit (7:17–18; cf. 12:33), forgiving others and living the ethic of the kingdom as sketched out in the teachings of Jesus. The benefits of Christ are thus not a warranty of divine grace, but an assurance of grace for those who follow him and become disciplined for the kingdom which is to come. Redemption is not grounded in his death as an atoning event, but in the authority of the risen Christ who does and will do what, according to the angel prior to his birth, he is supposed to do—save his people from their sins—by way of forgiveness.

The Gospel of Matthew addresses third-generation Christians in a particular social and religious setting. In spite of its own emphasis on a mission to all the nations (28:18–20), it was not written for those who had not yet heard the gospel.[45] It was written for a community which was already heir to previous evangelization and Christian tradition. The beginnings of Christianity at Antioch of Syria can be traced back to the early 30s (Acts 11:19–20).[46] In this setting the primary focus of Matthew is not upon delineating the benefits of Christ for Jews and gentiles outside the Christian movement—heralding what has been accomplished by God in Christ for their salvation. The focus is rather on formulating and institutionalizing community life and mission, and those efforts are carried out particularly through the discourses. It is precisely those who would look upon the benefits of Christ as their possession and as a guarantee of security who are challenged to see that his benefits include membership in the true Israel, a community of righteousness and mission, which both experiences salvation in part through the forgiveness of sins and awaits final salvation at the coming of the Son of Man.

THE GOSPEL OF LUKE AND THE
ACTS OF THE APOSTLES

Although separated in the sequence of New Testament books, the Gospel of Luke and Acts must be considered together when investigating

Lucan themes, including christology and redemption. Luke's two volumes are the work of a writer situated in the last two decades of the first century A.D.[47] The place of writing is not certain,[48] and the intended audience for his work is not clear either. At the outset of both volumes Luke addresses "Theophilus" as a presumed interested reader (Luke 1:3; Acts 1:1), but this address (or perhaps dedication) does not help much.[49] Is this an actual person? If so, is he a Christian? And if a Christian, is he of Jewish or of gentile heritage? Or is he a pagan of some importance whom Luke knows to be interested in the subject of which he writes? The name is found in other sources from pre-Christian antiquity for both Jews and gentiles.[50]

Although we cannot know the identity of Theophilus, Luke-Acts was written in any case for an audience far more extensive than a single individual. But there is no consensus about the nature of this broader audience. According to one proposal, Luke stands apart from most early Christian writers, whose works were written for use within Christian communities, and wrote "from the perspective of apologetics that also consciously appealed to pagan readership" in the Roman world.[51] Most interpreters, however, view Luke as writing primarily for a Christian readership. Even though he puts forth a "political apologetic" at various points in his Gospel and Acts (to establish that neither Jesus nor Paul was seditious toward the Roman Empire),[52] Luke wrote to strengthen and perhaps to reformulate Christian faith and thought for his generation.

Yet the composition of the church for which he wrote, its place within early Christianity, and the purpose which Luke sought to achieve in relationship to his audience are matters on which interpreters vary in their assessment. Hans Conzelmann has proposed that Luke wrote for a church which was by his day gentile in composition, located in the third generation of Christianity, and that he dealt with the question of how the church could "abandon" its link with Judaism and "yet remain within the continuity of redemptive history."[53] Jacob Jervell has suggested that for Luke the time of mission to the Jews was past, but that the church addressed by Luke contained a Jewish-Christian core, to whom gentiles had been added, and it retained a "Jewish-Christian stamp." Luke wrote in part to explain how it could be possible that the mission to the Jews was over, why an unbelieving Israel could exist alongside the church, and how the mission to the gentiles actually fulfilled the promises to Israel.[54] Other proposals which emphasize the Jewish-Christian composition of Luke's primary audience have been advanced by David Tiede and Donald Juel. Tiede suggests that Luke wrote from within the context of competing interpretations of Scripture by "messianists" (= Jewish Christians) and other Jews in the aftermath of the destruction of Jerusalem (A.D. 70); Tiede writes that Luke, dealing in part with the question whether God had remained faithful to his promises to Israel, affirmed the faithfulness of God by rehearsing the story of Jesus and the founding history of the church.[55] Juel suggests that Luke wrote for a predominantly Jewish-Christian community made up of persons who had separated themselves from the larger Jewish population and then experienced an influx of gentiles, which raised questions about the original community's heritage. Luke wrote to confirm their identity as the people of God.[56]

Yet the claim that Luke had a gentile readership in mind continues to persist. Nils Dahl has suggested that "we should certainly seek the prospective readers among the God-fearers" and that the purpose of Luke-Acts was that these gentile Christians "should be strengthened in their faith, praise God for the salvation sent to them, and take courage, so that the number of believers might continue to increase."[57] Joseph Fitzmyer has agreed with Conzelmann that the readers envisaged by Luke were essentially gentile Christians (among whom were some Jewish Christians), but he also draws upon the work of Jervell. While he rejects Jervell's view concerning the intended readers (Jewish Christians), he affirms Jervell's contention that Luke sought to explain the continuity of Israel and the church: Gentile Christians are not a "new people of God, but belong to the reconstituted people of God" which consisted of repentant Jews at the beginning and increasingly was made up of incoming gentiles.[58] It is not our purpose here to arbitrate among the various proposals. But it can be said that, in spite of their differences, these interpreters share in the view that Luke concerned himself with questions concerning lines of continuity and discontinuity between Israel and the church, the working of God in history in light of the Scriptures,[59] the relationship of believing Christians (whether Jewish or gentile) to those of Israel who did not and would not believe the gospel, and the church's understanding of itself in the third generation near the close of the first century.

Luke is conventionally known as a theologian of redemptive history (*Heilsgeschichte*). That is to say, for Luke there is a divine plan of salvation working itself out in history which becomes perceptible to faith in certain events and/or epochs, and which will come to its completion at history's end.[60] That Luke thought in terms of a divine purpose working itself out in history can be seen in several ways. God "has fixed" (RSV, or "established," *etheto*) certain "times and seasons" by his own authority (Acts 1:7). Events take place according to God's "plan" (*boulē*, Acts 2:23; 4:28) or by divine necessity (*dei*, "it is necessary")—both in the course of Jesus' ministry, death, and resurrection,[61] and in the church's mission.[62] Jesus' passion, death, and resurrection take place to fulfill the Scriptures (Luke

18:31; 22:37; 24:44; Acts 1:16). Purpose, necessity, and the fulfillment of the Scriptures are concepts employed by Luke to speak of God's redemptive purpose working itself out in history, particularly in the story of Jesus.

There is disagreement, however, among interpreters in their assessments of how Luke might have conceived epochs of redemptive history and construed them in his work. The pioneering work in this field is that of Conzelmann, whom several have followed (with variations).[63] Conzelmann has claimed that Luke thought in terms of three epochs: the "period of Israel" (from the creation of the world through the ministry of John the Baptist); the "period of Jesus" (from his baptism to his ascension), which is the "center of time"; and the "period of the church" (from the ascension to the parousia).[64] The starting point and primary basis for the division between the first two epochs is the statement of Jesus at Luke 16:16 that "the law and the prophets were until John; since then the good news of the kingdom of God is preached."[65] And the distinction between the second and third epochs is established because Luke does not expect an imminent parousia (cf. Luke 21:9; 17:20), but considers it to be delayed for an indefinite length of time. The life of Jesus is thus relegated to a past epoch, and "the time leading up to the parousia is built into God's saving plan as the time of the church."[66] The matter has been stated succinctly by Ernest Haenchen: For Luke "the life of Jesus was a self-contained epoch in the history of salvation, one which was distinct from the period which followed."[67]

Other interpreters, while indebted to Conzelmann for his stimulating proposal, have seen matters differently. They claim that for Luke there is essentially one continuous story of salvation within which there is the era of prophecy and the time of fulfillment, and the latter extends from Jesus' earthly ministry to the end of time, during which the risen Lord continues the saving work.[68] Against the view that there is a distinction to be made between an epoch of Christ and an epoch of the church, Otto Betz has put the matter crisply: "With the preaching of Jesus the kerygma is not completed; it is not restricted to a historical past, for with the preaching of the church its second phase has begun."[69]

There is merit to the view that, for Luke, there is essentially one continuous history of salvation consisting of prophecy and fulfillment.[70] It is doubtful that Luke 16:16 can be used as evidence for a sharp division of epochs in Lucan theology.[71] The verse reads: "the law and the prophets were until [mechri] John." Does this mean, as Conzelmann would have it, that for Luke there was an era—the period of Israel—which included John as its final representative? Or does it mean that such a period lasted only up to John, so that John himself is thought to belong to a subsequent era? The matter is not clear, and it may be that there is another possibility. Luke uses the preposition *mechri* on two other occasions. The first (Acts 10:30) does not shed light on the problem, but in the second instance (Acts 20:7) the word has an exclusive sense—that is, up to a point in time. This is admittedly slim evidence for Luke's usage of the preposition, but it opens up the possibility that at Luke 16:16 the evangelist means that the era of the law and the prophets extended up to, but not including, the ministry of John. This becomes the more natural rendering of the verse when the rest of it is considered: "from then" (*apo tote*, i.e., from the time of John's ministry) "the good news of the kingdom of God is preached" (16:16b). Rather than seeing a division of epochs at the point of John in Lucan theology, it is thus more fitting to see John as a transitional figure who marks the advent of the time of fulfillment.[72] John is considered by Luke to be not only a prophet (1:76; 7:26) but indeed "more than a prophet" (7:26); he "prepares the way" at the initial stage of fulfillment (7:27). This means then that Luke interprets redemptive history as being guided to its fulfillment in Jesus. The era of the law and the prophets is not essentially a closed epoch of the past in the Lucan perspective, but an era which is fulfilled in the total "Christ event." So at the outset of the Gospel of Luke there is portrayed a rebirth of prophetic and charismatic activity among the devout of Israel who make inspired utterances and prophesy in the Spirit (1:41, 67; 2:26–27); they are exemplary in their piety and are obedient to the law of the Lord (1:6, 9; 2:21, 22–24, 39). John is a prophet, and Jesus himself is a prophet, the eschatological prophet like Moses (Acts 3:22–23; 7:37; cf. Luke 7:16; 24:19). And in Acts the church is guided by the Spirit and prophecy (2:4, 17–18, 33, 43; 6:8; 8:29; 18:25; 19:6, 21; 20:22; 21:4, 9).[73] The story of Jesus is central to the story of redemption, for through him the saving work of God for humanity is made possible. But that Luke thinks in terms of three self-contained epochs does not follow. Such a conception can too easily be imposed on Luke by the modern interpreter looking back from afar.[74]

If one cannot think of a division of epochs between Israel and Christ in Lucan theology, the same is true for a division between periods of Christ and the church. There are passages in Luke in which the delay of the parousia is assumed or affirmed.[75] But there are others in which the parousia is considered an imminent prospect.[76] The degree to which Luke consciously sought to reconstruct early Christian thought so that the parousia would be thought of as far off into the future is debatable. We should not expect of Luke a precision on eschatological reflection that is possible after the passing of the centuries; he lived at a time when such reflection was less developed and probably less absolute in its claims than some interpreters have made it out to be. On balance it can be said that for Luke, when compared with Paul and Mark, there is less sense of an imminent parousia.

But is the distant futurity of the parousia his point, thereby making room for an epoch of the church? For Luke the parousia is still expected, but one cannot determine when it will occur (Luke 12:40, 46; cf. 18:8; 19:11), and the time between the resurrection and the parousia extends the age of fulfillment when the gospel of salvation is to be proclaimed to all nations (Luke 24:47). The risen Christ promises the gift of the Spirit (Luke 24:49) and declares that "repentance and forgiveness of sins should be preached in his name" (24:47), certifying that in the church's Spirit-led mission there is salvation for all who repent and believe. The risen Christ is himself the one who pours out the Spirit on the church (Acts 2:33), and the obedience of the church to his commission to proclaim repentance for forgiveness is documented many times in Acts (2:38; 3:19, 25–26; 5:31; 10:43; 11:18; 20:21). Rather than portraying precise, successive epochs of Christ and the church, Luke portrays a continuity of the era of fulfillment within the history of redemption, an era which has come in Christ and extends in its second phase to the end of time as the risen Lord effects the saving work of God through the proclamation of his witnesses. It is not so much in Luke's own outlook, but in consequence of it (as well as other factors), that the church would then soon have to make "arrangements . . . for the long period before the end comes"[77] by instituting a regularized teaching ministry and church structures,[78] attending to moral teaching based on traditional virtues of the Greco-Roman world and Christian tradition itself, and ultimately forming a canon of Scripture. To speak of an "epoch of the church" presupposes Christian reflection on the church's "place" within history at a distance removed from the church of Luke's day, even though Luke provides the conditions for it. Finally, that an essential continuity of redemptive history, consisting of promise and fulfillment, is uppermost in Luke's thinking can be illustrated in his version of Peter's speech concerning Christ at Acts 10:43: "To him all the prophets bear witness that every one who believes in him receives forgiveness of sins through his name." Christ fulfills the utterances of the prophetic witnesses, and he grants his benefits to all who believe in his name until the end of time. That is so because the so-called "epoch of the church" is not in fact a self-contained epoch following a closed epoch of the Christ, but because the risen Lord empowers the church through the Spirit to exercise his saving work on earth through the passing of time.

Luke's christology, and his redemptive christology in particular, must be set within the broader perspective of his redemptive history. Within his two volumes Luke makes use of a wide range of christological titles, more than any other New Testament writer. This may be accounted for largely by the sheer length of his two volumes, which cover over one-fourth of the New Testament,[79] and Luke's incorporation of many sources within them. Aside from nine other titles which are not often used (seven times or less),[80] Luke uses all the main christological titles, including "Christ" (thirty-eight times),[81] "Son of God" (twelve times),[82] and "Son of man" (twenty-six times).[83] In the other gospels the last title is used only in sayings of Jesus. That is so also in Luke's Gospel, but the title also appears once in Acts (the speech of Stephen, 7:56). But the title used most often by far in Luke-Acts is "Lord" *(kyrios)*. The term is used frequently for God, but in the Gospel of Luke it is used forty-one times in reference to Jesus,[84] and it is used in Acts on eighteen occasions when it definitely refers to Jesus,[85] and on another forty occasions when it most likely refers to him;[86] but then there are still another seventeen times when it is quite ambiguous (Jesus or God?), but probably refers to Jesus.[87] This means that the title is used in reference to Jesus in Luke-Acts on fifty-nine occasions for certain, and possibly 116 times in all (forty-one times in the Gospel, seventy-five times in Acts). Moreover, Luke frequently makes use of this title in his own redactional comments, as at Luke 7:13, "and when the Lord saw her" (the widow from Nain), and in various other places,[88] totaling fifteen times, none of which is taken over from Mark or Q. This title, which refers to Jesus in his exalted state (Acts 2:36), is thus retrojected back by Luke into the earthly ministry, indicating that the whole course of Jesus' ministry, death, and resurrection has a transcendent character.[89] It is the "most characteristic title of Jesus in Luke-Acts."[90]

In order to discern the Lucan portrayal of redemptive christology in his two volumes, one can begin with the speeches in Acts, for they set forth Luke's Gospel in miniature, particularly the speech of Peter in 10:34–43.[91] Among the points made in Peter's speech are that (1) after his baptism by John, Jesus (who is "Lord of all") proclaimed the word of God, the good news of peace, first in Galilee and than in Judea; (2) for this task, God has anointed Jesus of Nazareth with the Holy Spirit and power; (3) he went about doing good and healing all who were oppressed by the devil; (4) Peter and others were witnesses to all that he did; (5) "the Jews" put him to death by crucifixion; (6) but God raised him from the dead on the third day and made him manifest to the chosen witnesses (Peter and others), who ate and drank with him after his resurrection; and (7) he commanded these witnesses to preach "to the people" and to testify that Jesus is "the one ordained by God to be judge of the living and the dead." The speech closes with the statement that Jesus fulfills the witness of the prophets of Israel and whoever believes in him receives forgiveness of sins through his name.

All the items listed in this speech, and more, are elaborated by Luke in his Gospel and in Acts. A possible exception would be the statement that apostolic proclamation should include the claim that Jesus is the one ordained by God to be judge of the living and the dead (Acts 10:42), but even this relates to those passages in which Jesus speaks of himself as the Son of Man whose role is to exercise judgment at his coming (Luke 9:26; 12:8; 17:26–30; 18:8; 21:36; 22:69).

As in the case of the Gospel of Matthew, so Luke's work was not likely intended for the evangelization of those who had not yet heard the gospel of salvation. Yet Luke cannot avoid the question of the redemptive significance of Jesus, and he treats it in his own distinctive way. Jesus, endowed by the Spirit in his earthly ministry,[92] goes of necessity to the cross and his subsequent glorification according to the divine purpose and in order to fulfill the Scriptures. Decisive points in the narrative are the predictions of his passion, death, and resurrection (9:22; 18:31–33), or simply his passion (9:44), and Lucan interpretive statements at 9:31 and 9:51. In the first of these statements, set within the transfiguration scene, Luke says that Moses and Elijah spoke with Jesus concerning his "departure" (RSV; the Greek is *exodos*), which "he was to accomplish in Jerusalem"; and in the second, at the outset of the "travel narrative" (9:51—19:44), Luke says that Jesus' resolve to go to Jerusalem happened "when the days drew near for him to be received up" (RSV). What the RSV translates as a verb ("to be received up") is actually a noun in Greek, *analēmpsis,* which has the primary meaning of "ascension," but can also be a circumlocution for one's death (cf. "he was taken" or "passed on" in English).[93] Considered within the context of all that is to follow in the gospel narrative (fifteen more chapters), neither the reference to Jesus' "exodus" (9:31) nor his being "received up" (9:51) can be interpreted at these points simply as predictions of his ascension. They must rather portend the entire course of what is to transpire in the days to follow: Jesus' passion, death, resurrection, and ascension. But it is significant that the goal of his course is then not the cross but his ascension, his departure, when he is "taken up . . . into heaven" (Acts 1:11; cf. Luke 24:51).[94]

Luke does stress, even more than Mark, the innocent suffering and death of Jesus.[95] Yet he omits the saying of Mark 10:45 that the Son of Man would give his life as a "ransom for many." As interpreters have indicated time and again, Luke does not portray the death of Jesus as atoning.[96] The death of Jesus is portrayed as that of a perfect martyr who forgives his enemies (23:34; cf. Stephen in Acts 7:60) and commits his spirit to the Father (23:46; cf. Stephen again at Acts 7:59).[97] Luke looks upon Jesus' suffering and death as the means by which he might "enter into his glory" (24:26; cf. Acts 17:3; 26:23). As in the Gospel of John, the death and glorification of Jesus are therefore inseparably connected. They differ somewhat in that while for John the lifting up of the Son of Man on the cross is itself the beginning of the glorification (John 12:32–33; cf. 3:14; 8:28), for Luke the cross is the necessary step for glorification, which comes in consequence of his resurrection.

The redemptive significance of Jesus is seen by Luke to lie not in his bearing the consequences of the sin (or sins) of humanity on the cross, but by virtue of his authority as the exalted Lord who grants forgiveness of sins. In the post-resurrection account, which asserts the divine vindication of the crucified Messiah, the risen Lord interprets the Scriptures concerning himself and his sufferings (24:25–27, 32, 44–45) and declares to the eleven, "Thus it is written, that the Christ should suffer and on the third day rise from the dead, and that repentance and forgiveness of sins should be preached in his name to all the nations, beginning from Jerusalem" (24:46–47). Without recourse to specific texts, here the risen Lord declares that both his death and resurrection and the preaching to the nations are in accord with the divine plan set forth in the Scriptures. The proclamation is to present the good news that in the name of Jesus— that is, on his behalf and by his authority—there is forgiveness for those who repent and believe (cf. Acts 10:43). "The forgiveness that Jesus mediated in his earthly days through his personal involvement was now offered to all from his resurrection: 'through this man forgiveness of sins is proclaimed to you!' (Acts 13:38)."[98] In Luke's view christology and redemption are thus connected by virtue of the present and ongoing activity of the risen Lord who brings redemption through the forgiveness of sins to those who repent and believe in him in consequence of the proclamation of his witnesses.[99] The cross is not thereby dispensed with, but it is integrated into the larger drama of redemption.[100] It is not itself the means of atonement, but it is the necessary means by which the divine purpose of redemption can alone be achieved. It remains for Luke the sign of divine grace for humanity and the presupposition for the existence of the church (Acts 20:28). It culminates the ministry of Jesus as the one who forgave sins by divine authority in his earthly ministry (5:20, 24; 7:47–49; cf. 19:7–10) and is the means of his "exodus" (9:31) into glory that he might continue the ministry of grace to all humankind through the proclamation of his witnesses to Israel and then to all the nations (Luke 24:47; Acts 5:31; 13:38; 26:18).[101] He offers his promise of forgiveness of sins, and those who receive him are to understand that the eschatological kingdom has come among them (17:21); that is, the time of fulfillment is being realized, as demonstrated by the resurrection of the suffering Messiah and by the power of the Spirit in the community, and lacks only the final communion with Christ when the kingdom of God comes in its fullness (22:16, 18, 30). "The risen and exalted Christ represents the new world of God. In the word of grace (Acts 14:3; 20:32) and salvation (13:26) he is personally present. In the 'to-day' which marks the fulfilment of salvation he speaks to his own."[102]

RETROSPECT

Matthew and Luke stress the divine initiative in redemption, acting itself out in the ministry, death, resurrection, and reign of Jesus. The earthly ministry itself is seen to be redemptive in that Jesus heals, forgives sins, and does battle with Satan. But the thrust of both writers for readers in their own time is to emphasize the forgiveness of sins extended to believers by the risen Lord, who has authority to forgive sins and who grants authority to his emissaries to exercise forgiveness (Matthew) or to proclaim it in his name (Luke-Acts).

In this type of redemptive christology the redemptive purpose of God is confirmed through Christ. It is through Christ that the Scriptures of Israel have been fulfilled, and it is through Christ that the God of Israel has drawn near to humankind to forgive the penitent and to give them his pledge of final salvation. Beyond this general characteristic, there are several facets of this type of redemptive christology to highlight.

1. While in the first type of redemptive christology the death of Jesus is the means by which sin and its consequences are borne for the benefit of humanity, in this type the cross is essentially the means by which he gives up his life on the way toward his exaltation. He gives up his life in light of his coming resurrection, at which he assumes all authority in heaven and on earth (Matthew) or enters into his glory (Luke-Acts). The goal toward which Jesus moves is thus his heavenly reign. Redemption is made possible through Jesus' following the course of his divinely appointed destiny, which ends with his being the exalted Lord who grants forgiveness of sins, by divine authority, to his own.

It must be granted that Matthew and Luke-Acts differ in certain particulars in regard to soteriology, but they nevertheless conform to a single type of redemptive christology. Two points of difference can be illustrated. Matthew takes over the saying of Mark 10:45 ("the Son of man came . . . to give his life as a ransom for many") and incorporates it into his Gospel (20:28), but Luke does not; the saying does not appear in his corresponding pericope at 22:24–27. Second, Matthew attaches to the cup saying at the last supper ("my blood of the covenant, which is poured out for many," 26:28) the additional words, "for the forgiveness of sins," not found in the accounts of Mark and Luke. These two items could appear at first glance to indicate that Matthew attaches an atoning significance to the cross of Jesus in the manner of the first type of redemptive christology. But when the larger redactional framework of this Gospel is taken into consideration, these items become submerged into the totality. As Son of Man, Jesus gives his life sacrificially for the benefit of others, to be sure, but that is in anticipation of his resurrection and reign; it is as the risen Lord that he has authority to forgive sins, and his forgiveness of sins is enacted in the ongoing life of the church. Likewise, the saying in connection with the cup has to do with his ongoing ministry of forgiving sins in the eucharistic celebrations; forgiveness of sins is granted ever anew in the present on the basis of Christ's promise at the last supper. Matthew and Luke-Acts share in a common type of redemptive christology in that, for both, the cross is not regarded as the decisive moment at which sin or sins and their consequences were borne once for all for the benefit of others; it is the risen Lord who forgives.

2. Christ, in this type of redemptive christology, confirms the redemptive purpose of God, but redemption is essentially a future prospect. While Paul could say that in Christ God has reconciled the world to himself, and while both Paul and Mark could stress the "objective" character of redemption, to which the gospel bears witness, the second type of redemptive christology understands the gospel primarily as being a divine pledge of future redemption. Redemption is made possible by the death, resurrection, and reign of Jesus as Lord and Christ. This complex of events is the sole foundation of redemption, but it remains a foundation for future redemption, for none of the events within the complex is itself *the* decisive, redemptive act.

3. Yet the time between the resurrection of Jesus and his parousia is not devoid of redemptive significance. The life, death, and resurrection of Jesus are thought to mark the fulfillment of the promises given in the Scriptures to Israel and also to initiate the time of salvation. Salvation is granted in the act of forgiveness of sins to those who repent and believe, and the church is the earthly instrument for the mediation of salvation. It exercises forgiveness of sins in the name of the exalted Lord to its members (Matthew) or bears the good news of forgiveness for penitent believers in the name of Christ (Luke-Acts). It must be said, however, that salvation granted in the present era is explicitly conditioned in Matthew's view by the necessity of the believer to endure in faith and obedience to the end; those who endure to the end will be saved (10:22, 24:13). In Luke's view there is no corresponding contingency of salvation explicitly stated, but for him it is no less true that a life of constancy in

faith, penitence, and the performance of "deeds worthy of repentance" is expected on the way to the day of final salvation (Acts 26:20; cf. 17:30–31), when Christ will judge the living and the dead (Acts 10:42; 17:31).

4. The redemptive christology of the second type exhibits reflection not only on the place of Christ in redemptive history but on the place of the church in it as well. For Matthew the church—consisting of both Jews and gentiles—is the true Israel to whom the promises of old have been confirmed; obdurate Israel has forfeited its claim (21:43) and has become but "one people among many."[103] In the Lucan perspective the church at its beginning and core consists of the repentant of Israel, to whom the promises have been confirmed and to whom gentiles have been joined.[104] The church, in this way, does not replace Israel but fulfills Israel's destiny by receiving its Messiah and extending the messianic blessing to the gentiles, which, in Luke's reading of the Scriptures, was Israel's historic role.[105] In both cases, the struggle concerning identity in the purposes of God is apparent: Who constitutes the true heritage of Israel; who are the heirs of the divine promises put forth in Scripture? Confronting this question determines in part the outcome of redemptive christology. The redemptive work of God is set forth in accounts which rivet the career of Jesus to redemptive history, drawing lines of connection between the Scriptures and Jesus. Through him and him alone, God has confirmed his promises to Israel. But it is not possible to stop short of going on to speak of the community gathered about him—by now into its third generation. It is the community which gathers in his name that completes the historical phase of divine redemption. The consequence of such reflection is to lay less stress on the cross as the reconciling event, by which the consequences of sin are assumed for the benefit of humanity, and more stress on the living Lord present and worshiped in the community as the one who offers saving benefits, the forgiveness of sins. The believing community is the beneficiary of the saving work of Christ, for it is the true Israel (Matthew) or the repentant and believing people of God (Luke-Acts) who have affirmed that the promises of God have indeed been confirmed through his Messiah. Redemptive historical reflection, arising as it does with the passing of time and within the context of determining who now is heir to the divine promises, discerns the benefits of Christ chiefly in consequence of his exaltation and ongoing power to exercise forgiveness to his own.

5. Another aspect of the redemptive christology of the second type is that the benefits of Christ include not only the forgiveness of sins leading to final salvation, but also guidance for a life of fullness along the way to the end. In some ways this is more apparent in Matthew, in which the

discourses of Jesus can hardly be read without the reader sensing that they are being played to an audience, the church of Matthew's day. Luke is more subtle, but frequently the teachings of Jesus in his Gospel also provide instruction for Christians in the way of discipleship within the church and in the world.[106] Matthew and Luke are not unique, of course, in providing moral instruction, but they stress it and fill out the picture more than most New Testament writers do. They do not leave the believer suspended midair in a new self-understanding, but direct the believer into the community of faith and discipleship and into the world in which the demands of other people—and even the abuse or persecution of others in the world—call for response in words and deeds. In this regard the works of Matthew and Luke were programmatic in giving shape to the moral teaching of the church and then to the formation of the character of individual Christians. Through the passing of time there has been a change of effects; their works have given shape more to the character of individual Christians and, to a lesser extent, the moral teaching of the church. To say such is not to pass judgment on historical developments. It is simply the case that the later church incorporated more than these two books into its canon and developed its moral teaching on a broader base. Matthew and Luke tend in consequence to inspire the character formation of individuals and the ethos of small groups of Christians. In any case, from the standpoint of both evangelists the formation of Christian discipleship for life in its fullness is a portion of the benefits of Christ. And this is to be expected not simply because of the peculiar interests of the writers. The redemptive christology of the second type demands it. Since final salvation is contingent upon a life of fidelity to the end, the basic character of that fidelity has to be considered and to some extent spelled out.

6. In the perspective of this type of redemptive christology virtually no thought is given concerning the saving benefits of Christ for the rest of humanity, for those who have not heard the gospel. A cosmic redemptive christology does not come into view. Matthew, to be sure, considers the exalted Christ as a cosmic Lord to whom all authority in heaven and on earth has been given (28:18), and as Son of Man he will judge all the nations of the world (25:31–46). Luke also knows the risen Christ to be Lord of all (Acts 10:36) and the one who will judge the living and the dead (Acts 10:42; 17:31). But in neither case is the cross the means by which God has reconciled the world to himself. The saving benefits consist of forgiveness of sins, and the forgiveness of sins is extended to those who are incorporated into the believing community.

Having indicated major facets of the second type of redemptive christology, it is fitting to conclude our retrospection with a rejoinder to one way in which the Gospel of Luke in particular has been evaluated. Luke has been accused of having sacrificed a theology of the cross for a theology of glory.[107] Of course this is not a correct assessment. If we mean by a "theology of the cross" a doctrine about the cross as saving event, Luke is open to attack. But if we mean by the phrase, as we should, a way of thinking about the nature of God—the doing of theology itself—and how the relationship between God and humanity is restored to wholeness, and claim that that comes about purely by the grace of God through the suffering and death of his Son and not by reliance upon one's own righteousness, then Luke is a theologian of the cross. The same is true of Matthew, even if he does not seem to need defense at this point.

Both Matthew and Luke, more consciously and intently than other writers of the New Testament, stress the cortinuity of Jesus with the story of Israel. The God of redemption is the God who created all things, elected Israel to be his people, and guided his people through times of trouble, despair, and even rebellion. And in the fullness of time God confirmed his faithfulness and his redemptive purpose through Jesus. This claim is not unique to Matthew and Luke by any means, but it is they who stress it and fill out the picture more than the rest. They retain the historic underpinnings of the gospel story, portray Jesus as a vital and prophetic figure in his earthly ministry, and proclaim the risen Christ as the living Lord who is present with his church in its ongoing life and mission.

7

Redemption Won by Christ

THE REDEMPTIVE CHRISTOLOGY of the third type comes to expression at a literary level in various books written during the last third of the first century A.D., which means that they are contemporaries of the Synoptic Gospels and the Johannine writings. But this redemptive christology stands out sharply and has a distinct profile of its own. Although the God of Israel wills the redemption of humanity and even initiates the drama, Christ emerges more forthrightly as a redeemer figure. Sharing the divine glory in a preexistent state, he comes into the world from above to rescue humanity; he secures redemption and then returns to his former glory, which will be revealed to all the world at his parousia. The stress is therefore a christopractic one: Christ is the actor of the drama, and he is acclaimed as the one who has won redemption through his cross and victorious resurrection. This type of redemptive christology comes to expression in Colossians and Ephesians, the Pastoral Epistles, 1 Peter, Hebrews, and Revelation. It is therefore a widely attested type in New Testament writings of the final third of the first century. Since it appears in the deutero-Paulines (i.e., books written in the name of Paul by a person who seeks to represent the apostle in a post-Pauline situation), it manifests itself in the Pauline corpus, although it differs from Paul's own redemptive christology. And since this type of redemptive christology appears in the Book of Revelation, it also has a place in the Johannine writings, although the rest of these writings manifest a different type (which will be explored in the next chapter).

COLOSSIANS AND EPHESIANS

Colossians and Ephesians, both deutero-Paulines, share much in common in their redemptive christologies and can therefore be treated to-

91

gether. It is commonly thought that Colossians was the earlier of the two, written not long after the death of Paul (so in the decade A.D. 60–70), that Ephesians belongs to a later time (A.D. 80–100), and that the author of Ephesians was dependent upon Colossians, incorporating and recasting materials from it.[1]

Both letters use the three most commonly used christological titles—Christ, Lord, and Son of God. Colossians uses the term "Christ" twenty-five times,[2] "Lord" thirteen times,[3] and "Son of God" once (1:13). In addition to these, the author speaks of Christ as "head" *(kephalē)* of "the body, the church" (1:18) and also of the universe (2:10, 19). Ephesians, which is greater in length, uses the term "Christ" forty-six times,[4] "Lord" twenty-four times,[5] and "Son of God" once (4:13). At 1:6 Jesus is spoken of as "the Beloved" and at 5:23 as the church's "Savior." Finally, as in Colossians, the term "head" is used as a christological title: Christ is the "head of the church" (5:23), the "head" to whom the whole body is joined (4:15), and he is "head over all things for the church" (1:22).

Both letters seek to further the Pauline gospel and outlook in new situations which have arisen after the death of Paul within the gentile churches of Asia Minor (Col. 1:21–23, 27; 2:13–14; Eph. 2:11–22; 3:1; 4:17). The writers share with Paul a view of gentile Christianity free from the law (Col. 2:11, 16–17, 20–22; Eph. 2:13–18). And in certain respects they share the Pauline view that it is God who initiated and carried out the redemptive drama in Christ. It is God who has "delivered us" (Col. 1:14) or "accomplished his will" in Christ (Eph. 1:11). And it is God who raised Jesus from death (Col. 2:12; Eph. 1:20). Yet certain other Pauline emphases are lacking. Nowhere is it said that God sent his Son, that God gave him up for us all, or that in him God condemned sin in the flesh. To be sure, the shedding of Christ's blood on the cross is redemptive (Col. 1:20; Eph. 1:7; 2:13), but this is not placed in the Pauline perspective of God's action in Christ; the redemptive work is Christ's own (more on that below). While in Ephesians (as in Paul) it is clearly said that God has seated the resurrected Christ at his right hand (1:20) and placed all things under his feet (1:22), in Colossians it is simply said that the resurrected Christ is at God's right hand (3:1). Finally, the Pauline assertion that in Christ God has reconciled the world to himself (2 Cor. 5:18–19; cf. Rom. 5:10) is repeated in Colossians (1:20),[6] but in both letters it is also said that it is Christ himself who has accomplished reconciliation to God (Col. 1:22; Eph. 2:16).

The change which has come about in redemptive christology is determined by the settings for which these two letters were addressed. Paul saw the plight of humanity as bondage to sin (Rom. 5:12, 21; 6:12–13; 7:13–14; 8:2), the consequences of which are death. For him the redemptive work of God in Christ consisted of God's own coming to the rescue, sending his Son in human form and then making him "to be sin" for us (2 Cor. 5:21); that is, God made Christ to be the one in whom sin could be localized and identified; and in him God "condemned sin in the flesh" (Rom. 8:3). The results of Christ's obedience are justification and life (Rom. 5:16, 18–19) and reconciliation (Rom. 5:9–10; 2 Cor. 5:18–19).

In Colossians and Ephesians there is no concept of "sin" as a power of bondage. The terminology is in the plural: "sins" (Col. 1:14; Eph. 2:1), "trespasses" (Col. 2:13; Eph. 1:7; 2:1, 5), and "evil deeds" (Col. 1:21; cf. Eph. 5:11), for which there must be forgiveness, and that has been obtained in Christ's death (Col. 1:14, 22; 2:13; Eph. 1:7; 2:1, 5). The bondage from which humanity must be redeemed (or liberated) is of a cosmic order, redemption from the reign of the "principalities and powers."

Although the relationship of Christ to the cosmic powers is finally treated differently in the two letters, and these differences will be dealt with subsequently, the letters share a common perspective concerning the existence of such powers. Both speak of "dominions" (*kyriotētes*, Col. 1:16; Eph. 1:21), "principalities" (*archai*, Col. 1:16; 2:10, 15; Eph. 1:21; 3:10; 6:12), and "authorities" (*exousiai*, Col. 1:16; 2:10, 15; Eph. 1:21; 3:10; 6:12). Beyond this common terminology, each letter has its own specific terms as well. In Colossians the writer speaks of "thrones" (*thronoi*, 1:16), "the elements of the universe" (*ta stoicheia tou kosmou*, 2:8, 20), and the "worship of angels" (2:18). In Ephesians the terminology includes references to a cosmic "power" (*dynamis*, 1:21) and "the prince of the power of the air" (*ho archōn tēs exousias tou aeros*), who is "the spirit [*pneuma*] that is now at work in the sons of disobedience" (2:2). Moreover, the writer speaks of the "devil" (*diabolos*) who seeks opportunities to lead people into evil deeds by his craftiness (4:27; 6:11). This does not exhaust the list of cosmic powers, for the writer also mentions "every name [*onoma*] that is named" (1:21).

The apostle Paul himself had spoken of "the elements of the universe" (*ta stoicheia tou kosmou*, Gal. 4:3, 9), "principalities" (*archai*, Rom. 8:38; 1 Cor. 15:24), "powers" (*dynameis*, Rom. 8:38; 1 Cor. 15:24), and "angels" (Rom. 8:38; cf. 1 Cor. 4:9; 2 Cor. 12:7) as cosmic powers which seek to control human destiny.[7] Twice he refers to "the rulers of this age" (*archontes tou aiōnos toutou*, 1 Cor. 2:6, 8). Yet Paul denies that these powers are "gods" (1 Cor. 8:5; Gal. 4:8).

Belief in cosmic powers as rulers of both nature and history was current prior to the rise of Christianity. It was expressed both in gentile Hellenistic texts and in Jewish texts prior to and alongside of early Christianity.[8] The personification of the "elements" (*stoicheia:* earth, air, fire, and water) occurs in texts ranging from the classical era of Greece on into Hellenistic texts of the Christian era.[9] Within Hellenistic Jewish texts there are numerous references to the "elements [*stoicheia*] of the universe,"[10] as well as references to cosmic powers as "thrones,"[11] "dominions,"[12] "authorities,"[13] and "powers."[14] The names used are largely interchangeable,[15] but the "location" of these powers differs in various documents. In certain Hellenistic traditions these powers are the visible heavenly bodies (planets and stars) themselves, which may be regarded as gods.[16] In Judaism, however, such bodies are not considered to be gods, for they have been created by God. Nevertheless, even if the heavenly bodies have been created and set in their courses by God (Pss. 8:3; 136:9; Jer. 31:35), they are spoken of already in the Old Testament as "ruling" day and night (Gen. 1:16; Ps. 136:9). In Jewish traditions they are spoken of as "rulers,"[17] and it is said that the angel Uriel had been "appointed by God" over these bodies that they might "rule in the face of the sky and be seen on the earth to be guides for the day and night."[18] Nevertheless, it is also said that certain "stars of heaven have transgressed the commandments of the Lord"[19]—a conception which lies behind the reference to the "wandering stars" at Jude 13.

For Paul and the writers of Colossians and Ephesians, however, the cosmic powers are not identified with the visible heavenly bodies. Paul would not have assigned the heavenly bodies any divine status (cf. 1 Cor. 8:5; Gal. 4:8). In Colossians the cosmic powers are included within the heavenly, invisible realm of God's creation (1:16),[20] and in Ephesians the "location" of the cosmic powers is said to be "in the heavenly places" (3:10; 6:12)—a realm which is invisible to sight, for the same term is used in reference to the "location" of the risen Christ (1:10; 2:6). Yet there are gradations within this realm, for Christ has been raised "far above" (*hyperanō*) these powers (Eph. 1:20–21).

According to both Jewish and Christian traditions, these "powers" owe their being to God initially, but they have revolted. In Jewish sources the "powers" (*dynameis*) are personified and are subject to God (2 Esdr. 6:3; *3 Macc.* 5:51; 7:9), and they are summoned to bless the Lord (Pr. of Azar. 39). God is sovereign over "spirits" (*pneumata,* 2 Macc. 3:24), and angels are his servants. Yet, according to Jewish traditions,[21] various angels have revolted; this view is also expressed in Jude 6, where certain angels "did not keep their own position but left their proper dwelling," and in 2 Pet. 2:4, which speaks of angels who "sinned." This view of the rebellion of various angels against God, coming from Jewish tradition, is extended so that the "powers" of the cosmos—a Hellenistic (including Hellenistic Jewish) conception—are considered in the same light; they are essentially hostile to God and seek to reign over the earthly realm. Thus the ambiguity of human existence is addressed, if not solved. God has created the world as good, but experience knows that there is also hostility against God. How can this be? For Jewish and Christian thinking there can be no absolute and eternal dualism between God and the power of evil, for God is sovereign over all things, as well as their creator. Nor can one set up a polarity between a good God and an evil humanity, for it is impossible to think that God would have created humanity as either antithesis or adversary. The answer to the problem is to speak in terms of supernatural angels or powers which have been created by God, and indeed have been vested with power by God, but which have left "their own position" and abused this power by self-will.[22]

Such a conception is not designed to get humanity "off the hook" of responsibility so as to excuse humanity from its own self-centeredness and rebellion. It comes about through a deeper penetration of the human condition. Weakness, not overt hostility to God, is the character of human life; within the life of every human being, and in society at large, there are "powers" at work which lead to evil and destruction. Modern persons would not speak of these as "powers" in the way the ancients did, but the concept is not far away. People place their trust and commitments in, or they value, various things which, in turn, become "authorities" *(exousiai)* or "principles" *(archai)* which consume their attention; persons are "driven" by these things along certain paths. Good, mediocre, or bad, these things nevertheless have dominion over one's life, and the pursuit of them results in the fragmentation of human relationships and the loss of integration within the self. Ancient Jews and Christians were willing to acknowledge that human beings are not in control of their own lives and destinies—in a way that moderns are not always willing—and affirmed that individuals and nations are "driven" by forces outside their own control. In order to express this, and using vivid mythological images as conceptual tools to portray this reality, they claimed that "powers" are at work to ensnare persons in their weakness and frailty. Such powers must be resisted (Eph. 6:12). Even though one seeks to serve God, the flesh is weak, and powers contrary to God and God's rule are most willing to move in and have dominion.

The Letters to the Colossians and Ephesians portray redemptive christology within the context of a world view which takes for granted the existence of these cosmic powers. But there are differences between the respective recipients of the letters and the ways in which the authors address the issues. It can be seen, for example, that in Colossians the author is engaged in polemics with opponents within the community addressed, while the author of Ephesians is engaged in issues—and to that extent with a possible opposing view—but not with opponents who have unsettled the community. Therefore it is necessary to treat the letters separately from this point on.

1. The Letter to the Colossians. This letter warns against those who would make "a prey of you by philosophy and empty deceit" (2:8; cf. 2:4), and the beliefs and practices of such persons are described in 2:8–23. On the basis of this section it is not clear that these opponents are even Christians. What is clear—whether they are Christians or not—is that they promote a syncretistic world view made up of Jewish traditions and current cosmological thought which has entered certain Jewish and Christian traditions.[23] They regard the "elements of the universe" as governing human and cosmic destinies (2:8, 20), and they promote the worship of angels (2:18b, which they may have thought to be the powers moving the elements themselves),[24] mysticism (2:18b), and aspects of Jewish law, including circumcision (2:11), dietary regulations (2:16a), Sabbath and festival observances (2:16b), and laws of purity (2:20–21). All of these regulations have "an appearance of wisdom" in promoting discipline (2:23). And the implication is that through such a way of wisdom one can master the secrets of the universe and attain personal salvation. Wisdom and Torah had already been identified in Jewish tradition (Sir. 24:23–24; Bar. 4:1),[25] and the opponents were heirs of this tradition.

The author of Colossians engages this "philosophy" at several points. It is in Christ, he says, that the "treasures of wisdom and knowledge" are hid (2:2–3), and Christ is the "head of all rule [*archē*] and authority" (*exousia*, 2:10). In him believers have been "circumcised" (2:11), that is, incorporated into the people of the promise. Some of the author's most significant affirmations are made in 1:15–20, where a hymn has been incorporated, but revised by the writer. That the author makes use of a hymn at this point can be seen by the introductory word "who" (*hos* in Greek; RSV has replaced it with "he"), which introduces hymnic or creedal materials elsewhere (cf. Phil 2:6; 1 Tim. 3:16; Heb. 1:3), the rhythmic construction, and the fact that the unit contains a host of christological affirmations beyond what the context requires. It is possible, although not necessary, that the hymn was known to the community and that the author used it—and used it so early on in the letter—to obtain rapport with his readers. In any case, various interpreters have suggested that the author revised it by adding "the church" at 1:18 and "through the blood of his cross" at 1:20.[26]

What is striking, in light of the previous discussion on cosmology and the view of the opponents at Colossae, is that for the writer of this hymn the cosmic powers are said to have been created by God (along with all other things) "in" Christ as well as "through him" and "for him" (1:16). Nothing is said about the cosmic powers as having become hostile. In fact it is said that "in him all things hold together" (1:17), which assumes that the powers are subject to Christ and have been so from the beginning. In these instances the hymn writer has drawn upon wisdom traditions in which Wisdom is the agent of God's creative work (Prov. 8:27–30; Wisd. of Sol. 7:22; 8:6; 9:1–2) and in which *sophia* (wisdom) and *logos* (word) are identified (Wisd. of Sol. 9:1–2) and it is said that by God's *logos* "all things hold together" (Sir. 43:26; cf. Heb 1:3). It is surprising, in view of this picture of cosmic unity, that the writer of the hymn then goes on to say that "all the fullness of God" dwelt in Christ "to reconcile to himself all things" (1:19–20). Why would there need to be reconciliation of all things to Christ if "all things hold together" in him (1:17)?[27]

For this reason there is merit in the suggestion of Wayne G. Rollins (maintained on other grounds) that the original hymn consisted of 1:15–18a (ending with "he is the head of the body"), and that all of 18b (beginning with "the church") through 20 is the author's own composition, in which he sets forth his own soteriological emphases.[28] This would mean that by quoting from the hymn (1:15–18a) the author has first of all repudiated the view of the opponents that the "elements of the universe" reign over the lives and destinies of people, for it is Christ in whom and for whom all things were created, and in whom all things "hold together." For the author of the letter there can be only an either/or: It is either the elements of the universe or Christ (2:8) that is "head of all rule and authority" (2:10), and it is Christ alone who is such. But for the writer that is so not only in principle—that is, by virtue of Christ's preeminence and instrumentality in creation—but it has been confirmed in his death and resurrection. In spite of the fact that in Christ all things hold together and all things were created for him, the writer's point of view is that there is a "dominion of darkness" *(exousia tou skotous)* from which deliverance is needed (1:13), and under which "sins," "evil deeds," and "trespasses" are committed (1:14, 21; 2:13). Indeed the "principalities and powers" *(archai kai exousiai)* created "for him" have forsaken their position and have sought to rule, but God has triumphed over them in Christ (2:15). To grant such autonomy to the cosmic powers is to go beyond what is said in 1:15–18a; yet it is the presupposition of 1:18b–20, in which the reconciliation of all things in Christ is proclaimed. There is good reason, therefore, on the basis of the respective theological views, to take the former as a hymn used by the writer and the latter as his own composition.

The focus of the writer is clearly on the redemptive work of Christ in history and on the earthly plane through his cross and resurrection. The "fullness of God" dwelt in Christ and "through him" to reconcile all things unto him by making peace "through the blood of his cross" (1:20). He "has now reconciled" those who had been estranged, doing evil deeds, "in his body of flesh by his death" in order to present them "holy and blameless and irreproachable" (1:21–22). The view is that Christ—who represents God in the creation of the universe, and then to the world—took upon himself the sins of humanity and bore on himself the penalty upon sins to its ultimate conclusion, death. As a consequence, those formerly estranged stand blameless. Sins have been forgiven (1:14; 3:13). God has "forgiven us all our trespasses, having canceled the bond which stood against us with its legal demands . . . nailing it to the cross" (2:13–14). The law can no longer accuse, for trespasses brought to light by the law have been given their due in the atoning death of Jesus.[29] In the crucified Jesus the law as accusing testimony has itself been rendered dead.[30] Here Pauline theology is put to service against the opponents who propagate legal demands and denigrate those who do not observe them properly (2:18).

Risen from the dead by the power of God (2:12), Christ is now the "beginning" (*archē*), "the first-born from the dead" in order that he might "have first place in everything" (1:18).[31] In this verse Paul's conception of the risen Christ as the "first fruits of those who have fallen asleep" (1 Cor. 15:20, 23) is recalled, but not exactly. Paul's view presupposes a temporal succession of the ages, in which the new age has been inaugurated through God's raising Jesus from the dead, and it will come into its own at the parousia. For this writer too there are indications of a temporal conception, since the parousia is future (3:4), and the "inheritance" is yet to come (3:24). But equally apparent, this writer also thinks in terms of earthly and heavenly realms. Christ is in the realm "above" (3:1), and the "hope" of the Christian is laid up in heaven (1:5); "the forward-looking perspective becomes a perspective directed upwards, spatially: there the heritage is already laid up."[32] When Christ is spoken of as "the first-born of the dead," the nuance of temporality is of course there, but the accent can equally be upon his gain of preeminence (or rank) over the creation,[33] thus indicating his return to his former position: being "the first-born of all creation" (1:15). The fact that the author uses a purpose clause ("in order that in everything he might be preeminent") shows that this is indeed what he wishes to express.

The Pauline eschatological outlook is therefore not dispensed with in Colossians, but it is infused with an ontological and existential perspective not yet envisioned by the apostle. The reign of Christ has begun, for he is already preeminent over all things. His reign over creation takes on its specific, even visible, form in the church, of which he is head (1:18) and in which he is regarded as Lord (1:10; 2:6; 3:17, 20, 23–24).[34] The unseen cosmic powers have been subjected to him (2:10), but apart from the gospel this is not known. Consequently, there are those—the opponents, specifically—who continue to teach their vain philosophy, calling upon their hearers to submit to a way of life for salvation which regards the powers capable of benevolence.[35] But for the author of the letter, Christ is ontologically superior to the elements of the universe, for he is above them (2:10), and to follow the opponents' philosophy is but a worldly enterprise (2:20), giving attention to human precepts and doctrines (2:22). Christ reigns above all things, and his kingdom is a present reality (1:13), not simply a future hope. Rather than pressing temporal imagery in reference to Christ's reign, the author thinks primarily in terms of ontological categories. Worldly thinking and acting must be overcome. Christians are to "seek the things that are above" and "set their minds" on them rather than on earthly things (3:1–2; cf. 2:20). This is possible for them now, since from the divine side they have been reconciled (1:20), forgiven (1:14; 2:13), and transferred to the kingdom of God's Son (1:13) through baptism. And in their own consciousness they are to know that they have died (2:20; 3:3), been raised (3:1), and made alive (2:13) already. Their having been raised to life under the dominion of Christ is, however, a matter of faith (2:12), not sight, wisdom, or ecstatic experience (2:18), and this point maintains the Pauline caveat against an overblown realized eschatology which leads to being puffed up with conceit (1 Cor. 4:8)[36] and against the view to be confronted in post-Pauline Christianity that "the resurrection is past already" (2 Tim. 2:18).

The reign of the risen Christ over the cosmos will be seen publicly at the parousia—and here the temporal note has to be employed—when he appears in glory along with his saints (3:4), not to redeem them, but to certify their redemption. What faith knows already through the gospel will be made manifest to all. In fact, that which is to come is already coming upon the world now. The gospel of Christ's reconciling work and reign over all things "has been proclaimed to every creature under heaven" (1:23). This cannot mean (by use of the aorist passive) that the proclamation of the gospel in the world has been completed. Rather the point is that the gospel has been preached to all creation located "under heaven"—that is, the human race—and the "all" signifies that there has been no exclusion, and hence no exclusivism (as there is in the case of the opponents' "philosophy").[37] The "mystery hidden for ages and generations" (1:26) is not a mystery attained by a religio-philosophical elite through wisdom, but is disclosed through the word of God, which is to be made fully known (1:25) through proclamation to every person (1:28).

And the fact that the gospel "is bearing fruit and growing" in the world is cause for rejoicing (1:6).

The redemptive perspective of Colossians is christopractic,[38] in which Christ bears "all the fullness of God" (1:19; 2:9). Agent of creation, redeemer, and reconciler, he is acknowledged in the church as ruler over all things, and he is served as Lord by those who through baptism have been buried with him and raised to life with him (2:13–14). Yet the reconciling work of Christ extends to "all things," the whole creation, and therefore the gospel of his reconciling work is to be proclaimed to every person. In Christ, God—and here again a theopractic note is sounded—has disarmed the cosmic powers, made a public example of them, and triumphed over them (2:15).[39] The "dominion of darkness" has already been rent asunder by the deliverance of the redeemed from its power. There is admittedly a tension between the reconciliation (by Christ) of "all things, whether on earth or in heaven" (1:20) and God's triumph in him over the cosmic powers (2:15). But the purpose of the writer in the latter context is to stress that the cosmic powers no longer have any autonomous power; therefore those who hear the gospel should not live as though they belong "to the world" (2:20) in pursuit of redemption (or salvation) through wisdom. The triumph over the cosmic powers implies that their power to rule apart from Christ is not eternal. They were created "through" Christ and "for him" (1:16), and now Christ is also their "head" (2:10); "they are brought to an acknowledgement of his authority and of their rightful place under him"[40] whose work is peace (1:20). There is no vision of a final battle between Christ and the powers, nor does Christ destroy them. What remains is on the earthly plane in which believers are to put away all that is "earthly" (3:5) and to serve the Lord in word and deed as befits his servants (3:17). Ernst Käsemann, who has suggested that the Colossian Hymn (1:15–20) belonged originally to a baptismal context, has summarized the message of the letter to its readers in an eloquent way:

> You are reconciled and the cosmos is pacified, because the powers which swayed it have been despoiled and now follow in the train of the triumphal progress of Christ. They have lost their lordship and their position as mediators. For you are 'translated', you have entered into an immediate relationship to the Christ, you are his body.[41]

To submit to the opponents' way of thinking and living would be to deny that Christ's reconciling work had been accomplished.

The author knows, of course, that evil deeds are still a reality in the world and a possibility for the Christian. This would seem at first to deny that the powers have been vanquished and brought under the lordship of Christ. Yet that need not follow. Vices and evil are attributed to "the old nature" (3:9), which does not yet acknowledge the lordship of Christ. The reconciled world is nevertheless on a course toward its preeminent Lord who is above; all things move toward him, however imperfectly. Christians are those who see the goal above and ahead and move toward it in earnest, and so they are admonished to increase in the knowledge of God (1:10), not shift from their hope (1:23), become mature in Christ (1:28; 4:12), and seek the things which are above (3:1–2). God's wrath is coming upon those who continue to indulge in vices of an earthly nature (3:6; cf. 3:25). These warnings function to direct the Christian along the earthly pilgrimage toward the heavenly hope, which is above in heaven and is entered at its portal, death. Threat as well as promise must be given, and the threat is no less real than the promise. But the wrath of God, once having been exercised with justice, is finally but a portion of God's "whole fullness" which dwells in Christ (2:9), who in his death has reconciled all things and has made peace. There is no part of the creation which remains unreconciled to him and in him. The church is thus to embody this gospel in its own internal life (3:12–17), its proclamation (1:23, 28), and its conduct toward those outside (4:5–6). Christ is "the head of every [person], whether that [person] believes in Christ or not. . . . The image of headship asserts the sufficiency of Christ's atonement to redeem all [persons] from their bondage, and sets the church in the midst of the world as the sign of that sufficiency."[42]

2. *The Letter to the Ephesians.* Ephesians shares terminology with Colossians, and it appears to take over materials from Colossians and expand upon them,[43] but it differs from this letter in important respects as well. The letter—if one can call it a "letter" at all; it is as much a treatise placed within an epistolary framework—speaks to a situation within gentile Christianity (cf. 2:11; 3:1) of the Pauline sphere,[44] but it does not have the polemical tone of Colossians. At most there is a negative comment about (but hardly a warning against) being "tossed to and fro and carried about with every wind of doctrine, by people's cunning, by their craftiness and deceitful wiles" (4:14). Attempts to discern the purpose of the letter have led to many proposals but few certainties.[45] At a minimum, however, the letter clearly emphasizes the unity of the church (and "church" means not simply the congregation, but the church extending throughout the world)[46] and particularly the place of gentiles within it. The writer asserts that Christ has "broken down the dividing wall of hostility" between Jews and gentiles (2:14). He does not actually use the term "Jews" but speaks of "the circumcision" (2:11) and "the commonwealth of Israel" (2:12). For him, Christ confirms "the convenants of promise" (2:12) given to Israel. That is to say, "the circumcision"

101

or "the commonwealth of Israel" with which gentiles are united consists of those Jews who have come to believe in Jesus as the promised Messiah.[47]

It is surprising that gentile Christians in a post-Pauline situation[48] should need to be told that in Christ they have been "brought near" (2:13), or reconciled, to God on an equal footing with Jewish Christians. The explanation may lie in the fact that now gentile Christianity has become institutionalized and in need of an identity and outlook both for its own inner life and in its accounting of itself to the larger social and cultural setting. No longer could gentile Christians consider themselves simply a wild olive branch grafted into the tree of Israel (Rom. 11:17–24), awaiting the parousia when this rather unnatural situation would be resolved through the salvation of themselves and Israel together (Rom. 11:25–36).[49] Now a new conception has to be worked out in which gentile Christianity is seen to be a direct heir to Israel, and the solution is to say that in Christ "the law of commandments and ordinances"—that which publicly gives an enduring and unconverted Israel its identity—has been abolished (2:15) and that a unity has been created which consists of believing Israel and gentiles incorporated into her. These gentiles are "fellow citizens with the saints" (2:19), that is, with believing Israel. Gentile Christians can thus give an account of themselves to both themselves and the public. They are not Jews, even though they lay claim to the promises and heritage of Israel. Neither are they gentiles pure and simple, even though they are physically uncircumcised—in fact regarded as "the uncircumcision by what is called the circumcision" (2:11)—and do not observe "the law of commandments and ordinances" (2:15). Moreover, they live in a predominantly gentile culture. Yet they are in tension with it. Gentile Christians have thus become within the social and religious context a "third race"[50]—neither Jews nor adherents of gentile religious traditions. Whatever else the purposes of the letter may have been, it deals with the question of identity for these gentile Christians.

The ontological and eschatological perspectives differ from those in Colossians. As in the latter, Ephesians speaks of Christ as reigning above the cosmic powers (1:20–22; 3:10; 4:10). It too speaks of Christians as having been saved (perfect tense, *sesosmenoi,* 2:8), "made alive" (2:1, 5), and "raised up" to be with Christ (2:6), thus sharing with Colossians an emphasis on salvation as already having occurred for believers. Yet there is in Ephesians essentially a salvation-historical perspective.[51] The "day of redemption" is future (4:30). At present Christians have the gospel of their final salvation, and the Spirit is the guarantee of it (1:13–14). They have been called by the gospel and thereby been "enlightened" concerning their hope (1:18). But at present the days are evil (5:16), and the "evil day" is yet to come (6:13). There is a distinction made between "this age" and "that which is to come" (1:21). The "kingdom of Christ and of God" is a future inheritance (5:5).

There is also a shift of perspective concerning the cosmic powers. Although Christ has been raised above them, he has not yet subjected them.[52] True, he reigns "far above" them (1:21); all things are "under his feet," and he is "head over all things," but that is so "for the church" (1:22). That is to say, the effects of his reign "far above" the cosmic powers do not affect the powers yet—his kingdom is future—but his superiority over these powers signals that he is "positioned" to bring them into subjugation and that he will finally subject them for the sake of the church (which in the meantime he "nourishes and cherishes," 5:29). Still the devil (6:11), "the evil one" (6:16), is at work, and Christians contend against "principalities," "powers," the "world rulers of this darkness" *(hoi kosmokratores tou skotous toutou),* the "spirits of wickedness in the heavenly places" (6:12). The demonic powers are guided by the "prince of the power of the air, the spirit that is now at work in the sons of disobedience" (2:2). Here the author is an heir to Jewish traditions that distinguished between angels and demons, ranking them in their cosmic positions so that the "air" is the abode of the latter,[53] from which they penetrate and dominate people's thoughts, aspirations, and deeds from a position of intimacy.[54]

The redemptive work of Christ is spelled out from a Pauline basis but is extended. Although it is not said that God sent his Son or gave him up for us or for our sins, God's eternal purpose has been realized in Christ (3:11); in him God accomplishes his will (1:11); and it is God who raised him from the dead, seated him at his right hand, and placed all things under his feet (1:20, 22). But the work of redemption, rooted in God's purpose, is centered in the action of Christ[55] who "loved us and gave himself up for us [*paredōken heauton hyper hēmōn*], an offering and sacrifice to God, to be a fragrant offering" (5:2). In Christ "we have redemption through his blood [*apolytrōsis dia tou haimatos autou*], the forgiveness of our trespasses" (1:7). Moreover, it is said that Christ "loved the church and gave himself up for her [*heauton paredōken hyper autēs*]" (5:25).

In speaking of Christ as one who "gave himself up for us as an offering and sacrifice to God," the author conceives of the work of Christ in a rather non-Pauline way. Paul could use similar terminology ("a fragrant offering, a sacrifice acceptable and pleasing to God") in reference to the gifts sent to him by the congregation at Philippi (Phil. 4:18), but it would be uncharacteristic of him to think of Christ as giving up himself as an offering to God on behalf of humanity, since for Paul it is God who has

103

given up his Son for a redemptive purpose (Rom. 3:25; 4:25; 8:32). The thought expressed here in Ephesians is closer to that of Hebrews (cf. Heb. 9:23–26; 10:12) than to Paul's. Nevertheless, the degree to which the author sees the sacrificial death of Jesus to be a means of placating God on behalf of humanity must be held in check. For this writer the redemptive work of Christ is carried out not over against God, but on behalf of God who "has blessed us in Christ" (Eph. 1:3), has accomplished his purpose in him (1:19–20; 3:11), and shows "the immeasurable riches of his grace in kindness toward us in Christ Jesus" (2:7). The context of 5:2 is an exhortation to "walk in love," and this imperative is followed by the indicative of the love of Christ. The sacrificial death of Christ was an expression of his love, and it is in that respect that it was "a fragrant offering and sacrifice to God" (RSV). The idea lying behind the phrase is that acts of true devotion to God are sacrifices pleasing to him. This is found in the Old Testament (Deut. 33:19; Pss. 4:9; 51:17, 19; 107:22; 116:17; Sir. 35:6–7), and it is readily at hand for use in the New Testament. So Paul admonishes Christians at Rome to present their "bodies" (i.e., themselves) as "living sacrifices, holy and acceptable to God" (Rom. 12:1) and speaks of the gift of the Philippians as an offering and sacrifice (Phil. 4:18). Moreover, in the Epistle to the Hebrews the praise of Christians to God is spoken of as a sacrifice, and their doing good and sharing are sacrifices pleasing to God (13:15–16). It is in this deeper sense of the meaning of sacrifice that Eph. 5:2 must be understood: The very act of Christ's giving himself up for his own in love is a sacrificial act pleasing to God.[56] The syntax of the verse implies of course that Christ was himself the "offering and sacrifice." But that is so in consequence of his love and service on behalf of his own. As Christians can be "living sacrifices" themselves, that is so through their sacrificial deeds. In the same way, Christ—in his act of love and sacrificial death—is himself the offering and sacrifice. He has given himself over to the will and purpose of God so that there might be "redemption through his blood, the forgiveness of our trespasses" (1:7). Through the use of the *hyper*-formula, the author portrays the death of Christ as an act "on behalf of us" (5:2) or "on behalf of [the church]" (5:25). In this, as in Paul before him (cf. Rom. 5:8; Gal. 3:13; 1 Thess. 5:10), the writer conceives of Christ as having assumed the consequences of "sins" (but "sin" in Paul) in himself on behalf of others. The results are forgiveness (1:7; 4:32) and reconciliation to God (2:16).

The risen Christ is "far above" all cosmic powers and "head over all things" (1:21–22). Yet, as indicated previously, this does not mean that "all things" have been reconciled to God. Within Ephesians attention is directed primarily upon Christ and his church. The benefits of Christ for the present—between his resurrection and parousia—are the reconciliation of Jews and gentiles into one body, and this one body to God. Formerly humanity was divided into two parts—Jews and gentiles—and the gentiles were without hope in the world (2:12). Between Jews and gentiles there had been "the dividing wall of hostility" (2:14, RSV; literally, "the dividing wall of the fence, the enmity"),[57] which in context refers to the law (2:15).[58] Judaism, in this view, had separated itself off from gentiles through its observance of the Torah—not simply its moral teaching, but its ceremonial and dietary traditions—and gentiles looked upon such separation as an offense. But Christ has broken down this wall, creating "one new being in place of two, so making peace" (2:15). In this way the writer claims that "the commonwealth of Israel" has itself been renewed and that those formerly "far off" (i.e., gentiles) have joined with it in fellow citizenship in the one household. There are no longer two entities but one new entity. And all in this one body have been reconciled to God through the cross (1:16). Reconciliation is accomplished in two directions: Jews and gentiles have been reconciled into one body, and this one body has been reconciled to God. Thus the church becomes the instrument and locus of reconciliation, constituting the totality of reconciliation in the era between Christ's resurrection and parousia.

The focus on the church as the reconciled entity tends to push cosmic reconciliation in Christ to the periphery. The picture portrayed is one of Christ sitting "far above" the cosmic powers; his reign does not affect the cosmic powers in the present, but extends down—not as rays of light through the universe, but as power through the Spirit (3:16; 4:4, 30; 5:18; 6:17, 18; cf. 1:13; 2:18)[59]—among believers in the one body on earth. It is through the church that the witness to Christ's reign is made to "the principalities and powers in the heavenly places" (3:10) and that Christ's lordship is realized on earth.[60] This means that Christ and his church are fused together. But they are not totally identified, nor are they interchangeable, for the church is always under the lordship of Christ, who is its head and upon whom the church is dependent for its existence and life (4:15–16; 5:29).

But the scope of the redemptive work of Christ is envisioned in Ephesians to extend finally beyond the church. God is the creator of all things (3:9), and the risen Christ has ascended "in order that he might fill all things" (4:10; cf. 1:23). He is head over all things "for the church" in the present era (1:22) in order that the church might be empowered in its mission—not threatened by the cosmic powers, but strengthened by the Spirit to contend against them and to stand firm (6:10–20). But there is to come a future "day of redemption" (4:30) and "the kingdom of Christ and of God" (5:5). God's "purpose" has been displayed in Christ; the plan of salvation which God brings to reality through Christ is "to unite" *(anakephalaiōsasthai)* "all things in him, things in heaven and things on earth" (1:10). The meaning of the Greek verb is notoriously difficult to translate and interpret; it has been rendered as "to unite" (or "to sum up"), "to make [Christ] head" over all things, and "to renew."[61] The nearest parallel to the verse is Col. 1:20 in which the verb "to reconcile" *(apokatallaxai)* is used, and it is said that Christ reconciles "all things . . . whether on earth or in heaven." Most likely the writer of Ephesians has essentially the same meaning in mind in using the verb *anakephalaiōsasthai,* relating the idea of reconciliation to the supremacy of Christ, who is "head" *(kephalē)* over all things (1:22). This will then mean that, according to the writer, God's purpose is to give to "all things" a supreme head in Christ, under which they are united.[62] In all of this the vision of Ephesians, for all its ecclesiological-redemptive emphasis, looks out upon wider horizons.[63] The writer is aware that the mass of humanity is currently alienated from God due to its ignorance and hardness of heart (4:18) and that cosmic powers, inspired by the evil one, still seek to fulfill their own purposes in the heavens and upon the earth. The reconciling work of Christ remains a secret unknown among the powers and most of humanity upon the earth, but it is to be made known in both arenas by the church (3:9–10),[64] through which Christ exercises his reign until the final day of redemption. But since Christ fills all things and displays God's purpose and plan of salvation, the church as the new creation (2:10; 4:24) does not represent the sum total of the redemptive work of Christ, but it is the instrument of his reign in the world and the sign of that which is to come on the day of redemption. A wider hope and expectation are therefore expressed in Ephesians, even if the details are left to God. That which occupies the writer's concern in the present circumstances is that the church be faithful to Christ in demonstrating the reconciliation that has already been accomplished through Christ's breaking down the barrier between Jew and gentile, creating one new body, and reconciling this one body to God. By attending to the reconciled life within its own earthly setting, the church bears witness that beyond and above all that is seen and unseen, there is a power at work to reconcile the universe itself, a power that manifested itself in the resurrection of Jesus from the dead (1:19–20).

THE PASTORAL EPISTLES

The Pastoral Epistles (1 and 2 Timothy, Titus) purport to be letters of the apostle Paul written to colleagues and treating matters of doctrine, ethics, and church order. Nevertheless, they are generally regarded as pseudonymous and are classified as deutero-Pauline, that is, written in the name of Paul by a person who seeks to represent the apostle in a post-Pauline situation.[65] This classification can be established chiefly on the grounds of a comparison of their language, theological outlook, and prescribed church order with what is found in these matters among those letters which no one disputes as genuinely Pauline. Not all of the results of such a comparison can be reviewed here.[66] Suffice it to say that over 38 percent of the words in the Pastorals do not appear in the undisputed letters of Paul;[67] theological concepts also differ, so that, for example, the term "faith" generally means in the Pastorals "the Christian faith," whereas in the undisputed letters it generally has the meaning of "trust" in God, Christ, or the gospel;[68] and the church order reflected in the Pastorals—with recognized officials bearing the titles of bishop, presbyter, or deacon—is not found in the letters of Paul, but corresponds more closely to what one finds in certain Apostolic Fathers. The Pastorals were most likely written ca. A.D. 100 and most certainly in Ephesus or its vicinity, and addressed to churches in the Pauline field of Asia Minor.[69]

The Pastorals contain relatively few christological titles. The term "Son of God" is lacking altogether. Titles which do appear are "Christ" (thirty-two times),[70] "Lord" (*kyrios,* eighteen times),[71] "Savior" (four times: 2 Tim. 1:10; Titus 1:4; 2:13; 3:6), and "Mediator" (once: 1 Tim. 2:5). Of these terms, special attention has to be given to "Savior" (*sōtēr*). Although this term appears as a christological title at various other places in the New Testament (Luke 2:11; John 4:42; Acts 5:31; 13:23; Eph. 5:23; 2 Pet. 1:1, 11; 2:20; 3:2, 18; 1 John 4:14) and has come to be one of the most common titles for Christ in subsequent history, it appears in Paul's own letters only once (Phil. 3:20). Moreover, the author of the Pastorals uses it on six more occasions referring to God (1 Tim. 1:1; 2:3; 4:10; Titus 1:3; 2:10; 3:4). This usage is of course rooted in the Old Testament (e.g., Isa. 45:15, 21; Ps. 62:2, 6).[72] By using the term for both God and Jesus, the writer asserts that God wills to save and does save (cf. 1 Tim. 2:4; 4:10; Titus 2:11), but this action is carried out by Christ. Christ is the manifestation of the "goodness and loving kindness of God our Savior" (Titus 3:4). In him "the grace of God has appeared for the salvation of all people" (Titus 2:11).

The Pastorals portray a high christology. The humanity of Christ is affirmed (1 Tim. 2:5; 6:13; 2 Tim. 2:8). It is not likely that the title "Mediator" carries ontological significance. It is used (once only) to speak more of the function of Christ than his nature: There is but "one Mediator," not many, "between God and humanity, the man Christ Jesus, who gave himself as a ransom for all" (1 Tim. 2:5–6). On the other hand, the Pastorals assert a status of Christ in which he is exalted above the human race, and that is reflected through both the use of christological titles and the portrayal of a "three-stage christology" of preexistence, incarnation, and exaltation.[73] An explicit statement of the preexistence of the Son of God or logos (titles lacking in the Pastorals) cannot be found. Nevertheless, the writer says that Christ "was manifested in the flesh" (1 Tim. 3:16), and he speaks of the appearance of the grace of God in Christ, a grace which existed "before the ages" (or before temporality, 2 Tim. 1:9; cf. Titus 2:11). Preexistence and incarnation are linked in various expressions in which the author says that "Christ Jesus came into the world" (1 Tim. 1:15) or that Christ appeared for a redemptive purpose (2 Tim. 1:10; Titus 3:4). And following his crucifixion Christ was exalted (1 Tim. 3:16; 2 Tim. 1:10; 2:12), so that he shares in the divine glory. In such an exalted state he also shares titles which are otherwise applied to God, such as "Lord" and "Savior." In fact, he is even called "God" in one place: Christians await their "blessed hope, the appearing of the glory of our great God and Savior Jesus Christ" (Titus 2:13).[74]

The application of the term "God" to Christ is in many respects surprising for two reasons. First, such usage is notoriously rare in the New Testament as a whole; the only other places where the term is applied unambiguously to Jesus are at John 20:28 and Heb. 1:8. Second, the writer of the Pastorals himself makes clear-cut distinctions between God and Christ at several places (cf. 1 Tim. 1:1; 2:5–6; 5:21; 2 Tim. 4:1; Titus 1:4; 3:4–6). Yet it must be said that, for the writer of the Pastorals, the distinction does not imply a separation; God and Christ are intimately related even in passages in which they are distinguished. And so at Titus 2:13 it is said that at his parousia Christ will bear the divine glory to complete the saving work of God, and in that sense he will be "God and Savior." And already in his first coming, he was the manifestation of "the goodness and loving kindness of God our Savior" (Titus 3:4).

The redemptive christology of the Pastorals portrays Christ as a vigorous redeemer figure who comes to the rescue of humanity. Salvation is willed by God (1 Tim. 2:4), and it is due purely to God's grace and mercy (Titus 2:11; 3:5, 7). Nevertheless, the redemptive christology is of the christopractic type, in which Christ performs the saving work on behalf of humanity. In the view of the writer, as in the case of his hero Paul, the whole human race is sinful. But there is a shift away from Paul. Paul speaks of "sin" in the singular and considers it a power which reigns over all persons (Rom. 3:9; 5:12, 21; 7:14; Gal. 3:22). In the Pastorals, on the other hand, the author never speaks of "sin" but thinks in terms of particular "sins" which people commit (1 Tim. 5:22, 24; 2 Tim. 3:6).

Nor can he think then of sin as a dominating power. He thinks of sins essentially as vices, of which he gives a long list (2 Tim. 3:2–5), and considers these to result from a life disoriented from serving God and keeping the godly virtues, of which many are mentioned throughout the letters (e.g., faith, love, purity of heart, good deeds, moderation, civic and domestic duties, contentment, generosity, respect for others, and self-control).[75] Vices are due essentially to serving self and the passions which arise from selfish desires (2 Tim. 2:22; Titus 2:12; 3:3).

The thinking here appears to be rooted in various Jewish and Hellenistic traditions outside of the Pauline stream. Above all, the author appears to be heir of that Jewish tradition which thought of sins to be caused by the "evil impulse" (*yeṣer ha-ra'*), which is in perpetual conflict with the "good impulse" (*yeṣer ha-ṭob*). This tradition can be traced back to Genesis (6:5; 8:21), but was developed in pre-Christian times (Sir. 15:11–20, particularly 15:14) and is found also in texts contemporary with the rise of Christianity (2 Esd. 3:21; 4:30–31) as well as in rabbinic literature.[76] Likewise, in Stoicism it was taught that one must learn to exercise control over one's passions—ever prone to vices—by renouncing them and striving for *autarkeia* (self-sufficiency).[77] This term also appears in the Pastorals (1 Tim. 6:6), although here it probably has the meaning of "contentment" (RSV). In any case, the writer shares the outlook of these Jewish and Hellenistic traditions in his view that there is a conflict within the heart of every person between good and evil impulses, and the Christian is called to purity of heart (1 Tim. 1:5; 2 Tim. 2:22) and to engage in the struggle toward righteousness and godliness (1 Tim. 6:11; 2 Tim. 2:22).

Salvation, however, does not come about by a victory of the "good impulse" over the "evil impulse" or virtue over vice. It comes purely by the grace of God and "not because of deeds done by us in righteousness" (Titus 3:5; cf. 2 Tim. 1:9). It is grounded in the purpose of God and carried out by Christ who "came into the world to save sinners" (1 Tim. 1:15). In his death Christ "gave himself as a ransom [*antilytron*] for all [*hyper pantōn*]" (1 Tim. 2:6); further, "he gave himself for us [*hyper hēmōn*] in order that he might redeem [*lytrōsētai*] us from all iniquity" (Titus 2:14). In these statements the writer affirms that Christ, in his sacrificial death, has set humanity free from the consequences of sins committed, and these consequences are judgment and death. The terms "ransom" and "to redeem" refer to the act of liberation, and the *hyper*-formula—used already in pre-Pauline traditions (cf. 1 Cor. 15:3) and by Paul himself (see p. 48)—implies that Christ himself has borne the divine judgment against sins for the benefit of others. In one of the most explicit statements in the entire New Testament on Christ as the one who has won redemption for others, the writer declares that Christ "abolished death and brought life and imperishability to light" (2 Tim. 1:10, the aorist tense is used for both verbs). The accent in this passage is primarily on the resurrection (not the death) of Christ. By his resurrection death has been overcome, and that means that "life and imperishability" come into their own, into the light of day. Previously there was only perishability leading to death, but now the imperishability and life which God intends for his people have been gained.

The Pastorals therefore stress the "objective" character of the redeeming work of Christ. He has borne sins and their consequences for the benefit of others, and he has abolished death that people might have life and imperishability. Further, the Pastorals stress the "universal" character of the redeeming work of Christ, "who gave himself as a ransom *for all*" (1 Tim. 2:6). In so doing, Christ has taken up the divine cause, for God "desires all persons to be saved" (1 Tim. 2:4). In fact, the writer says, the hope of Christians is set on God, "who is the Savior of all people, especially of those who believe" (1 Tim. 4:10). The scope of redemption is here said to be universal, but various interpreters have sought to tone it down with other proposals. There are essentially four interpretations of the verse. First, some have argued that the writer simply wanted to stress the term "all" over against Gnostic Christian claims that only an elite group is capable of salvation, but of course the writer claimed that believers alone will be saved.[78] Second, some have suggested that the writer meant that God is potentially the Savior of all (cf. 1 Tim. 2:4) or is Savior of all in the sense of being their preserver, but that in the end only believers will be granted salvation.[79] Third, there are those who say that the writer did indeed envision the universal salvation of all people, but believers are singled out (in the phrase "especially those who believe") as those who have certainty of salvation in the present world.[80] Finally, it has been suggested that the phrase "especially those who believe" is a scribal addition.[81] The last of these will probably have to be dismissed, since it is purely a conjecture; all known Greek witnesses contain the phrase. The first two can be dismissed also as attempts, arising from nervousness over theological universalism, to get around the plain meaning of the text. When translated from Greek in a very literal fashion the clause speaks of God as "all persons' Savior, especially believers' [Savior]." Believers are distinguished from all persons in the sense that they know God as their Savior, for they have heard the gospel. Or to put it another way, believers know God as their Savior, so he is "especially" their Savior. This means that the author holds in tension, on the one hand, the universality of God's grace and saving power—a grace and a power which know no limits (cf. Rom. 5:18–19; 11:25–32; 1 Cor. 15:22–28; 2 Cor.

5:19; Phil. 2:10–11; Eph. 1:9–10; Col. 1:19–20; 1 John 2:2)—and on the other, the particularity of faith which accepts this grace and power for oneself. The writer thus encloses within his view both the human race as a whole and the community of faith; his focus is "especially" on the community of faith as the beneficiary of God's salvation, but the focus is only that—a focus, not a limit.

It is the gospel alone that attests the redemptive work of Christ. The gospel is the "testimony" that Christ gave himself as a ransom for all (1 Tim. 2:6), and it is "through the gospel" that one hears that Christ has abolished death and brought imperishability to light (2 Tim. 1:10). Faith is the acceptance of the gospel as true, and in that acceptance of the truth persons "take hold of the eternal life" to which they are called (1 Tim. 6:12; cf. 6:19).

Salvation is thought in the Pastorals essentially as a future hope, life in the "heavenly kingdom" (2 Tim. 4:18). For now Christians are "heirs in hope of eternal life" (Titus 3:7; cf. 1:2), expecting salvation to come (1 Tim. 4:16) and enduring until its arrival (2 Tim. 2:10, 12). Yet the writer can also speak of salvation as a present reality. Twice he declares that God "saved us" (2 Tim. 1:9; Titus 3:5), and just as many times he tells his readers to "take hold of" eternal life (1 Tim. 6:12, 19). The picture which emerges is that the redemptive work of God has already been accomplished by Christ's death and resurrection (so God "saved us'). In the present Christians "take hold of" the new life which has been won for them, and of which they are heirs, and they shall enter into that life in its fullness, the eternal kingdom, at the time of their "departure" (2 Tim. 4:6) or at the parousia of Christ (Titus 2:13), should that take place before death.

To this point nothing has been said about the polemics of the Pastorals. The writer refers frequently to heretical teachers and gives some indication of their teachings. It is not possible to cover this in detail here,[82] except to say that they seem to have taught an ascetic way of life (1 Tim. 4:3), were engaged in speculative teaching based on the Scriptures (1 Tim. 1:3b–7; 4:7; Titus 1:14; 3:9), and claimed that "the resurrection has taken place already" (2 Tim. 2:18). Most likely these persons represented an early gnostic movement which promoted a syncretism of Jewish and Christian traditions.[83] In regard to the claim that the resurrection is past already they must have considered themselves and their adherents to have risen into the new life already, a view that came to expression fully in the Nag Hammadi Treatise on the Resurrection (1.4.48–49):

> The resurrection . . . is the revelation of what is, and the transformation of
> things, and a transition into newness. For imperishability [descends] upon

the perishable; the light flows down upon the darkness, swallowing it up. . . . Therefore do not . . . live in conformity with the flesh . . . but flee from the divisions and the fetters, and already you have the resurrection. . . . Why not consider yourself as risen and [already] brought to this?[84]

The writer of the Pastorals combats the heretical teachers in the name of the apostle Paul, calling upon his readers to avoid them (1 Tim. 4:7; 6:20; Titus 3:9) and setting forth the view found in Paul that although there is a newness of life for those who are in Christ (2 Cor. 5:17; 6:2), salvation in its fullness is a future prospect (Rom. 10:9; 13:11; Phil. 2:12; 3:20; 1 Thess. 5:8–9), and the believer awaits it in fellowship with the body of Christ and in obedience to the Lord.

The redemptive christology of the Pastorals, however, differs in important respects from that of the mentor they claim, the apostle Paul. It reflects a later situation in which Christianity has become a "religion" on its own, fostering piety or godliness, a structured community, and an emerging orthodoxy. Christ is portrayed as the one who comes to rescue humanity from its sins and mortality for the heavenly kingdom. He bears the titles "Lord" and "Savior," which are found also in Paul's Epistles, but he also bears the "glory" (or dignity) of "God" as well.

As indicated already, the redemptive christology of the Pastorals stresses both the "objective" and "universal" character of the work of Christ. This, of course, is in keeping with the Pauline view, even though the way in which it is all expressed differs. It is on the basis of Christ's own work that humanity's redemption has been won. The gospel of the church declares what he has done, and those who hear it are able already to "take hold" of eternal life in the present, live within his community— which is a social reality on earth, a community of mutual love, virtue, and respect for those outside—and finally enter into the heavenly kingdom. At the same time, while the author's focus is on the community of believers, their life and faith, humanity in general is neither forgotten nor considered out of range of the scope of the benefits of Christ, who gave himself as a ransom for all on behalf of God, the "Savior of all people, especially of those who believe" and know God as such through the work of Christ.

THE FIRST EPISTLE OF PETER

Judged by critical scholarship generally as a pseudonymous work and written from Rome (cf. 5:13),[85] the actual date of composition of 1 Peter in its final form is disputed. The tendency is to place it in the last two decades of the first century,[86] although some would put it early in the second.[87] In any case, the letter belongs to the "subapostolic" period (the era in which works were written in the name of deceased apostles or anonymously, prior to the "postapostolic" age when persons such as Clement and Ignatius wrote again under their own names).[88]

The letter makes use of only two major New Testament christological titles. Most commonly it simply uses the term "Christ" (twenty-two times).[89] In the nine instances at which "Jesus" is coupled with this term,[90] it is always "Jesus Christ" and never "Christ Jesus" that is written—a contrast from Paul's usage, in which both forms appear. A second title used is "Lord" (*kyrios,* on two occasions: 1:3; 3:15).[91] Conspicuously lacking is the title "Son of God" (which is also lacking in the Pastorals).

Beyond these major New Testament christological titles, the author uses a variety of christological imagery. What is striking about this imagery is that in each instance it is not employed to assert christological emphases so much as to deal with aspects of the community's life and self-understanding. Although the members of the community had been formerly "straying like sheep," they have now returned to the "Shepherd" (*poimēn*) and "Bishop" (*episkopos,* RSV, "Guardian") "of souls" (2:25). Thus Christ protects, guides, governs, and guards the members of the Christian fellowship. Within the context of a treatment of community leadership (5:1–5), the author says that elders (presbyters) are to tend the flock of God, not domineer, and set examples to the flock; then they will receive their reward at the parousia, the manifestation of the "Great Shepherd" (*archipoimēn,* 5:9). Members of the community must be willing to "suffer for righteousness' sake" (3:14) or "for doing right" (3:17), for the "righteous one" died for the unrighteous (3:18). Members of the community are called to holiness of life (1:15), for they have been ransomed by the death of Jesus, whose death, recalling Old Testament sacrificial regulations (Exod. 12:5; 29:1; Lev. 22:19–21), is compared to the offering of "a lamb without blemish or spot" (1:19). Christians are exhorted to be as "living stones" making up a "spiritual house" (or household, 2:5), and Christ himself is designated the (true) "living stone" (2:4), rejected by humanity, but designated by God as a "cornerstone chosen and precious" (2:6) and the "head of the corner" (2:7). All of these images—Shepherd, Chief Shepherd, Bishop, righteous one, lamb, and living stone—are christological. They appear within hortatory contexts, however, and are not developed for their own sake. That does not make them insignificant for the christology of this letter, for they extend christological thought and portraiture beyond what the major titles have to offer or even suggest, and they function to apply christological reflection to the church's life and self-understanding. The writer uses symbols for Christ which have social cohesiveness under the domain of Christ as their goal.

The letter recalls aspects of the redemptive christology set forth by

Paul.[92] This is seen above all in 3:18: "Christ also died for sins once for all, the righteous for [*hyper*] the unrighteous." The *hyper*-formula—used several times by Paul (Rom. 5:6, 8; 2 Cor. 5:14; Gal. 3:13; 1 Thess. 5:10)— also appears in 2:21: "Christ suffered for you." Moreover, the Pauline accent is heard in the statement that it is God who raised Jesus from the dead (1:21; cf. 1:3; 3:18b). Although it is not said that God sent his Son— a Pauline assertion (Rom. 8:3, 32; Gal. 4:4–5)—it is said that God "destined" Christ (the term "Son" is not used) for his saving action "before the foundation of the world" (1:20).

Yet the emphasis in the letter regarding redemption is upon the action of Christ.[93] It is the "Spirit of Christ" (meaning the Holy Spirit) which was already operative in the prophetic predictions of the Old Testament era concerning his sufferings and subsequent glory (1:11). Christ "died for sins once for all, the righteous for the unrighteous, in order that [*hina*] he might bring us to God" (3:18). Here the Pauline accent—that Jesus was made (by God) to be sin (2 Cor. 5:21), that in him God condemned sin in the flesh (Rom. 8:3), and that God has reconciled the world to himself in Christ (2 Cor. 5:19)—is overshadowed.[94] The accent is rather upon Christ as the one who has acted to break down the barrier between humanity and God. That barrier is due to the "sins" (not "sin," as in Paul) of unrighteous humanity. These "sins" Christ "himself bore . . . in his body on the tree" (2:24). The intensive "himself" is not to be overlooked, pointing to a christopractic conception. The language recalls Isa. 53:12 (LXX), "he bore the sins of many."[95] Christ thus bore the consequences of human sins on behalf of humanity. By so doing, he opened up the pathway to God, even bringing the redeemed to God (3:18). In all of this Christ is portrayed as a victorious redeemer figure, who cancels the barrier between humanity and God and conducts the redeemed into the presence of God in the heavenly kingdom. Moreover, resurrected from the dead, Christ "has gone into heaven"—preceding those to follow in his pathway—"and is at the right hand of God, with angels, authorities, and powers subject to him" (3:22). The contrast with Paul can again be seen. Paul speaks of Christ's being "at the right hand of God" in consequence of his having been raised by God (Rom. 8:34). Of course for this writer too the resurrection of Jesus is unmistakably a consequence of God's having raised him from the dead (1:21; 1:3; 3:18b). But the focus of attention in 3:18 is on Christ as the victorious redeemer figure "who has gone into heaven and is at the right hand of God." Christ has borne the consequences of sins, has gone into heaven, and brings the redeemed to God. Redemption is won by Christ, who was destined before the foundation of the world, who was manifested at the end of times (1:20), and who now reigns as Lord of the cosmos (3:22).

Even more distinctive to this writer are the assertions that Christ, although put to death in the flesh, was made alive in the Spirit and went and preached to "the spirits in prison, who formerly did not obey" (3:19), and that the gospel was proclaimed "even" to the dead in order that "they might live in the spirit like God" (4:6). There is no exegetical consensus concerning the meaning of these verses, and the various nuances and positions taken cannot be reviewed here.[96] The author has declared already that Christ "died for since once for all [*hapax*], the righteous for the unrighteous" (3:18). The author sees no limitations to the redemptive effects of Christ's death. The position taken by interpreters is persuasive which claims that the "spirits in prison," to whom Christ preached (3:19), are to be taken as the disobedient of Noah's generation—considered in Jewish tradition among those most certainly condemned[97]—and that "the dead" to whom the gospel was proclaimed (4:6) include all the dead from the beginning of time.[98] As Leonhard Goppelt has summarized, these verses deal with the question: "What significance does Christ have for those who have not come to a conscious encounter with him in this life? Its reply was that we could leave them to the grace of the One who died for the unrighteous ones and was raised; we could leave them to the grace for which the community of faith lived."[99]

The letter was written to encourage Christians to stand fast in the grace of God (5:12). These Christians are gentiles (2:10; 4:3) of Asia Minor (1:1). They have been called through the gospel (1:15; 2:9, 21; 3:9; 5:10) of Christ, in whom they believe (1:8; 2:7). Although they suffer (2:10; 3:14; 4:19; 5:9–10), doing so as Christians (4:16), and are reviled and reproached for the name of Christ (3:16; 4:14), they are to know that they constitute the "people of God" (3:9, 10) of the last days; they are "a chosen race, a royal priesthood, a holy nation" (3:9). The author exhorts his readers to holiness (1:15), love (1:22; 2:17; 3:8; 4:8), the renunciation of vices (2:1, 11), good conduct (2:12; 3:16), and above all to suffer patiently for the sake of righteousness (2:20–21; 3:14, 17) and to be prepared to defend the hope they have (3:15). Suffering is required of Christians throughout the world (5:9). Christ has himself left an example of righteous suffering for his followers (2:21–23).

In the face of this situation, the author's redemptive christology makes common cause with the realities of human experience. Drawing upon select christological traditions,[100] the writer of the letter presents them anew in light of these realities. His redemptive christology does not treat the benefits of Christ for the disturbed conscience, burdened by guilt, so much as for the disturbed consciousness of living as exiles in a world of abuse.[101] How can the community consider itself to be God's people? The answer is that Christ did indeed die for "our sins" once for all, and he did so in order to "bring us to God" (3:18). And risen from the dead, he "has gone into heaven and is at the right hand of God, with angels, authorities, and powers subject to him" (3:22). He is Lord over the entire cosmos, reigning in glory, and he shall be revealed and made manifest at the last day (1:7, 13; 4:13; 5:1, 4), which is expected soon (4:7). Then he will "judge the living and the dead" (4:5).[102]

The redemptive christology of 1 Peter is thus one of redemption won by Christ. Through his death he bore the sins of humanity bodily to the cross, went into heaven, assumed the status of Lord over all things, and will come to judge the living and the dead. He left an example of suffering for those who follow him. But such suffering is for an interim only (5:10), an era of abuse toward those who bear the name of Christ, and this suffering is due to the activities of the devil, who seeks to entice believers to fall (5:8–9). But the outcome of Christ's redemptive work is to bring those who are called into his fellowship to God, delivering them over to God the Father in his heavenly kingdom. That fellowship consists of the present "flock of Christ" (5:2) and—if our exegetical judgment is correct—those who, although dead, have had the gospel proclaimed to them (3:19; 4:6). But "the end of those who do not obey the gospel" (4:17) is perilous; they are left with him who is to judge the living and the dead. Concerning those who have not heard—or will not have the opportunity to hear—the gospel beyond the spatial and temporal horizons of the letter, nothing is said, although it is possible that the writer would have thought of these persons in the same way as he thought of humanity prior to the advent of the gospel, so that the scope of Christ's benefits extends even to them. On this, however, we cannot be certain, even if the author's position leads logically in this direction. What is set forth is the good news that Christ is the victorious Lord through his suffering, bearing sins, going to heaven, reigning, coming to judge, and bringing his own into God's heavenly kingdom.

THE EPISTLE TO THE HEBREWS

The Epistle to the Hebrews can be considered an epistle only in a quite general sense. It has features of an epistle in two respects: (1) It has an epistolary ending (13:22–26), and (2) it appears to be addressed to a community of Christians at some distance from the writer (13:24), encouraging them in a rather specific, and critical, situation. Otherwise, however, the document does not conform to the usual letter form of antiquity. This is most obvious at the very outset, since Hebrews lacks an epistolary introduction. It opens in the manner of a treatise, and it has features frequently of a homily (cf. 2:5; 5:11; 8:1; 9:5; 11:32). Nevertheless, for convenience we shall refer to it as an epistle or letter.

The title given to the work, *Pros Hebraious* ("To Hebrews"), was known at Alexandria in the second half of the second century.[103] The title is modeled on the form of titles given to the letters of the Pauline corpus. This can be accounted for on the basis of claims made for the letter by certain Alexandrians. Eusebius quotes from Clement of Alexandria (ca. A.D. 150–215) who speaks in terms of a "blessed presbyter" before him (who may be Pantaenus, who flourished ca. A.D. 185), and according to this "blessed presbyter" the document was written by Paul "to the Hebrews."[104] Clement himself went on to claim that it was written by Paul to the Hebrews, asserting further that it was written by him originally in Hebrew and then translated into Greek by Luke.[105] All of these judgments at Alexandria appear to be based on the contents of the document rather than on factual information about its authorship and intended readers. Certainly the document was not written by Paul; even Origen (also of Alexandria, A.D. 182–254) denied the claim, concluding that God alone knows who wrote it.[106] It was composed in the Greek language, not Hebrew, which can be established above all on the grounds that some of the author's arguments are based on a Greek version of the Scriptures.[107] Whether the readers envisioned were Jewish Christians (as "Hebrews" probably suggests; non-Christian Jews are not likely to be meant, for even a cursory reading shows that Christians are addressed) is not certain. What is more certain is that the letter was written prior to the close of the first century, since it was quoted by Clement of Rome (who does not refer to it by title, however) in A.D. 96,[108] and that it belongs to the subapostolic era (not earlier).[109] Various interpreters therefore place its time of composition about A.D. 80–90.[110] It appears to have an association with Rome, not only because Clement of Rome quotes from it, but also because of 13:24 ("Those from Italy greet you"). While some scribes of antiquity concluded that Rome was the place from which it was sent elsewhere,[111] it is more likely (on the basis of Clement's use and 13:24) that Rome was its destination.[112]

The christology of Hebrews is elaborate and multifaceted. Christological titles abound. The writer employs the three most commonly used christological titles of the New Testament letters: "Christ" (fifteen times),[113] "Lord" (five times),[114] and "Son of God" (four times)[115] or simply the term "Son" (nine times),[116] meaning "Son of God." But in addition to these conventional titles, the writer uses "high priest" (ten times)[117] or "priest" (seven times).[118] Priestly imagery and titles dominate the christology of Hebrews. Another seven titles are used less frequently: "mediator of a new covenant" (9:15; 12:24), "pioneer" (*archēgos*, 2:10; 12:2), "apostle" (3:1), "surety" (or "guarantee," *enguos,* 7:22), "forerunner" (6:20), "perfecter" (12:2), and "Good Shepherd" (13:20). Moreover, at 2:5 the title "Son of Man" is implicitly applied to Christ in a quotation from Ps. 8:4, and at 1:8 the title "God" is given to him indirectly in a quotation from Ps. 45:6.

The christology of Hebrews is of a mature type in which the functional aspects of christology are giving way to more consistent reflection on the person and nature of Christ as the basis for his redemptive work. It is on the basis of who Christ is—indeed, what kind of being he is—that he is able to do what he does. Practically all of the "christological moments" of the later ecumenical creeds are to be found in the letter: Christ was preexistent and is the one through whom all things were created (1:2; 2:10); he partook of human nature (2:14) for the redemption of humanity (2:9); he suffered and died by crucifixion (2:9, 10, 14; 5:8; 12:2; 13:12), and his death was atoning (1:3; 7:27; 9:12, 28; etc.); he was raised from the dead (13:20; cf. 7:16); he passed from earth into heaven (4:14; 9:24) where he is seated at the right hand of God (1:3, 13; 8:1; 10:12; 12:2); there he reigns over all things in subjection to him (2:5, 8; 7:26; 8:1); and he will appear again to save those who wait for him (9:28). In all of this it can be seen that Hebrews provides an abundant quarry of possible prooftexts for the ecumenical creeds and orthodox christology. Essentially all that is lacking are assertions of a virginal conception, the "third day" as the moment of resurrection, and the descent into Hades, but the other major christological moments are there, as well as interpretations of the redemptive significance of his incarnation, death, and coming again. The matter of the two natures of Christ in later orthodoxy is not yet defined with precision, but even here the author stands at the threshold of orthodoxy. For on the one hand, the writer stresses the humanity of Christ;[119] on the other, he makes bold assertions of Christ's divinity when he applies utterances of the Psalms to him: "Thy throne, O God, is for ever" (1:8, from Ps. 45:6); and "Thou, Lord, didst found the earth in the beginning" (1:10, from Ps. 102:25).[120] Nevertheless, it would be inappropriate to regard Hebrews as displaying a fully orthodox christology; its christology is proto-orthodox. It is not quite orthodoxy because it distinguishes between the earthly and heavenly, and the human and the divine, aspects of the career of the Son of God, rather than simply his two natures. In his partaking of flesh and blood (2:14), he was actually "made lower than the angels" for his earthly career (2:9)—that is, was truly human and devoid of divine status—and the essential christological title of "priest" was bestowed upon him in consequence of his death and resurrection (7:16; cf. 5:5).[121] Furthermore, he was made perfect through his suffering and obedience (5:8–9).[122] The picture which emerges is that, while Christ shared a divine status with the Father from eternity, he partook of human nature in his earthly career, then moved toward his former status through his obedience and suffering, becoming both priest and victim in his sacrificial death, and finally resumed his former status in consequence of his work. This is the basis on which the writer, standing later at the other side of the resurrection/exaltation of Christ, looks back upon the whole Christ event as a priestly ministry.

While the redemptive work of Christ is founded upon the "grace of God" (2:9; cf. 10:9–10), it is Christ himself who accomplishes it.[123] It is Christ who "has secured an eternal redemption" (9:12). It is he who is "the source of eternal salvation" (4:9), who in his service to God makes "expiation for the sins of the people" (2:17), and who "delivers" humanity from its bondage (2:15). He "offered himself without blemish to God" (9:14) and has entered into heaven "to appear in the presence of God on our behalf" (9:24). And it is he who is "able for all time to save those who draw near to God through him, since he always lives to make intercession for them" (7:25).

In his presentation of redemptive christology, the author draws upon Old Testament texts and Jewish traditions concerning sacrifices, priesthood, and covenant. Particularly in regard to sacrifices there is a blending of motifs related to the cultus, and these stem from three types of sacrifice: covenant sacrifice, daily sacrifices, and the sacrifices offered annually on the Day of Atonement. Sometimes these motifs are blended together in a confusing way, as when the author clearly alludes to the sacrifices of the annual Day of Atonement and yet speaks of such sacrifices as taking place "daily" (7:27), although he knows full well that such occur only once a year (cf. 9:7, 25; 10:1, 3).[124]

The concept of Christ's priesthood, so important for the redemptive christology of the writer, may have developed from earlier traditions in which it is affirmed that the exalted Christ intercedes for his own before God (cf. Rom. 8:34; 1 John 2:1).[125] In any case, the writer of Hebrews developed it to a degree found nowhere else in the New Testament, and he did so by a midrashic use of Ps. 110:4 and Gen. 14:17–24. Psalm 110, particularly verse 1 ("The Lord says to my lord: 'Sit at my right hand, till I make your enemies your footstool'"), had for long been used in christological affirmations, and the concept of Christ as intercessor had already been combined with it, as Rom. 8:34 shows. The writer of Hebrews quotes this psalm verse himself (5:5), but then he goes on immediately (5:6) to quote from Ps. 110:4, which became for him the essential key to his christology: "You are a priest for ever after the order of Melchizedek." So important is this verse that he quotes it four times in his work (5:6; 7:13, 17, 21) and alludes to it four more times (5:10; 6:20; 7:11, 15).

119

Especially in chapter 7, the christological significance of the verse is developed, and it is developed in connection with the story of Abraham and Melchizedek in Genesis 14. The point made by the writer is that the sacrifice which Christ has offered is superior to the sacrifices offered by the Levitical priests of the old covenant: Christ's sacrifice secures an eternal redemption, for it is offered by a priest who is able to offer a complete and perfect sacrifice once and for all. The author of Hebrews makes a series of interpretive moves to get to his conclusion. There can be little doubt that his focus on Ps. 110:4 led to his use of Genesis 14, for he had already fastened attention on the former (5:6), and it is also toward this verse that his argument moves.[126] Nevertheless, the author begins with comments on Genesis 14 and then moves toward the verse from the Psalms in order to clinch his argument concerning the superiority of Christ's priesthood.

Regarding Genesis 14, he says that Abraham, the father of all Israel, and therefore of the tribe of Levi as well, presented a tithe to Melchizedek (7:2, 4). Melchizedek was not, of course, of Abrahamic descent (7:6)— as are the Levitical priests—but "without father or mother or genealogy" (7:3). The fact that he received this offering from Abraham and blessed him shows his superiority to him (7:6–7). Moreover, by virtue of the fact that Abraham presented a tithe to Melchizedek, it can be said that the Levitical priests themselves "paid tithes through Abraham" to him (7:9–10), for Abraham, as their progenitor, represented them. This attests that the Levitical priests conceded the superiority of Melchizedek's priesthood to their own. And now, the author affirms, "another priest" has risen "in the likeness of Melchizedek, who has become a priest, not according to a legal requirement concerning bodily descent but by the power of an indestructible life" (7:15–16).

At this point the author moves to the verse from the Psalms, which he takes to be an oracle of God concerning the Son.[127] In this verse the author finds two major points for the case he is making. First, God has appointed Christ a priest by a solemn oath (7:20–21; cf. 7:28), while the Levitical priests "took their office without an oath" from God. And second, Christ has been appointed a priest "for ever" (7:17, 21) and therefore "holds his priesthood permanently, because he continues for ever" (7:24), whereas the "former priests . . . were prevented by death from continuing in office" (7:23). On the basis of all these assertions drawn from the Scriptures—the concession of superiority of Melchizedek by Abraham and, through him, the Levitical priests; the divine oath concerning Christ's priesthood; and the promise from God of its permanence—the priesthood of Christ is shown to be superior to that of the Levitical priesthood.

The link between Melchizedek and Christ is not, of course, precise. Christ cannot be thought of as a "successor" of Melchizedek,[128] nor can the author think that Melchizedek is an eternal form or archetype to which Christ conforms—for then he would be superior to Christ. At 7:3 the author says that Melchizedek, "resembling *(aphōmoiōmenos)* the Son . . . continues a priest for ever," and at 7:15 he speaks of Christ as being "in the likeness *(homoitēta)* of Melchizedek." The imprecision of these verses, as well as that which makes Christ a priest after the "order" *(taxis)* of Melchizedek (7:11), shows that the author is not really interested in establishing the status of Melchizedek beyond what he gives and what is necessary:[129] that Melchizedek's priesthood is superior to that of the Levitical priests. Other than that, the author's interest is fixed on what can be said about Christ. He is a priest after the order of Melchizedek—a truth based on the word of God concerning the Son (Ps. 110:1, 4)—rather than the order of the Levitical priests, and that order to which he belongs consists of permanent eternal priesthood.[130]

This priesthood qualifies Christ to offer "for all time a single sacrifice for sins" (10:12), which occurred at his death. There "by a single sacrifice he has perfected for all time those who are sanctified" (10:14). The writer insists that, because the sacrifices of the Levitical priesthood were performed repeatedly, they obviously (to him) did not "take away sins" (10:4, 11); "otherwise," he asks, "would they not have ceased to be offered?" (10:2). In his own case, however, Christ as the perfect priest (without sins of his own to atone for first)[131] offered a sacrifice to God on behalf of others which secures an eternal redemption (9:12). As both sacrificing priest and sacrificial victim, he offered "his own blood" (9:12), even "himself" (9:14, 26), "without blemish to God" (9:14).

The redemptive work of Christ is thus spoken of primarily through the use of images drawn from Israel's worship, but not exclusively. There are five major ways in which the writer speaks of this work. We shall review these, beginning with a way which does not draw precisely upon cultic imagery, but which nevertheless touches upon it; it also appears early on in the letter.

The first way of speaking of the redemptive work of Christ is to portray him as one who deals with the devil and his power. In chapter 2 the writer says that Jesus partook of human nature "in order that [*hina*] he might render him powerless who has the power of death, that is, the devil, and deliver all those who through fear of death were subject to lifelong bondage" (2:14–15). The verb translated here as "render powerless" *(katargein)* is "destroy" in the RSV, but here it does not likely have the meaning "annihilate."[132] The author knows that people still experience temptation (2:18; 4:15; cf. 3:8). The point is that Christ has effectively eliminated the devil and his power over humanity in terms of ultimate destiny. The thought of the writer is that, due to the consequences of sin, humanity had fallen under the dominion of the devil, who having power over death causes terror among all and exercises that power by bringing death upon them. Here the writer adopts a particular strain of Jewish and Christian tradition. In one stream, while sin may be due to the temptation of a rebellious power, or simply to human rebelliousness itself, God passes the sentence of death upon humanity (2 Esdr. 3:7; 7:118–19; Sir. 25:24; Rom. 5:16–17; 6:23). In the other stream, which the writer of Hebrews picks up, the rebellious power carries humanity away from God into the devil's own dominion. This is expressed, for example, in the Wisdom of Solomon: "for God created humanity [*ton anthrōpon*] for incorruption, and made humanity [*auton,* "him"] in the image of his own eternity, but through the devil's envy death entered the world, and those who belong to his party experience it" (2:23–24).

Christ's redemptive work consists of rendering the devil powerless and thereby liberating humanity from his dominion. The fact that people still die physically is of no consequence in this perspective. The point is that the devil's reign has no abiding force either at death or beyond the threshold of death for the redeemed. Hebrews portrays the life of such persons as a pilgrimage from the earthly, temporal, and perishable sphere into the heavenly, eternal, and incorruptible world, to which Christ has gone as pioneer (2:10; 12:2) and forerunner (6:20), and to which he beckons those who belong to his fellowship. This is possible on the basis of the nature and work of Christ. He alone was without sin (4:15; 7:26), and that means that he was never under the power of the devil. He did, of course, "taste death for every one" (2:9). But his purpose was not to give himself over to the devil and his dominion. His purpose was instead to share in physical death for the benefit of others—the author uses the *hyper*-formula (*hyper pantos,* "on behalf of every person")—and to open up for them a way which leads from the earthly, temporal, and physical realm into the heavenly, eternal, and spiritual one. He tasted death and entered directly into the heavenly sanctuary (9:24; cf. 4:14; 8:1–2). This means that death is in principle no longer the victory of the devil over humanity any more than it was for Christ himself. "We have confidence to enter the sanctuary by the blood of Jesus, by the new and living way which he opened for us" (10:19–20). Death is now but a threshold into the heavenly sanctuary, the presence of God and of the reigning Christ, for the redeemed. It cannot be considered a triumph of the devil. For Christ has gone before his people, by way of death itself, from the earthly to the heavenly realm without becoming a victim of the one who has power over death. There is a "way" around him, which means that his power has been effectively eliminated. And that power is eliminated not only in regard to Christ, but for others as well. In the same section the writer says that in his death Christ made "expiation for the sins of his people" (2:17). The sinless Christ is the first to break through a pathway to the heavenly realm, and in his death, by which he made expiation for the sins of others, he rendered them sinless; the devil is therefore powerless over them as well.[133] Thus Christ does not engage the devil in battle, destroying him, but renders him powerless by doing away with that which provides evidence and legitimization for his rule over humanity, namely, sins. Where there are no sins, the devil has no claim, and persons are "delivered" or "redeemed" from his power.

A second way in which the author treats the redemptive work of Christ is to speak of him as one who was "offered once to bear the sins of many" (9:28). Here the image of the Servant in Isa. 53:12 is recalled and applied to the crucified Christ. Though without sin himself, the crucified Christ is the one upon whom the sins of others are transferred and by whom the consequence of sins, death, is borne on their behalf. The verse is of interest because of its use of the passive voice ("Christ, having been offered") and its use of the Servant concept from Isaiah. Elsewhere it is said that Christ offered himself (7:27; 9:14, 24), or that he offered a sacrifice (10:12), and the Servant concept is not otherwise significant for the author's treatment of the work of Christ.[134] But this verse shows that, for the redemptive christology of the writer, Christ's death was in accord with the divine purpose, which is implied by the passive voice, and that it was a means by which sins and their consequences have been dealt with effectively by a "blessed interchange" in which Christ becomes the one in whom sin is concentrated, leading to his death; sinful humanity is thereby no longer under the sentence of death.

A third way of speaking of the work of Christ is to portray him as a priestly figure who performs an atoning act. Here Christ is the one who makes a sacrificial offering. The conceptual background is that of the sacrifices of the Old Testament, particularly on the Day of Atonement, in which the priest does an act before God on behalf of the people. As the high priest entered the Holy of Holies before God with the sacrificial blood, thereby making expiation (Leviticus 16), so Christ "entered once for all into the Holy Place, taking . . . his own blood" (9:12), thereby making expiation (2:17). Christ's entrance into the Holy Place (or Holy of Holies) is said to be his entrance into heaven itself (9:24). This does not mean that, in the view of the writer, Christ died, entered heaven, and then offered his sacrifice.[135] His death itself was atoning (2:9; 9:15, 28)—the death which took place outside the city of Jerusalem—for he "suffered outside the gate in order to sanctify the people through his own blood" (13:12).

The author, much like the writers of Luke and John, looks upon the death and exaltation of Jesus as a unitary event. Christ's going to the cross to offer a sacrifice is at the same time his entry into the heavenly sanctuary.[136] The cross stands midway between two worlds. What happened there in history and on earth happened as well in the presence of God who inhabits the heavenly sanctuary. And that which happened was an act of atonement, by which Christ as both priest and victim offered his own blood (9:12) or himself (9:14, 26). The writer does not theorize concerning how this sacrificial act makes atonement. He simply asserts that it is redemptive, expiatory, and a means of purification (9:12; 2:17; 1:3). Here he relies on the self-evident significance of the liturgy of the Day of Atonement. According to Lev. 16:30, both a command and a promise are given to Israel: "on this day shall atonement be made for you, to cleanse you; from all your sins you shall be clean before the Lord." In the estimation of the author of Hebrews, of course, the annual offerings of the Day of Atonement actually failed to take away sins (10:4, 11). What was instituted under the law was but a shadow of the good things to come (10:1). But now Christ has "appeared as a high priest of the good things that have come" (9:11), and that to which the law points has been fulfilled in him. In sum, the author moves within the framework and presuppositions of the Day of Atonement, as he conceives it. The offering of the high priest is envisioned in Leviticus as one which makes atonement. The principle is not disputed. But that which is envisioned is but "seen from afar"—to borrow the language of 11:13—in the annual sacrifices. It is only in Christ's offering of his own blood once for all that what is envisioned becomes effective, "securing an eternal redemption."

A fourth way in which the writer speaks of Christ's sacrificial work is in terms of a covenant sacrifice. This discussion is often intertwined (and even confused, in the sense of fused together) with his use of Day of Atonement imagery. This is so particularly in chapter 9 where the writer breaks off using the imagery of the Day of Atonement and speaks of Christ no longer as a priest but as the mediator of a new covenant (9:15), going on in 9:18–22 to draw upon Exodus 24, the account of the ratification of the covenant. This covenant, he says, was ratified with blood (9:18; cf. Exod. 24:6–8). Surprisingly, the author does not go on here to draw out the analogy, but at several places he presupposes what could have been said explicitly: that the blood of Jesus signifies that a new covenant has been ratified. Christ is the mediator of a better and new covenant (8:6; 9:15; 12:24; cf. 7:22; 10:9, 13), fulfilling the promise of God of a new covenant uttered in Jer. 31:31–34 (Heb. 8:8–12). Through his death his blood became the basis for an "eternal covenant" (13:20), and the redemptive significance of this covenant ratification is spelled out in the divine oracle: "I will remember their sins and their misdeeds no more" (10:17, quoting Jer. 31:34).

Finally, a fifth way of speaking of the work of Christ is through the frequent use of the *hyper*-formula, signifying that the death of Jesus was "for" or "for the benefit" *(hyper)* of others. As in the case of the Pauline writings,[137] so in Hebrews the *hyper*-formula has both persons and "sins" as its object. Christ tasted death "for every one" (2:9); he has entered into heaven as a forerunner "on our behalf" (6:20); he always lives to make intercession "for them" (i.e., those who draw near to God through him, 7:25); and he has appeared in the presence of God "on our behalf" (9:24). On the other hand, he offered for all time a single sacrifice "for sins" (10:12). It can be seen that in these cases the *hyper*-formula is used in connection with two separate functions. In certain cases a soteriological use is made when it is said that Christ tasted death "for every one" (2:9), that he offered a sacrifice "for sins" (10:12), and that he was a forerunner into heaven "on our behalf" (6:20). In the other cases, however, the redemptive work has already been accomplished, and Christ is intercessor for his people before God (7:25; 9:24). Concerning the first usage, no more need be said than that these passages cohere with the redemptive christology of Hebrews as a whole; that is, through his sacrificial death and his exaltation, Christ has secured redemption for others. But concerning the second, his work of intercession, more needs to be said. His role of intercession is not to plea on behalf of others for the forgiveness of their sins, as in 1 John 2:1 ("if any one does sin, we have an advocate with the Father, Jesus Christ"). No, the redemptive work of Christ has been finished "once for all" *(ephapax,* 7:27; 9:12; 10:10). The intercession of Jesus is for divine help for his own, who experience suffering and temptation in their earthly pilgrimage.[138]

Before leaving Hebrews, it is necessary to ask how the writer considers the benefits of Christ's redemptive work to be received by others and the scope and limitations of his work. The burning focus of the writer is on Christ and his redemptive work. Repeatedly he asserts that the redemptive work of Christ took place "once for all" *(ephapax,* 7:27; 9:12; 10:10; *hapax,* 9:26, 28)—an assertion found also in Paul (Rom. 6:10) and 1 Peter (3:18). The appearance of Christ was an eschatological event, for Christ "has appeared once for all at the end of the age to put away sin by the sacrifice of himself" (9:26). His death and exaltation signal that the dawn of the new age has broken, though the full day of the final rest has not yet arrived.[139] Christians are exhorted to strive to enter that rest by fidelity to Christ in their earthly sojourn (4:11). In general it can be said that in the christological parts of the letter the emphasis is on the "already" (or realized) aspect of eschatology, while in the hortatory sections the "not yet" aspect is emphasized.[140] The promised inheritance is future (6:12; 10:36), and salvation is also spoken of as a future reality (1:14; 6:8; 9:28).[141] The one possible exception to this view is at 12:22–24 ("But you have come to Mount Zion . . ."), but even here the indicative is followed by the exhortation not to reject the messenger of the good news and what is promised (12:25–26); the community is at the threshold of the heavenly kingdom, not yet within it.

So emphatic is the writer on the "once for all" character and all-sufficient quality of Christ's redemptive work that the writer assumes without further ado that it is effective for others as a gift (6:4). His emphasis is thus, in principle, on the "objective" character of redemption. And yet there is a way in which he involves the believer in the appropriation of Christ's benefits. He does not do so by speaking explicitly of faith in Christ, or of faith in the gospel, as the means; faith in this letter is primarily faithfulness (or fidelity) and patient endurance.[142] Rather, he speaks of Christians as persons who have been "enlightened" (6:4; 10:32) through hearing the gospel of the redemptive work of Christ and who have thereby "tasted the heavenly gift, and have become partakers of the Holy Spirit, and have tasted the goodness of the word of God and the powers of the age to come" (6:4–5). Such persons "share in Christ" and his benefits—if they hold fast their confidence to the end (3:14). With the enlightenment they receive, they understand themselves and their ultimate destiny in terms of pilgrimage and its goal; they are persons who have a "heavenly call" (3:1). The way is set before them toward the goal, and they need to endure to arrive at it (10:36).

In this form of presentation, the redemptive work of Christ, though accomplished totally apart from human initiative, is not envisioned as effective for those who have not been "enlightened" to hear the call to follow after Jesus to where he has gone; it is effective only for those who are willing to set off on the pilgrimage. In short, it has no significance for humanity outside the community which has heard the gospel and responded to it,[143] or at best it can be said that the redemptive work of Christ is potentially effective for humanity as a whole and becomes actually effective for those persons who have opportunity to hear the call and respond to it. Exception is made for the saints of the old covenant who are "perfected," in the sense that their hope is brought to completion with the present generation of Christians (11:39–40); this implies that the saints of old also share in the destiny of Christ and his people. On the other hand, even those who have once been enlightened can lose the inheritance promised if they commit apostasy (6:4–6; 10:26–31; cf.

12:16–17). Such persons crucify the Son of God and hold him up to contempt (6:6), thereby rejecting his benefits and forsaking the pilgrimage (10:26, 29). The loss of the inheritance by such persons is dreadful beyond imagining. The author says that "it is impossible to restore again to repentance" such persons (6:4). This is often taken to mean that the author precludes the readmission of persons into the church who commit apostasy and then have a change of heart and mind; they can never be restored, nor can they ever receive forgiveness from God.[144] But of course the passage does not say that (nor does any other in Hebrews). In the context of the passage the writer says that he intends to leave aside "elementary doctrine" and go on to more mature subjects (6:1). There is no use going over the basics again, he says, for "it is impossible to restore again to repentance" those who are apostates: They simply will not listen; one cannot induce them to repent (the passage says nothing about God's refusal to grant mercy again)—so it is time to go on to other matters. Having said this, however, the principle remains for the writer that those who commit apostasy have excluded themselves from final salvation.

The Epistle to the Hebrews consists chiefly of christological elaboration and hortatory address to its readers to persevere in difficult times. The christological teaching and the exhortation are closely intertwined. In fact, one senses that readers are exhorted to believe the teaching and, conversely, that the teaching calls for a response—the response the exhortation seeks.[145] This focus leads to a construal of the indicative and imperative in a peculiar direction. The indicative concerns what Christ has done, but it is not applied to the condition of humanity such that now, in consequence of what Christ has done, humanity (not even believing humanity) stands in a new world; at most, believers stand at the threshold of the new world. True, there are steps made in that direction, as can be seen in our survey of how the writer speaks of the redemptive work of Christ. But the imperative (expressed through exhortations) is so strongly sounded throughout the letter that the believer is led to consider himself or herself as one who has "tasted" the "heavenly gift" and the "powers of the age to come" (6:4–5), but not as one who belongs to the age to come.[146] The "world to come" (2:5), the "age to come" (6:5), and the "city which is to come" (13:14) are all future, and the present life is one of pilgrimage thereto. One needs to endure to receive what is promised (10:36). In all of this it can be said that "the imperative is here not truly founded upon the indicative."[147]

There are obvious strengths to such a message. Above all, grace and salvation cannot be considered permanent, eternal possessions. Hebrews prescribes a vigorous form of Christian discipleship; it calls for integrity and fidelity. Yet it sets up the possibility of moral and intellectual elitism, which praises vigor and maturity as near ends in themselves, overlooking that side of the Christian tradition which portrays Jesus as the friend of sinners, the weak, and the despised, and sees in his redemptive work an act of grace for those who have nothing to offer, justifying the ungodly and reconciling the world to God.

All this means that Hebrews must be seen in context. It is not an address to those who have not heard the gospel. It is an address to persons who belong to the third generation of Christianity; it calls upon them to 'lift [their] drooping hands and strengthen [their] weak knees" (12:12) and to "run with perseverance the race that is set before [them]" (12:1), while living in difficult times of suffering and abuse for the name of Christ. Yet even in this time of crisis, the writer is able to step back and give a creatively new and fresh interpretation of redemptive christology. The author is surely one of the most brilliant writers of the subapostolic period. He is so overcome by the magnificence of the sacrifice of Christ and his benefits for humanity—this beautiful and holy mystery of divine grace—that he presents it all within the context of a "word of exhortation" (as he describes his work, 13:22) to strengthen his contemporaries in their understanding and perseverance in the apostolic faith. His legacy is enormous in enriching christology and the interpretation of the work of Christ, even if it is less so in an understanding of the gospel, when it is compared to others of the New Testament era.

THE REVELATION TO JOHN

There is a widely held, but by no means unanimous, consensus among interpreters concerning the authorship, date, and setting of the Book of Revelation: that it was written by a Jewish-Christian prophet, who probably bore the name John (1:1, 4, 9; 22:8), but who is not to be identified with John, son of Zebedee and one of the Twelve, or with the author of the Fourth Gospel; that it was written toward the close of Domitian's reign (the years of which are A.D. 81–96), most likely within the time frame of A.D. 90–96; that it speaks words of encouragement, hope, and valiant resistance against the Roman state to Christians who have known persecution already among their membership (cf. 2:13; 3:10; 6:9); and that it was composed in western Asia Minor, either at the place of John's vision (Patmos, 1:9) or subsequently on the mainland (such as at Ephesus).[148]

The author's christology is presented more through the use of pictures than titles, and some of the titles found in this book appear nowhere else in the New Testament.[149] The familiar titles include "Christ" (eight times),[150] "Lord" (six times),[151] and "Son of God" (once, 2:18). As in the Fourth Gospel (1:1, 14), Christ is called the "Word" (*logos,* 19:13). Although the term "son of man" appears twice (1:13; 14:14), it would not be appropriate to speak of this as a christological title in Revelation (as in the Gospels); in both instances in Revelation it is said that the exalted Jesus appears "like a son of man," that is, like a human being (as in Dan. 7:13; Ezek. 2:1, 8; etc.). Scattered throughout the book, a variety of terms are used as designations of Christ: the "Amen" (3:14), the "faithful witness" (1:5; 3:14), the "first-born of the dead" (1:5), the "ruler of kings" (1:5), the "beginning of God's creation" (3:14), the "living one" (1:18), the "holy one" (3:7), the "Lord of lords and King of kings" (17:14; 19:16), the "Lion of the tribe of Judah" and "Root of David" (5:5), and the "root of the offspring of David" and "bright morning star" (22:16). But above all, Christ is spoken of as the "Lamb" (twenty-eight times).[152] The Greek term differs from that in the Gospel of John, where Jesus is spoken of as the "Lamb of God" (1:29, 36).[152] In the latter the term for Lamb is *amnos,* whereas in Revelation it is always *arnion.* This Lamb has been slain (5:6, 12; 13:8; cf. 7:14; 12:11), but now lives; the apostles are spoken of as "apostles of the Lamb" (21:14); the redeemed community consists of the Bride of the Lamb (21:9; cf. 19:7, 9); and the name of each person in this community is "written in the Lamb's book of life" (21:27).

The christology of Revelation is developed around two principal foci. On the one hand, it is rooted in and grows out of the common Christian kerygma. Jesus, of Jewish heritage (5:5), was crucified (11:8; 1:18; 2:8), raised (1:5, 18; 2:8), and now reigns over the cosmos (3:21; 11:15). But there is a shift of emphasis and terminology away from the common kerygma. The use of the term "raised" is misleading if left to itself. The familiar verbs used elsewhere in the New Testament for the raising of Jesus from the dead (*anistēmi* and *egeirō*) are missing in Revelation. Instead, Christ is spoken of as the "first-born of the dead" (1:5, as at Col. 1:18) and the one who, although he had died, is "alive for evermore" (1:18) or "came to life" (2:8). And rather than having been raised from death by the power of God, Christ is said to have conquered death (3:21; 5:5) and now to possess the keys of death and Hades (1:18). The second principal factor in the development of the christology of Revelation is the thrust of the book as a whole. Its focus of attention is the conflict between the reign of God and Christ on the one side, and the reign of Satan and the beast on the other, a reign made manifest in the power and seductions of "Babylon," the Roman Empire. In conjunction with this attention to conflict, Christ is portrayed as a powerful world ruler, to whom God has entrusted the carrying out of his plan for history. He is the one to whom the scroll with the seven seals is given (5:7), a scroll which contains the fixed, redemptive purpose of God.[154] It is Christ who opens the seals (6:1, 3, 5, 7, 9, 12; 8:1), inaugurating the events to come portrayed in the vision. And he is acclaimed ruler over the world (11:15) and designated the one who destroys Satan, death, and Hades (19:20; 20:10, 14).

These two foci—kerygmatic tradition and the writer's confessional commitment to the present and future reign of Christ in the midst of conflict—permeate the Book of Revelation, and they form the substructure of its redemptive christology. For all of its future orientation, the book is not lacking in references to the "already" of redemption. And in these instances the emphasis is upon Christ as the actor—as is also the case with that which is to come. It is Christ who "has freed us from our sins by his blood and made us a kingdom, priests to his God and Father" (1:5–6). It is by his own blood that he "ransomed people for God" from every tribe, tongue, people, and nation and "made them a kingdom and priests" to God (5:9–10). The basis for this action is Christ's love (1:5).

But how does the death of Christ "do" the work of redemption? The verbs used in the passages cited are *luein* (to "free" or "set free," 1:5) and *agorazein* (to "purchase" or "redeem," 5:9), followed in each case with "creation" language (*poiein,* to "make"): Christ created a kingdom of a priestly people (1:6; 5:10). Furthermore, in each case it is "by his blood" (= by means of his death) that the redemptive act has taken place. The redeemed are those who "have washed their robes and made them white in the blood of the Lamb" (7:14; cf. 22:14).

Although it is difficult from all this to discern just how the death of Christ is thought to be redemptive, a proposal can be made. The author of Revelation is heir to the common kerygmatic tradition that Christ's death was "for our sins." Moreover, the association of the death of Christ with Isa. 53:7 ("like a lamb that is led to the slaughter") is clear at 5:9. Starting with the kerygmatic tradition and the association with Isa. 53:7, images from Exodus are drawn upon which have to do with priesthood, washing, and the use of the blood of a ram. At Exod. 19:6, after the exodus event itself, the Lord tells Moses to announce to Israel that "if you . . . keep my covenant, you shall be my own possession among all peoples, . . . and you shall be to me a kingdom of priests and a holy nation." Further, Moses is directed to consecrate the people and "let them wash their garments, and be ready by the third day; for on the third day the Lord will come down upon Mount Sinai in the sight of all the people" (19:10–11). The priestly people are thus created by God, and their consecration as a priestly people is to be attested by the washing of their garments. Then in Exodus 29 the consecration of the Aaronic priesthood itself is instituted. This involves the killing of a ram and the sprinkling of its blood on Aaron and his garments, and upon his sons and their garments. "And he and his garments shall be holy, and his sons and his sons' garments with him" (29:21).

The author of Revelation never quotes passages word-for-word from the Old Testament. What he does, however, is pick up phrases, clauses, and images and use them in the service of what he writes.[155] These pervade virtually everything, and they are connected together by verbal and pictorial associations conceived in the mind of the author, who seems to think out of the Scriptures in their entirety. And so in this case, when he writes about the redemptive work of Christ, which he knows from the kerygma to entail redemption from sins in consequence of the cross, he associates the death of Christ the Lamb with the consecration of priests and the sanctification of them and their garments through the blood of a ram, as well as the consecration of the people as a whole to be a community of priests, who wash their garments to await the theophany at Mount Sinai on the third day. The community of faithful Christians, for this writer, now consists of a consecrated and sanctified people, a kingdom of priests, who have washed their garments in the blood of the Lamb. In chapter 14, where the author depicts the community of the redeemed, he makes further associations with Exodus 19. His vision contains a christophany (corresponding to the expected appearance of the Lord in Exodus 19) of the Lamb on Mount Zion (14:1); the "third day" of eschatological expectation has been fulfilled. Further, he speaks of the redeemed as persons "who have not defiled themselves with women" (14:4). The passage is undoubtedly an allusion to Exod. 19:15,[156] in which the males of the consecrated, priestly community of Israel are commanded not "to go near a woman" as they await the theophany. In the perspective of the writer of Revelation, his designation of the redeemed by such terminology is most certainly to be taken as symbolic;[157] they have resisted the seductions of "Babylon the great, mother of harlots and of earth's abominations" (Rev. 18:5), the one who has led astray kings and other dwellers on earth (17:2); even some Christians have been led astray into harlotry (= idolatry, 2:20).

If this is a correct appraisal, it means that the author's understanding of the work of Christ is based on a collage of images and terms from the Old Testament, which he associated with the received kerygma, rather than on a systematic doctrine of redemption. Although he uses familiar redemptive terminology (1:5; 5:9; 14:3–4), his understanding of the work of Christ is more precisely that of sanctification than redemption, as usually understood, at this point. That is to say that through his death, the pouring out of his blood, the Lamb has provided a means by which people can wash their garments and become a holy, consecrated, priestly people. Just how people do this act of washing is not explained. The reason why this is so may be that the writer is not interested in the question of how to proclaim and explain the gospel to those outside the church. He writes for those who are already Christians and seeks to have them understand themselves as the priestly people.[158] That Christ offers salvation (deliverance from sins and ultimate death) is self-evident and needs not to be explained; moreover, his gift of salvation is given freely to those who are baptized and continue in fidelity to him. The author then speaks of the death of Christ and his benefits in terms of consecration and the sanctification of a kingdom of priests, drawing upon consecration and sanctification traditions in the Old Testament which entail the use of blood. All this is to equip the community of believers with a renewed understanding of their status before God and to encourage them for fidelity in hope. It is those who have become the priestly people through the blood of the Lamb who shall reign with him.

This "already" aspect of the redeeming work of Christ, however, is only one part of the picture, and so is the sanctifying work of Christ. From what has been said so far, it might be concluded that sanctification precedes final redemption in this book. But more must be said. The author speaks of the redemptive work of Christ more specifically in other imagery, and here both the "already" and "not yet" aspects come into view. There can be no doubt that the writer portrays the exaltation of Christ as the turning point of history.[159] The exalted Christ declares, "I myself conquered and sat down with my Father on his throne" (3:21; cf. 5:5). Again, after the casting down of Satan from heaven,[160] which for the writer coincides with the crucifixion (cf. 12:11), a heavenly voice declares that "now" (*arti*) have come God's salvation, power, and kingdom "and the authority of his Christ" (12:10). And elsewhere a hymn of heavenly voices declares: "The kingdom of the world has become the kingdom of our Lord and of his Christ, and he shall reign for ever and ever" (11:15). Finally, the exalted Christ is acclaimed as "King of kings and Lord of lords" (19:16; cf. 17:14).

It is on the basis of the crucifixion and exaltation of Christ, which inaugurate his reign, that the Christian community is "already" redeemed. "Salvation belongs to our God who sits upon the throne, and to the Lamb" (7:10). Satan, the accuser of the saints before God in heaven, has been thrown down; there is no room in heaven for both Satan and the exalted Christ. And in that sense it can be said that "by the blood of the Lamb" the saints themselves have conquered Satan (12:11). They have access to life (2:7; 22:14) and shall reign with Christ in his heavenly kingdom (5:10; 20:4, 6; 22:5).

But there is also a "not yet" aspect to the redemptive work of Christ. While there is cause for rejoicing for heaven and all who dwell therein with the casting down of Satan, there is now anguish for "earth and sea," for Satan has come "in great wrath, because he knows his time is short" (12:12). In the perspective of this book, echoed over and again, Satan manifests his power chiefly through the earthly powers (imperial Rome) to oppress the saints who dwell on the earth. The author portrays the manifestation of his power through two beasts. The first (13:1–10)— which has great authority over all people, demands worship, and is "allowed to make war on the saints" (13:7)—represents the Roman Empire itself. The second (13:11–18)—which enforces emperor worship (13:12) and slays all who resist (13:15)—is identified later as a "false prophet" (16:13; 19:20; 20:10) and here with the number 666, a cryptogram most likely representing the emperor.[161]

Although Christ has entered into his heavenly reign through his death and resurrection, and is therefore victor over Satan both in the heavenly world and for the saints, his victory over Satan has yet to be won on the earthly plane. Revelation therefore has a redemptive-historical perspective which allots final redemption to the "not yet" of the future.[162] But the certainty of Christ's ultimate triumph is secure. At 19:20 the capture of the two beasts ("the beast" and the "false prophet") by Christ is envisioned, and they are thrown into the lake of fire. Satan himself is bound (20:2) and ultimately thrown into the lake of fire (20:10). Then the seer portrays the judgment of the nations (by God): The dead are raised and judged according to what they have done (20:12–13; cf. 22:12). Yet only those whose names have been written in the book of life share in the new Jerusalem (21:27), while those whose names are not found there are thrown into the lake of fire along with death and Hades (20:14–15). In short, no one judged according to works passes the test; only those whose names are in the book of life are acquitted in the judgment.[163]

Nevertheless, subsequent to the vision of universal judgment, there is a vision of universal grace. In 22:1–5, a portion of the vision of the new Jerusalem, the author tells of a "river of the water of life" flowing from the throne of God and of the Lamb, on either side of which is the tree of life. Proceeding from the tree are leaves "for the healing of the nations" (22:2), and there is no longer anything accursed (22:3). Matthias Rissi has drawn attention to this passage, maintaining that here there is a final vision of the "universalism of salvation" in which life and healing are imparted to all the nations.[164] Further, he points to other passages of the Book of Revelation which cohere with this vision of final universal redemption.[165] At 5:13, containing a vision of the absolute victory of the Lamb that was slain, and set prior to the opening of the scroll with seven seals, "every creature in heaven and on earth and under the earth and in the sea" acclaims his lordship. And at 15:3–4, prior to the outpouring of the final plagues (the wrath of God), the song of Moses and "of the Lamb" declares: "Who shall not fear and glorify thy name, O Lord? For thou alone art holy. All nations shall come and worship thee, for thy judgments have been revealed." In addition, there is the declaration of God, "Behold, I make all things new" (21:5). Rissi goes on to say that in all of this, of course, the judgment to come is not to be minimized, but for the writer of Revelation "neither in its historical nor in its eschatological form is the judgment God's last word, but rather serves in the final analysis as the agent of his grace."[166] God is the creator of all things (4:11), and the unleashing of his wrath against the opposing forces is not for the destruction of his creation, but for the overthrow of Satan. Only so can humanity be set free from oppression and delusion, be healed, and join in the worship of God and the Lamb.[167] "In 21:1—22:5," writes Elisabeth Schüssler Fiorenza, "the seer describes with the image of the New Jerusalem the perfected community, to which the whole world belongs (21:14; 15:4)."[168]

The redemptive christology of Revelation, as already indicated, is developed around the two foci of the received tradition (that Christ's death was for our sins) and the conflict with the unimaginable evil oppressing the Christian community and bringing death to those who refuse to worship the emperor. The combination of factors could lead to two possible results. First, the writer could offer an escapist view. Christians could, after all, submit to the demands for devotion outwardly on the grounds that this world is without reality or importance anyway; or, taking a different path of escapism, they could seek martyrdom as the way of release from earthly into heavenly existence. But these alternatives are not for a moment contemplated. The earthly plane is the home of Christians until the parousia, and they are called upon to resist and endure in the midst of horrible conditions. A second possible result of the factors could be a purely vindictive attitude. The Book of Revelation has been charged again and again of having such, and the charge is not without foundation. Yet the vindictiveness which does exist is aimed primarily against Satan, not humanity or creation. The book ends on the note of renewal and healing, not destruction. If the core of the canon is the love of God in Christ for the fallen world, and if this is lifted up as a lantern, the Book of Revelation lies at the outer edge of the illuminated space, but not in the darkness outside the circle.

The redemptive christology is construed in a way that is unusual. It is clear that in the death and exaltation of Christ there are redemptive benefits already. Without saying how this is true, Christians are regarded as having been redeemed from sins while living on the earthly plane in history. It appears that the writer has not reflected on the question of how that is so,[169] but accepts their redemption as true, and the visions of martyrs living in the presence of God confirms it (6:9–11; 20:4). Those on earth consider themselves as persons forgiven and as having been enrolled in the book of life, which assures them of acquittal at the judgment. Otherwise the redemptive work of Christ is portrayed as future, when Satan is overthrown and the stage is set for the new creation and the new Jerusalem where God's servants worship God without hindrance or fear.

It has been said that "the seer has in mind only the church and the evil powers. So this book is the most ecclesiocentric in the whole of the New Testament."[170] That would be so if we have misinterpreted the note of grace to the nations in 22:1–5; one would have to say then that the writer's focus of attention is solely upon the church and its vindication as the only thing that mattered for God and his Christ. And, to be sure, there is much in the book to support such a view. But the entire substance of the book was put together in the context of oppressive conditions, calling for fidelity, patience, and endurance in the certain hope that those who endure will not lose their reward. They will reign with Christ in the presence of God forever. Their own vindication can hardly be described in a book of images in any other way than through contrasts portraying the fall of their enemies, and great indeed is their fall. And yet, as we have seen, there are places at which the tension is relaxed and a larger vision of the redemptive work of Christ is portrayed. So even for this writer God's purpose is not to destroy his larger creation, but to renew it. And in the meantime—and this is certainly the primary thrust of the book—Christians are called to faithful witness to God and to Christ through their confession and conduct in the world. Christ thus exercises his reign on earth through his church in its struggle against those powers which claim divine honors for themselves, as Domitian did in bearing the title "Lord and God."[171] The way to the future is filled with peril and probable suffering, but it is clearly illuminated by the vision of the new Jerusalem, where God's glory is the light and the healing of the nations is assured.

RETROSPECT

The works surveyed in this chapter are exceedingly diverse. They all belong to the latter part of the first century A.D., the subapostolic era, and each in its own way presupposes the development of Christian tradition to the point where "the Christian movement" has become "the Christian religion," distinct from Judaism, in the geographical areas represented by them. These areas lie most certainly in Asia Minor for Colossians,

Ephesians, the Pastorals, 1 Peter, and Revelation; in the case of Hebrews the question will have to remain open. In any case, these documents portray the flowering of redemptive christology along quite different lines and in creative ways. Yet, for all their diversity, there are commonalities among them. We shall indicate six ways in which they cohere.

1. In each case redemption is in accord with the will of God,[172] but the perspective is christopractic; that is, Christ is portrayed as a vigorous redeemer figure who acts decisively to redeem humanity. In none of these writings is it said that God sent his Son, that he gave him up for the benefit of others, or that God condemned sin in him—assertions found in the writings of Paul. We hear the christopractic accent being made in various ways, but it is present in each of the books: Christ is the one who has reconciled all things to himself through his death on the cross, establishing peace (Col. 1:20–22); he "loved us and gave himself up for us" (Eph. 5:2), reconciling both Jew and gentile "to God" (2:16), and he is the means of access to the Father (2:18); he "came into the world to save sinners" (1 Tim. 1:15) and "abolished death and brought life and imperishability to light" (2 Tim. 1:10); he died as the righteous for the unrighteous "in order that he might bring us to God" (1 Pet. 3:18); he "has appeared once for all at the end of the age to put away sin by the sacrifice of himself" (Heb. 9:26), having "entered once for all into the Holy Place, taking not the blood of goats and calves but his own blood, thus securing an eternal redemption" (9:12); and he declares, "I myself conquered and sat down with my Father on his throne" (Rev. 3:21).

Each of the writers discussed considers (or assumes) Christ to have been preexistent.[173] Christ came into the world for a redemptive purpose, representing God and winning redemption for humanity. Each document also speaks of his exaltation, but the exaltation is spoken of in different ways. In some cases the traditional formula is used, which asserts that God raised him from the dead (Col. 2:12; Eph. 1:20; 1 Pet. 1:21); in other cases the same thought is expressed, even if the precise language differs (1 Tim. 3:16; 2 Tim. 2:8; Heb. 13:20). But one also finds in the Book of Revelation the bolder assertion that Christ has died but has conquered death and lives again (1:18; 2:8; 3:21; 5:5). There are other phrases in these documents which move in the same direction to speak of Christ's exaltation as a victory which he has won: He has abolished death and brought life and imperishability to light (2 Tim. 1:10); he has "gone into heaven and is at the right hand of God" (1 Pet. 3:22); and "when he had made purification for sins, he sat down at the right hand of the Majesty on high" (Heb. 1:3).

The redemptive christology of the type discussed in this chapter is the foundation of what has been called the "Christus Victor" theme, which was to become even more pronounced in the era of the Apostolic Fathers and Apologists.[174] This theme comes to expression also, for example, in the *Te Deum Laudamus,* where the exalted Christ is addressed directlv as a redeemer figure. Apart from its reference to the virgin birth of Christ (not asserted in the documents reviewed in this chapter), its lines are inspired by this type of redemptive christology:

> You, Christ, are the king of glory, the eternal Son of the Father.
> When you became man to set us free, you did not abhor the Virgin's womb.
> You overcame the sting of death, and opened the kingdom of heaven to all believers.
> You are seated at God's right hand in glory.
> We believe that you will come and be our judge.
> Come, then, Lord, and help your people, bought with the price of your own blood,
> and bring us with your saints to glory everlasting.[175]

2. A second feature of this type of redemptive christology is a pronounced connection between the nature and function of Christ. In fact, the nature of Christ is beginning to enter as the basis for his work. As already indicated, each writer alludes to Christ's preexistence. Beyond that, the nature of Christ is spoken of in two main ways. In the case of 1 Peter it cannot be said that there is a full-fledged ontological estimation of Jesus as being the manifestation of God; in fact, God and Christ are distinguished (3:18). What does appear, however, is that Christ "was destined before the foundation of the world" for his redemptive work (1:20). Ephesians moves a step closer to an ontological unity, saying that God has realized his eternal purpose in Christ (3:11) and that to know Christ's love is to experience the "fullness of God" (3:19). In these cases the work of Christ is founded upon his nature as the one who manifests God's purposes and nature in the world, even if Christ is ontologically distinguished from God. But the other writers gathered under this type of presentation move considerably farther to assert an ontological unity— even if a distinction remains—between God and Christ. In Colossians Christ is "the image of the invisible God" (1:15) and "the whole fullness of deity dwells bodily" in Christ (2:9). In the Pastorals Jesus shares the titles of "Savior" and even "God" with God himself (2 Tim. 1:10; Titus 1:4; 2:13; 3:6). In Hebrews Christ is the agent of creation, the one through whom God created all things (1:2; 2:10), and the term "God" is ascribed to him (1:8). And in the Book of Revelation the designation for God as "Alpha and Omega" (1:8) is applied to Christ as well (22:13; cf. 1:17). The concept of preexistence appears of course already in the writings of Paul (1 Cor. 8:6; 2 Cor. 8:9; Phil. 2:6). But these writers move farther than Paul to speak of the nature of Christ, and they begin to think

of his nature as a presupposition for his work. This way of thinking develops further after the New Testament era and gains added force in the history of christology. The great controversies up to the Council of Chalcedon (A.D. 451) concern themselves chiefly with the nature of Christ. It becomes thought that the question of his nature has to be determined in order to speak of his work. The point to observe here is that the beginnings of that history can be traced to the New Testament, particularly—although neither for the first time nor exclusively—to the type of redemptive christology considered here.

3. The redemptive work of Christ under this type is concerned essentially with the liberation of humanity from "sins," thereby setting persons free for life in the world to come. Each writer speaks of "sins" in the plural;[176] each uses the terminology of "redemption" to speak of Christ's liberating act;[177] and four of the writers (the exceptions being the authors of Colossians and Revelation) use the traditional *hyper*-formula (*hyper*, "for" or "on behalf of" persons or sins).[178] Generally lacking is the profound Pauline sense of "sin" (singular) as a power reigning over humanity, although the writer of Hebrews speaks of "the deceitfulness of sin" (3:13) and the "struggle against sin" (12:4).[179]

The way in which Christ does his redeeming work is portrayed differently by the various writers. In each case, however, Christ is spoken of in one way or another as the one who has borne sins and their consequences for the benefit of others. There is no concept of his making "satisfaction" for sins or of his appeasing God through his redemptive work. His redemptive work is grounded consistently in the will and purpose of God. And his bearing of sins for the benefit of others takes place through his death: Persons have been reconciled to God "in his body of flesh by his death" (Col. 1:22); they "have redemption through his blood" (Eph. 1:7), and reconciliation takes place "through the cross" (2:16); he "gave himself as a ransom for all" (2 Tim. 2:6); "he himself bore our sins in his body on the tree" (1 Pet. 2:24); in his death he bore the sins of many (Heb. 9:28); he "has freed us from our sins by his blood" (Rev. 1:5), and by his blood he ransomed people for God (5:9).

In some of the writings discussed the redemptive work of Christ includes liberation from the rule of cosmic powers or of the devil as well. But it is treated differently among them. The triumph of Christ over the cosmic powers is affirmed in Colossians (2:8–10, 15), so that Christians need no longer fear them. But in Ephesians, while Christ is exalted above these powers (1:20–23), Christians must still contend with them (6:12). In Hebrews (2:14–15) Christ is said to have rendered the devil powerless, and yet that does not mean that there is no more temptation; it means rather that Christ has provided a way around death, which is the manifestation of the devil's power. In the Pastorals and 1 Peter it is taken for granted that the devil is still active, seeking to ensnare and devour persons in moments of weakness (1 Tim. 3:7; 2 Tim. 2:26; 1 Pet. 5:8). And in the Book of Revelation the devil has been cast down, giving way to the reign of Christ in heaven (12:9–10), but now the devil rages on earth (12:12), and it is only at the manifestation of the reign of Christ in its fullness at the end of this world that he will be destroyed (20:10). Therefore it can be said that the motif of the liberation of humanity from the rule of cosmic powers and of the devil generally belongs to a future stage of redemptive history in the view of these writers, with the author of Colossians being an exception. What is common to them all is that they see that redemption by Christ is more than a matter of liberation from sins and their consequences. There are cosmic and/or demonic powers that must be undone as well in order for humanity to enter into the fullness of life in the world to come. Human life is not set on a stage, an earthly plane, which is neutral or benign. Humanity is drawn—however subtly (the mode of operation of these forces)—by powers which lead it away from the life for which it is destined by God. Christ, risen from the dead and reigning over all things, is above these powers, but humanity does not yet find relief from them. Liberation from them is a future prospect with the parousia of Christ.

4. A fourth feature of this redemptive christology is that, although the redemptive work of Christ has been done once and for all, its effects are essentially future. Each of the writers uses language which signifies the "already" aspect of the believer's salvation,[180] and in certain cases this "already" most likely coincides with baptism (Col. 1:13; Eph. 2:6; 5:26; 1 Pet. 1:3, 23; 3:21; Heb. 6:4–5). But there is a proliferation of terms to speak of salvation as (1) future and (2) in the heavenly realm. Every writer discussed here speaks of salvation as a future "inheritance" (Col. 3:24; Eph. 1:14, 18; 5:5; Titus 3:7; 1 Pet. 1:4; Heb 1:4; 6:12; 9:15; Rev. 21:7); the writer of 1 Peter, for example, says that Christians have "an inheritance which is imperishable" and "kept in heaven" (1:4). Beyond this common language of "inheritance," there is an abundance of terminology signifying the "future" and "heavenly"—the temporal and spatial—realms of salvation. According to Colossians, Christians have a "hope laid up . . . in heaven" (1:5), and in Ephesians they are "sealed with the promised Holy Spirit," which guarantees their "inheritance" until they possess it (1:13–14); they are "sealed for the day of redemption" (4:30), and then they shall be with Christ who is in the "heavenly places" (1:18–21). According to the Pastorals, Christians expect to be saved for Christ's "heavenly kingdom" (2 Tim. 4:18); they expect to "obtain salvation," enter into "eternal glory," and "reign" with Christ (2:10, 12). The

writer of 1 Peter likewise speaks of Christians as persons who expect to "obtain salvation" and to enter into "eternal glory" (1:9; 5:10), gaining their inheritance in heaven (1:4). According to Hebrews, Christians have a "heavenly call" (3:1) and expect to enter into a final "rest" (4:11) in the heavenly realm and there receive what has been promised to them (10:36). And in the Book of Revelation the expectation is that the saints will receive the heritage of those who conquer (21:7) and will inhabit the new Jerusalem that comes down from heaven (21:10) and where their names are written in "the Lamb's book of life" (21:27).

This collage of passages illustrates that, although they can speak of the "already" aspect of salvation, all of these writers of the subapostolic era consider the benefits of Christ's redemptive work to be essentially future. This in itself is not different from Paul, who also speaks of salvation as future (Rom. 5:9–10; 13:11; Phil. 2:12). Yet there is a change of emphasis. Paul could speak of the believer as a new creation already (2 Cor. 5:17). These writers can also, of course, speak of Christians as belonging to Christ and in communion with him (especially at Col. 1:13; Eph. 2:6), and in that regard Christians are endowed with the power of the new age. But the emphasis lies upon the future inheritance; there is a proliferation of terms expressing the futurity of salvation and its realization in the heavenly realm. This means that the present, earthly life of the Christian is essentially preparatory to that which is to be realized. The Christian has been set on a course leading to salvation, must not depart from it, and expects its realization in the heavenly realm (or, in the imagery of Revelation, the new Jerusalem).

5. The scope of Christ's redemptive work is universal, but the writers differ in regard to the universality of final salvation. In principle Christ's redemptive work is seen to be at least potentially effective for all humanity. That he gave himself for all or that through his death he has reconciled all humanity is asserted by each of the writers.[181] But on the question whether Christ's redemptive work is actually effective for all there is a division among them. It must be said that no writer makes a clear statement on the matter; one can only draw inferences from what is said or from what is not said within the larger presentation of redemptive christology. As previous discussions of the texts have indicated, universal final salvation is implied in Colossians, Ephesians, the Pastorals, and Revelation. In 1 Peter there are no limitations to the redemptive work of Christ; even those who have died prior to his coming have the gospel proclaimed to them. Yet the writer of 1 Peter does not seem to have considered the question of the living who have not heard the gospel, and he says explicitly that those who have heard but "do not obey the gospel" will be judged (4:17). And in Hebrews the focus is so centered on the faithful, believing

community as constituting those destined for salvation that the question of the larger hope for humanity in general is not dealt with. What is said is that those who have committed apostasy have excluded themselves from final salvation.

What is remarkable about these writers is that, although they lived in an era of an increased sense of Christian identity, when Christianity had become a "religion" set apart from Judaism and distinct from various gentile religious traditions, there remained among them still the conviction that Christ gave himself for the redemption of all humanity. The fact that Christians actually made up such a small proportion of the population wherever they existed makes their redemptive-christological convictions all the more striking. Christ is not thought of from the inside of the Christian movement as the founder and teacher of a philosophical school or as a god of the Christian cult—a competitor among other cult heroes— through whom the devotee could gain a state of higher consciousness or eternal blessedness by communion with him.[182] Rather, Christ is thought of as a universal figure, the source of salvation for all humanity. Salvation, it is believed, is founded purely on the grace of God, which has been made manifest in the atoning death and resurrection of Jesus, and the scope of grace and salvation is extended to all humanity through the proclamation of the gospel. But how far does that scope reach beyond the limits of proclamation in history? Here there is a division among the writers. In the case of 1 Peter and Hebrews there is silence; the limitations are set, by implication, at the circumference of proclamation; further, the disobedient are judged (1 Peter), and the apostates have excluded themselves (Hebrews). But in the case of the other writers there are no implied limits to the scope of final salvation; no part of humanity is left unaffected by the benefits of Christ, who gave himself for all. The gospel bears witness to his redemptive work, and those who hear it and believe are regarded as claimants to the inheritance to come and are, in that sense, those who are saved.

6. A final feature of this redemptive christology is that Christ, exalted above the heavens, already exercises his reign over the universe through the church. This is spelled out in various ways: (1) His lordship is confessed in the church (1 Tim. 3:16; 1 Pet. 3:15; 4:14–16; Heb. 4:14; 10:23; Rev. 1:5; 2:3); (2) Christ strengthens Christians for witness or the struggle against evil powers (Col. 1:28–29; Eph. 6:10–12; Heb. 13:21); or (3) the Spirit is given to Christians for their witness and struggle (Eph. 3:16; 1 Pet. 1:2). In all of the writers discussed there is an emphasis on confession, solidarity, and struggle against evil powers (or, in Colossians, gaining maturity). The church is Christ's body (Col. 1:18; Eph. 1:23), the household of God (1 Tim. 3:15; Heb. 3:6), or a priestly

or royal kingdom (1 Pet. 2:9; Rev. 1:6). It follows from this that the church is expected to mirror the rule of Christ in its own inner life and in its attitude and conduct toward those outside.

The redemptive christology discussed in this chapter is expressed in a relatively large body of literature from the subapostolic era. In addition to the books already surveyed, it can also be seen to come to expression in other places, for example, at 2 Pet. 2:1, which speaks of the "Master" *(despotēs)* as having "bought" persons, and at 2 Thess. 2:8, which speaks of the "Lord Jesus" as the one who will destroy the "lawless one" at his parousia. Traces of its substructure can be seen also in the Philippian Hymn (Phil. 2:5–11) of an earlier generation, for its first stanza (2:5–8) is christopractic, speaking of Christ's emptying himself and taking human form, and its second (2:9–11) speaks of his cosmic reign. But the hymn in fact does not speak of his bearing of sin or delivering humanity from sin or cosmic powers, in spite of the fact that it speaks of his death (2:8); his redemptive work can only be inferred from it. Moreover, the exaltation of Christ is based solely on an act of God (so here the theopractic accent is made) in response to his obedience. The redemptive christology in which redemption is portrayed as won by Christ—a figure who comes from above to rescue humanity—is developed in a subsequent era, in which reflection on the kerygma of his death as "for us" or "for our sins" has taken place within the context of an emerging religious community that has achieved a place for itself in distinction from Judaism and Hellenistic religious traditions and has a place and identity within the larger society, whether perilous or acceptable.

The degree to which language and concepts of the Greco-Roman culture (particularly the emperor cult) influenced the development goes beyond the purposes of this study. It is clear that the emperor cult is very much on the mind of the writer of Revelation, and some of the terms found in the Pastorals (e.g., "Savior" and "epiphany") may have been used in part because of it. But generally terms from the emperor cult are avoided by New Testament writers,[183] and that the cult was a direct influence on the development of the third type of redemptive christology—as a type—is doubtful. Essentially the impulses for the development come from within the Christian tradition itself. The "raw materials" were available in the tradition—the concepts of preexistence, incarnation, atoning death, exaltation, reign, and parousia. But the existence of these concepts alone does not account for the shift from a theopractic to a christopractic emphasis. There had to be other factors. A major factor must have been a developing "Christian" self-consciousness, in which the third generation—now predominantly gentile in composition—considered itself to be identified both by its own membership and by those outside as devotees of Christ. Moreover, the use of liturgical, hymnic, and creedal materials concerning Christ and his redemptive work—fragments of which can be detected in all of these writings[184]—must have impelled thought and devotion to focus on Christ all the more. It is Christ who is the Redeemer. He is the one who brings humanity to God (1 Peter), offers his own blood in a priestly sacrifice (Hebrews), brings life and imperishability to light (the Pastorals), conquers Satan, death, and Hades (Revelation), and reconciles all things to himself or to God and triumphs over the cosmic powers (Colossians and Ephesians). This redemptive christology is heir to traditions found elsewhere, particularly from Paul in the case of the deutero-Paulines and 1 Peter, but it is clear that a transformation has taken place so that Christ emerges all the more sharply as the one who wins redemption—not apart from the will and purpose of God, but as the one who performs the action on God's behalf for the benefit of humanity.

8

Redemption Mediated
by Christ

THE FOURTH MAIN type of redemptive christology expressed in the New Testament shares the christopractic emphasis of the third. But here we enter into a quite different world of theological reflection and spirituality. Christ is portrayed as the one who reveals the Father and mediates salvation from God to those who believe in him. He is in union with the Father, who has given him authority to exercise judgment and to grant life to his own. This redemptive christology is expressed primarily in the Gospel of John, but it also appears in the Letters of John, which presuppose the redemptive christology of John's Gospel, but they also amend it in interesting ways.

THE GOSPEL OF JOHN

It is generally agreed among interpreters that the Fourth Gospel was completed in its present form during the last decade of the first century A.D.; that it contains traditions concerning Jesus which have been given their characteristic Johannine stamp by its author, who sought to present Jesus not simply as a figure of the past, but also Jesus as he *is* for Christian faith, so that when Jesus speaks to his disciples in this book he addresses the church of the evangelist's time as well; that the Gospel of John shows the marks of having been written and revised by its author, and then supplemented (and perhaps revised again) by an editor; and that the Fourth Evangelist and the final editor are anonymous. The place (or places) of composition, revision, and editing are disputed, but Syria and Ephesus are most commonly proposed.[1] Since matters of the Gospel's sources, composition, and editing will not be a concern in this study, but rather the Gospel itself in its present form, we shall speak as though

145

there was a single author and call him "John" or the "Fourth Evangelist," even though such terminology implies no commitment to a single authorship of the entire Gospel, nor does it contest the view that the writer is anonymous.

The Gospel of John shares the main christological titles found in the Synoptic Gospels: "Christ" (nineteen times),[2] "Son of man" (thirteen times),[3] "Lord" (thirty-seven times),[4] and "Son of God" (nine times).[5] At times Jesus is designated simply as "the Son" (nineteen times),[6] which is for John virtually equivalent to "Son of God,"[7] but with a special nuance to it, referring to the relationship of the Son to "the Father," the term used for God so frequently in this Gospel. Other titles appear less frequently. John alone of the New Testament writers uses the Semitic title "Messiah" for Jesus, and he does so twice (1:41; 4:25), providing a translation for it ("Christ") on both occasions. He alone uses the christological designation of "the Word" (*logos,* four times in the prologue, 1:1–18).[8] He also uses the designation "Lamb of God" (twice, each instance in a saying of John the Baptist, 1:29, 36). The title "the prophet" (or "the true prophet") is applied to Jesus in a special (eschatological) sense at 6:14 and 7:40;[9] it is a christological designation which is based on a typological reading of Deut. 18:15–18, where Moses declares that the Lord "will raise up for you a prophet like me," and which surfaces as a christological concept elsewhere in the New Testament as well.[10] Once Jesus is called the "Savior of the world" (4:42), and at the close of the Gospel the risen Jesus is called "God" by the disciple Thomas (20:28). Finally, the title "King" is applied to Jesus. Often this term or the full phrase "King of the Jews" is applied to Jesus in the passion narrative, such as when Pilate asks "the Jews" whether Jesus is their king, or when "the Jews" deny that he is. It is also used in mockings and in the inscription on the cross (18:33, 37, 39; 19:3, 12, 14, 15, 19, 21). But the term "King of Israel" is applied to Jesus in a positive way by Nathanael (1:49) and by the crowds at his entry into Jerusalem (12:13).[11]

The christological titles do not convey John's christology apart from both their usage in context and the basic christological substructure underlying the Gospel. This substructure becomes apparent primarily in sayings embedded in longer discourses of the Johannine Jesus. Here there are two types of sayings. First, there are sayings about the descending and ascending of the Son of Man. John shares the Son of Man designation with the Synoptics, but his usage differs. There are, for example, no "future" (or apocalyptic) Son of Man sayings in John;[12] the emphasis is upon his having come already. John uses the term to speak of the origin and destiny of Jesus and of his authority to exercise judgment. The Son of Man has "descended from heaven"—which designates his preexistence—and through his death and exaltation has "ascended into heaven" (3:13) where he was previously (6:62). As Son of Man Jesus is the one who has shared an intimacy with the Father prior to his descent to earth and is therefore able to reveal the Father. The ascent of the Son of Man takes place through the crucifixion, his being "lifted up" (3:14; 8:28; 12:34), which is his glorification (12:23; 13:31). And as Son of Man he has received "authority to execute judgment" (5:27)—an allusion to Dan. 7:13–14, where "one like a son of man" receives power and authority.[13]

The second type of sayings has to do with Jesus' having been sent and his going (or returning) to the Father. Here John uses two different verbs for sending (*apostellō* and *pempō*), but there is, practically speaking, no distinction in their meaning (cf. 17:18 and 20:21).[14] John also uses two verbs for Jesus' going to the Father or to heaven (*hypagō* and *poreuomai*). In these instances a christological title occurs only twice (3:17; 5:23), and in both cases it is "the Son" who is the one sent by the Father. More frequently there is simply a clause designating Jesus as the one whom the Father has "sent," and in the clauses which speak of Jesus' going to the Father no titles are given. That Jesus, or the Son, has been sent from the Father is stated forty-one times in the Fourth Gospel,[15] and that he is going to the Father is stated twenty times.[16] The concept of Jesus as having been sent "is the most characteristic christological formula in the Fourth Gospel."[17] The purposes of Jesus' having been sent and his returning to the Father are manifold. He was sent by the Father above all "not to condemn the world, but that the world might be saved through him" (3:17). In order to carry out this saving function, he was sent to reveal the Father (12:44–45), speak "the words of God" (3:34; cf. 7:16), and do the will of and accomplish the work assigned to him by the Father (4:34; 5:36). He returns to the Father to resume his place of honor, but also to prepare a place for his own (14:2), send the Paraclete (16:7), and enable believers to perform works in his name through prayer (14:12–14).

We leave aside for the moment those discourses in which Jesus speaks of himself as the Bread of Life, Good Shepherd, etc., and go on to a consideration of John's redemptive christology. The Fourth Evangelist does not use the noun "redemption" or those verbs conventionally translated "to redeem." His soteriological language consists primarily of three terms: (1) the verb "to save" (*sōzō*, 3:17; 5:34; 10:9; 12:47); for example, the Father sent the Son to save the world (3:17), or the Son came to save the world (12:47); (2) the verb "to live" (*zaō*, 5:25; 6:51, 57, 58; 11:25; 14:19); and (3) the noun "life" (*zōē*) or "eternal life" (*zōē aiōnios*), the former used sixteen times,[18] and the latter seventeen.[19] That the two

147

terms are equivalent can be seen by their interchangeableness (as at 5:24, 39–40; 6:53–54).

The terms "life" and "eternal life" appear already with a soteriological reference in the Synoptic Gospels (fifteen times, including parallels),[20] but in general they designate a future existence, as in the question put to Jesus, "Teacher, what must I do to inherit eternal life?" (Mark 10:17). But in the Gospel of John two things are striking. First, there is the sheer abundance of the terminology (thirty-three instances) in comparison to the Synoptics. Second, in the Fourth Goseph "life" or "eternal life" is predominantly a present possession of the believer. To be sure, there are references to life as a future possession (5:25; 6:27; 12:25), just as there are references to the futurity of the resurrection (5:29; 6:39–40, 44, 54; 11:24; cf. 12:48); John therefore retains from the received tradition a "future eschatology." Yet, as interpreters have emphasized so frequently, the primary perspective of John is that of a "realized" or "present eschatology."[21] Eternal life is a gift given already to the one who believes in Jesus as the one he claims to be. It is not simply a future gift, but it is in fact a present possession: "whoever hears my word and believes him who sent me has eternal life; this one does not come into judgment, but has passed from death to life" (5:24). This emphasis on the present gift of life to the believer is repeated again and again (3:16, 36; 5:24; 6:40, 47, 53, 54, 68; 10:28; 17:2–3). Although physical death is to be expected (cf. 11:25) and resurrection and judgment are certain (5:28–29; 12:48), the decision concerning a person's standing has already been determined; the final judgment simply confirms what has taken place. Whoever rejects the Son and his words will be condemned (12:48), but in fact this person is condemned already in the present (3:18). And those who believe in the Son of God not only will have life; they have it already. In all of this, the Fourth Evangelist presents warning for those who refuse to believe, and he extends a promise to believers. But more is involved: the portrayal of the life of the believer as a new existence. Although living "in" the world, the believer is no longer "of the world" (17:14, 16) and its standards. The believer has been "born from above" (by the Spirit, 3:1–8), is freed from sin and its bondage (8:36), and has life abundantly (10:10)—it endures from the moment of faith into eternity.

But how does Jesus, in the Johannine view, effect redemption? As for all other New Testament writers, for John there is no redemption or salvation apart from the cross and resurrection of Jesus. Further, the saving work of Jesus is according to the will and purpose of God. This point is brought out in various ways, and we shall mention three. First, the very fact that John emphasizes so often that Jesus is the one sent from God confirms that his work is divinely intended. God sent the Son in order to save the world (3:17), and Jesus declares, "My food is to do the will of him who sent me, and to accomplish his work" (4:34; cf. 9:4). The second way the motif appears is in the theme concerning the unity of the Father and the Son (10:30, 38; 14:8–9), by which the Son knows the will of the Father and thereby speaks and acts not by his own authority but by the will and authority of the Father (5:30; 8:28; 12:49; 14:10). The third way is that, for John, God guides not only the ministry of Jesus, but the actions of others as well. For example, John the Baptist was sent by God to bear witness to the light (1:6–8), and even Pilate is said to have power given him "from above" in his treatment of Jesus in the passion narrative (19:11). God is thus involved in the whole complex of events and persons surrounding Jesus, whether for good (as in the case of his herald, John) or for peril (as in the case of his governor and interrogator, Pilate).

The human race, in the Johannine perspective, lives in a state of being overcome by sin, darkness, falsehood, and death. These are what must be overcome or canceled for redemption to take place. In keeping with the common Christian tradition, John uses language which portrays Jesus' death as beneficial. Above all, he uses the *hyper*-formula: Jesus lays down his life "for [*hyper*] the sheep" (10:11, 15), and even in the words of Caiaphas, who "prophesied" (11:51), it is said that Jesus would die "for [*hyper*] the people" (11:50; 18:14; cf.11:51). In these passages, however, it is not clear that Jesus' death is considered a means by which he bears sin and its consequences for others; it has been maintained that within the Johannine perspective such passages simply express the self-giving love of Christ for others.[22] On the other hand, Jesus is designated once as the "Lamb of God who takes away the sin of the world" (1:29). In this instance it is clear that the Johannine tradition knows a cultic and atoning estimation of the death of Jesus, although it is only here that the view is expressed.[23]

The concept of Jesus' death as an atoning sacrifice is not the primary thrust of the Fourth Gospel.[24] The death of Jesus on the cross is given new content. The cross is the means by which Jesus is "lifted up" from the earth (3:14; 8:28; 12:34). The physical act of lifting Jesus up on the cross is taken to have a deeper meaning. It is the moment of his departure to the Father as well.[25] John does not of course use the term "moment," but he uses the term "hour" to signify the time appointed—which coincides with the crucifixion—for both Jesus' departure to the Father (13:1) and his glorification (17:1). Thereby John connects the death and exaltation of Jesus together as a single event: The cross is the means of his death (19:13), but also the means of his return to the Father, his glorification. "Hence passion, resurrection, exaltation, ascension, and glorification are all seen together as one event."[26]

The saving work of Christ, in the Johannine perspective, consists primarily in the nexus between historical event, as interpreted in its true (i.e., Johannine) significance, and present proclamation. The historical event of Jesus is to be taken as the unique event in which the Son was sent into the world by God, revealed the Father, and returned to the Father; this is summed up at 13:3: Jesus was the one who "had come from God," the one to whom "the Father had given all things," and the one who "was going to God" (cf. 8:14; 16:28). In his historical ministry Jesus revealed the Father through his deeds and teaching. The teaching he gave was primarily about himself (the discourses), but it was not simply his own teaching, for, he says, "the word which you hear is not mine but the Father's who sent me" (14:24; cf 3:32; 8:26, 38; 12:49). Again, he says, "My teaching is not mine, but his who sent me" (7:16). Already in his historical ministry the word of Jesus caused division: There were those who believed (4:41; 17:6) and those who rejected him and his message (8:37, 43; 10:19). But when John composed his Gospel, the earthly ministry of Jesus had been concluded. The Proclaimer (the earthly Jesus) had become the Proclaimed (the Christ of proclamation). In the development of the Johannine tradition presumably, but in any case at the level of the writing of the Fourth Gospel, the author has cast (or recast) sayings of Jesus so that the Johannine Jesus speaks about the church's proclamation about himself. He declares in his prayer to the Father concerning his disciples, "I have given them thy word" (17:14), and they have indeed "kept thy word" (17:6)—the condition of being a true disciple (8:31; 14:23). It is expected that the disciples will proclaim the word (15:20), and it is through such proclamation that others come to believe (17:20). And by believing in this word there is salvation: "If anyone keeps my word, that person will never see death" (8:51); "if anyone loves me, that person will keep my word, and my Father will love him, and we will come to him and make our home with him" (14:23); and "whoever hears my word and believes him who sent me has eternal life" (5:24). On the other hand, whoever rejects the Son proclaimed in the word will be judged (i.e., condemned,[27] 12:48).

This means that, while John thinks of the Jesus event in history as the decisive turning point in time for salvation, that event must be seen in its deeper significance. The historical career of Jesus of Nazareth was a time of revelation. It was the earthly course of the Son who was sent by the Father and who revealed the Father. The claim that he revealed the Father was made by Jesus himself, in John's view, and it was accepted as true by those who heard and believed, while others rejected both claim and claimant. Now in the present (the time of the Fourth Evangelist) those who hear—through the church's proclamation—and believe that Jesus truly is what is proclaimed are saved; they have eternal life. Salvation, in other words, is the result of believing the word which testifies that Jesus is the revelation of the Father.[28] Or to use the language of "knowing" instead of "believing" (for John these are closely related concepts, since faith leads to understanding and becomes knowledge):[29] "this is eternal life, that they know thee the only true God, and Jesus Christ whom thou has sent" (17:3).

Salvation comes then by way of revelation and its reception. Jesus' saving work is that of revealing the Father and at the same time revealing himself to be the Revealer of the Father. This way of thinking has been attributed to a gnostic influence,[30] but it can be attributed primarily to christological and soteriological reflection and to the author's purpose in writing his gospel. Whatever the exact situation and purpose, interpreters have maintained on good grounds that the Gospel had its rise in a community in which various contending groups of persons were addressed. The major battles were over the question of the identity of Jesus in relationship to God, and these had serious implications for the relationship of the community, at various stages of its history, to nonbelieving Jews, who had expelled Christian Jews from their synagogues, and even for the relationship of the community to other Christian groups, which were thought to have an inadequate christology in the view of the Fourth Evangelist.[31] The "dominant dispute" reflected in the Gospel of John is over the question of the divinity of Jesus.[32] Jesus is portrayed as one who is accused of making himself equal to God (5:18; 10:33; cf. 19:7), which can be taken as an indicator that it was precisely the status of Jesus in relationship to God that was the issue dividing Johannine Christians and Jews, and perhaps Johannine Christians and other Christians as well. The Johannine Christians were under suspicion of proclaiming and worshiping Jesus as a second God and urging others to do the same.[33]

Given the polemical situation in which it was written, the Gospel of John treats Christ and his benefits in an exclusivistic way. The Johannine Jesus declares, "No one comes to the Father, but by me" (14:6). Since the Son and the Father are one (10:30, 38), it is by "seeing" Jesus, and him only, that one "sees" the Father (12:45; 14:9). There is in the Fourth Gospel—to borrow a term from C. K. Barrett—a "Christology of mediation."[34] That is to say, "the Son of man is the one true mediator between heaven and earth; he passes from one to the other, and through his earthly sojourn he bestows upon [people] the revealed knowledge and the eternal life in virtue of which they in turn come to the life of heaven."[35] Salvation is mediated to humanity by the Redeemer, Revealer, and Mediator, the one sent by the Father. Those who receive him receive the salvation he brings. Implicit in all this, of course, is that the risen Christ can do as he wills, and indeed that is affirmed. He has authority, given by God, to execute judgment (5:27). Therewith is the authority to grant life to those who hear his word and believe in him. In his prayer to the Father, Jesus declares: "Thou hast given [the Son] power over all flesh, to give eternal life to all whom thou hast given him" (17:2). In sum, just as Christ is the Mediator of creation (1:3), so he is the Mediator of salvation.

That Jesus is the exclusive Revealer of the Father and the only Mediator of salvation is brought out in a particularly striking way in the seven "I am" discourses which contain predicates ("Bread of Life," etc.). Each of the seven predicates contains Old Testament and Jewish imagery,[36] including messianic imagery in connection with the Bread and the Shepherd.[37] In the Johannine contexts the discourses are christological and soteriological, pointing to Jesus as the sole Revealer and indicating that he is the Mediator of life to believers. Each of the seven is related to the theme of life,[38] and believing in him is often stated explicitly as the means of gaining the life he gives. Jesus is "the Bread of Life" (6:35, 41, 51) who has come down from heaven (6:41), the "living Bread," and whoever believes in him "will live for ever" (6:51; cf. 6:47). He is "the Light of the World" (8:12; 9:5), and whoever follows him "will have the light of life" (8:12). He is "the Door of the Sheep" (10:7, 9), and whoever enters by him "will be saved," for he came in order that people might "have life, and have it abundantly" (10:9–10). He is "the Good Shepherd (10:11, 14) who gives his "life" for the sheep (10:11, 15). He is "the Resurrection and the Life" (11:25), and whoever believes in him "shall never die" (11:26). He is "the Way, the Truth, and the Life" (14:6), and by him— and only by him—do people gain life and the way to the Father. He is "the True Vine" (15:1, 5) who (by implication) gives life to the branches (15:4–5)—those who abide by faith in him—for apart from him they wither away (15:6). Thus it is said seven times that Jesus brings life, and the counterpoint to this claim is that the life he brings is accessible to those who believe in him, and to them alone.

It was said previously that John considers humanity to be locked up in sin, darkness, falsehood, and death. Yet that estimation, while true,[39] must now be nuanced somewhat. John's use of this terminology at the level of writing his Gospel is not due so much to a theological analysis of the general human condition as it is to his polemical stance against those who have not believed, or will not believe, in Jesus as the Son sent from the Father. Such persons belong to "the world" (8:23), which is ruled by the devil (12:31), and "the world" has nothing but hatred for Christ and his disciples (15:18; cf. 7:7; 16:20). Each of the terms used for the negative estimate of unbelievers has its antithesis in faith. Sin is essentially the refusal to believe in Jesus; so unbelievers are those whom Jesus says the Paraclete will convict of sin, "because they do not believe in me" (16:9), and he says to the Pharisees, "You will die in your sins unless you believe that I am he" (8:24; cf. also 9:41; 15:22). Darkness is dispelled by belief in Jesus: "I have come as light into the world, that whoever believes in me may not remain in darkness" (12:46). Jesus is the Light of the World and says that "the one who follows me will not walk in darkness, but will have the light of life" (8:12; cf. 12:35–36). Falsehood is attributed to those who cannot bear to hear the word of Jesus (8:43–47), while those who are his disciples and continue in his word know the truth (8:31–32). To die is the obverse of gaining life, and life comes through believing in Jesus (11:26), but unless one believes in him, the result is to die in one's sins (8:24).

John's use of these symbols in writing his Gospel then is not due primarily, as so often thought, to his analysis of the existential needs of humanity. His Gospel was not written to address people's needs for meaning ("life") on the basis of a prior assessment, which finds humanity lost in sin, darkness, falsehood, and death. F. s aim is much more limited, and that is to contend for the claim that Jesus is the Revealer of God and the Mediator of salvation. Refusal to believe in him is to belong to the realm of sin, darkness, falsehood, and death. The Gospel of John is more polemical than existential, and that accounts for its harshness, which is too often overlooked by those who find in it a lofty spirituality. It accounts for those passages where Jesus describes unbelieving Jews as children of the devil (8:44), unable to understand the Scriptures (5:39), and devoid of God's love (5:42). It accounts for those passages in which Jesus tells the Pharisees that they are guilty of not responding to the truth revealed by him (9:40–41) and then speaks of the leaders of the Jewish people as "thieves and robbers" (10:1, 8).

The purpose of John is not so much to present Jesus as the one in whom God has reconciled the world to himself, or to show how Jesus fulfills the divine purpose of salvation, or to portray Jesus as the one who enters into the human condition and bears sin and its consequences for the benefit of others (even if the author uses the *hyper*-formula and has the Baptist declare that Christ "takes away the sins of the world"); nor is the Fourth Gospel a missionary document.[40] Rather, the burning issue for John is how one will respond to Jesus (represented through the word of proclamation): will it be a response of belief, leading to salvation, or disbelief, leading to condemnation? Sin is not alienation from God in a general sense; it is disbelief and, more specifically, disbelief of the Johannine message (not the gospel in a more general sense) about Jesus.

153

Rather than proclaiming that there is salvation from God, assured in the cross and resurrection of Jesus, available to those who believe, the approach of John might better be described as proclamation that those who believe in Jesus as the Revealer obtain salvation. The syntactical nuances are slight in such a statement, but the theological nuances are great. It is therefore only partially correct to say that "John intends to draw the complete picture of Jesus as faith sees him, and *to this extent* his presentation makes the claim to offer the perfect testimony to Christ."[41] The intention of John is also to engage his readers in issues of christology and to sharpen issues which divide the community and the larger Jewish environment as well as divide the community and the larger Christian community. His "testimony to Christ" is not "perfect" in the sense that it is timeless; it is an embattled testimony, and his redemptive christology is polemicized.[42]

This means that the message of John must be seen to be directed, like that of any other New Testament book, primarily to its own situation. It is not a message spelled out on the basis of reflection on the gospel and the human condition and which is directly applicable for persons in every time and place. What is contingent and what is consistent and abiding in the New Testament are vexing problems. But if we were to sketch out what may well be consistent in John with the rest of the New Testament— a task which is finally necessary—the following themes would be included. John stresses the love of God for the world, the divine purpose of redemption, God's self-expression through Jesus of Nazareth, who ministered to people on earth, was crucified, and raised from the dead, and the promise of life to humanity in consequence of the Christ event. For all its exclusivism of life only for those who believe in Jesus as the Revealer, it should be pointed out that even in this Gospel there are assertions made concerning the scope of the benefits of Christ as extending to all humanity. He is the one "who takes away the sin of the world" (1:29), who was sent not to condemn the world but to save it (3:17; 12:47), who is "Savior of the world" (4:42), and who declares that "I, when I am lifted up from the earth, will draw all persons to myself" (12:32). The will of God, for John, is clearly the salvation of all humanity. Yet the actual mediation of salvation is consistently interpreted to take place solely through belief in Jesus. Even the most "universalistic" saying ("I will draw all persons to myself," 12:32) does not finally cancel out the consistent view. In the only other place at which Jesus speaks of the "drawing" of people he says that "no one can come to me unless the Father who sent me draws him; and I will raise him up at the last day" (6:44). And elsewhere, when Jesus speaks of his being lifted up, he declares immediately that whoever believes in him will have eternal life

(3:14–15), but then whoever does not believe is condemned (3:18). John's consistent view on the mediation of the benefits of Christ is rooted in his christology, forged in a polemical situation. He does not set forth a redemptive christology which portrays the redemptive work of God in Christ as the foundation for trust and love for God (i.e., salvation), but portrays Christ as a challenge. Only those who believe him to be the Revealer sent from the Father receive life; and they receive life because he is able to grant it to them. Although John affirms the unconditional love of God for the world, it must finally be said that, in spite of the oneness of the Son with the Father, the love manifested by the Johannine Jesus is limited to "his own" (13:1), those intimately bound up with him (11:5; 13:23, 34; 15:9, 12): "He who loves me will be loved by my Father, and I will love him" (14:21).

Such an assessment of the redemptive christology of the Fourth Gospel may be misunderstood without further comment. There can be no doubt that the Gospel of John represents one of the richest, most considered christologies within the New Testament, manifesting a genuine and awesome development. And the Gospel of John was one of the most important books, perhaps the most important book, in the New Testament to influence christological doctrine from the second century to the fifth, the era in which orthodoxy grew and matured.[43] Our point has to do with (1) the time and setting of the composition of the Gospel of John and (2) its redemptive christology only (not its christology in general). Then and there it is appropriate to say that the Gospel of John reflects a redemptive christology which is polemical in its stance, and the message which arises out of it is largely a summons to believe in Jesus as the Revealer of the Father and the Mediator of salvation. The gospel of God's sending his Son is of course the basis without which there can be no saving faith, and therefore the Gospel of John is truly evangelical. Nevertheless, the accent of the Fourth Gospel falls more on the act of believing the word testifying to the Son, and thus believing in the Son himself, than on the act of God in Christ for the salvation of the world. Those who believe have life; those who do not are condemned. There are similarities to that way of thinking in the synoptic tradition, as when Jesus declares that "every one who acknowledges me before others, the Son of man also will acknowledge before the angels of God, but every one who denies me before others will be denied before the angels of God" (Luke 12:8–9// Matt. 10:32–33). But in the Gospel of John the precondition of faith in the Son for salvation becomes so prominent and pervasive that the news of the unconditional love of God for the world—which is exhibited by the earthly Jesus himself in his fellowship with outcasts (the synoptic tradition) and declared by Paul (cf. Rom. 5:8)—recedes into the background.

That is so because of the aim of the Fourth Evangelist: to confront those who do not see things the way he does and to give assurance to those who belong to his own community.

THE EPISTLES OF JOHN

The Johannine Letters are generally considered to have been written by a member of a "Johannine school" after the writing of the Gospel of John and, presumably, in the same locality (Ephesus or Syria). Interpreters generally agree also that they were written around the turn of the century, the outside dates being ca. A.D. 90–110. Areas of disagreement among interpreters are whether all three letters were written by the same person[44] and whether the writer of any or all was the Fourth Evangelist or the final editor of the Gospel of John.[45] Perhaps the most plausible view is that of Raymond E. Brown. He has suggested that the letters were written by a single author who was someone other than the Fourth Evangelist (or editor)[46] and who wrote after the exit of secessionists from the Johannine community (cf. 1 John 2:18–19). These secessionists were seeking to undermine the essentials of the Johannine Christian faith through, among other things, their denial of the incarnation and humanity of Jesus (1 John 4:2–3; 2 John 7),[47] their claim that they and their followers were without sin (1 John 1:8, 10), and their disregard of ethical teaching ("commandments," 1 John 2:3–4; 3:22, 24; 5:2–3) and the practice of love (1 John 2:9–11; 3:11–18; 4:20).[48] This means that a shift of adversaries has taken place between the Gospel and the Epistles of John. While in the former the adversaries were essentially "outsiders" (i.e., "the Jews" and perhaps other church groups), they are now "insiders" in the sense of being members of the Johannine community who claim to continue and to represent the Johannine understanding of the Christian faith, but who are considered a threat to it and are opposed by the writer of the letters.[49]

The christological terminology of the letters is similar in many respects to that of the Gospel of John. Frequently, as in the Gospel, Jesus is designated simply as "the Son" (sixteen times)[50] or "the Son of God" (seven times);[51] once he is called "the Son of the Father" (2 John 3). The other main title is "Christ" (eleven times).[52] Just as Jesus is once called "the Savior of the world" in the Gospel of John (4:24), so he is called such in the letters on one occasion (1 John 4:14). He is designated once also as "the Holy One" (1 John 2:20),[53] which resembles Peter's declaration in the Gospel that Jesus is "the Holy One of God" (6:69). And as Jesus is frequently designated in the Gospel of John as the Son whom

156

the Father "sent" (forty-one times), the same appears three times in the letters (1 John 4:9, 10, 14).[54]

But there are striking differences in terminology as well. Once Jesus is called the Paraclete (*paraklētos*, translated as "advocate" in the RSV, 1 John 2:1), which is never assigned to Jesus in the Gospel of John; there the term refers instead to the Holy Spirit (cf. John 14:16–17, 26). Although it is not used as a christological title, twice Jesus is spoken of in the letters as an "expiation for our sins" (*hilasmos peri tōn hamartiōn hēmōn*, 1 John 2:2; 4:10), which does not occur in the Fourth Gospel. While Jesus is spoken of as the Son sent by the Father in the letters and it is said that he has "come" into the world (implicitly from the Father, 1 John 4:2; 5:6; 2 John 7), there are no passages which speak of his "going" (or "returning") to the Father. This can most likely be accounted for on the grounds that the letters contain no discourses. Nor does one find in the letters the title "Son of man" and therefore statements about his descent and ascent. This too can be attributed to the lack of discourses in the letters, for the term Son of Man in the Gospel of John (as in the Synoptics) is used only in sayings of Jesus. The letters never use the title "Lord" (*kyrios*) for Jesus, which appears thirty-seven times in the Gospel of John. Perhaps the most interesting thing of all in a survey of the letters is that 3 John contains no christological terminology at all; in fact, it does not even mention Jesus.

The redemptive christology of the Epistles of John is portrayed chiefly in 1 John (and unless indicated otherwise, references will be to that letter). The redemptive christology stands in basic agreement with that of the Gospel of John, setting forth the view that salvation is mediated by Christ. The author asserts that God sent his Son into the world in order that people "might live through him" (1 John 4:9; cf. 1:2). There is "eternal life" in the Son, and those who believe in him receive it (5:11–13). Indeed those who believe have passed out of death into life (3:14). In all of this the author clearly echoes themes familiar in the Gospel of John.

In the affirmation that life is mediated from the Son of God to believers there would be complete agreement between the writer and the secessionists. It is in other matters, however, that there were severe and unreconcilable differences. Some of these have been indicated already. In terms of redemptive christology the writer reverts to other aspects of the Christian tradition which are only implicit in the Fourth Gospel, lifts them to a dogmatic status, and presses them against the secessionists, whom the writer brands as "false prophets" (4:1), "deceivers" (2 John 7), and representatives of the "spirit of antichrist" (4:3; cf. 2 John 7). Above all, he stresses the incarnation of the Son (already in the Fourth

Gospel) and the death of Jesus as an atoning event, which is not explicit in the Gospel of John, although it is implicit in the Johannine traditions which speak of Jesus as the Lamb of God who takes away the sin of the world (John 1:29) and in which Jesus speaks of laying down his life for the sheep (10:11, 15). The writer of the letters insists that the touchstone of Christian truth and faith is whether one "confesses that Jesus Christ has come in the flesh" (4:2), which is denied by the secessionists (2 John 7). And he asserts forthrightly that the death of Jesus was an atonement for sin. In the Fourth Gospel the crucifixion of Jesus is portrayed essentially as the "hour" of the Son's glorification and return to the Father, or as the lifting up of the Son of Man. It would be possible for the secessionists to look upon the crucifixion purely as the culmination of Jesus' revealing his glory, and not as an atoning event.[55]

Another unreconcilable difference between the writer and the secessionists would have arisen over their possible belief that the saving significance of Jesus was his communication of life to those who believe in him, by which they become "like him" (3:2) in the present. This is possible on the basis of a reading of the Gospel of John, and it can be fortified by another concept in the Gospel as well, which is picked up in the letters. The secessionists claim to have "fellowship" with God (1:6) and say that they "abide" in Jesus (2:6), who had indeed commanded his disciples to "abide" in him (John 15:4–7) or be bereft of the life he gives. The author of the letters chides his opponents on this matter. Those who truly abide in the Son "ought to walk in the same way in which he walked" (2:6)—the way of love and obedience to the Father. They ought to keep that which was taught from the beginning (2:24), observe the commandments of Jesus (3:24), practice love for others in the community (4:12–13, 16), and make the true confession of faith (4:15). In short, they must keep "the doctrine of Christ" to abide in him (2 John 9). Furthermore, it is only at the appearance (or parousia) of Christ that Christians will "be like him"; for only then will they "see him as he is" (3:2). The secessionists, who do not share this view, must therefore have taught that salvation is a matter of a spiritual communion with the glorified Jesus, an abiding in him. They claim thereby to share already in his glorified existence and to be without sin (1:8, 10). Seen under this perspective, the crucifixion of Jesus is not thought to have atoning benefits for sin. The significance of Jesus was not that of dealing with sin,[56] but of providing redemption for the true, spiritual self which is enlightened (as the opponents claim to be, 2:9) and freed from death for life through believing in Jesus and abiding in him. The person who thus abides in him has overcome the world and is in fact incapable of sin.

In response to such a view, the author of the letters spells out what it means to abide in Christ. Moreover, he insists that the crucifixion of Jesus was an atoning death in accord with the will of God: "the blood of Jesus his Son cleanses us from all sin" (1:7); "he is the expiation for our sins" (2:2); "he appeared to take away sins" (3:5) and "to destroy the works of the devil" (3:8); God "loved us and sent his Son to be the expiation for our sins" (4:10). By means of such statements the author asserts the essentials of the kerygma appearing prior to the Epistles of Paul, including both the declaration of the *hyper*-formula (although this writer uses the preposition *peri* instead of *hyper*), that the death of Christ was for the benefit of others, and the simple declaration that "Christ died for our sins" (1 Cor. 15:3). That is to say that Christ, the Son of God, was sent by the Father into the world to bear the consequences of sin for the benefit of others.

It is this "faith," taught from the beginning and reasserted by the writer, that "overcomes the world" (5:4). It does not follow that persons no longer commit sin. Sin is an ever present possibility, and it is by way of confession of sins that there is forgiveness (1:9). Sins are forgiven for the sake of Christ (2:12), who has borne their consequences already and who intercedes before the Father for those who sin (2:1). Twice the author exhorts his readers to refrain from sin in language which comes close to that of the opponents: "no one who abides in him sins" (3:6) and "no one born of God commits sin; for God's nature abides in him, and he cannot sin because he is born of God" (3:9; cf. 5:18). The difference of this position from that of the opponents, however, is that such passages are hortatory; they are not claims made by the writer about himself or his followers.

By way of summary, it can be said that the author of the letters takes over the Johannine view that salvation is mediated by Christ to believers and that this is his starting point. But he makes modifications. That eternal life is given to believers continues to be asserted, but that truth is shown to be fundamentally possible in consequence of the atoning death of Jesus. Further, the gift of eternal life continues to be spoken of as a possession of believers in the present (5:11–13), so that they are "born of God" (3:9; 4:7; 5:4, 18) and are "God's children now" (3:2; cf. 5:1), but the futurity of salvation is brought out more strongly than in the Gospel of John. It is on the basis of abiding in Christ that one can have "confidence" of salvation at his coming (2:28; 3:21) and at "the day of judgment" (4:17), which is taken to be future (not, as in the Gospel of John, an event which takes place also in the moment of a hearer's possible response). It is only at the appearing of Christ that believers will be like him (3:2), sharing in the fullness of salvation.

The redemptive christology of the Fourth Gospel is thus the basis for that which is in the Epistles of John, but it is revised. Like the Fourth Evangelist, the writer of the letters stresses the love of God for the world and the redemptive work of Christ as being in accord with the purpose of God. But he goes beyond the evangelist in his estimation of the scope of Christ's benefits when he says that Christ is "the expiation for our sins, and not for ours only but also for the sins of the whole world" (2:2). The benefits are thus universal in scope. This truth, of course, would be considered by the author to be known only through the gospel. Yet, in a surprising move, the author himself qualifies his own assertion by excluding his opponents. Those who do not practice love for others in the community abide in death (3:14) and walk in darkness (1:9, 11). Further, those who commit "mortal sin" (5:16) appear to be excluded from life, and these persons are most certainly the secessionists.[57] The author might have entertained the expectation of the final salvation of all humanity through the universal and all-sufficient expiation of sins by the crucified Christ: "The darkness is passing away and the true light is already shining" (2:8). But at the moment of writing his letter, in any case, he sees the secessionists as persons who have excluded themselves. This is of interest for the treatment of redemptive christology in the early church as a whole. These persons profess to be Christians, even if they do not profess the truth in the view of the writer. They claim to have fellowship with Christ and to abide in him. Further, if our assumption is correct that they were themselves former members of the Johannine community, they would have been known personally to the writer; they would not have been abstractions ("heretics" in general), but persons known by name (such as Diotrephes, 3 John 9). Here is a most interesting case therefore in which a New Testament writer claims that the redemptive benefits of Christ are effective not only for his own community of Christians, but for the whole world as well, and yet makes an exception: there is no hope, short of repentance, for known Christians considered heretical.

RETROSPECT

The Gospel of John and the Epistles of John have obvious differences in perspective. To gather them under one common type of redemptive christology causes some strains on the type itself, for the letters revise the redemptive christology represented by the Gospel of John. Yet they build upon the foundation provided by the Fourth Gospel. The situation calls for an approach which entails reflection on a number of aspects of the basic type of redemptive christology shared by both the Gospel and the Epistles, but then identifies the strains upon it.

1. The fourth type of redemptive christology shares with the other three the fundamental conviction that redemption is rooted in the purpose of God. The Father has sent the Son for the salvation of the world. Nevertheless, like the third type, the fourth has an essentially christopractic orientation and emphasis. Attention is fastened upon Jesus, the Son, as the one who comes into the world from above to reveal the Father and to mediate salvation to humanity. This theme is made explicit in both the Gospel and the Epistles. The Fourth Evangelist declares that the Son reveals the Father (12:45; 14:9) and that he has authority from the Father to give eternal life to all whom the Father gives him (17:2). And in the letters it is said that "the eternal life which was with the Father. . . was made manifest to us" in the Son (1 John 1:2). The Son is thus the one who mediates salvation (or "life") from the Father to his own.

2. The mediation of salvation by the Son from the Father takes place when and where persons believe in the Son. This is affirmed repeatedly in the Gospel of John (3:16; 5:24; 6:47; etc.), and it is expressed also in the letters: "God gave us eternal life, and this life is in his Son. Whoever has the Son has life; whoever does not have the Son does not have life" (1 John 5:11–12). It is by receiving the Son, that is, by believing the testimony of proclamation about him and thereby believing in the Son himself as the one who reveals the Father, that a person passes from death into life. Not to believe is to remain not only in disbelief but in sin as well. What is involved here is more than a matter of right knowing (*gnōsis*) and right believing. True, the person who does not believe in the Son is in darkness and implied ignorance. But equally important is the christological conviction that the risen, glorified Christ has power to give life (salvation) to those who believe in him. The confidence of believers is not in their knowing and believing, but in the Son himself who came from the Father to give life to those who belong to him. Both the Gospel and the Epistles proclaim to their readers that the one who believes in the Son can be certain of the gift of life (John 5:24; 20:31; 1 John 5:13).

3. As in the other types of redemptive christology, so here the cross and resurrection of Jesus are the presupposition and foundation of redemption. The cross is seen in this type of redemptive christology essentially to mark the end of the Son's earthly career and his return to the Father in heaven, and it is in his exalted state that he is able to grant life to those who believe in him. This has been shown, in the discussion of the Gospel of John, to be a major theme of the Fourth Evangelist. But this way of thinking about the cross is also implicit in the view of the author of the letters. It is not the sum total of the latter's interpretation of the cross, but it provides the foundation for his view—consistent with

the evangelist— that it is the Son in his exalted state who gives life to those who believe in him.

4. The message which flows from this type of redemptive christology consists of both gospel and summons. This is true of all types, but it is particularly pronounced in this type. The message consists of the good news of the love of God for the world and of God's sending the Son for its salvation. But it also consists of a summons to believe in the Son as the one who reveals the Father and who alone mediates salvation. The degree to which both gospel and summons are heard is contingent upon the state of the hearer. Those who are already believers hear the good news, and so the Gospel and Epistles of John have been prized through the centuries within the Christian community as setting forth the gospel with utmost clarity, and probably that would have been so for insiders within the history of the Johannine community as well. But for those on the outside, both the Gospel and the Epistles provide a challenge and a summons to believe in the Son for salvation, and that aspect of the message is not due simply to the writers' manner of expression. It arises out of the nature of this type of redemptive christology, for the type has been forged in a polemical setting. It has been shaped deliberately in such a way that the Christ portrayed comes from above, reveals who he is, gives life to those who accept him, and returns to the Father above. Or, as it is expressed in literary form, the Son has already returned to the Father, and it is through the Son's word proclaimed that the claims for him are made: that is, that he came from the Father and has returned to him, that he has revealed the Father, and that he gives life to those who believe the message. Revelation, or the claim to be a bearer of revelation, calls for a response. For those who hear the message for the first time and for those who stand on the outside of the circle of witnesses, the message consists largely of a proposal and a summons. It cannot be said in the first instance of the proclamation of this type that in Christ God has already reconciled the world to himself or that the sins of the world have been borne by Christ. Rather, the view is that God has given his Son with a view toward the salvation of the world, which is contingent upon faith on the part of individual persons. The overarching message is that whoever believes the Son to be what the message declares him to be— thus authenticating the message for oneself—receives the life he brings. The hearer is thus summoned to believe in Christ, and on the basis of coming to believe can one be first granted the good news of salvation. This means that in the structure of the soteriological message a summons precedes the gospel. The sequence is summons, belief, and then the declaration of the gospel that a person has the gift of life.

5. The redemptive christology of the fourth type, which states more

clearly than any other that salvation is mediated by Christ solely to those who believe in him, is the most exclusivistic of all. Exclusivism is of course built into the very structure of this type. The structure was constructed within the arena of polemics, in which black-and-white distinctions were made between what was considered true and what was considered false. There can be no compromise. Either one accepts the word of revelation, the truth itself, and receives the life promised, or one rejects the word and its truth, remains in sin, and reaps condemnation. It is sometimes thought and said that the significance of the Johannine writings is that they are concerned with the question of truth. But it goes without saying that the truth of which this literature speaks is not the truth of philosophers, the sciences, and courts of law. It is the particular truth claims about Jesus—who he is—as asserted in a unique christology. Those who do not share the estimate given of Jesus by this christology are judged to be in sin and heading for condemnation; in the language of the Gospel of John, they are condemned already (3:18). The magnificence of this type of redemptive christology is its power to give assurance of life to those who believe what is declared about Jesus. But this assurance is forged against the backdrop of its opposite, which considers the world—those who have not heard and those who do not believe—to be lost. There lies its exclusivism, and there too may be its greatest liability when it is compared with the other types.

The redemptive christology of the fourth type was expressed in both the Gospel and Epistles of John, but it did not endure without amendment by the author of the letters. There were those in the Johannine community who accepted the teachings of the Fourth Gospel but drew conclusions concerning Christ and the way of discipleship which were not considered acceptable by the author of the letters. This writer essentially retained the redemptive christology of the Gospel of John. He continued the christopractic orientation and even extended it in speaking of Christ as the "Advocate" of the Christian with the Father (1 John 2:1) and as the one who "appeared" to take away sin (1 John 3:5). The writer also retains the mediatorial view, since eternal life, he says, was made manifest by the Son (1 John 1:2); "this life was in his Son" (1 John 5:11). And it is given to those who believe (1 John 5:12–13). But the author revived and restored the older theme (which, even if this was not a major theme of the evangelist, had left its mark on the traditions contained in the Gospel of John, e.g., at 1:29; 10:11, 15) of the atoning significance of the death of Jesus, and he looked upon the gift of eternal life also as a future inheritance for those who believe and who abide in the Son and the fellowship of his community. He was able to see in the death of Jesus an expiatory event in which Jesus bore sins and their consequences for the benefit of others (1 John 1:7; 2:2; 3:5; 4:10). And the corollary of this is that the good news (or gospel) of Christ's redemptive work now becomes more fully integrated with the summons to believe. The redemptive work of Christ is centered in the cross, and it is asserted as the basis for salvation. The message is heard once again that it is on the basis of an action done, once and for all, that sins and their consequences have been assumed by Christ. Yet the features of summons and exclusivism, so firmly embedded in the redemptive christology presupposed, are not fully submerged. The secessionists are summoned to right thinking about the Son and to a life of love and keeping his commandments. Even though they profess to abide in Christ, they remain outside the scope of the benefits of Christ, unless (by implication) they repent and return to the community of the writer. There is the exclusivist note. It is not the world which is excluded from the benefits of the redemptive work of Christ; in fact, it is declared that Christ is the expiation not only for "our sins" but even "for the sins of the whole world" (1 John 2:2). But those who are excluded are the secessionist Christians. What had been the basis of salvation in the Fourth Gospel—belief in the Son—can now actually be the basis for condemnation if it is erroneous. It is correct belief that is decisive for salvation.

The redemptive christology of the fourth type is thus most clearly expressed by the Fourth Evangelist. He may not have been the first to give it expression, for it may have come to expression already in the Johannine community prior to the writing of the Gospel. But he gave it expression on a literary level in his own Gospel in any case. This type of redemptive christology was subject, more than the others, to early gnostic developments within the Christian movement. The writer of the Johannine Epistles sought to refute such tendencies.[58] Without dismantling the redemptive christology represented in the Gospel, but building upon it, he revived soteriological interpretations which had become dormant. These caused strains upon this type of redemptive christology, but did not burst it asunder, and the effect of his work in the long run was to preserve this type for its reception in the "catholic, orthodox church" (as viewed in retrospect) which was coming into its own.

PART THREE

CHRISTOLOGY AND REDEMPTION IN HISTORY AND THEOLOGY

9

Basic Questions About Redemptive Christology in the New Testament

HAVING REVIEWED THE four main types of redemptive christology in the New Testament, it is our purpose now to step back, look at what has emerged, and seek answers to some basic questions. We shall ask four: Why are there different types? Is there a unity to be found in the diversity? What differences remain? And what does all of this mean?

WHY ARE THERE DIFFERENT TYPES?

The most obvious answer to the question why there are different types of redemptive christology among the books of the New Testament is that these books were written by different authors at different times and places and for different purposes. But while that is true, it is not by itself sufficient. Take the matter of chronology. The first type of redemptive christology emerges in New Testament books earlier than the other three, since it is represented by Paul, the earliest New Testament author. Yet the third type emerges already in Colossians, and that book may antedate the Gospel of Mark, a representative of the first type. The second, third, and fourth types are virtually coeval, and the Gospel of John, an example of the fourth type, may antedate the Pastoral Epistles (exemplifying the third type). Or we can take up the matter of geographical locale. The third type comes to expression in Asia Minor, since the deutero-Paulines (at least the Pastorals, if not all in this group) and the Book of Revelation were undoubtedly written there. But it is quite possible that the Gospel and Epistles of John, representing the fourth type, were composed there as well. The third type is expressed also in 1 Peter and Hebrews, and both of these may have associations with Rome: as the place of authorship in the case of 1 Peter or destination in the case of Hebrews. The point

167

to be made from this is that one cannot think of a "growth" or "development" of redemptive christology through successive stages from the first type to the fourth (as though the types represent stages) in a straight-line course of development of a unified tradition shared among all Christian communities, nor can one say that one type represents, say, Roman Christianity, while another represents Christianity in Asia Minor and still another represents Syrian Christianity.

An accounting for the different types must remain modest in what it seeks to accomplish. It must take into account the factors mentioned already—authorship, chronology, locale, and purpose—but it must consider other factors as well, and these may differ case by case. In each case, however, the factors brought in must include the aims of the authors who give expression to a particular type, plus an assessment of their respective places within the history of early Christianity—a history which is not unilinear, but variegated.

1. The first type of redemptive christology, represented by Paul and Mark, reflects moments of thought and expression which are presumably several years apart (ten to fifteen years), but the two writers share a theopractic emphasis and the view that in Christ God has accomplished his saving activity. The factors affecting each writer's coming to this type of redemptive christology differ. Paul had been a Pharisee, but in his encounter with the risen Christ he was at the same time called to be an apostle to the nations. He saw in Christ the fulfillment of the promises of God to enact a saving deed—the revelation of his righteousness—for the world at the coming of the Messiah or messianic age. He considered his time also to be the era in which the nations would be converted to the worship of the God of Israel, as foretold by the prophets. Paul could not think of himself as a participant in, or a propagator of, a new religion, Christianity. For him, the God of Israel—the only God, who is God of both Jews and gentiles—has sent the Messiah for the redemption of the world. God put forth his Son-Messiah as a means of atonement, and in him God has reconciled the world to himself. By emphasizing the theopractic foundation and thrust of Paul's redemptive christology, we do not deny that his thinking in other respects is highly christocentric. His letters attest an overwhelming sense of the presence of the risen Christ in his own life and in the lives of others; for him, there is newness of life for those who are "in Christ." Moreover, he speaks of Christ's giving himself for a redemptive purpose: "at the right time Christ died for the ungodly" (Rom. 5:6). Yet Paul does not go so far in his letters as those who subsequently were to speak of Christ's offering himself up as a sacrifice (Hebrews), or as one who brings the redeemed to God (1 Peter), or as one who reconciles all things (Colossians and Ephesians). It is God who

reconciles and justifies humanity in the Christ event, his cross and resurrection. Paul belongs more clearly than later writers to the heritage of Israel, thinking thoughts from the "inside" of this heritage, and therefore he expresses a redemptive christology that is theopractic in character.

The evangelist Mark stands at a later historical moment, and he produces a Gospel in which he gives an account of the earthly ministry, passion, death, and reported news of the resurrection of Jesus. Therefore Jesus appears front and center in the story, and he appears furthermore as the Son of Man who acts and teaches with authority. Yet the redemptive christology of Mark is also essentially theopractic; redemption is accomplished by God in Christ. A major factor in Mark's production of this redemptive christology is the aim he set for himself in the actual writing of his Gospel. He sought to provide an account of the "beginning [*archē*] of the gospel" (1:1) proclaimed—or to be proclaimed—in the church, and for him this is the gospel of the crucified and risen one. Mark follows the old canon that the nature of a phenomenon (in this case, the gospel) is disclosed by its origins. An understanding of the gospel entails the view that Jesus came to give his life as a ransom for others, that he was crucified in weakness and raised by God. Although a christopractic note is sounded in the saying that the Son of Man "came to give his life as a ransom for many" (10:45), in fact Jesus is more often spoken of as the one who is (or must be) "given over" to the events which transpire (9:31; 10:33; 14:41; cf. 14:42). And although Jesus foretells his own passion, death, and resurrection three times in the course of the story (8:31; 9:31; 10:33–34), he does not say (contra John 10:18) that he has power to lay down his life and take it up again. The redemptive work is grounded securely in God who initiates and determines the course of events. Jesus acts in accord with the divine necessity (*dei*, "it is necessary") and in accord with the Scriptures. His passion and death are portrayed as moments of his being abandoned by his disciples and even—from the standpoint of the dying Jesus—by God (15:34). His resurrection is due to an act of God (*egērthē*, "he was raised," 16:6), and the news of it to the women at the tomb causes astonishment and numinous awe ("fear," 16:8). For Mark the origins of the gospel are to be found in the divine work of redemption centering on the cross and resurrection; here is the foundation on which the "beginning" rests. Mark knows nothing of the preexistence of Jesus[1]—or at least makes nothing of it—which might qualify Jesus to do the redemptive work by coming to earth from above to rescue humanity. For him Jesus is declared God's Son at his baptism by John, which sets him on a course to be the agent in whom God accomplishes redemption, guiding the obedient Son to the cross, where he dies a miserable death, and then vindicating him and the stated redemptive meaning of his death through the resurrection. Christ is the one in whom the action is carried out, but the principal actor of the drama is God, the unseen, whose glory is revealed in that which he does.

2. The second type of redemptive christology, represented by Matthew and Luke, comes to expression at a time not far removed from Mark, and its beginnings may reach back prior to the writing of these Gospels quite near to Mark's own time. Nevertheless, these two writers stand both in chronology and theological outlook more clearly in the third generation of Christianity when the Christian movement has taken on a discrete identity over against Judaism. For all their differences in purpose and presentation, both set the story of Jesus within the context of redemptive history, seen from a consciously Christian perspective. This may be true of other major writers of the New Testament as well, but it is particularly true of Matthew and Luke. Each in his own way draws lines of continuity from Jesus back into the Old Testament and from Jesus forward to the end of time.

As soon as a redemptive-historical perspective is introduced in a thoroughgoing way, there are consequences for the expression of redemptive christology. Issues of continuity and identity arise, and the "not yet" aspect of salvation has to be stressed in ways not required formerly. The church is then considered the true Israel (Matthew) or the community of the repentant and believing people of God (Luke), in either case the heir of the divine promises. The cross and resurrection, while they are thought to mark the end of the age of promise and the onset of the time of fulfillment, begin to be relegated to the past of an ongoing history which is expected to continue, and the attention of the communities shifts now to the presence of the living Lord in their midst and to the final salvation to come at history's end.

But the most significant point in regard to this type of redemptive christology emerges precisely when one asks the question: What now has happened in consequence of the Christ event? In one sense, nothing has happened. Salvation is considered a future expectation more than a deed accomplished; one cannot say, for example, that in Christ God has reconciled the world to himself. Salvation is a potentiality. It is given to the faithful, the people of God, in consequence of repentance. But this is nothing new, for it had long been taught in Judaism before the Christian era that God freely forgives the repentant and will grant salvation to the penitent at the final judgment. Yet, of course, there is a new element, Jesus. Already in his historical ministry Jesus exercised divinely given authority to forgive sins (Matt. 9:2, 6; Luke 5:20, 24; 7:47–48). And both Matthew and Luke, and so also the communities they serve, consider the risen Jesus to be endowed with authority to grant forgiveness of sins to all persons, and this forgiveness is mediated and exercised in the communities themselves. At this point—where the forgiveness of sins is enacted, exercised by believers in the name of Christ—a step has been taken that ventures beyond the practices of the synagogue, and it is an offense to the latter. In sum, this type of redemptive christology portrays Christ as the one in whom the redemptive purposes of God are confirmed. Salvation is essentially future, and it is contingent upon a person's fidelity to the end, but its assurance is certified in the present to the faithful.

In this type of redemptive christology the theopractic emphasis is less clear than in the first, but it is still there. History is seen to be a totality, a course of events directed by God in which the Scriptures of old reach their culmination in the era of Christ and his church, an era extending to the end of time. In neither Matthew nor Luke is Christ portrayed as preexistent, or as one who comes from heaven to earth to rescue humanity (as in the third and fourth types), or even as one who gives himself through an atoning death for the benefit of others (as in the first and third types). He is rather the one through whom the divine pledge of forgiveness of sins and final salvation has been confirmed. Yet there are strains on the theopractic emphasis. It is giving way to a christopractic one, for Christ has been exalted by God, grants forgiveness to his own because he has authority to do so, and will act on God's behalf at the final judgment (Matt. 25:31–46; Acts 10:42; 17:31). Yet this redemptive christology retains the theopractic accent in two ways: (1) in its re-demptive-historical framework, by which history (including the story and destiny of Jesus) is regarded as divinely ordered; and (2) in its view that Christ does not actually accomplish redemption for humanity through his cross and resurrection, but that God confirms his purposes to do so through him. Salvation is a future prospect, for which divine forgiveness exercised by Christ through his church is a preparation.

3. The third type of redemptive christology is expressed in various documents of the subapostolic era: the deutero-Paulines, 1 Peter, Hebrews, and Revelation. Common to all of them is that, although redemption is thought as a matter of course to be founded in the will and purpose of God, it is Christ who acts decisively and victoriously to redeem humanity. All of these documents speak of Christ's preexistence, his coming to earth from above to rescue humanity, and his exaltation and reign over the cosmos. It is Christ who reconciles all things in heaven and on earth to himself (Colossians) or to God (Ephesians); who appears, gives his life for others, abolishes death, and brings life and imperishability to light (the Pastorals); who brings humanity to God (1 Peter); who offers his own blood as a sacrifice for sins (Hebrews); and who is victorious over the devil, death, and Hades (Revelation).

Since there are several documents expressing this type of redemptive christology and since they differ from one another greatly in terms of genre, setting, and aim, it is more difficult to discern the factors which go into the expression of this type. Nevertheless, there are certain factors which can be considered determinative. The first is the chronological factor. This should not be pressed too far, for other writings portraying different types of redemptive christology coincide with these writings. Yet all the writers in this group are heirs to a developing Christian theological tradition. The era of the apostles and others of the first generation is over, and the subapostolic era is one in which redemptive christology must be expressed within new contexts, drawing upon but refashioning traditional formulations. The second factor, very closely related, is that the writers themselves reflect a maturity of christological reflection from long acquaintance with the Christian faith, which may be lifelong in some or even all cases. The situation is quite different from that of Paul and others of the first generation who were in the position of having to formulate redemptive christology at the dawn of the Christian movement, forging it by the fusion of proclamation, scriptural traditions, and traditions about Jesus for both themselves and those whom they addressed. Now the older formulations are in place as a foundation on which to build, and the various edifices built upon the foundations must be habitable for distinctly Christian communities which are made up primarily of gentiles and which are devotees of Christ. The third factor, again very closely related, is that these writers inherit liturgical, creedal, and hymnic compositions. These are all "second person" in focus,[2] speaking of Christ as a redemptive figure—preexistent, appearing on earth for a redemptive purpose, dying, being exalted, and reigning.[3] Of course it is true that liturgical, creedal, and hymnic materials were in existence from very early times and were therefore available for writers expressing other types of redemptive christology. So Paul, for example, incorporated a hymn in his letter to the Philippians (2:5–11) and undoubtedly much more throughout his letters, and the Synoptic Gospels employed liturgical materials, such as the Lord's Prayer (Matt. 6:9–13; Luke 11:2–4) and the liturgically formulated account of the last supper (Mark 14:22–25; Matt. 26:26–29; Luke 22:14–21). But in the case of Paul the theopractic accent, as already indicated, continues to predominate, and the writing of the Synoptic Gospels did not lend itself to the use of liturgical, creedal, and hymnic materials which would—in the words of Pliny the Younger—render honor "to Christ, as to a god."[4] But the writers expressing the third type of redemptive christology could and did draw upon the rich heritage of materials available, and it is likely that this factor was the main source and catalyst in the expression of redemptive christology in this form within communities quite firmly established in the last third of the first century. A fourth factor must have been the christological use and adaptation of a model, found already in the Jewish wisdom tradition, which assigns a role for intermediary figures.[5] In the Wisdom of Solomon, for example, there is a transfer of divine attributes and actions to Wisdom herself, including the creation of the world (9:1–2) and the deliverance of Israel from Egypt (10:15–21). This tradition of ascribing divine attributes and functions to intermediaries would have provided a conceptual basis and even legitimation for a christopractic redemptive christology in the course of development.

Were there additional factors? Could it be that the development of this type of redemptive christology was also dependent on concepts from the emperor cult and the so-called gnostic redeemer myth? In regard to the first, the writer of Revelation is clearly aware of the emperor cult, and the writer of the Pastorals uses terminology similar to it.[6] Yet the rise of the type itself antedates these documents, and it can be attributed to the factors already listed. In regard to the second, the same judgment can be applied. The existence of a gnostic outlook in the era being considered can hardly be denied, for traces of it can be found in the New Testament itself.[7] But that a gnostic redeemer myth antedated the rise of this type of redemptive christology is doubtful.[8] Again, the rise of this type can be attributed to the factors already considered. But finally we must ask whether the development of this type of redemptive christology arose in response to persecution, so that Christians sought to portray Christ as a figure of strength and final victory. Again, the answer must be negative, for while 1 Peter, Hebrews, and Revelation provide evidence that the communities addressed have known, or presently experience, persecution, that is not so in the case of the deutero-Paulines—certainly not in Colossians and the Pastorals at least (in the case of Ephesians the matter is less clear, depending on the meaning of 6:12). Colossians attests the rise of this type prior to any general persecution of Christians.

4. The fourth type of redemptive christology, expressed by the writers of the Gospel and Epistles of John, shares features with the third type. The theopractic note is not lacking, for God has sent the Son. Yet the christopractic emphasis is there, and it dominates. Christ is the Revealer and the Redeemer, the one who descends from above, reveals the Father, and mediates salvation to his own (Gospel of John). Or he is portrayed as the "Advocate" of Christians before the Father and the one who "appeared to take away sins" (1 John 2:1; 3:5). The factors which affected the presentation of each writer—the evangelist and the writer of the letters—would include those already mentioned for the third type: a third-generation setting; authors who have long been Christians themselves

and who have reflected intently on the Christian tradition to which they are heirs; the existence of liturgical, creedal, and hymnic materials which speak of Christ as a redemptive figure; and the tradition of ascribing divine attributes and functions to intermediaries (to Jesus in Christian tradition). These factors do not of course account for the writing of the Johannine Gospel and Epistles any more than they or other factors do for the writing of any other books in the New Testament, but they have a formative influence on the type of redemptive christology that is given expression.

In addition to these four factors there is another. That is the polemical setting of the Fourth Evangelist and, at a later time, that of the author of the Epistles. The history of the Johannine community is one of polemics with Jews who do not share belief in Jesus as the Christ, perhaps with other Christians who do not share the heights of christology developed here, and—when the letters were written—most certainly with those of the community who go farther than the letter writer is willing to go, denying the essential humanity of Jesus and his saving work through the cross, and who have actually left the community by the time the writer produced the letters. Given their polemical contexts, the writers of the Gospel and Epistles of John portray a type of redemptive christology in which the burning focus is on Christ as the one who mediates salvation from God to those who believe in him. Those who believe have life. In this perspective there is no room for the view that in Christ God has reconciled the world to himself. The world is portrayed as lost. Moreover, those who hear the gospel but do not believe are condemned already (the Gospel of John), and even those who profess to be Christians but belong to the secessionist party are excluded from life as well (the Epistles of John).

IS THERE UNITY WITHIN
THE DIVERSITY?

A review of the different types of redemptive christology exposes the diversity among them. Much of the diversity, as indicated in the preceding section, can be accounted for because different factors influenced the development of each type. Yet it is obvious that all types, and the documents which express them, are bound together in a common interest, which is to speak of Christ and his benefits. They belong to the same religious movement, which is rooted in the story and people of Israel, but which has been given its peculiar character within the heritage of Israel in consequence of the ministry, death, and resurrection of Jesus of Nazareth. So, in spite of the different factors influencing them and the diversity of their expressions, we are asking here whether the four types share a common theological perspective. Undoubtedly there are many commonalities, but we shall itemize four which have to do with redemption in particular.

1. Redemptive christology is always grounded in the purposes of the God of Israel. This is made clear particularly in the first two types, but is not lacking in the other two. As indicated previously, there was a tendency already in some circles and traditions of Judaism prior to the rise of Christianity to ascribe divine attributes and functions to intermediaries, particularly to Wisdom. Judaism was flexible enough to allow for intermediaries to act on God's behalf without losing its monotheistic character and confession. Christians were able likewise to speak in a christopractic way without cutting themselves off from their monotheistic moorings. Christ never replaces the God of Israel, nor does he become a second god. And regardless of how far certain types of redemptive christology went to focus on Christ as the one who does the redemptive work, they did not weaken the conviction that redemption is willed and initiated by the God of Israel. In fact, all the writers affirm it without reservations.

2. Redemptive christology in the New Testament is then never expressed in such a way that Christ performs an action on behalf of humanity over against God. There is no thought, for example, of Christ's appeasing the wrath or justice of God. The apostle Paul says on one occasion that Christians will be saved by Christ from the wrath of God on the basis of justification through Christ's blood (Rom. 5:9), and yet this statement comes immediately after the assertion that God has shown his love in the death of Christ for "sinners" (5:8). There is no thought of a split between God and Christ in which Christ steps in to avert the wrath of an angry God. This is true even in the third type in which Christ is portrayed as the agent of redemption most clearly. In 1 Peter it is said that Christ died for sins "in order that he might bring us to God" (3:18). Yet it was God who had destined him for this purpose and caused his manifestation "at the end of times" for the sake of humanity (1:20). Again in Hebrews Christ is the one who offered himself up (7:27) by means of his own blood, securing an eternal redemption (9:12). Yet it was God who appointed him for his task and designated him a priest who is competent to offer such a sacrifice (5:5–6). A "satisfaction theory" of the atonement cannot therefore be derived from the New Testament. Christ is indeed portrayed as the one who bears sins, dies on behalf of others in order to redeem them, and is even the one in whom sin is concentrated and condemned (Rom. 8:3). But the work of Christ is finally and invariably the work of God in him, through him, or by him.

3. Redemptive christology in all its forms presupposes the cross and

resurrection of Jesus. The only question is where the cross and resurrection fit into the panorama. In the first type the cross is seen to be the atoning event, the moment at which Christ bears sin and its consequences in himself for the benefit of others, and the resurrection is his vindication and the inauguration of his reign and the new age of salvation. The same note is struck in the third type, although here the tendency is to think of the resurrection of Jesus as inaugurating his reign over the cosmos, and less emphasis is placed on the dawn of the new age; the communities look toward a future inheritance. In the second type the cross and resurrection are set within the context of redemptive history, and no atoning significance is assigned to the cross explicitly at the redactional level. Nevertheless, the cross and resurrection are presupposed as the means by which Christ is exalted to a status of having competence (authority) to grant forgiveness of sins. And in the fourth type, while again the cross is not a means of atonement in itself, it is the means by which the Son is glorified and returns to the Father—which the post-resurrection narrative certifies—so that he can grant life to those whom the Father gives him, those who believe in him.

The fact that the cross and resurrection play so important a role in the various types of redemptive christology has implications for our study as a whole. If it were the case that the "most primitive Christology of all" (as described by John A. T. Robinson; see chapter 2) attached redemptive significance only to the "Christ elect," and not to the cross and resurrection, then we would have to conclude that a major transformation came about very early and that it was pervasive, affecting all transitions and types of redemptive christology. It seems that a better approach is to broaden our understanding of what we mean by redemptive significance. If we mean simply an interpretation of the death of Christ as an atoning event by which sin is borne or canceled at the cross, we can say that such an interpretation may indeed have been lacking at the outset, for in fact it is lacking in later documents and types of redemptive christology as well. But that is to write the rules too narrowly. The question is whether there was a development of redemptive christology which initially looked solely to the future (the parousia) for redemption and then at a later stage (as in a straight-line development) looked back to the cross. That can be demonstrated not to be the case, as shown in chapter 2. Rather, from the outset and then in all types of redemptive christology, the cross and resurrection—taken together as a unity—are seen to be the event in which redemption is achieved (as in types one and three) or made possible (as in types two and four). Whether or not an atoning significance is attached specifically and solely to the death of Christ, a redemptive significance is universally attached to the death and resurrection as a unity. A new world is made possible for humanity through Christ who has been crucified and raised, now reigns, and is present through the Spirit in the communities of those who acclaim him as Lord.

4. Redemptive christology in all its forms also asserts that a decisive turn of the ages has taken place in the cross and resurrection of Jesus, that a new age has been inaugurated, and that it is possible for persons to participate in this new age through fellowship with the risen Christ and one another. This is sometimes more an assumption than a claim, but it is always present in one way or another. It is expressed clearly in the first type, particularly in the writings of Paul, and also in the fourth type, especially in the Gospel of John. In these two types those who have heard the gospel and believe it live "in Christ" (Paul) or "abide" in Christ (John) and understand themselves to have been created anew (Paul) or to have passed from death to life (John). In the second and third types the concepts of the turn of the ages and the inauguration of the new age are present as well, even if these are bound up more with Christ and his destiny than with the self-understanding of believers. In the redemptive christology of the second type, represented by Matthew and Luke, the Christ event marks a moment of transition. The times have been fulfilled, and the present is a phase of the era of Christ, in which forgiveness of sins is exercised in the name of Christ. And in the redemptive christology of the third type Christ is the one who has appeared "once for all at the end of the age" (Heb. 9:26); and since he has won redemption and has authority over the cosmos, it follows that a new age has come into being, even if it is essentially a future inheritance "kept in heaven" (1 Pet. 1:4) for the redeemed. The degree to which each type succeeds in explicating the full implications of a turn of the ages varies, and that issue will be taken up in the next chapter, but at this point it can be said that all four types come to terms with it in one way or another.

WHAT DIFFERENCES REMAIN?

Granted that there is a unity among the types of redemptive christology, there are obvious differences as well. Here one could provide an extensive list, including such items as the degrees of theopractic or christopractic emphasis in each, whether Christ is portrayed as engaging cosmic powers or not, differences in nuance concerning the nature of Christ as a prerequisite for his work, and so on. But our interest here will be confined to three issues which emerge from a study of all four types and which bear directly on the benefits of Christ.

1. The first issue we cite has to do with what we might call the christological "moments" of redemption, those points along the course of the

redeeming work of Christ: his preexistence, incarnation, earthly ministry, passion and death, resurrection/exaltation, ascension, reign, and parousia. Of these various moments, it is striking that the second type of redemptive christology, expressed by Matthew and Luke, stands alone in lacking an affirmation of the preexistence and incarnation. (The Gospel of Mark lacks the same, but this lack is not characteristic of the first type as type, for Paul affirms Christ's preexistence and incarnation. This type neither requires nor precludes these moments.) If the question is raised whether there is a New Testament consensus on where the focus of redemptive action lies, it is clearly on the cross and resurrection, not the incarnation. The second type of redemptive christology portrays the "coming" of Christ into the world through a virginal conception by the Holy Spirit some nine months before his birth. Prior to that, by implication, there was no Son from eternity. And without a preexistent Son there can be no incarnation.

2. The second issue concerns time. In all expressions of redemptive christology both the "already" and "not yet" aspects of salvation are touched upon. But the emphases differ. The first and fourth types emphasize the "already" aspect without losing sight of the "not yet"; conversely, the second and third types emphasize the "not yet" without losing sight of the "already." It is no accident—indeed it is to be expected—that modern existentialist theology has found Paul and the Gospel of John to be preeminent in the New Testament for giving significance to the present life of the believer, so that the believer understands himself or herself to have entered already into newness of life (or "authentic existence" in the modern terminology). But this insight is due not only to an existentialist reading of the New Testament, even if such a reading has underscored it. There is a difference to be seen. The second and third types, while they assert no less that the cross and resurrection mark a turning point, look upon salvation as essentially future. The time between the resurrection and the parousia is under the reign of Christ, and Christ exercises his reign through the believing community. But the radicality of Paul and John is lacking, for Paul could say that whoever is in Christ is a new creation (2 Cor. 5:17), and John could say that the believer has passed from death to life (5:24). In the second type salvation is assured for those who receive forgiveness of sins from Christ and remain faithful to the end. And in the third type salvation is a future "inheritance"—a term they all use. To be sure, Paul uses the language of a future inheritance too (cf. 1 Cor. 6:9–10; Gal. 5:21). But he also speaks of believers as already heirs of the promises of God given to Abraham (Gal. 3:29; 4:7) and fellow heirs with Christ (Rom. 8:17). In short, he can speak of Christians as already having received an inheritance, for the inheritance

of which he speaks is the fulfillment of the promises to Abraham in the past. In all four types it can be said that salvation in its unrestricted fullness is future, but in the case of Paul and John it is realized in the present as well by those who believe. The era between the resurrection and the parousia, for those who believe, is not primarily the final stage of the old era, but rather the initial stage of the fullness of life in the new age which has dawned.

3. The third issue has to do with the scope of redemption. Here there is little agreement, and types alone do not determine the results. A zigzag pattern runs through them. Paul envisions the redemption accomplished in Christ as effective for all humanity. To be sure, there are places at which Paul can speak of eschatological peril, but these are in hortatory contexts. In those places at which he treats Christ's redemptive work most thoroughly he speaks of God's reconciling the world to himself, the justification of all persons in Christ's death, the final salvation of Israel, and the universal acclamation of Jesus as Lord. The scope of redemption as reaching out to all humanity is also affirmed or envisioned in Colossians, Ephesians, the Pastoral Epistles, and the Book of Revelation. But other books do not share in this breadth of redemptive benefits. Concerning those who have never heard the gospel there is silence in the Gospels of Mark, Matthew, and Luke, and also in 1 Peter and Hebrews. In the Gospel of John it must be concluded that the world is lost; salvation is given only to those who hear the word of Jesus and believe in him. And in certain books the worst off of all people are those who have heard the gospel but do not believe it (the Gospel of John), "do not obey" it (1 Peter), commit apostasy (Hebrews), or—even if they do believe—do not believe as they ought (the Johannine Epistles).

WHAT DOES THIS MEAN?

We have four main types of redemptive christology in the New Testament. When they are analyzed and examined, it is clear that they cannot be harmonized. This has implications for the study of the New Testament in the context of the community of those who have a vested interest in it, the church. It is appropriate to recognize points of similarity—which everyone wants to do—but it is necessary to acknowledge and come to terms with points of disagreement too. The result is that the church is then forced to step back, once the work of observation has been done, and seek to think through a redemptive christology for its own time which is responsive and responsible both to the New Testament and to its own time and place. This will involve an affirmation of the central and unified claims of the New Testament, but beyond that it may involve saying yes to some things and no to others when these are disputed within the New Testament itself. The closing chapter seeks to offer a responsible sketch of what that might entail. But first we shall make an assessment of the four types as a basis for that endeavor.

10

An Assessment of the Four Main Types of Redemptive Christology in the New Testament

GIVEN THE DIFFERENT types of redemptive christology in the New Testament, the question arises concerning the strengths and weaknesses of each. Perhaps that is the inevitable consequence of constructing typologies. We begin to ask whether any one type within a typological presentation is more adequate than the others in giving expression to the matter under study.

THE SEARCH FOR CRITERIA

The problem we face in evaluating the types of redemptive christology in the New Testament is considerable. What criterion or criteria could possibly be used to assess their strengths, weaknesses, and adequacy? Some options come to mind. First, one could ask: Which type is the most common, or catholic, expression of the faith of the Christian church in the New Testament era? Here one would probably settle on the third type, which portrays Christ as the one who wins redemption. This type comes to expression in the largest number of writings, is the most consciously "Christian," and continues to be expressed in writings of the Apostolic Fathers and Apologists.[1] But is the question posed the right one? One could ask second, for example: Which type preserves continuity most clearly with the proclamation of Jesus? Here the third type would be seen to be less adequate. One could ask as a third possibility: Is any one type the presupposition on which the others rest? Here it might be tempting to claim that the first is the presupposition of the others, and one might then consider the other three to be dependent upon it. But this would not work. While the deutero-Pauline letters and probably 1 Peter are dependent upon Pauline Christianity, the type of redemptive christology they express, along with Hebrews and Revelation, has an integrity of its own. And the types represented by Matthew and Luke (type two) and the Johannine Gospel and Epistles (type four) are not dependent on the first. Each of the four types should be considered to be a facet or angle of vision on redemptive christology, each in its own way giving expression through different avenues of reflecting theologically on both the common tradition and traditions peculiar to the various writers, each pursuing different goals, and each influenced by other factors as well.

The question of adequacy can be asked in another way altogether: Is the redemptive christology of each type adequate for the purposes intended? Here it may well be that each of the types would be assessed as equally adequate. The intentions of the writer of Revelation differ from those of Paul, for example, and therefore the former is constrained by his own goals to express redemptive christology in the way he does, adopting a type of redemptive christology clearly distinct from the type found in the Pauline letters. He does not belong primarily to a missionary situation, but to a situation in which those already evangelized are exhorted to endure under the reign of Christ in the face of horrible conditions of persecution.

But having said that, it is proper to ask the question of adequacy in still another way. This involves asking theological and historical questions. First, it is appropriate to ask whether each type portrays the redemption of humanity within the context of decisive emphases of the Scriptures (Old and New Testaments), the canonical context. Second, it is fitting to ask whether each type takes seriously the historical ministry of Jesus of Nazareth as one who was answerable to God for others—a concept which we shall develop later. By asking such questions we inevitably leave the descriptive task behind, enter into theological and historical criticism, and run the risk of bringing our own discernent of what we consider the "heart of the matter" into the discussion. We could easily assign theological priority to one or more types and imply that others are less significant. In response to this, it must be emphasized that all four types deserve equal hearing, that all four types offer valid ways of looking at the matter, and that all four not only have, but ought to have, an enduring place in constructive theological work and in the proclamation of the church. But if theological inquiry is to be an instructive and constructive discipline, it is fitting to place the four types under the spotlight of theological and historical criticism. Our suggestion of (1) the redemption of humanity within the canonical context and (2) the historical ministry of Jesus as the two critical foci may not be the only way of approaching the matter; one can ask about the adequacy of the criteria.

But these two criteria are basic for a critical assessment, for the way in which redemptive christology is expressed ought to cohere with the larger panorama of Scripture and with the historical ministry of Jesus, insofar as the latter can be known.

CRITERION ONE: THE REDEMPTION OF HUMANITY WITHIN THE CANONICAL CONTEXT

The question raised here is whether the various types portray the actual redemption (or liberation) of humanity through the cross and resurrection of Jesus and do so against the background of the Scriptures of Israel and the rise of the Christian community. We shall ask five questions in regard to this and make brief responses.

1. Does a given type preserve the theopractic character of the Scriptures so that the God of Israel is the one who acts to redeem humanity? While it is certainly the case that each of the four types grounds the work of redemption securely in the purposes of God, this is seen to be asserted most clearly in types one and two. Types three and four tend to present Christ as the actor in the drama of redemption, either as the one who enters the world from above to rescue humanity (type three) or as the one who is the sole mediator of salvation (type four). They are christopractic in their essential thrust.

2. Does a given type set forth the cross and resurrection of Christ as the focal point of divine redemption? The cross and resurrection is presupposed for redemption in all four types; there can be no redemption otherwise. But the cross and resurrection is not universally understood to be *the* focal point in the sense that the death of Christ itself is given redemptive significance. Such an interpretation appears explicitly in the first and third types, but it does not appear in the second (Matthew and Luke) and in the primal expression of the fourth (the Gospel of John). The author of the Johannine Epistles is able to incorporate it into his thought and expression, but it does not belong to the type in and of itself.

3. Does a given type maintain the conviction that in the cross and resurrection of Christ something decisive was actually done for humanity as an act of liberation? Again a judgment must be made which corresponds to our answer to the second question. The answer to our question is clearly affirmative in the first and third types. But the second type, expressed by Matthew and Luke, lacks the claim that something was actually done—in the sense of relief from bondage once and for all—for humanity in the cross and resurrection. In the view of this type Christ has been exalted and given authority to exercise forgiveness of sins in the time between the resurrection and parousia, and the beneficiaries of the exercise of forgiveness are members of the church who repent and remain steadfast disciples (and continue to ask for forgiveness; cf. Matt. 6:12; Luke 11:4) to the end when the final judgment will take place. And in the fourth type, as expressed by the Fourth Evangelist, Christ is the one who has, by means of his cross, returned to the Father and from his glorified position gives life to those whom the Father gives him, but a once-for-all act of liberation has not been made. On the other hand, the writer of the Johannine Epistles recovers the redemptive significance of the death of Christ which had left its mark on the Johannine tradition earlier. Here there are strains on the type itself, for the claim of a redemptive deed having been done is not integral to the structure of the type itself.

4. *Does a given type assert the view that the Christ event marks the "turn of the ages," so that the resurrection of Jesus signals the inauguration of the new age?* All four types assert such to one degree or another. It is most explicit in the first type, expressed by Paul and Mark, but it is also expressed clearly in the fourth type, even if in a different way, where it can be said that a "turn of the ages" has occurred for the believer, who passes from death to life. In the second and third types, however, the new age which has dawned tends to be assigned to the supratemporal and supraspatial sphere into which the risen Christ has entered, while for the Christian the new age remains essentially a future and otherworldly prospect. Christ has entered into his reign and has authority over all things in heaven and on earth, so his resurrection signals the turn of the ages in regard to his own destiny, and it certifies the destiny of Christians. But it cannot be said that Christians have already entered into the life of the new age. The whole Christ event can be seen as a time of fulfillment, to be sure, and in the era between the resurrection and the parousia the church comes into being and receives certain benefits of the new age (the gospel, the Spirit, and forgiveness) in consequence of Christ's reign. But this era is understood to be primarily an anticipation of the new age of redemption. That which has been confirmed through Christ (type two) or won by Christ (type three) is, in the words of 1 Peter, "an inheritance . . . kept in heaven" (1:4). In the meantime the Christian community is called to fidelity, endurance, struggle, and witness, aided by power from above. Redemption has been confirmed or even won by Christ for others, but in the second and third types it cannot be said that believers themselves are already a new creation (as in Paul) or that they have passed from death to life (as in John). Any thought of newness of life having been given is set within the context of a course of life leading to the promised goal, aided by the Spirit; and

the place of believers along that course can be thought of as (1) near the beginning in hortatory contexts or (2) near the end in passages which address and encourage those facing persecution.

5. *Does a given type provide an integral place for the emergence and preservation of a community which understands itself to be the immediate beneficiary of redemption?* Here it must be said that each of the four types envisions the emergence and preservation of a community, the church. But there are differences in perspective. When we ask whether a given community considers itself to be the "immediate" beneficiary of redemption—in other words, that it has been set free in the manner of an exodus into a new world—that applies to the first and fourth types which accent the "already" aspect of redemption (without losing its futurity), whereas the second and third types understand the day of redemption, the event of liberation into a new world, to be in the future.

It will be seen from this brief analysis that of the four types it is the first which meets the criterion proposed most adequately. It could of course be argued that the five questions raised are all "Pauline" in orientation, so that the argument is actually circular. But that is not the case, for each of the five items can be seen to have either their implicit or explicit manifestation in all four types, even if not with equal success. Paul is not then the model by which the others are measured. He is simply the one who gives expression to all five points most explicitly.

CRITERION TWO: THE HISTORICAL MINISTRY OF JESUS

Each type should also be measured against at least two facets related to the historical ministry of Jesus: (1) whether it takes the humanity of Jesus with utmost seriousness; and (2) whether it preserves continuity with what was most characteristic of his ministry.

1. In regard to the first point, it is the first type of redemptive christology which takes the humanity of Jesus most seriously. In both Paul and Mark, to be sure, there are elements of a high christology. Paul alludes to the preexistence of Christ, and Mark portrays Jesus as having knowledge of his forthcoming passion, death, and resurrection, which could imply so-called "divine foreknowledge"—but then it might imply only prophetic discernment.

Yet in both cases the humanity of Jesus is essentially preserved. In the case of Paul, "nowhere is it suggested" that in his earthly ministry Christ "brought with him any of the glory of his earlier status or that he enjoyed any freedom from the limitations of our human lot."[2] Paul emphasizes rather the lowliness, weakness, and scandalous death of the Christ, and he declares that his resurrection was an act of God; Christ "was raised" or God "raised" him from the dead (Rom. 6:4; 8:11; 10:9; 1 Cor. 15:4, 15, 20; Gal. 1:1; etc.). There is no thought that Jesus himself had power to lay down his life and to take it up again as he does in the Gospel of John (10:18). Likewise Mark, who knows nothing of a doctrine of preexistence, asserts that Jesus, with a sense of being abandoned by his own and seemingly by God himself, truly suffered and died an excruciating death, but was raised through an act of divine vindication.

To leave types aside for a moment, it must be granted that none of the New Testament writers would likely have denied the humanity of Jesus if asked about it. But in the documents we have, there are none, with the possible exception of Hebrews, which go as far as Paul and Mark to take the humanity of Jesus seriously, that is, to think of him as a flesh-and-blood person, as one who, in the words of Ignatius, "was really born, ate, and drank; was really persecuted under Pontius Pilate; was really crucified and died."[3] While Matthew and Luke write accounts of his ministry—and they undoubtedly thought that they were writing about an earthly, historical figure—in fact they portray a figure who had been conceived by the Holy Spirit and not by a human father, who goes to the cross with regal bearing (Matthew) or as an exemplary martyr (Luke) and in both cases with controlled consent, who incarnates Wisdom (Matthew) or who is called "the Lord" frequently by the narrator (Luke). The writers who express the third type of redemptive christology tend to lose sight of the humanity of Jesus too. They portray a Christ who, as a preexistent figure, comes from above to rescue humanity and then returns to his former place of glory over the creation. This Christ can hardly be said to share fully in the human condition or to be a human being in the ordinary sense of the term. While it would be said later in the history of christological reflection that Christ cannot redeem that which he has not first assumed,[4] it must be said that in the third type of redemptive christology Christ is portrayed as one who does in fact rescue what he does not fully share. A possible exception among writers belonging to this group is the author of Hebrews, who claims that Chist partook of human nature and tasted death (2:14), was "made like his brethren in every respect" (2:17), and was even "tempted as we are, yet without sin" (4:15). At least in a formal way the writer seems to claim that Christ dispensed with his former, preexistent dignity at the point of his incarnation. Whether the writer actually succeeds in carrying this out in a material way is debated,[5] but in any case the writer asserts the humanity of Jesus to a degree seldom matched among writers of the New Testament. Finally, it is not possible to say in regard to the fourth type of redemptive christology, represented by the Gospel and Epistles of John, that the Jesus presented shares fully in the human condition, in spite of John 1:14 and 1 John 4:2. The verdict of Ernst Käsemann continues to stand, in which he says that in his Gospel "John changes the Galilean teacher into the God who goes about on earth";[6] he is "the one who walks on earth as a stranger, as the messenger sent by the Father, the one who passes through death without turmoil and with jubilation, because he has been called back to the realm of freedom."[7] Or one may put the matter in another way, as James Dunn has: Jesus is portrayed as the preexistent "divine being who was sent into the world and whose ascension was simply the continuation of an intimate relationship with the Father which neither the incarnation nor crucifixion interrupted or disturbed."[8]

2. In regard to the question whether a given type of redemptive christology preserves continuity with what was most characteristic of the ministry of Jesus, it is necessary to preface the discussion with a crisp indication of what can be considered most characteristic. Whatever else Jesus said or did, he declared forgiveness and salvation from God to those who were considered by contemporaries to be unworthy of either.[9] Further, although it is not likely that he spoke of himself as the Messiah, he identified with a redefined messianic role from the time of his baptism by John and in his own words and deeds actualized the coming of the kingdom.[10] Jesus, the prophet of the kingdom, revealed the nature of the messianic kingdom by acting out the role of one who embodies the features of life in the messianic kingdom, representing the kingdom proleptically to his contemporaries. In this regard it can be said that he was more than a prophet of the kingdom. For as one who represented the kingdom to others by his own words and deeds, and who embodied in his own life the features of the kingdom, he was a figure standing on the boundary between this world and the kingdom to come. And although he was a flesh-and-blood person in this world, it was possible for those who followed him to perceive a transcendent quality in him and to regard him as one who was destined already to have a leading role, and therefore a preeminence, in the kingdom to come. He acted with divine authority to forgive sins and declare salvation to others—persons who then went away believing that they had forgiveness and salvation. *In so doing, Jesus freed men and women by assuming to himself the burden of sins and their consequences; he acted as one who was answerable to God for others, and who expected the vindication of his actions by God. And the vindication of his actions would certify that he had truly acted on God's behalf, that God was in him, liberating and reconciling the estranged to himself.* He went on to accept crucifixion on the basis of the charge of being the Messiah, a charge which he did not reject. To put it as crisply as we can,

Jesus so identified with a redefined messianic role that the line of de-
marcation was worn away and even crossed; he was, in his own way, a
redemptive, messianic figure. It is only a very small step from this for
his disciples to understand later that his death and resurrection, considered as a unity, was redemptive as well. For after his death and resurrection his followers experienced both his presence among them and
newness of life through the presence and power of the Spirit.[11] From this
vantage point it could be seen that it was precisely through Jesus' cross
and resurrection that redemption had been accomplished. *The one who
had assumed the burden of others in his historical ministry had assumed
the burden of all people once and for all, for his resurrection and the
pouring out of the Spirit mark the beginning of the new age, which has
universal, cosmic dimensions.* The cross and resurrection event is so
decisive and disruptive that the universe is no longer the same as it was
previously. A new world has been opened up.

Each of the four types of redemptive christology can be regarded as
continuing the essential character of the ministry of Jesus as sketched
out here. But there are profound differences among them. The first type,
represented by Paul and Mark, is again the most explicit. Paul does not
of course present an account of the ministry of Jesus, but the Christ of
whom he speaks is the one who assumes the burden of others in his
crucifixion and whose resurrection inaugurates the age of salvation. The
Gospel of Mark, on the other hand, portrays Jesus as the one who assumes
the burden of others in both his earthly ministry and his death as a
"ransom for many." The second type, represented by Matthew and Luke
at the level of their redaction of traditions, represents Jesus as the one
who assumes the burden of others in his earthly ministry and who continues to do so in his exalted state, but it lacks the claim that something
was actually done for human redemption in his cross and resurrection
in the sense of attaching a redemptive significance to the cross or to the
cross and resurrection as a unity. The third type, which portrays Christ
as the one who wins redemption, continues the theme that Christ assumed the burden of others in his redemptive death. Moreover, the christopractic emphasis of this type can be seen to have its roots in the historical ministry of Jesus himself, for Jesus assumed the burden of others.
But what has happened is that what can be assigned to the historical
ministry of Jesus has been extended both backward and forward, so that
Christ is seen as the preexistent one who comes from above to redeem
humanity and carries out his work in his death and resurrection, with
the result that the whole of redemption is given a christopractic stamp
and the theopractic emphasis of the Scriptures begins to recede. Finally,
the fourth type of redemptive christology, in which Christ is the mediator

of salvation, preserves by definition the tradition that Jesus offers salvation to God for humanity. Yet, as indicated previously, it assigns no atoning significance to his death per se. His death is the means of his return to the Father, from whose side he offers salvation (life) to those who believe in him, those whom the Father gives to him. In spite of the claim that God loves the world, the love of Jesus is circumscribed to include only those who believe in him, and salvation is precluded for the world (Gospel of John) and even for those who do not share the christology of those considered to be orthodox, although they claim to be Christians (Epistles of John).

CONCLUSION

The result of examining the four types of redemptive christology in light of these two criteria—how well they cohere with the larger canonical context and the historical ministry of Jesus of Nazareth—is that the first type emerges as the least problematic and as meeting the criteria to a degree greater than the rest. The other three bear the marks of advanced reflection in service of communities of faith more firmly established in the third generation of Christianity, when an accounting of the gospel of redemption is not so acutely needed. But Paul and Mark stood closer to a missionary situation. That is especially true of Paul. In the case of Mark's Gospel, although it was not written for a missionary purpose, its author sought to give an account of the beginnings of the gospel proclaimed in the church. In both cases the aim was to provide and commend an understanding of the divine redemption of humanity through the death and resurrection of the man Jesus of Nazareth in light of, and in continuity with, God's own purposes. Reflection on redemptive christology did not stop there, and indeed it could not, for in the passing of time the Christian movement took on a character and identity of its own, not independent of its Jewish heritage, but understanding itself as the true continuation of Israel and often over against Judaism and the various Greco-Roman cults. It is in the changed situation that the other types were expressed. They are not therefore to be evaluated in a negative way. But if one asks the question of strengths and weaknesses in light of the criteria presented, it can be said that a theological priority can be attached to the first type because it provides a way of expressing redemptive christology which coheres most consistently with the canon and the historical ministry of Jesus of Nazareth. Other criteria would lead to different judgments and conclusions. But at least these criteria seem to be necessary for any discussion in the critical task of theology.

11

The Challenge of New Testament Redemptive Christology

THROUGHOUT THE WORLD Christians confess that Jesus as the Christ is Lord and Savior. But the confession has been learned by rote. When a person is asked to explain this confession, there is often silence, even if the person has had a formal theological education. We belong no longer to the period of the emergence of the Christian movement when things seem to have been more clear. It is foreign territory. In this chapter we shall review some of the problems the distance causes and then go on to attempt a statement of what can be said in the modern world about Christ and his benefits in light of the New Testament.

NEEDS AND NORMS THEN AND NOW

It is frequently said that modern persons are not preoccupied with the religious questions of the past. In the first century people were concerned about salvation from sin, death, and the grip of malevolent cosmic powers. In order to obtain salvation (eternal bliss), they thought, it is necessary to have sin forgiven or removed and the power of death and the elements of the universe relativized and made ineffective. Then there can be eternal happiness with God or the gods. The strength of the Christian gospel was that it proclaimed a Redeemer who bore sins, broke the power of death, conquered the oppressive powers, and thereby liberated his followers for life in God's eternal kingdom.

Modern persons, however, do not share the old world view in which Christianity appeared. This is true not only in terms of modern cosmology, which has discarded the view that the universe consists of a heaven above, an earthly habitation, and an underworld below; it is true also in a fundamental existential way. The thought of an eternal life with God above the world and beyond one's natural life is often not entertained for long among thoughtful people. The concept of sin as a condition of being far from God, or as a sense of being inadequate in the presence of God— sin in its *religious* meaning, its primary meaning in the Bible—is hardly entertained among ordinary people. It is recognized that there are immoral actions, that there are offenses aplenty against other persons, and that there ought to be compensation for these offenses and even forgiveness from the injured party. But just as the concept of "sin" in the singular is hardly considered vital to human experience, so also the idea that particular offenses toward others ("sins" in the old language) are offenses on a cosmic scale ("before God") is not thought to follow. To be sure, the immoral act of one person can have consequences for many innocent persons, reaching unimaginable proportions (for example, the action of terrorists or the willful negligence on the part of persons responsible for the health and safety of others). But the offense is still considered to be against others, not a supreme being.

Perhaps most difficult of all for moderns to understand or appreciate is the New Testament view concerning "principalities and powers." It is difficult for persons to believe today that there are benevolent and/or malevolent powers encircling the universe, ruling the movements of the stars and planets, and guiding the destinies of people on earth. In spite of the interest in astrology, thoughtful persons generally consider it to be primarily an amusement. Today the powers which are feared and served alike are much closer at hand and located on earth. We live in the "nuclear age" and sense the near autonomous rule of a power and threat beyond our control. Or in the economic realm there are those who speak of "market forces" or "market factors" as though these are autonomous powers at work, determining the rise and fall of industries and the employment and unemployment of individuals. Yet it must finally be said that these powers, on closer inspection, should not be thought of as autonomous. They are the result of human ingenuity and political priorities and processes. They are beyond the grasp of individuals, to be sure; and every person is affected by them for good or for ill—and there lies the threat they pose. Yet they are earthbound and the product of human culture. One cannot think of them in the way the ancients thought of the "principalities and powers," that is, as vital entities—angelic or demonic—exercising control over the cosmos. Although some interpreters of the New Testament have sought to draw parallels between the ancient world view concerning the cosmic powers and the modern sense of bondage to scientific, technological, social, political, and economic powers that be,[1] the parallels are only proximate, and it is questionable whether the analogies should be pressed in hermeneutics. There may be other and better approaches, but at present there does not seem to be a way known which can captivate and provide a meaningful interpretation.

We must come to terms with the stark fact that many modern people do not share with the ancients a sense of their need for redemption at all. The world is not considered a place from which one needs to be rescued. One can say that that portion of the biblical tradition which asserts that the earth is the habitation given to humanity—a place where persons should therefore feel at home—has prevailed. Yet in fairness it must also be said that that view has been superseded as well. Modern secularism shares with the biblical tradition that this *saeculum*—this "age" or this "world"—has its own satisfactions, but it differs in that it does not understand this *saeculum* to be a habitation given to humanity *by God,* and it sees this *saeculum* to encompass and exhaust the totality of existence and values. Nothing transcendent remains.

With the dominance of the secular outlook, "redemption"—if the old word can be used at all—becomes a prospect and project within history, not beyond it. What is needed is a transformation of this world, not its replacement by another, a transformation in which there is liberation of both inner and outer aspects of life from the constraints imposed upon the spirit and body, individually and collectively. The shorthand for this is liberation from oppression, so that persons individually and corporately are set free from mental and spiritual captivity—prejudices, illiteracy, feelings of inferiority and superiority, the intolerance of ideologies, the denial of human rights, the censorship of ideas, information, and expression—and from bodily captivity imposed by political and economic systems which bring poverty and prevent the equitable distribution of food, water, sanitation, medical care and technology, and disaster relief, as well as the care of the elderly, the homeless, and the weak.

Yet even while the secular outlook dominates, there are those who are heirs to the Christian tradition, or who have adopted it, who find within the Christian message as nowhere else the resources and vision for meaning and service in the world. Although there are some who are attracted to the Christian tradition and message as a bulwark against thought and action—a refuge from reality and an escape from citizenship in the world—there are also those who are captivated by the story of Israel and the Christ as a window which for them opens up a way of seeing all things in a way that makes life into life. Their essential outlook could be stated thus:

> I believe that, in spite of all in nature and history which would seem to disprove it, at the basis of all things there is a Power which sustains life, affirms it, and also affirms and vindicates love, justice, and reconciliation among people. This conviction is common to many, even if latent, for it

would be virtually impossible to account for either individual or corporate human existence without its presence. To believe that death, hatred, injustice, and alienation must and will prevail would lead only to the dissolution of both individual and corporate life. The conviction of which I speak is thus not sectarian, for it belongs to the public realm. But it is given its classic expression in the Scriptures of the Christian church, and above all in the story of the sacrificial death and resurrection of Jesus. I find in these Scriptures, as nowhere else, both the invitation to hold such a conviction and the most compelling reason to do so. For the gospel of Jesus as the Christ, in all its simplicity and profundity, declares forthrightly that the Power of all being, the God of Israel and the world, has acted to affirm life, love, justice, and reconciliation; that these are values to which one should therefore be committed in this life; and that the One who called all things into being will refashion the creation beyond history through a renewal of life and community that has been signaled and promised in the resurrection of Jesus from the dead.

The person who thinks essentially along these lines articulates a biblically grounded theology. But it must be granted that such a theological perspective is derivative; that is, it is a systematic elucidation of major themes in Scripture. And although that is entirely appropriate, it can be objected that such a procedure tends to overlook the diversity of perspectives found in actual biblical texts. In major Christian traditions, if not all, it is held that one cannot simply pick and choose those aspects of the Bible which are most congenial to one's preconceptions and discard the rest. One must attend to the Scriptures in their entirety *(scriptura tota)*, the "whole counsel of God." But that dictum can have different meanings. It can mean that one must consider every single one of the thousands of verses of the Old and New Testaments as equal in importance. John 3:16 is then neither more nor less important than Lev. 3:16. The Letter to the Romans is no more important than the Song of Solomon. But actually no Christian thinks this way. The Christian who reads the Bible finds that certain pages of the Bible at hand are smudged after years of use more than others; some are rather clean. And if one checks the index of Scripture passages actually used in volumes of systematic theology or examines the passages cited or alluded to in documents which set forth the normative theology of a particular church body (such as the *Book of Concord* for Lutherans, the *Thirty-Nine Articles of Religion* for churches of the Anglican communion, or more recently, the *Documents of Vatican II* for Roman Catholics), it will be found that certain books and passages of Scripture are used more than others; some things are neglected altogether. Therefore, when one says that Scripture is to be used in its totality, that does not mean that every passage has equal weight, but rather that all passages are to be understood within the totality of the overarching canopy of the Scriptures. Scripture is used critically within the life of all churches, and it must be so used.

Modern Christians face realities which the ancient writers did not. One example, and perhaps the most acute, is modern religious pluralism, and we stress the word "modern." It is true, of course, that the ancient Christians faced pluralism, but the situation was different. The early Christians came to realize over the course of the first century that they were becoming irreversibly set apart from Judaism and that Judaism would indeed continue as a religious tradition with its own commitments and institutions along with Christianity. They were also obviously aware of Greco-Roman cults. But what modern Christians face is somewhat different. Modern Christians are heirs to a long history particularly from the time of Constantine up to quite recent times in which Christianity expanded and came to dominate the Western world, served as the spiritual and ideological center for the majority, and showed promise of reaching to the ends of the earth, bringing all of humanity to acknowledge Jesus as Lord. The Christian mission spread from the Mediterranean cradle north and west across Europe and also over major areas of the East, and then in times of tremendous missionary zeal it made its way into other lands as well. But that zeal and even its success can be attributed in part to the opening of doors by colonial expansion. That era is over. And what Christians of the West face is the loss of promise held by persons of only a short time ago. They realize that other major religious traditions continue to dominate large areas of the world—religious traditions which cannot be dismissed as unworthy of anyone's adherence, but which in their mature developments offer their adherents both dignity and meaning, and whose adherents in many cases are rediscovering the vitality of their own traditions, looking upon Christianity as not only foreign but unacceptable (or even decadent) as well. Moreover, these religious traditions exist in areas of the world which have achieved political and economic strength. Beyond that, there is the aforementioned secularism which will not yield to what seems to many to be a legacy and world view of an era that has passed away.

Although we would not agree with the prescription he offers for a cure, the diagnosis of John Hick is painfully precise, and it deserves a hearing:

> The problem which has come to the surface in the encounter of Christianity with the other world religions is this: If Jesus was literally God incarnate, and if it is by his death alone that [people] can be saved, and by their response to him alone that they can appropriate that salvation, then the only doorway to eternal life is Christian faith. It would follow from this that the large majority of the human race so far have not been saved. But is it credible that the loving God and Father of all [people] has decreed that

only those born within one particular thread of human history shall be saved? Is not such an idea excessively parochial, presenting God in effect as the tribal deity of the predominantly Christian West?[2]

If we grant that Hick makes a disturbing yet valid point here, we see that modern Christians are placed in a difficult situation, in which the need for a world-embracing outlook and the norms of Christian faith seem to be on a collision course. On the one hand, there is the conviction of thoughtful Christians that theological reflection and the church must come to terms with a pluralism that is, by all appearances, here to stay. On the other hand, there is the conviction of thoughtful Christians that one cannot dispense with the particularity of Christian claims—the norms—without losing the heart and soul of the faith itself. Hick goes on to envision the Christian mission as a way of deepening the understanding of others in their own traditions: "The specifically Christian gift to the world is that [people] should come to know Jesus and take him into their religious life—not to displace but to deepen and enlarge the relationship with God to which they have already come within their own tradition."[3] But this, we submit, is not the appropriate response. What gives religious traditions their vitality, grandeur, and worthiness of commitment is precisely their particularity. An attraction for Jesus may well be found by others living in their own traditions. But that will be Jesus the teacher, not the risen and universally reigning Christ whom the New Testament and Christians ever since proclaim. It is difficult to envision Christians putting their efforts into recommending Jesus as one who can enrich the religions of others without making claims for his ultimacy. Moreover, it would be the height of arrogance to say that Jesus can enrich the faiths of others without granting that elements (and figures) of their traditions would do the same for Christianity. The consequence of the Hick proposal is finally the abolition of all religions in their particularity in favor of a universal syncretism. The proposal seems to presuppose that religious particularism leads only to conflict, rivalry, and exclusivism. And, of course, there is no end to the amount of documentation that can be gathered to support the view that often—but not always—particularism occasions such things. But one can also claim on good grounds that those who are not willing to recognize particularist diversity, and at times outright contradictions between religious traditions, will inevitably fail to appreciate other religious traditions and their values, and they will find little to appreciate or value in their own—or the one they have abandoned.[4] Furthermore, one can argue on good grounds that those who have immersed themselves fully into the particulars of their own tradition have emerged as the most universal and benevolent in their outlook and actions. It is our view that such an emergence can be inspired by the New Testament.

THE CHALLENGE TO THOUGHT
AND ACTION

In all of its diversity the redemptive christology of the New Testament challenges Christian thought and action in our time. The church can be bound to its own culture in any generation, and to some extent that is inevitable. But the Scriptures offer a challenge, a corrective, and impulses from the dawn of the Christian movement. We shall indicate five ways in which that is so.

1. The Challenge to Free the Heart and Mind. The redemptive christologies of the New Testament illuminate the human condition in ways that can still be understood. It may be true that modern persons do not generally share with the ancients the view that they must be saved from sin and death and for eternal bliss with God or the gods. Yet, modern persons do think of themselves on occasion as burdened by failure, worthlessness, weakness, and finitude. The Christian tradition offers a terminology and a symbol system which allow for the expression of these feelings. It gives permission and even encouragement to speak of these feelings, and it does so in such a way that persons are linked with all previous generations, as well as with those present and to come, and with a body of believers who do not censor such feelings, but welcome their utterance. The Christian tradition is able to do this because it both acknowledges that these feelings are common to all and gives unconditional assurance that these feelings do not stand in the way of life's renewal, ultimate significance, and destiny. The primacy of grace, justification, and life sets those who hear the gospel into a new world, a world that is believed to endure even beyond the finitude of this life. Even though persons may not go about from day to day hoping and longing for an eternal bliss beyond this life, the unconditional promise of life with God and with a renewed humanity in the world to come provides life in the present with a transcendent quality of commitment and vitality, not an escape from it. One of the most inspiring of phenomena one encounters in modern times is the testimony of oppressed Christians. Exactly in those conditions where Christians might have been expected to say that it is action, not faith, that is needed to relieve their misery—the liberation from human oppressors, not a spiritual opiate of peace with God—it has been the gospel of God's self-giving love in Jesus Christ and its promise of life through his victory that has sustained them. And whether action is perceived to be possible or not, in either case strength to endure is

197

inspired by the conviction that the victory of God in Jesus Christ has relativized all earthly powers of oppression. "The body they may kill," but "his kingdom is forever."[5]

2. *The Challenge to Declare the Gospel Afresh.* The redemptive christologies of the New Testament challenge thoughtful Christians, and particularly those who preach and teach, to speak of Christ and his benefits in idioms which make sense. We have seen that within the New Testament itself there are different ways of portraying Christ and redemption. The manner of expression is important in each case, and that is instructive—for the same holds true for our own times. The texts will and should be read in the churches in all their particularity. But thought and proclamation for modern times will have to do more than repeat the old words. They will also have to do more than repeat dogmatic formulations constructed in the history of Christian thought. In a very bold—and helpfully offensive—way Michael Goulder has characterized and chided statements on the work of Christ:

> Alas for those whose task is the defence of the traditional doctrines of the atonement! Better Skid Row than the endless round of empty speculations that run from the implausible to the irreligious: the theories that point to demons more powerful than God (unless he can cheat them), and those that posit a faceless justice more powerful than God; those that make Christ a whipping boy, and those that make him an international banker in merit, with resources enough to pay off the world's balance of payments deficit.[6]

The way forward is to go back to the beginning. Within the New Testament there is no thought that God seeks to have justice done for offenses against him, that Christ steps in to appease God's wrath on behalf of humanity, and that Christ's sacrifice, being perfect, satisfies the divine justice. Even in those places at which sacrificial and cultic terminology is used, it is clear that it is God who has put forth Christ for the sake of human redemption. There is an indissoluble solidarity between God and Christ. Christ's bearing of sin and its consequences for others is itself grounded in the divine purpose of self-giving love. Sin is not simply endured by God, so that no action is called for. Instead sin is borne by God, taken into himself, as it is borne by the crucified Christ. From one perspective the cross is not necessary; God can forgive sin without it. But from another perspective—and here we presume to speak of the hidden heart of God—it is God's own need to bear the sin of humanity for the sake of his children which makes it necessary. The necessity of the cross flows from the character of God. God can do no other. To make such a claim as this is audacious, but if God is what God does, it follows as true.

3. *The Challenge to Expand One's Hope and Vision.* The redemptive

christologies of the New Testament challenge thoughtful Christians to consider the scope of redemption. As pointed out in the quotation from John Hick above, a widely held view of late modern Christianity is that there can be final salvation only for those who respond to the Christian message positively; all others are lost. Those who hold such a view can find warrant for it in various passages of the New Testament. But many thoughtful Christians are uneasy with such a view, and over the centuries the church has allowed for exceptions. For example, when the church was the dominant religious institution of a homogeneous culture, it had to deal with the question of what happens to infants who die prior to baptism or a conscious faith, and it concluded that since these children do not have the opportunity to refuse baptism or the gospel, and since they would no doubt be bapitized and believe the gospel if they had the chance, they will be saved. It has also been held that persons who are ignorant of the gospel—whether the great thinkers of the past (such as Plato) or persons of the present who have not heard the gospel—can be saved. After all, God should be as fair as he expects us to be, and it would be unjust of God to abandon such persons. But then the question is raised whether God will condemn some persons after all, and if so, on what grounds. One approach is to say that the decisive point at which people are and will be condemned is unbelief, and then certain passages of Scripture (particularly from the Gospel of John) are brought forth to substantiate it.[7] But of course the logic of such thinking is absolutely baffling. The corollary is that many people are then better off if they do not hear the gospel. Hearing the gospel gives them the opportunity to say no and puts them into eternal jeopardy. Never mind the scriptural commands to proclaim the gospel. The Christian can presumably receive forgiveness for not proclaiming it. For the sake of those for whom Christ died, silence is better. The gospel is not good news of what God has done in Christ for all, but a summons to believe or be condemned. In other words, the gospel is not gospel.

The way forward is not to relativize the Christian claim about salvation in Christ and him alone. The way forward is to go back to the beginning when Christianity was a minor movement in a highly pluralistic age. Within the New Testament itself—particularly in Paul and in the deutero-Pauline letters, but not only there—we hear a different message, a message which challenges the mindset of a religion which gained the upper hand in a "Christian" culture but now sees itself again as a minority in a larger world. There, at the source, we see redemptive christology manifested in different ways, but the larger hope for humanity and even the whole creation is sounded forth. Paul could declare that in Christ God was reconciling the world to himself, no longer (that is, never again) counting trespasses (2 Cor. 5:19), that in Christ's act of righteousness there is justification and life for all (Rom. 5:18), and that the whole creation will be set free from bondage to enjoy the liberation which Christians have already (Rom. 8:21). And in Colossians and Ephesians the reconciling work of Christ embraces the whole creation. In these types of expression the deed is said to have been done. The gospel of the church is then not a message that people can be saved ultimately only on the basis of their personal profession of faith. It is rather the good news of what God has done in Christ (Paul) or what Christ has done on God's behalf (the deutero-Paulines) for all. Those who hear the good news have already, in the act of hearing and believing, that which God has prepared for them. But those who have not heard, and even those who refuse to believe what they have heard—while they cannot be spoken of as those who have been saved (that is, who live in a right relationship, peace, and communion with God)—are still heirs to what God in Christ has accomplished for all. Therefore Paul can speak of the final salvation of unbelieving Israel (Rom. 11:25–32) and, when at the end all persons see what has been done for them in the lowly, crucified, and risen Christ, the eruption of praise and the universal acclamation of Jesus as Lord (Phil. 2:10–11).

It can be objected that such a view is one-sided. Where now is the totality of Scripture in this? The totality is precisely recognized at this point. It is acknowledged that the redemptive christologies of the New Testament are different and that they cannot be harmonized. The universal thrust of the Pauline tradition and the exclusivism of the Gospel of John, for example, do not cohere. One is forced to make a decision. The case for Paul can be made on the basis of his perception that the God of Israel, the God of all humanity, has done an act of redemption in Christ which has actual benefits, so that the destiny of the world has been permanently altered. This is the presupposition of all the redemptive christologies, indeed of the Christian movement itself, even if its consequences are not consistently spelled out due to other interests and the particular purposes of the writers. Further, it is consistent with the Scriptures of Israel in which God is the creator and ruler of the whole world, will not abandon it, and is expected to transform it in the messianic age. The case against John can be made on the basis of his polemics against unbelieving Jews and other Christians who do not share his christology. Paul and the deutero-Pauline writers could look out upon the whole world as the domain of God and his risen Christ. John could see the world only as permanently lost; God has withdrawn from the world and is known and effectively present only in the word of Jesus' disciples. That is a departure from the testimony of the Scriptures of Israel, in which God remains ruler of the world and is expected to redeem it. The Johannine exclusivism cannot be raised to a dogmatic level. It can be understood, however, as the testimony of one who was embattled by those who opposed all that he stood for.

What is proposed here is that it is possible, on the basis of the New Testament, to assert the *particularism* of the Christian gospel—that in Jesus Christ God has redeemed humanity—without drawing consequences of *exclusivism* from it. If ultimate salvation depends solely on what a person thinks and believes in this life, then exclusivism follows from particularism. But if it depends rather on the grace and power of God, it does not. It is possible to think of Jesus as the Redeemer of the world and have the words mean what they imply. Such has been expressed in various ways in the history of Christian thought. So Irenaeus wrote that the incarnate Son of God "commenced afresh"—or "recapitulated" *(recapitulavit)*—"the long line of human beings, and furnished us, in a brief, comprehensive manner, with salvation; so that what we had lost in Adam . . . we might recover in Christ Jesus."[8] Christ has comprised in himself the "original man" in order that, "as our species went down to death through a vanquished man, so we may ascend to life again through a victorious one."[9] And Athanasius wrote that "the incorruptible Son of God, being conjoined with all by a like nature, naturally clothed all with incorruption, by the promise of the resurrection."[10] Or one can cite the eucharistic prayer of Thomas Cranmer in *The Book of Common Prayer* of 1549, in which it is said that on the cross Jesus "made there (by his one oblation once offered) a full, perfect and sufficient sacrifice, oblation, and satisfaction, for the sins of the whole world."[11] The specific words of Cranmer, although they speak of an atonement with universal effects, are heavily laden with a specific view of the atonement (a satisfaction theory), and so the prayer has been revised (but retaining the scope) to read that on the cross Christ "made there a full atonement for the sins of the whole world, offering once for all his one sacrifice of himself."[12] Similarly, in the Proper Preface of the Liturgy for the Passion, Christ is spoken of as the one "who on the tree of the cross gave salvation to all, that, where death began, there life might be restored, and that he, who by a tree once overcame, might by a tree be overcome."[13]

The affirmation that the scope of God's grace in Christ reaches out to all humanity is firmly fixed in the Christian tradition from the earliest times, and it has a secure place in the theological tradition and the most solemn moments of the church's worship. Yet there are voices raised in protest against it, or the affirmation is amended so that it turns out to mean only that, while God's grace is intended for all, it is effective only for those who believe. It must be recognized by thoughtful Christians today that there is a conflict of traditions within the larger Christian tradition itself and that that has been so from the New Testament era as reflected in its writings. One is universal in outlook; the other is exclusivistic. We must ask why it is that those who adopt the former are generally accused of selling out the particularism of the Christian faith and put on the defensive by those who adopt the latter. That alleged sellout simply is not the case. Perhaps the position a person or a community of persons adopts says more about that person or community than it does about the Christian faith itself. Those who adopt the exclusivist view may do so for reasons running all the way from lack of information to the unworthy belief that there must be some advantage to being a Christian ("If God's grace extends finally to all, and if he will save all, why be a Christian?"). And those who adopt the universal outlook may do so for reasons running all the way from lack of information (or its censorship) to an egalitarian view derived from modern thought (all decent persons ought to have God's approval, and those who are not decent are sick, and God should rehabilitate them). But in the final analysis it is necessary to come to terms with the two traditions, recognize that they are finally not compatible, and subject the whole matter to theological critique informed by the canonical sources. Conclusions will continue to differ, but our point is that some of the sources themselves authorize the point of view which seems to need greater defense: namely, that in the crucified and risen Christ God has acted to restore his creation. We would argue, furthermore, that this view is in touch with the vital impulses of the kerygma and the most profound theological reflection on it from the earliest times. The resurrection of Christ signaled not simply the inauguration of a new world within the interiority of the earliest Christians, but the inauguration of a new world into which believers have entered already in part by the transforming power of the Spirit and into which the whole present world will enter when it is transformed by the One who has power to subject all things to himself. This is not the whole of the biblical witness, but it is that which cannot be overlooked by thoughtful Christians who have a global and pluralistic consciousness and still seek to maintain essential norms with integrity—above all, the claim that in Christ God has acted to redeem humanity with a grace that surpasses all human judgments and the inclination to impose limits upon it. "The point of Christology is to explicate the uniqueness of Jesus, not the uniqueness of Christians."[14]

This way of thinking holds promise for establishing continuity between creation and redemption. The God of creation is involved in the re-creation of all that he has made—even to the extremities of its fallenness. The resurrection of Jesus from the dead is a new and decisive occasion by which God begins the re-creation of the world by bringing life into being out of death (cf. Rom. 4:17). Through the gospel and the Spirit God continues that work of re-creation, for those who hear and believe enter into newness of life, even while living under the conditions of the old age. The church is the sign and promise of God's redemptive work, his new creation. And God's work of re-creating the world anew will be finished at the parousia.

4. *The Challenge to Mission.* The redemptive christologies of the New Testament challenge thoughtful Christians to mission. If, as maintained, the benefits of Christ can be thought, on the basis of New Testament sources, to be ultimately for all of humanity, it follows that the Christian church is to bear witness to what has been done. It would be wrong to think that, since God has acted to reconcile and redeem humanity and will finally deliver his whole creation and refashion it into a new heaven and earth, all is well with the world; one way of thinking and acting is as good as another—Christian, secular, or religious in another way. No, darkness and evil abound; ignorance and oppression are evident. As in the beginning, so now the church of Jesus Christ is to bear witness to the gospel of God's self-giving love and redemption in Christ. This is no longer possible from a position of privilege and power. It is possible only from a position of obedience to its Lord and in service of the One who was crucified and now reigns over the world incognito but seeks to show himself in the world through his servant community. This community reads its Scriptures, baptizes, celebrates Christ's presence, proclaims his gospel, shares his sacrament of self-giving and edifying love, and represents Christ to others in word and deed. It has no power except that which is given: the gospel and the Spirit. It has no sense of an us/them way of thinking, which looks upon itself as the people of God, while others are less so. It does not expect success as measured by conventional criteria, but looks only to the inherent value and captivating power of its message and life to commend itself to others. It does not withdraw from the world and its day-to-day concerns but, being set free and disengaged from the interests of nationalism, classism, ethnicism, and sexism, it engages these interests and seeks the enhancement of life for all. It does not draw in upon itself, considering the world to be lost, but reaches out to the whole world. It does not seek to prove its superiority to other religions, but bears witness in hope and in a coherent way to the truth it knows—and expects both assent and rejection of its claims.

5. *The Challenge to Public Witness.* The redemptive christologies of the New Testament challenge thoughtful Christians to public witness on the basis of their confession. According to all four redemptive christologies, Jesus crucified and raised is now Lord over the entire creation.

That such is the case, however, is a matter of faith, not sight, awaiting its eschatological verification. In the meantime the reign of Christ is realized on earth in communities of faith created by the gospel and the Spirit which gather in his name and acclaim him Lord.

In its act of confessing Jesus as the Christ and Lord of all, the church in principle relativizes all other authorities, temporal and spiritual (including the "spirit" of any age). But the goal is not to seek a "christocracy" in the social and political spheres. The Fourth Gospel is consistent with the rest of the New Testament outlook in its claim that Christ's kingship is "not of this world" (18:36; cf. Matt. 4:8–10; Luke 4:5–8). Just and lawful authority on earth through temporal rulers is affirmed by various New Testament writers (Rom. 13:1–7; 1 Tim. 2:1–3; 1 Pet. 2:13–17). The degree to which the language of christology and redemption in the New Testament has political overtones is debatable, and it differs in any case from book to book. Our time awaits a full-scale study of the matter. But at least it can be said that the redemptive christologies share two things in common.

First, since the Christ event is grounded in the purposes of God, who wills the salvation of the world, there is an implicit claim that a just and lawful order is willed by God and that it will be sought by believers. To be sure, neither a robust social ethic nor a specific political or economic program is spelled out in the New Testament. In fact, its eschatological expectations might seem to preempt long-term efforts for Christian participation in building a just and lawful order in the public sphere. Yet the vision of a coming kingdom has within it the implication that those who await its coming will align themselves with its essential features already in the time before its coming. They will be on the side of the future. And being on the side of the future means that Christians will promote policies and processes which seek to establish justice, peace, and order in the world.

A second point which has bearing on the public witness is that an "eschatological reserve" is maintained by all four redemptive christologies. That is to say that the kingdom of God, or redemption in its fullness, is consistently held as a future prospect and a divine gift, never as a human achievement on earth. Attempts at establishing justice, peace, and a lawful order on earth are never envisioned to be wholly successful. What can be achieved in the historical struggle is always relative, not absolute, proximate, not final. The implication of this is that thoughtful Christians, even while promoting policies and processes for human betterment, will realize that these do not guarantee perfection. The "not yet" of the Christian witness gives vitality and force for continuing efforts at reform, and this "not yet" must be declared whenever a nation or society glories in its achievements while there are still persons who do not share in them. The "eschatological reserve" is then not a warrant for resignation to the way things are, but a powerful force for continuing reform.

The challenge to public witness is affected by, and directly related to, the projected scope of redemption which a person or community has. The christology which a person or community has arises in part out of deeply held values. Conversely, personal and social values can be informed and reformed by christology. Exclusivistic redemptive christologies and exclusivistic world views—views which claim superiority for one's self or religious community and tradition— tend to go hand in hand. One's own way of life is then to be protected, and the world in all its pluralism is evaluated as a problem or a threat; therefore it must be won over to one's own ways—or else it is assigned to eternal damnation; it is beyond the scope of redemption. But a redemptive christology which affirms that in the cross and resurrection of Jesus as the Christ a new situation has been created by God for all of humanity—a redemptive christology which claims that the entire cosmos has been reconciled to God—has within it the power to refashion and renew thinking and action toward and in the world. If Christ has been given for the redemption of the world, the thoughtful Christian and the church will look upon all persons and every people as reconciled to God in principle, awaiting final redemption. Then the calling of Christians is both to affirm final redemption and to exert energies to the fullest extent possible before the end in the direction of that final redemption. Ever since the resurrection of Jesus from the dead and the giving of the Spirit, God has inaugurated the era of redemption of all that he has made, working through a people who are called and created as the new humanity, and who are enlisted in the service of his redemptive work already in the time before the end, when the redemption of all things in its fullness will come into its own. The words of the prayer are appropriate in which the community prays: "We . . . dedicate our lives to the care and redemption of all that you have made, for the sake of him who gave himself for us, Jesus Christ our Lord."[15]

THE WHOLE OF THE MATTER AND
THE HEART OF THE MATTER

We began our study with a quotation from Philipp Melanchthon, who said that to know Christ is to know his benefits. Such an assertion may be assessed by some to be reductionistic, for knowing Christ involves an ongoing pilgrimage of discovery, just as it does in "getting to know" any other person. And to discern Christ and his benefits is itself a complex task as one goes down the main streets and side alleys of the redemptive christologies of the New Testament.

Twentieth-century study has uncovered innumerable facets of the christologies of the New Testament. Attention has been given primarily to christological titles and the christological perspectives of the traditions and the various writers of the New Testament. But generally it has not touched specifically upon what seems so obviously to be the heart of the matter: what the christologies have to do with the redemptive framework for which they were cast and placed into service.[16] It is hard to imagine that the christologies would have been expressed apart from their being conceived as ways to portray the decisive, salutary significance of Christ for human life. That is not the whole of the matter, of course, for christological thought develops well beyond the limits of a soteriological or redemptive concern, but it can be considered the heart of the matter. The work presented here does not pretend to be a study of the christologies of the New Testament toward their outer limits; it is concerned with only one aspect, "redemptive christology," that is, discourse on Christ as a redemptive figure.

The study has shown that there are four main types of presentation in spite of the manifold portraits of Christ and the specific terminology used by each writer concerning the redemptive work of God or Christ. An accounting for the differences has been attempted. Further, it has been suggested that while there is a measure of unity among the various types—and indeed among the writers themselves—there are also areas in which dissonance is to be found. But that is cause for neither alarm nor despair. It is to be expected. The challenge of the redemptive christologies of the New Testament for thoughtful Christians in the present age, as for those in the past, is to discern critically what the heart of the matter is: what is it, in light of the common claims and the competing claims of the New Testament, that one can say about Christ as the one in whom God has acted for the redemption of humanity? The proposal offered in this chapter is that, whatever else is said, it should begin with the claim that in the crucified and risen Christ God has reconciled the world to himself—totally and unconditionally—and that the gospel, the good news, declares that that is so. The way forward is to go back behind the centuries of tradition and to reclaim the good news.

Notes

CHAPTER 1

1. Philipp Melanchthon, *Loci Communes, 1521,* in *Melanchthons Werke,* ed. Hans Engelland, 7 vols. (Gütersloh: C. Bertelsmann Verlag, 1951–75), 2:7; Eng. trans.: *The Loci Communes of Philipp Melanchthon,* trans. Charles L. Hill (Boston: Meador Pub. Co., 1944), 68.

2. Cf. Leander E. Keck, "Toward the Renewal of New Testament Christology," *NTS* 32 (1986): 363: "There would be no christology if there were no soteriology because it is what Christians claim about Jesus as the bringer or effecter of salvation that generates the question of his identity. . . . At the same time, christology is not reducible to soteriology because . . . Christ is always more than saviour." The soteriological connection has been recognized previously. Cf. Oscar Cullmann, *The Christology of the New Testament,* rev. ed. (Philadelphia: Westminster Press, 1963), 3: "The New Testament hardly ever speaks of the person of Christ without at the same time speaking of his work." Cf. also John K. Mozley, "Christology and Soteriology," in *Mysterium Christi: Christological Studies by British and German Theologians,* ed. G.K.A. Bell and A. Deissmann (London: Longmans Green, 1930), 171: "There is in the New Testament no speculative Christology divorced from the Gospel of the Saviour and of the salvation He brings." That christology and soteriology are inextricably intertwined is also asserted by various systematic theologians, e.g., Paul Tillich, *Systematic Theology,* 3 vols. (Chicago: Univ. of Chicago Press, 1951–63), 2:150–51; and Edward Schillebeeckx, *Interim Report on the Books* Jesus *and* Christ (New York: Crossroad, 1981), 11–13. The limitations of soteriology as the beginning point of christology are outlined by Wolfhart Pannenberg, *Jesus—God and Man,* 2d ed. (Philadelphia: Westminster Press, 1977), 47–49.

3. G.N. Stanton, "On the Christology of Q," in *Christ and Spirit in the New Testament: In Honour of Charles Francis Digby Moule,* ed. Barnabas Lindars and S.S. Smalley (Cambridge: Cambridge Univ. Press, 1973), 27–42; Athanasius Polag, *Die Christologie der Logienquelle,* WMANT 45 (Neukirchen-Vluyn: Neukirchener Verlag, 1977); and Arland D. Jacobson, "Wisdom Christology in Q" (Ph.D. diss., Claremont Graduate School, 1978).

4. Among the many studies of creeds and hymns, those which deal explicitly with christology include Oscar Cullmann, *The Earliest Christian Confessions* (London: Lutterworth Press, 1949); Vernon H. Neufield, *The Earliest Christian Confessions,* NTTS 5 (Grand Rapids: Wm. B. Eerdmans, 1963); Reinhard Deichgräber, *Gotteshymnus und Christushymnus in der frühen Christenheit: Untersuchungen zu Form, Sprache und Stil der frühchristlichen Hymnen,* SUNT 5 (Göttingen: Vandenhoeck & Ruprecht, 1967); Ralph P. Martin, *Carmen Christi: Philippians ii. 5–11 in Recent Interpretation and in the Setting of Early Christian Worship,* SNTSMS 4 (Cambridge: Cambridge Univ. Press, 1957; rev. ed., Grand Rapids: Wm. B. Eerdmans, 1983); Jack T. Sanders, *The New Testament Christological Hymns: Their Historical Religious Background,* SNTSMS 15 (Cambridge: Cambridge Univ. Press, 1971); Klaus Wengst, *Christologische Formeln und Lieder des Urchristentums,* SNT 7 (Gütersloh: Gütersloher Verlagshaus Gerd Mohn, 1972); Elisabeth Schüssler Fiorenza, "Wisdom Mythology and the Christological Hymns of the New Testament," in *Aspects of Wisdom in Judaism and Early Christianity,* ed. Robert L. Wilken (Notre Dame: Univ. of Notre Dame Press, 1975), 17–41; and Martin Hengel, "Hymns and Christology," in *Between Jesus and Paul: Studies in the Earliest History of Christianity* (Philadelphia: Fortress Press, 1983), 78–96.

5. Aspects of pre-Pauline Christianity, including christology, are treated by A.M. Hunter, *Paul and His Predecessors,* rev. ed. (Philadelphia: Westminster Press, 1961); Werner Kramer, *Christ, Lord, Son of God,* SBT 50 (London: SCM Press, 1966); Peter Stuhlmacher, *Das paulinische Evangelium: I. Vorgeschichte,* FRLANT 95 (Göttingen: Vandenhoeck & Ruprecht, 1968), 266–82.

6. H. J. Cadbury, "The Hellenists," in *The Beginnings of Christianity,* ed. F.J. Foakes Jackson and K. Lake, 5 vols. (London: Macmillan Co., 1920–33), 5:59–74; Marcel Simon, *St. Stephen and the Hellenists in the Primitive Church* (London: Longmans Green, 1958); Robin Scroggs, "The Earliest Hellenistic Christianity," in *Religions in Antiquity: Essays in Memory of Erwin Ramsdell Goodenough,* ed. Jacob Neusner, SHR 14 (Leiden: E. J. Brill, 1968), 176–206; and Martin Hengel, "Between Jesus and Paul: The 'Hellenists,' the 'Seven' and Stephen (Acts 6.1–15; 7.54—8.3)," in *Between Jesus and Paul,* 1–29.

7. Jean Danielou, *The Theology of Jewish Christianity* (Philadelphia: Westminster Press, 1965; reprinted, 1977), 147–72; Hans-Joachim Schoeps, *Jewish Christianity: Factional Disputes in the Early Church* (Philadelphia: Fortress Press, 1969), 59–73; Joseph A. Fitzmyer, "Jewish Christianity in Acts in Light of the Qumran Scrolls," in *Studies in Luke-Acts: Essays Presented in Honor of Paul Schubert,* ed. Leander E. Keck and J. Louis Martyn (Philadelphia: Fortress Press, 1980 [1966]), 233–57; the essay is reprinted in Fitzmyer's *Essays on the Semitic Background of the New Testament,* SBLSBS 5 (Missoula, Mont.: Scholars Press, 1974), 271–303; Richard N. Longenecker, *The Christology of Early Jewish Christianity,* SBT 2/17 (London: SCM Press, 1970; reprinted, Grand Rapids: Baker Book House, 1981); and Hans Conzelmann, *History of Primitive Christianity* (Nashville: Abingdon Press, 1973), 29–77.

8. John Knox, *The Humanity and Divinity of Christ: A Study of Pattern in Christology* (Cambridge: Cambridge Univ. Press, 1967), x.

9. Ibid., 1–18.

10. Reginald H. Fuller, *The Foundations of New Testament Christology* (New York: Charles Scribner's Sons, 1965); the patterns are summarized on 243–47. Although the patterns are not delineated so sharply, the three categories concerning strata are used also by Ferdinand Hahn, *The Titles of Jesus in Christology: Their History in Early Christianity* (Cleveland: World Pub. Co., 1969).

11. The major, classic treatments of the main titles are by Cullmann, *Christology NT;* Fuller, *Foundations of NT Christology;* and Hahn, *Titles of Jesus.* A smaller range of titles—those which have a bearing on incarnation—is treated by James D. G. Dunn, *Christology in the Making: A New Testament Inquiry into the Origins of the Doctrine of the Incarnation* (Philadelphia: Westminster Press, 1980).

12. The most far-reaching critique of the title approach in recent times has been made by Keck, "Toward the Renewal of NT Christology," 368–70. His criticisms are that the approach reflects an inadequate view of language, that it actually hampers the effort to understand the christology of texts (and he provides five reasons why that is so), and that it bypasses christology itself (reflection on the identity and significance of Jesus). Cf. also Horst R. Balz, *Methodische Probleme der neutestamentlichen Christologie*, WMANT 25 (Neukirchen-Vluyn: Neukirchener Verlag, 1967), 46; and the remarks made (particularly in regard to the christologies of the Gospels in relation to titles) by Howard C. Kee, "Christology and Ecclesiology: Titles of Christ and Models of Community," in *Society of Biblical Literature 1982 Seminar Papers*, ed. Kent H. Richards, SBLSPS 21 (Chico, Calif.: Scholars Press, 1982), 227–42.

13. Barnabas Lindars, *Jesus Son of Man: A Fresh Examination of the Son of Man Sayings in the Gospels in the Light of Recent Research* (London: SPCK, 1983; Grand Rapids: Wm. B. Eerdmans, 1984), 85.

14. This of course is the point of Reginald H. Fuller, who speaks of the titles as "tools of Christology," which the early church used for its "christological response." See his *Foundations of NT Christology,* 16.

15. Cf. Keck, "Toward the Renewal of NT Christology," 369.

16. Balz, *Methodische Probleme*, 46; translation mine.

17. Among others, the following (all British writers) can be cited: John A. T. Robinson, *The Human Face of God* (Philadelphia: Westminster Press, 1973); A. T. Hanson, *Grace and Truth: A Study in the Doctrine of the Incarnation* (London: SPCK, 1975); *The Myth of God Incarnate*, ed. John Hick (Philadelphia: Westminster Press, 1977); *Incarnation and Myth: The Debate Continued*, ed. Michael Goulder (London: SCM Press, 1979); and Dunn, *Christology in the Making.*

18. Dunn, *Christology in the Making,* 258.

19. Ibid., 256.

20. Ibid., 46, 125–28, 182–83, 194–96, 254–56. Concerning the work of Dunn, a major critique has been written by Carl A. Holladay, "New Testament Christology: Some Considerations of Method," *NovT* 25 (1983): 257–78. On Dunn's rejection of the concept of preexistence in Paul, Holladay has aptly stated: "While this way of reading Paul must be regarded as the most novel feature of Dunn's reconstruction, so is it the least convincing" (268). At the other extreme is the suggestion that Paul was the originator of preexistence christology, as proposed by Seyoon Kim, *The Origin of Paul's Gospel*, WUNT 2/4 (Tübingen: J. C. B.

Mohr [Paul Siebeck], 1981: Grand Rapids: Wm. B. Eerdmans, 1982), 114. This does not hold up, since preexistence is affirmed in the pre-Pauline Philippian Hymn (Phil. 2:5–11) and the "sending formula" (see chapter 5 below).

21. This becomes clear at various points in his book, and only a few instances can be cited here. He states early on that there is no evidence in Ancient Near Eastern sources for "the idea of a god or son of god descending from heaven to become a human being in order to bring men salvation" (*Christology in the Making,* 22); the author of the Wisdom of Solomon, he declares, would not have thought of Wisdom "as an independent divine being" (173); concerning early wisdom christology, he says, "it would be inaccurate to say that Christ was understood as a pre-existent being become incarnate" (211); he asks whether Paul would have thought of Christ "as a heavenly being who had pre-existed with God" (255); he distinguishes between "ideal" and "real" preexistence (256) and says that only at the end of the first century (with the Gospel of John) do "we find a concept of Christ's real pre-existence beginning to emerge" (258).

22. Ibid., 209–12.

23. Ibid., 176.

24. See Fuller, *Foundations of NT Christology,* 72–75, who offers more references in Jewish literature and discusses the concept of wisdom in Judaism.

25. For similar expressions of the meaning of the preexistence of Christ, see Rudolf Bultmann, *Theology of the New Testament,* 2 vols. (New York: Charles Scribner's Sons, 1951–55), 1:304; Knox, *Humanity and Divinity of Christ,* 107–8; Hans Conzelmann, *An Outline of the Theology of the New Testament* (New York: Harper & Row, 1969), 200–204; and Reginald H. Fuller, "Pre-Existence Christology: Can We Dispense with It?" *Word & World* 2 (1982): 29–33.

26. The noun *lytrōsis* appears at Luke 1:68; 2:38; and Heb. 9:12; *apólytrosis* appears at Luke 21:28; Rom 3:24; 8:23; 1 Cor. 1:30; Eph. 1:7, 14; 4:30; Col. 1:14; Heb. 9:15.

27. The noun *lytron* appears at Mark 10:45//Matt.20:28; *antilytron* at 1 Tim. 2:6.

28. At Rom. 11:26, however, the term "the deliverer" (*ho hryomenos*) could refer to Christ, or does it refer to God? In any case, *lytrōtēs* is never used in reference to Christ.

29. The verb *lytrousthai* is used at Luke 24:21; Titus 2:14; and 1 Pet. 1:18; *exagorazesthai* at Gal. 3:13; 4:5; and *hryesthai* at Matt. 6:13//Luke 11:4; Matt. 27:43; Luke 1:73; Rom. 7:24; 11:26; Col. 1:13; and 1 Thess. 1:10. The verb *hryesthai* is used at other places as well (Rom. 15:31; twice at 2 Cor. 1:10; 2 Thess. 3:2; 2 Tim. 3:11; 4:17, 18; 2 Pet. 2:7, 9), but in these instances the term does not have the meaning of redemption or deliverance from sin and/or death, but from mortal enemies on earth.

30. For a crisp treatment of genuine and deutero-Pauline letters, see Günther Bornkamm, *Paul* (New York: Harper & Row, 1971), 241–43. Cf. also Willi Marxsen, *Introduction to the New Testament: An Approach to Its Problems* (Philadelphia: Fortress Press, 1968), 17–109; and Helmut Koester, *Introduction to the New Testament,* 2 vols. (Philadelphia: Fortress Press; Berlin: Walter De Gruyter, 1982), 2:52–56.

31. On the matter of authorship of the Epistles of John, see chapter 8 where they are treated.

32. On the nuances between these terms and how the two concepts cannot be separated totally, see Fuller, *Foundations of NT Christology*, 247–50. Among other writers who make such distinctions can be mentioned Cullmann, *Christology NT*, 4; Willi Marxsen, *The Beginnings of Christology: Together with The Lord's Supper as a Christological Problem* (Philadelphia: Fortress Press, 1979), 81–85, 89–91; and Balz, *Methodische Probleme*, 119–27.

CHAPTER 2

1. Rudolf Bultmann, *Theology of the New Testament*, 2 vols. (New York: Charles Scribner's Sons, 1951–55), 1:37.

2. Ibid. 1:36.

3. Ibid. 1:33; the italics appear in the text.

4. Ibid. 1:42–47.

5. John A. T. Robinson, "The Most Primitive Christology of All?" *JTS*, n.s. 7 (1956):177–89; reprinted in *Twelve New Testament Studies*, SBT 34 (London: SCM Press, 1962), 139–53. Page references subsequently are to the latter edition.

6. Ibid., 145–46.

7. Ibid., 144.

8. Ibid., 148.

9. Ibid.

10. According to K. G. Kuhn, "Maranatha," *TDNT* 4:467–72, on linguistic grounds the term could mean "Our Lord, come," "Our Lord has come," or "Our Lord is present." He finally rejects the second on the basis of context.

11. Major reasons for this rendering—rather than an indicative *(maran atha)* —are that (1) the Greek imperative form is used at Rev. 22:20 and (2) the formula is clearly used in prayer (or petition) at *Didache* 10.6 (even though its use at 1 Cor. 16:22 could be either a prayer formula or an indicative statement). Cf. Oscar Cullmann, *The Christology of the New Testament*, rev. ed. (Philadelphia: Westminster Press, 1963), 208–10; Ferdinand Hahn, *The Titles of Jesus in Christology: Their History in Early Christianity* (Cleveland: World Pub. Co., 1969), 93–96; Werner Kramer, *Christ, Lord, Son of God*, SBT 50 (London: SCM Press, 1966), 100–101; Reginald H. Fuller, *The Foundations of New Testament Christology* (New York: Charles Scribner's Sons, 1965), 157; Hans Conzelmann, *An Outline of the Theology of the New Testament* (New York: Harper & Row, 1969), 82; Werner G. Kümmel, *The Theology of the New Testament: According to Its Main Witnesses, Jesus-Paul-John* (Nashville: Abingdon Press, 1973), 112; Joseph A. Fitzmyer, "New Testament *Kyrios* and *Maranatha* and Their Aramaic Background," in *To Advance the Gospel: New Testament Studies* (New York: Crossroad, 1981), 218–35; and Leonhard Goppelt, *Theology of the New Testament*, 2 vols. (Grand Rapids: Wm. B. Eerdmans, 1981–82), 2:23. Cf. also BAGD, 491.

12. Cf. Kuhn, "Maranatha," 471; Cullmann, *Christology NT*, 211–13; Siegfried Schulz, "Maranatha und Kyrios Jesus," *ZNW* 53 (1962): 125; F. Hahn, *Titles of Jesus*, 94–96; Kramer, *Christ, Lord, Son of God*, 100, 105, 107; Fuller, *Foundations of NT Christology*, 157; Kümmel, *Theology NT*, 112; and Goppelt, *The-*

ology NT 2:23. A modification of its significance which, however, does not deny its eucharistic setting has been proposed by C. F. D. Moule, "A Reconsideration of the Context of *Maranatha*," *NTS* 6 (1959): 307–10; reprinted in *Essays on New Testament Interpretation* (Cambridge: Cambridge Univ. Press, 1982), 222–26.

13. Cf. Cullmann, *Christology NT,* 211–13; Hahn, *Titles of Jesus,* 95–100; Kramer, *Christ, Lord, Son of God,* 100, 106–7; Fuller, *Foundations of NT Christology,* 157–58; Kümmel, *Theology NT,* 112; and Goppelt, *Theology NT* 2:23.

14. So Cullmann, *Christology NT,* 212.

15. So Hahn, *Titles of Jesus,* 99, 102; Kramer, *Christ, Lord, Son of God,* 104–7; Schulz, "Maranatha und Kyrios Jesus," 138; and Goppelt, *Theology NT* 2:23.

16. Edward Schillebeeckx, *Jesus: An Experiment in Christology* (New York: Crossroad, 1981), 407.

17. Hahn, *Titles of Jesus,* 100.

18. Ibid., 97.

19. Ibid.

20. A critical reconstruction of Q has been offered by Athanasius Polag, *Fragmenta Q: Textheft zur Logienquelle* (Neukirchen-Vluyn: Neukirchener Verlag, 1979). A listing of passages conventionally assigned to Q has also been made by Howard C. Kee, *Jesus in History: An Approach to the Study of Gospels,* 2d ed. (New York: Harcourt Brace Jovanovich, 1977), 84–87. For a survey of research on Q, particularly devoted to its christology, for the first half of the twentieth century, see H. E. Tödt, *The Son of Man in the Synoptic Tradition* (Philadelphia: Westminster Press, 1965), 235–46. Surveys of more recent studies include Ronald D. Worden, "Redaction Criticism of Q: A Survey," *JBL* 94 (1975): 532–46; and Frans Neirynck, "Recent Developments in the Study of Q," in *Logia: The Sayings of Jesus: Mémorial Joseph Coppens,* ed. Joël Delobel, BETL 59 (Louvain: Louvain Univ. Press, 1982), 29–75.

21. For a discussion of the issue whether Q actually existed, see Werner G. Kümmel, *Introduction to the New Testament,* rev. ed. (Nashville: Abingdon Press, 1975), 63–76.

22. But see T. W. Manson, *The Sayings of Jesus* (London: SCM Press, 1949; reprinted, Grand Rapids: Wm. B. Eerdmans, 1979), 16, who offers a strong case for his claim "that in Mt. and Lk. we have preserved for us substantially all that Q ever contained"; and Arland D. Jacobson, "The Literary Unity of Q," *JBL* 101 (1982): 365–89.

23. Tödt, *Son of Man,* 264.

24. Ibid., 249. Cf. Dieter Lührmann, *Die Redaktion der Logienquelle,* WMANT 33 (Neukirchen-Vluyn: Neukirchener Verlag, 1969), 96.

25. Manson, *Sayings of Jesus,* 16.

26. Tödt, *Son of Man,* 250.

27. Helmut Koester, *Introduction to the New Testament,* 2 vols. (Philadelphia: Fortress Press; Berlin: Walter De Gruyter, 1982), 2:148.

28. Richard A. Edwards, *A Theology of Q: Eschatology, Prophecy, and Wisdom* (Philadelphia: Fortress Press, 1976), 149–50.

29. William Wrede, *Paul* (Boston: American Unitarian Assoc., 1908), 161.

30. Ibid., 178.

31. Ibid.
32. Ibid., 179.
33. Cf. Kümmel, *Introduction,* 71; and Kee, *Jesus in History,* 83.
34. For a summary of the teaching of the Gospel of Thomas, see Koester, *Introduction* 2:150–54. Thomas is published in English translation, among other places in Kurt Aland, ed., *Synopsis Quottuor Evangeliorum* (Stuttgart: Württembergische Bibelanstalt, 1964), 517–30. The "trajectory" of a sayings tradition collection as a genre from Jewish literature to Gnosticism, and which includes Q and the Gospel of Thomas in its path, has been traced by James M. Robinson, "LOGOI SOPHON: On the Gattung of Q" in J. M. Robinson and H. Koester, *Trajectories through Early Christianity* (Philadelphia: Fortress Press, 1971), 71–113.
35. Joachim Jeremias, *The Eucharistic Words of Jesus,* rev. ed. (Philadelphia: Fortress Press, 1977 [1966]), 101–3; Harald Riesenfeld, "Hyper," *TDNT* 8:509–10; Kramer, *Christ, Lord, Son of God,* 19; Hahn, *Titles of Jesus,* 175–86; Fuller, *Foundations of NT Christology,* 160–62; Kümmel, *Theology NT,* 98; and Goppelt, *Theology NT* 2:41. Conzelmann considers the formula indeed primitive and allows for the possibility that it was composed in Jerusalem or else that it incorporated Jerusalem tradition, but he maintains that it was composed, at any rate, in a Greek-speaking, Jewish-Christian community; more than this one cannot say. His discussion is in his commentary, *First Corinthians,* Hermeneia (Philadelphia: Fortress Press, 1975), 252–54; idem, *Outline,* 65–66.
36. These include Fuller, *Foundations of NT Christology,* 161; and Leonhard Goppelt, "The Easter Kerygma in the New Testament," in L. Goppelt, Helmut Thielicke, and H.-R. Müller-Schwefe, *The Easter Message Today: Three Essays* (New York: Thomas Nelson & Sons, 1964), 36.
37. Koester, "The Structure and Criteria of Early Christian Beliefs," in Robinson and Koester, *Trajectories,* 205–31.
38. Ibid., 225.
39. Cf. also ibid., 211: "This belief is probably the most primitive"; and James D. G. Dunn, *Unity and Diversity in the New Testament: An Inquiry into the Character of Earliest Christianity* (Philadelphia: Westminster Press, 1977), 219: "In short, so far as we can tell, the christology (and soteriology) of the first Christians seems to have been essentially forward looking."
40. Cf. Martin Hengel, *Acts and the History of Earliest Christianity* (Philadelphia: Fortress Press, 1979), 104.
41. These are reviewed by Richard F. Zehnle, *Peter's Pentecost Discourse: Tradition and Lukan Reinterpretation in Peter's Speeches of Acts 2 and 3,* SBLMS 15 (Nashville: Abingdon Press, 1971), 44–60, who concludes that Luke was dependent on source material for the composition of Acts 3:12–26.
42. Pss. 50:1, 9; 108:14 (51:1, 9; 108:14 in Hebrew); Prov. 6:33; Sir. 23:26; 40:12; 46:20; Isa. 43:25; Jer. 18:23; 2 Macc. 12:42; 3 Macc. 2:19. There are forty-seven references for the use of the verb (but frequently having to do with the blotting out of life, etc., not sin) listed in E. Hatch and H. A. Redpath, *A Concordance to the Septuagint* (Oxford: Clarendon Press, 1897), 486–87.
43. Cf. Martin Dibelius, "The Speeches in Acts and Ancient Historiography," in *Studies in the Acts of the Apostles* (New York: Charles Scribner's Sons, 1956),

179. Cf. also Eduard Lohse, "Lukas als Theologe der Heilsgeschichte," *EvT* 14 (1956):270; reprinted in *Die Einheit des Neuen Testaments: Exegetische Studien zur Theologie des Neuen Testaments* (Göttingen: Vandenhoeck & Ruprecht, 1973), 159; and Goppelt, *Theology NT* 2:271–72.

44. Dibelius, "Speeches," 165.

45. Eduard Schweizer, "Concerning the Speeches in Acts," in *Studies in Luke-Acts: Essays Presented in Honor of Paul Schubert,* ed. L. E. Keck and J. L. Martyn (Philadelphia: Fortress Press, 1980[1966]), 208–9, 212.

46. Cf. also the argument, on different grounds, of Stephen S. Smalley, "The Christology of Acts Again," in *Christ and Spirit in the New Testament: In Honour of Charles Francis Digby Moule,* ed. B. Lindars and S. S. Smalley (Cambridge: Cambridge Univ. Press, 1973), 80.

47. Jacob Jervell, "The Divided People of God: The Restoration of Israel and Salvation for the Gentiles," in *Luke and the People of God: A New Look at Luke-Acts* (Minneapolis: Augsburg Pub. House, 1972), 43.

48. Ibid., 68.

49. Ibid., 43.

50. Cf. C. F. D. Moule, "The Christology of Acts," in *Studies in Luke-Acts,* ed. Keck and Martyn, 169.

51. J. A. T. Robinson, "The Most Primitive Christology of All?" 152.

52. At Acts 3:20 (Nestle-Aland text; 3:19–20 in RSV) there is a shift in subject. First, the "times of refreshment" will come; then "he" (the Lord) will send the Christ. There are two separate stages. The first is brought on by repentance. The parousia, however, is not brought on by repentance, but is prepared for by it. Cf. Hans Conzelmann, *Die Apostelgeschichte,* HNT 7, 2d ed. (Tübingen: J. C. B. Mohr [Paul Siebeck], 1963), 34 (Eng. trans.: Hermeneia; Philadelphia: Fortress Press, 1984).

53. Hahn, *Titles of Jesus,* 100.

54. Edwards, *A Theology of Q,* 149–50.

55. Cf. Athanasius Polag, *Die Christologie der Logienquelle,* WMANT 45 (Neukirchen-Vluyn: Neukirchener Verlag, 1977), 165; and Schillebeeckx, *Jesus,* 416.

56. In spite of the similarity of this verse to Mark 8:34, there are differences, and it is judged to be not from Mark but from Q. See Manson, *Sayings of Jesus,* 131–32; and Polag, *Fragmenta Q,* 70.

57. Cf. G. N. Stanton, "On the Christology of Q," in *Christ and Spirit in the NT,* ed. Lindars and Smalley, 40.

58. Edwards, *A Theology of Q,* 149.

59. Cf. Polag, *Die Christologie der Logienquelle,* 85.

60. Cf. Tödt, *Son of Man,* 119: "There is no forgiveness—in the post-Easter situation—for the one who sets himself in opposition to the manifest activity of the Holy Spirit."

61. Cf. Polag, *Die Christologie der Logienquelle,* 20–21, who concludes that the Q material would not have been used for missionary purposes.

62. Kümmel, *Introduction,* 74. For dissent, see Lührmann, *Die Redaktion der Logienquelle,* 94–97, 103. He maintains that the continuity between Jesus and the community lies in eschatology, not the kerygma, and says, "Jesus is not the proclaimed one, but rather the content of the proclamation is the coming judg-

ment, in which Jesus as the Son of man will save his community" (96–97; translation mine). But it simply does not follow that an emphasis on eschatology and coming judgment in the Q material precludes the kerygma as a presupposition in the community. One must ask concerning the function of Q—the task it (as a document) was designed to do.

63. Cf. Ernst Käsemann, "On the Subject of Primitive Christian Apocalyptic," in *New Testament Questions of Today* (Philadelphia: Fortress Press, 1969), 119–20.

64. Bultmann, *Theology NT* 2:199–200.

CHAPTER 3

1. Norman Perrin, *A Modern Pilgrimage in New Testament Christology* (Philadelphia: Fortress Press, 1974).

2. Most notable are Philipp Vielhauer, "Gottesreich und Menschensohn in der Verkündigung Jesu," in *Festschrift für Günther Dehn zum 75. Geburtstag am 18. April dargebracht,* ed. Wilhelm Schneemelcher (Neukirchen: Neukirchener Verlag, 1957), 51–79; reprinted in Vielhauer's *Aufsätze zum Neuen Testament* (Munich: Chr. Kaiser Verlag, 1965), 55–91; Ernst Käsemann, "The Problem of the Historical Jesus," in *Essays on New Testament Themes,* SBT 41 (London: SCM Press, 1964), 43; idem, "Sentences of Holy Law in the New Testament" and "The Beginnings of Christian Theology," in *New Testament Questions of Today* (Philadelphia: Fortress Press, 1969), 76–78, 101–2; H. M. Teeple, "The Origin of the Son of Man Christology," *JBL* 84 (1965): 213–50; W. O. Walker, Jr., "The Origin of the Son of Man Concept as Applied to Jesus," *JBL* 91 (1972): 482–90; and Hans Conzelmann, *Jesus* (Philadelphia: Fortress Press, 1973), 43–46.

3. Perrin, *A Modern Pilgrimage,* 5–6, 26, 35, 45, 57.

4. Ibid., 45, 60–77. He also claims (6) that all christological titles stem from the early church—none from Jesus himself.

5. Ibid., 10.

6. Ibid., 5, 12, 34–36, 55.

7. Ibid., 12–13, 34, 55.

8. Ibid., 36.

9. Ibid., 13–15, 34.

10. Ibid., 100–103.

11. Ibid., 101.

12. Ibid., 76.

13. Ibid., 76 n. 36, where he cites and disagrees with Reginald H. Fuller, *The Foundations of New Testament Christology* (New York: Charles Scribner's Sons, 1965), 119.

14. Perrin, *A Modern Pilgrimage,* 34.

15. A critique of Perrin's view along a different line has been offered by Eduard Schweizer, "Towards a Christology of Mark?" in *God's Christ and His People: Essays in Honour of Nils Alstrup Dahl,* ed. Jacob Jervell and Wayne A. Meeks (Oslo: Universitetsforlaget, 1977), 38, who asks: "If the Son of Man title originated

in scribal interpretation of Old Testament texts, why does it not appear in statements of the church, as Son of David, Lord or Christ do?"

16. Edward Schillebeeckx, *Jesus: An Experiment in Christology* (New York: Crossroad, 1981), 380–92.

17. Ibid., 382.

18. Ibid., 387.

19. Ibid., 390–91.

20. Martin Hengel, *The Atonement: The Origins of the Doctrine in the New Testament* (Philadelphia: Fortress Press, 1981), 65–75.

21. Ibid., 67.

22. Ibid., 69.

23. Ibid., 72.

24. Cf. Eduard Schweizer, *The Lord's Supper According to the New Testament*, FBBS 18 (Philadelphia: Fortress Press, 1967), 10–17; and Willi Marxsen, *The Beginnings of Christology: Together with The Lord's Supper as a Christological Problem* (Philadelphia: Fortress Press, 1979), 93–95.

25. Cf., among others, Hans Conzelmann, *An Outline of the Theology of the New Testament* (New York: Harper & Row, 1969), 57–58; and Marxsen, *Beginnings of Christology*, 92.

26. Ferdinand Hahn, *The Titles of Jesus in Christology: Their History in Early Christianity* (New York: World Pub. Co., 1969), 59.

27. Matthew alone adds "with you" to the saying of drinking in the Father's kingdom (26:29).

28. Cf. Günther Bornkamm, *Jesus of Nazareth* (New York: Harper & Brothers, 1960), 160; Schweizer, *The Lord's Supper*, 18–22; and I. Howard Marshall, *Last Supper and Lord's Supper* (Grand Rapids: Wm. B. Eerdmans, 1980), 94–97, 152–53.

29. Leonhard Goppelt, *Theology of the New Testament*, 2 vols. (Grand Rapids: Wm. B. Eerdmans, 1981–82), 1:221.

30. On the matter of performing miracles of healing, these are attested in all four strands of the synoptic tradition (Mark, Q, L, and M) and in the Gospel of John. The historicity of Jesus as a miracle worker has been established by various interpreters, most notably, Gerd Theissen, *The Miracle Stories of the Early Christian Tradition* (Philadelphia: Fortress Press, 1983). On the unique character of Jesus' miracles, see ibid., 277–80.

31. This point has been established beyond doubt and most forcefully by Nils A. Dahl, "The Crucified Messiah," in *The Crucified Messiah and Other Essays* (Minneapolis: Augsburg Pub. House, 1974), 23–24. Cf. also A. E. Harvey, *Jesus and the Constraints of History: The Bampton Lectures, 1980* (Philadelphia: Westminster Press, 1982), 13–14. The charge and reasons for it are discussed by E. P. Sanders, *Jesus and Judaism* (Philadelphia: Fortress Press, 1985), 294–318.

32. Cf. Eduard Schweizer, *The Holy Spirit* (Philadelphia: Fortress Press, 1980), 51.

33. Texts are cited by Rudolf Meyer, "Prophētēs," *TDNT* 6:812–19.

34. Quoted from *The Tosefta: Translated from the Hebrew Third Division:*

Nashim (The Order of Women), trans. Jacob Neusner (New York: KTAV, 1979), 201.

35. Text in *Josephus*, trans. H. St. John Thackeray et al., LCL, 9 vols. (Cambridge, Mass.: Harvard Univ. Press, 1926–65), 1:178–79.

36. This work is dated by A. F. J. Klijn to the late (post-70) first century or the first two decades of the second century A.D. in *OTP* 1:616–17. The text quoted is from *OTP* 1:651.

37. See Wilhelm Bousset, *Die Religion des Judentums im späthellenistischen Zeitalter*, ed. Hugo Gressmann, HNT 21, 3d ed. (Tübingen: J. C. B. Mohr [Paul Siebeck], 1966), 394–99; Meyer, "Prophētēs," 819–28; Martin Hengel, *Die Zeloten: Untersuchungen zur jüdischen Freiheitsbewegung in der Zeit von Herodes I. bis 70 n. Chr.*, AGSU 1 (Leiden: E. J. Brill, 1961), 239–51; Peter Schäfer, *Die Vorstellung vom heiligen Geist in der rabbinischen Literatur*, SANT 28 (Munich: Kösel Verlag, 1972), 147–49; David Hill, *New Testament Prophecy* (Atlanta: John Knox Press, 1979), 21–43; and David E. Aune, *Prophecy in Early Christianity and the Ancient Mediterranean World* (Grand Rapids: Wm. B. Eerdmans, 1983), 103–52.

38. See Geza Vermes, "Jesus and Charismatic Judaism," in *Jesus the Jew: A Historian's Reading of the Gospels* (Philadelphia: Fortress Press, 1981), 58–82. The prophetic role of Jesus and the forms of his prophetic speech are reviewed extensively by Aune, *Prophecy in Early Christianity*, 153–88.

39. Cf. Str-B 2:615–17, where rabbinic texts are cited; and Schäfer, *Die Vorstellung vom heiligen Geist*, 112–14, 147–4S.

40. *Sotah* 9:15; for text, see *The Mishnah*, ed. Herbert Danby (Oxford: Clarendon Press, 1933), 306–7.

41. Cf. Schweizer, *Holy Spirit*, 24–27.

42. Book 3 of the *Sibylline Oracles* is judged to be composed in mid-second century B.C. by J. J. Collins. See his introduction, in *OTP* 1:355. The text is on *OTP* 1:379.

43. In *NT Prophecy*, David Hill has concluded that the expectation of a new era of prophecy was but "a peripheral element in the hopes of Judaism" (35–36) and says that Joel 2:28–29 was "an oracle to which late Judaism gave little importance" (96). In contrast, Aune, *Prophecy in Early Christianity*, 193, writes in connection with the use of this passage in Acts 2:15–21: "There was an apparently widespread view in early Judaism that at the end of the present age or in the age to come the Spirit of God would be poured out on all Israel and all Israelites would have the gift of prophesying." Aune quotes from *Numbers Rabbah* 11.29: "In this world some men have prophesied, but in the world to come, all Israelites will prophesy" and indicates that the same comment is made of Joel 2:28 in the *TB Baba Meṣia* 59b.

44. Cf. Goppelt, *Theology NT* 1:248.

45. Cf. Rudolf Bultmann, *Theology of the New Testament*, 2 vols. (New York: Charles Scribner's Sons, 1951–55), 1:155; and Ernst Käsemann, "On the Subject of Primitive Christian Apocalyptic," in *NT Questions of Today*, 116.

46. Cf. Dahl, "The Crucified Messiah," 32–33. Dahl writes (33) that "we may take it as a historical fact that Jesus did nothing to avoid his condemnation as 'King of the Jews.'" Cf. also Harvey, *Jesus and the Constraints of History*, 18.

47. So John Knox, *The Humanity and Divinity of Christ: A Study of Pattern in Christology* (Cambridge: Cambridge Univ. Press, 1967), 1–9; cf. Bultmann, *Theology NT* 1:27.

48. Hahn, *Titles of Jesus*, 106–7, 246–58, in connection with his studies of Acts 2:36 and Romans 1:3–4.

49. Cf. Martin Hengel, "Between Jesus and Paul: The 'Hellenists,' the 'Seven' and Stephen (Acts 6.1–15; 7.54—8.3)," in *Between Jesus and Paul: Studies in the Earliest History of Christianity* (Philadelphia: Fortress Press, 1983), 1–29.

CHAPTER 4

1. James M. Robinson and Helmut Koester, *Trajectories through Early Christianity* (Philadelphia: Fortress Press, 1971). On the method itself, see especially J. M. Robinson, "The Dismantling and Reassembling of the Categories of New Testament Scholarship," in ibid., 13–14.

2. On the christology of James in particular, see Peter H. Davids, *The Epistle of James: A Commentary on the Greek Text*, NIGTC (Grand Rapids: Wm. B. Eerdmans, 1982), 39–41. Davids writes: "Given the author's view of Jesus as the ascended Lord, one notes the absence of a *theologia crucis*, a son-of-God Christology, or a savior Christology" (40).

3. Observations on the christology of 2 Peter are made by Frederick W. Danker, "The Second Letter of Peter," in *Hebrews, James, 1 and 2 Peter, Jude, Revelation*, ed. Gerhard Krodel (Philadelphia: Fortress Press, 1977), 85–89.

CHAPTER 5

1. These statistics are based on their occurrences in the twenty-sixth edition of the Nestle-Aland Greek text, as give in the *Computer-Konkordanz zum Neuen Testament Graece von Nestle-Aland, 26. Auflage und zum Greek New Testament, 3rd Edition,* ed. Institut für neutestamentliche Textforschung und vom Rechenzentrum der Universität Münster, with special assistance from H. Bachmann and W. A. Slaby (Berlin and New York: Walter de Gruyter, 1980), 1918–27, 1082–87, and 1825. On four occasions (Rom. 16:25, 27; 1 Cor. 1:8; Gal. 1:6) there is uncertainty on text-critical grounds whether "Christ" (or at Rom. 16:25–27 whether the verses themselves) should be included, but these instances have been included in the computation above.

2. *Kyrios* is used in addition on eighteen occasions to designate God (as in the LXX); twice it means "master"; and once it refers to pagan deities. The 168 instances referred to are christological.

3. Werner Kramer, *Christ, Lord, Son of God*, SBT 50 (London: SCM Press, 1966), 203–6; Nils A. Dahl, "The Messiahship of Jesus in Paul," in *The Crucified Messiah and Other Essays* (Minneapolis: Augsburg Pub. House, 1974), 38; Martin Hengel, "'Christos' in Paul," in *Between Jesus and Paul: Studies in the Earliest History of Christianity* (Philadelphia: Fortress Press, 1983), 66, 181–182. According to Kramer, Paul uses "Christ Jesus" when a genitive or dative is required, while in the nominative "Jesus Christ" is the rule.

4. Kramer, *Christ, Lord, Son of God*, 127.

5. Ibid., 190–94.

6. It does not mean "instead of " in christological contexts. See BAGD, 838–39; Harald Riesenfeld, "Hyper," *TDNT* 8:508–9; C. F. D. Moule, *The Origin of Christology* (Cambridge: Cambridge Univ. Press, 1977), 111–26; cf. Leonhard Goppelt, *Theology of the New Testament*, 2 vols. (Grand Rapids: Wm. B. Eerdmans, 1981–82), 2:92–94; and Gerhard Friedrich, *Die Verkündigung des Todes Jesu im Neuen Testament*, BTS 6 (Neukirchen-Vluyn: Neukirchener Verlag, 1982), 72–76.

7. Other instances of the *hyper*-formula outside of Paul are at John 6:51; 11:51–52; Eph. 5:2, 25; 1 Tim. 2:16; Titus 2:14; Heb. 2:9; 1 Pet. 2:21; 3:18; 1 John 3:16.

8. Kramer, *Christ, Lord, Son of God*, 111–23, divides the passages into "sending" and "giving up" categories. That is appropriate in terms of a material difference (however slight), but the formal structure is the same, and the instances are few (only three passages), so we are treating them together.

9. Other instances in the New Testament are chiefly in the Johannine writings, e.g., John 3:17; 1 John 4:9. A similar pattern is found in Matt. 15:24 and Luke 4:18.

10. Contra Kramer, *Christ, Lord, Son of God*, 27, who does not survey all the *hyper*-formulas in Paul but, nevertheless, says, "The christological title used is *Christ* in every instance."

11. Ibid., 26.

12. Another formulation is that atonement is made for a person for his sin, e.g., Lev. 4:35; 5:6, 10; etc.

13. This of course is disputed in the work of James D. G. Dunn, *Christology in the Making: A New Testament Inquiry into the Origins of the Doctrine of the Incarnation* (Philadelphia: Westminster Press, 1980), who claims that Paul does not assume or assert the preexistence of Christ. See our review and critique of his work in chapter 1 (7–8) and the accompanying notes.

14. Cf. Reginald H. Fuller, *The Foundations of New Testament Christology* (New York: Charles Scribner's Sons, 1965), 204, and the literature cited by him (234–35). To this can be added the studies of Dieter Georgi, "Der vorpaulinische Hymnus Phil 2, 6–11," in *Zeit und Geschichte: Dankesgabe an Rudolf Bultmann zum 80. Geburtstag*, ed. Erich Dinkler (Tübingen: J. C. B. Mohr [Paul Siebeck], 1964), 263–93; and Günther Bornkamm, "On Understanding the Christ Hymn: Philippians 2.6–11," in *Early Christian Experience* (New York: Harper & Row, 1969), 112–22.

15. Cf. Ernst Lohmeyer, *Der Brief an die Philipper*, MeyerK 9, 9th ed. (Göttingen: Vandenhoeck & Ruprecht, 1953), 97; Ernst Käsemann, "Kritische Analyse von Phil. 2,5–11," in *Exegetische Versuche und Besinnungen*, 2d ed., 2 vols. (Göttingen: Vandenhoeck & Ruprecht, 1960–65), 1:51–95 (esp. 84–88); and Georgi, "Der vorpaulinische Hymnus," 289–91.

16. Cf. G. Stählin, "Nun," *TDNT* 4:1117.

17. Cf. Ernst Käsemann, "'The Righteousness of God' in Paul," in *New Testament Questions of Today* (Philadelphia: Fortress Press, 1969), 168–82; Peter Stuhlmacher, *Gerechtigkeit Gottes bei Paulus*, FRLANT 87 (Göttingen: Vandenhoeck & Ruprecht, 1965); Karl Kertelge, *"Rechtfertigung" bei Paulus*, NTAbh

n.s. 3 (Münster: Aschendorf, 1967); John Reumann, *"Righteousness" in the New Testament: "Justification" in the United States Lutheran–Roman Catholic Dialogue* (Philadelphia: Fortress Press, 1982), 41–123, 187–89; J. Christiaan Beker, *Paul the Apostle: The Triumph of God in Life and Thought* (Philadelphia: Fortress Press, 1980), 262–64; Goppelt, *Theology NT* 2:140–41; and Arland J. Hultgren, *Paul's Gospel and Mission: The Outlook from His Letter to the Romans* (Philadelphia: Fortress Press, 1985), 12–46.

18. Some examples are Ps. 72:1–4, 7 (LXX, 71:1–4, 7); Isa. 9:7 (LXX, 9:6); 11:1–2, 5; 61:11; Jer. 23:5–6; Wisd. of Sol. 5:18; *Pss. of Sol.* 17.28–35, 42; *T. Judah* 24:1–6. For additional passages and treatment of the theme, see Hultgren, *Paul's Gospel and Mission,* 21–26.

19. Such is the position of Rudolf Bultmann, *Theology of the New Testament,* 2 vols. (New York: Charles Scribner's Sons, 1951–55), 1:46; Ernst Käsemann, "Zum Verständnis von Römer 3, 24–26," *ZNW* 43 (1950–51): 150–54; idem, *Commentary on Romans* (Grand Rapids: Wm. B. Eerdmans, 1980), 96–99; A.M. Hunter, *Paul and His Predecessors,* rev. ed. (Philadelphia: Westminster Press, 1961), 120–22; Stuhlmacher, *Gerechtigkeit Gottes bei Paulus,* 86–91; idem, "Zum neueren Exegese von Röm 3,24–26," in *Jesus und Paulus: Festschrift für Werner Georg Kümmel zum 70. Geburtstag,* ed. E. Earle Ellis and Erich Grässer (Göttingen: Vandenhoeck & Ruprecht, 1975), 315–16; Hans Conzelmann, *An Outline of the Theology of the New Testament* (New York: Harper & Row, 1969), 166; and many others. For a survey of those who subscribe to this position and still other possible positions, see Hultgren, *Paul's Gospel and Mission,* 78 n. 93.

20. Reasons for rejecting the view are stated in Hultgren, *Paul's Gospel and Mission,* 60–69.

21. The interpretation of the term *hilastērion* at Rom. 3:25 is disputed. Three main interpretations are held: "mercy seat," "propitiation," and "expiation." For a survey and critique of these positions and for reasons presented in favor of "mercy seat" as most fitting, see ibid., 47–81.

22. This translation ("justification resulting in life") is taken from C. E. B. Cranfield, *A Critical and Exegetical Commentary on the Epistle to the Romans,* ICC (Edinburgh: T. & T. Clark, 1975–79), 269, 289. Cf. BAGD, 198.

23. Cf. W. Michaelis, "Piptō," *TDNT* 6:172; and Cranfield, *Epistle to the Romans,* 284.

24. This can be established for four reasons: (1) The parallel in 5:18 speaks in its favor, where "many" clearly means "all"; (2) within 5:19 itself "many were made sinners" obviously applies to all humankind, so "many will be made righteous" applies to all as well; (3) the same parallelism appears in 5:15 at which "many" refers to "all"; and (4) the phrase "for many" is a Semitism which means "for all," as in Isa. 53:11, 12; Mark 10:45; 14:24. For a discussion of "for many" as a Semitism "for all," cf. Joachim Jeremias, "Polloi," *TDNT* 6:536–45 (esp. 540–43); Otto Michel, *Der Brief an die Römer,* MeyerK 4, 11th ed. (Göttingen: Vandenhoeck & Ruprecht, 1957), 123; and Egon Brandenburger, *Adam und Christus: Exegetisch–religionsgeschichtliche Untersuchung zu Röm. 5:12–21(1 Kor. 15),* WMANT 7 (Neukirchen-Vluyn: Neukirchener Verlag, 1962), 221.

25. Romans 5:17 appears at first sight possibly to set limits when it says that "those who receive the abundance of grace and the free gift of righteousness

[will] reign in life." Does this restrict the scope of grace and its gifts to believers alone? The answer is no. The contrast is between the reign of death and the reign in life of those who receive God's grace. A shift of ages has taken place. The reign of death is over, and now grace reigns (5:21), and that grace has "abounded for many" (5:15). No restriction is implied. The view that in Rom. 5:12–21 Paul envisions the justification of all humanity and that 5:17 poses no restriction is held by many interpreters, including Adolf Schlatter, *Gottes Gerechtigkeit: Ein Kommentar zum Römerbrief,* 2d ed. (Stuttgart: Calwer Verlag, 1952), 192; Michel, *Der Brief an die Römer,* 126; C. H. Dodd, *The Epistle of Paul to the Romans,* MNTC (New York: Harper & Brothers, 1932), 116–17; C. K. Barrett, *A Commentary on the Epistle to the Romans,* HNTC (New York: Harper & Row, 1957), 117; Nils A. Dahl, "Two Notes on Romans 5," *ST* 5 (1951): 42–48; idem, "Christ, Creation and the Church," in *The Background of the New Testament and Its Eschatology: In Honour of Charles Harold Dodd,* ed. W. D. Davies and D. Daube (Cambridge: Cambridge Univ. Press, 1956), 436; Käsemann, *Romans,* 155–57; Cranfield, *Epistle to the Romans,* 290, 830; and Ulrich Wilckens, *Der Brief an die Römer,* EKKNT 6, 3 vols. (Cologne: Benziger; Neukirchen-Vluyn: Neukirchener Verlag, 1978–82), 1:325–28.

26. Cf. Günther Bornkamm, "The Revelation of Christ to Paul on the Damascus Road and Paul's Doctrine of Justification and Reconciliation: A Study in Galatians I," in *Reconciliation and Hope: New Testament Essays on Atonement and Eschatology Presented to L. L. Morris on His 60th Birthday,* ed. Robert Banks (Grand Rapids: Wm. B. Eerdmans, 1974), 102.

27. These and other passages on eschatological peril are treated at length in Hultgren, *Paul's Gospel and Mission,* 98–111.

28. Material in the closing paragraphs of this section is a summary of the more detailed treatment of Paul's mission in ibid., 125–50.

29. See Isa. 2:2–4; 12:3; 25:6–8; 51:4–5; 60:3; 66:18; Jer. 16:19; Mic. 4:1–3; Zech. 8:20–23; Tob. 13:11 (LXX, 13:13); 14:6; Wisd. of Sol. 8:14; and Sir. 39:10.

30. The background for the imagery of Rom. 15:16 is Sir. 50:12–13.

31. Cf. Walther Eichrodt, *Theology of the Old Testament,* 2 vols. (Philadelphia: Westminster Press, 1961–67), 1:152; and Gerhard von Rad, *Old Testament Theology,* 2 vols. (New York: Harper & Row, 1962–65), 1:254.

32. Johannes Pedersen, *Israel: Its Life and Culture,* 2 vols. (London: Oxford Univ. Press, 1926–40), 2:301.

33. The term "creation"(*ktisis*) in Rom. 8:21 includes humanity. On this, see Michel, *Der Brief an die Römer,* 172–73; F. F. Bruce, *The Epistle of Paul to the Romans,* TNTC (London: Tyndale Press, 1963), 173; John G. Gibbs, *Creation and Redemption: A Study in Pauline Theology,* NovTSup 26 (Leiden: E.J. Brill, 1971), 39–42; John G. Gager, "Functional Diversity in Paul's Use of End-Time Language," *JBL* 89 (1970): 327–30; Käsemann, *Romans,* 232–33; and Wilckens, *Der Brief an die Römer* 2:157–58.

34. Paul does not mean here that the salvation of Israel depends on the conversion of Jews; it depends purely on the grace of God and his election of Israel. On this, see (among others) Barrett, *Epistle to Romans,* 227; Bruce, *The Epistle of Paul to the Romans,* 223; Oscar Cullmann, *Salvation in History* (New York: Harper & Row, 1967), 162; Günther Bornkamm, *Paul* (New York: Harper & Row,

1971), 151; Ulrich Luz, *Das Geschichtsverständnis des Paulus*, BEvT 49 (Munich: Chr. Kaiser Verlag, 1978), 286–300; Käsemann, *Romans*, 314; Krister Stendahl, *Paul among Jews and Gentiles* (Philadelphia: Fortress Press, 1976), 4; Nils A. Dahl, "The Future of Israel," in *Studies in Paul* (Minneapolis: Augsburg Pub. House, 1977), 153–58; Cranfield, *Epistle to the Romans*, 577; W. D. Davies, "Paul and the People of Israel," in *Jewish and Pauline Studies* (Philadelphia: Fortress Press, 1984), 139–43; and Wilckens, *Der Brief an die Römer* 2:254–56.

35. The seven instances are at 1:1; 8:29; 9:41; 12:35; 13:21; 14:61; 15:32.

36. These are at 1:11 ("my beloved Son"); 3:11 ("Son of God"); 5:7 ("Son of God"); 9:7 ("my beloved Son"); 13:32 ("the Son"); 14:61 ("Son of the Blessed"); and 15:39 ("Son of God").

37. These fall into three categories: the coming of the Son of Man (8:38; 13:26; 14:62); the suffering Son of Man (8:31; 9:9, 12, 31; 10:33, 45; 14:21 [twice], 41); and the earthly ministry of the Son of Man (2:10, 28).

38. These occur at 10:47, 48; 12:35.

39. These are at 15:2, 9, 12, 18, 26, 32. In the last of these six instances, the term is "King of Israel."

40. These are at 2:28; 11:3; 12:37; and 13:35. In each of these Jesus is in view when the term *kyrios* is used. In the saying of 5:19 it is probable that "the Lord" refers to God.

41. "Rabbi" is used three times (9:5; 11:21; 14:45) and "rabboni" once (10:51); "teacher" is used twelve times (4:38; 5:35; 9:17, 38; 10:17, 20, 35; 12:14, 19, 32; 13:1; 14:14); and "prophet" is used three times (6:4, 14; 8:28).

42. Vincent Taylor, *The Gospel according to St. Mark* (New York: St. Martin's Press, 1952), 120–22; Conzelmann, *Outline*, 144; and Jack D. Kingsbury, *The Christology of Mark's Gospel* (Philadelphia: Fortress Press, 1983), 47–155.

43. Norman Perrin, "The Creative Use of the Son of Man Traditions by Mark" and "The Christology of Mark: A Study in Methodology," in *A Modern Pilgrimage in New Testament Christology* (Philadelphia: Fortress Press, 1974), 84–93, 104–21; and Paul J. Achtemeier, *Mark* (Philadelphia: Fortress Press, 1975), 46.

44. Contra Taylor, *The Gospel according to St. Mark*, 152; Hugh Anderson, *The Gospel of Mark*, NCB (London: Oliphants, 1976), 66; Rudolf Pesch, *Das Markusevangelium*, HTKNT 2, 2 vols. (Freiburg: Herder, 1976–77), 1:74–75; Conzelmann, *Outline*, 141; Edward Schillebeeckx, *Jesus: An Experiment in Christology* (New York: Crossroad, 1981), 108; and Lamar Williamson, Jr., *Mark*, Interpretation Commentary (Atlanta: John Knox Press, 1983), 2, 28. A critique of this view has been presented by Joachim Gnilka, *Das Evangelium nach Markus*, EKKNT 2, 2 vols. (Zurich: Benziger Verlag, 1978–79), 1:42.

45. Contra C. E. B. Cranfield, *The Gospel according to St. Mark*, CGTC (Cambridge: Cambridge Univ. Press, 1959), 34–35; William L. Lane, *The Gospel according to Mark*, NICNT (Grand Rapids: Wm. B. Eerdmans, 1974), 42; and James M. Robinson, *The Problem of History in Mark and Other Marcan Studies* (Philadelphia: Fortress Press, 1982), 71.

46. Cf. Willi Marxsen, *Mark the Evangelist: Studies on the Redaction History of the Gospel* (Nashville: Abingdon Press, 1969), 148, who writes that "for Mark, Jesus is the subject and object of the gospel."

47. Ibid., 128, 131–32.

48. Cf. Sherman E. Johnson, *A Commentary on the Gospel according to St. Mark*, HNTC (New York: Harper & Row, 1960), 31; Leander E. Keck, "The Introduction to Mark's Gospel," *NTS* 12 (1965–66): 359, 366–68; Marxsen, *Mark the Evangelist*, 131–32; Eduard Schweizer, *The Good News according to Mark* (Richmond: John Knox Press, 1970), 30; Achtemeier, *Mark*, 48–50; Gnilka, *Das Evangelium nach Markus* 1:42–43; and Kingsbury, *The Christology of Mark's Gospel*, 55–56.

49. This is debatable. Some interpreters have maintained that Mark sought to combat and correct a false christology. But the degree to which Mark's christological instruction presupposes polemics, and not simply the need for catechesis, can scarcely be determined from the Gospel of Mark itself. One of the major works taking the view that Mark sought to combat and correct a false christology is that of Theodore J. Weeden, *Mark: Traditions in Conflict* (Philadelphia: Fortress Press, 1971). See also Norman Perrin, "Towards an Interpretation of the Gospel of Mark," in *Christology and a Modern Pilgrimage: A Discussion with Norman Perrin*, ed. Hans Dieter Betz (Claremont, Calif.: The New Testament Colloquium, 1971), 51–55; idem, "The Christology of Mark," 110–13.

50. The Gospel of Mark was composed ca. A.D. 70, according to most interpreters, either just prior to the destruction of Jerusalem or shortly after. Those who place it prior include Taylor, *The Gospel according to St. Mark*, 31–32; Dennis E. Nineham, *The Gospel of Mark* (Baltimore: Penguin Books, 1963), 42; Lane, *The Gospel according to Mark*, 18–21; Willi Marxsen, *Introduction to the New Testament* (Philadelphia: Fortress Press, 1968), 143; Reginald H. Fuller, *A Critical Introduction to the New Testament* (London: G. Duckworth, 1966), 106; Howard C. Kee, *Community of the New Age: Studies in Mark's Gospel* (Philadelphia: Westminster Press, 1977), 100–105; Anderson, *The Gospel of Mark*, 24–26; and Schweizer, *The Good News according to Mark*, 25. Those who place it after A.D. 70 include Étienne Trocmé, *The Formation of the Gospel according to Mark* (Philadelphia: Westminster Press, 1975), 244; Norman Perrin and Dennis C. Duling, *The New Testament: An Introduction*, 2d ed. (New York: Harcourt Brace Jovanovich, 1982), 257; and Werner Kelber, *The Kingdom in Mark: A New Time and A New Place* (Philadelphia: Fortress Press, 1974), 138–44. Others who simply place the Gospel to about A.D. 70 are Werner G. Kümmel, *Introduction to the New Testament*, rev. ed. (Nashville: Abingdon Press, 1975), 98; and Achtemeier, *Mark*, 116–17.

51. Cf. Nils A. Dahl, "The Purpose of Mark's Gospel," in *Jesus in the Memory of the Early Church* (Minneapolis: Augsburg Pub. House, 1976), 58, who writes concerning Mark: "His goal is not to persuade readers to believe in the message but to remind them of what is contained in it in order that they might understand what has been given to them. The purpose is not kerygmatic in the word's narrower sense, but rather theological or—to coin a word— anamnetic."

52. Cf. Kingsbury, *The Christology of Mark's Gospel*, 57–58, 68, 99, 101, 115–18, 120, 134, 143–44, 158, who shows that at decisive events (the sending of John, the designation of Jesus as God's Son at his baptism and transfiguration, the transfiguration as a tranformation, and the death and resurrection) it is God who is the initiator and director of the action. "For Mark . . . Jesus is the decisive

figure in the whole of God's history of salvation, and he alerts the reader to this as early as . . . the first verse of the Gospel" (58).

53. Other instances of the use of *dei* to indicate that events are taking place according to divine purpose are at 9:11; 13:7, 10.

54. Additional ways in which Jesus is portrayed by Mark as the one who fulfills the Scriptures are surveyed by Howard C. Kee, *Jesus in History: An Approach to the Study of the Gospels,* 2d ed. (New York: Harcourt Brace Jovanovich, 1977), 145–49.

55. Mark's "theology" (doctrine of God itself) and the relationship between theology and christology have been given treatment by John R. Donahue, "A Neglected Factor in the Theology of Mark," *JBL* 101 (1982): 563–94.

56. William Wrede, *Das Messiasgeheimnis in den Evangelien* (Göttingen: Vandenhoeck & Ruprecht, 1901; 3d ed., 1963); Eng. trans.: *The Messianic Secret* (London: James Clarke, 1971).

57. A history of research on the theme since Wrede has been written by James L. Blevins, *The Messianic Secret in Markan Research, 1901–1976* (Lanham, Md.: Univ. Press of America, 1981); a shorter survey and critique of various positions have been provided by Christopher Tuckett, "Introduction: The Problem of the Messianic Secret," in *The Messianic Secret,* ed. C. Tuckett, Issues in Religion and Theology 1 (Philadelphia: Fortress Press, 1983), 1–28. The volume contains essays in English (or in English translation) by N. A. Dahl, J. B. Tyson, T. A. Burkill, G. Strecker, E. Schweizer, U. Luz, W. C. Robinson, Jr., J. D. G. Dunn, and H. Räisänen. Another brief treatment and critique of various positions is offered by Kingsbury, *The Christology of Mark's Gospel,* 1–23.

58. É. Trocmé, "Is There a Markan Christology?" in *Christ and Spirit in the New Testament: In Honour of Charles Francis Digby Moule,* ed. B. Lindars and S. S. Smalley (Cambridge: Cambridge Univ. Press, 1973), 8–10. Trocmé states flatly that "under close scrutiny, the theory of the Messianic Secret simply vanishes for lack of evidence" (10).

59. Hans Conzelmann, "Present and Future in the Synoptic Tradition," in *God and Christ: Existence and Province,* ed. Robert W. Funk, *JTC* 5 (New York: Harper & Row, 1968), 42–43; translated from the German version, "Gegenwart und Zukunft in der synoptischen Tradition," *ZTK* 54 (1957): 293–95.

60. Cf. C. Tuckett, "Introduction: The Problem of the Messianic Secret," 17, who writes: "This theory, that the secret reflects the central importance of the cross as the only valid key for interpreting the person of Jesus, has found widespread support," and he cites works by H. Conzelmann, P. Vielhauer, U. Luz, J. Schreiber, J. M. Robinson, H. Koester, L. E. Keck, R. H. Fuller, H. D. Betz, G. Minette de Tillesse, A. M. Ambrozic, J. Lambrecht, D. A. Koch, and H. Anderson. To this list could be added many others, including Dahl, "The Purpose of Mark's Gospel," 59; Achtemeier, *Mark,* 81; and Maria Horstmann, *Studien zur markinischen Christologie,* NTAbh, n.s. 6 (Münster: Verlag Aschendorff, 1969), 113–28, 138.

61. Trocmé, "Is There a Markan Christology?" 11–13, gives attention to this theme, calling it a "christology of awe" and a "religious type of christology." On the other hand, J. M. Robinson, *The Problem of History in Mark,* 116–21, also

gives attention to the theme and concludes that Mark had serious reservations about the numinous—at least as a form of piety.

62. So Achtemeier, *Mark,* 80, who says that the "majority of miracle stories have no word about secrecy."

63. Cf. Jeremias, "Polloi," 536–45; idem, *The Eucharistic Words of Jesus,* rev. ed. (Philadelphia: Fortress Press, 1977 [1966]), 179.

64. The term is used to designate a fee given to purchase freedom for a slave (Lev. 25:51–52), to save a person from the death penalty (Exod. 21:30), or to compensate for a crime (Num. 35:31–32).

65. Cf. BAGD, 73; Schweizer, *The Good News according to Mark,* 222; Anderson, *The Gospel of Mark,* 257; Joachim Jeremias, *New Testament Theology: Part One, The Proclamation of Jesus* (New York: Charles Scribner's Sons, 1971), 292–94; and Moule, *The Origin of Christology,* 119. The sense of the preposition is illustrated clearly at Matt. 17:27

66. So H. E. Tödt, *The Son of Man in the Synoptic Tradition* (Philadelphia: Westminster Press, 1965), 204. Jeremias, *Theology,* 291; and Goppelt, *Theology NT* 1:196, assume that the allusion is clear.

67. These include Rudolf Bultmann, *The History of the Synoptic Tradition,* 2d ed. (New York: Harper & Row, 1968), 275–84; Martin Dibelius, *From Tradition to Gospel,* 2d ed. (New York: Charles Scribner's Sons, 1934), 178–217; Taylor, *The Gospel according to St. Mark,* 653–71; Jeremias, *The Eucharistic Words of Jesus,* 89–96; Ernest Best, *The Temptation and the Passion: The Markan Soteriology,* SNTSMS 2 (Cambridge: Cambridge Univ. Press, 1965), 89–102; and Helmut Koester, *Introduction to the New Testament,* 2 vols. (Philadelphia: Fortress Press; Berlin: Walter de Gruyter, 1982), 2:49, 165, 167.

68. Kümmel, *Introduction,* 84–85; Eta Linnemann, *Studien der Passionsgeschichte,* FRLANT 102 (Göttingen: Vandenhoeck & Ruprecht, 1970), 171–75; John R. Donahue, *Are You the Christ? The Trial Narrative in the Gospel of Mark,* SBLDS 10 (Missoula, Mont.: Scholars Press, 1973); Werner Kelber, "Conclusion: From Passion Narrative to Gospel," in *The Passion in Mark,* ed. W. Kelber (Philadelphia: Fortress Press, 1976), 153–59, who sums up the views of others as well; and Achtemeier, *Mark,* 82–91.

69. Cf. Philipp Vielhauer, "Erwägungen zur Christologie des Markusevangeliums," in *Zeit und Geschichte,* ed. Dinkler, 164. The rending of the temple curtain also signified the end of the temple and its cultus, as maintained by Donald H. Juel, *Messiah and Temple: The Trial of Jesus in the Gospel of Mark,* SBLDS 31 (Missoula, Mont.: Scholars Press, 1977), 140–42.

70. Cf. Eduard Schweizer, "Die theologische Leistung des Markus," *EvT* 24 (1964): 353–54.

71. John D. Crossan, "Empty Tomb and Absent Lord (Mark 16:1–8)," in *The Passion in Mark,* ed. Kelber, 149, writes, "This is no temporary response of numinous awe [and t]he women . . . fail to communicate the message." Cf. also Anderson, *The Gospel of Mark,* 358; Schweizer, *The Good News according to Mark,* 372–73; and Williamson, *Mark,* 285. A survey of critical views of the scene is provided by Robert H. Smith, *The Easter Gospels: The Resurrection of Jesus according to the Four Evangelists* (Minneapolis: Augsburg Pub. House, 1983), 43–45.

72. Cf. Smith, *The Easter Gospels*, 40–43; and J. R. Donahue, "A Neglected Factor," 569, who says that 16:8 "reinforces the numinous awe with which one should respond even to the resurrection proclamation." Other interpreters who express similar views include Cranfield, *The Gospel according to St. Mark*, 358; and Lane, *The Gospel according to Mark*, 590–91.

73. Cf. C. F. D. Moule, "St Mark XVI. 8 Once More," *NTS* 2 (1955–56): 58–59; and Smith, *The Easter Gospels*, 43.

74. Cf. Ferdinand Hahn, *The Titles of Jesus in Christology: Their History in Early Christianity* (Cleveland: World Pub. Co., 1969), 37–42; and N. Perrin, "The Use of (Para)didonai in Connection with the Passion of Jesus in the New Testament," in *A Modern Pilgrimage*, 100, who assigns these passages to passion apologetic.

75. The saying does not imply preexistence. It reflects rather a "prophetic motif" in which Jesus is God's messenger; cf. Donahue, "A Neglected Factor," 588–89. The view that the passage presupposes the preexistence of Christ is maintained by Johannes Schreiber, "Die Christologie des Markusevangeliums: Beobachtungen zur Theologie und Komposition des zweiten Evangeliums," *ZTK* 58 (1961): 166–67. That the Gospel of Mark has no concept of the preexistence of Christ is held by James D. G. Dunn, *Christology in the Making: A New Testament Inquiry into the Origins of the Doctrine of the Incarnation* (Philadelphia: Westminster Press, 1980), 46–48.

76. Cf. Jeremias, *NT Theology*, 292–94; Tödt, *Son of Man*, 202–11; Hahn, *Titles of Jesus*, 56–58; Perrin, "The Use of (Para)didonai," 102–3; and Goppelt, *Theology NT* 1:193–99.

77. Cf. Dahl, "The Purpose of Mark's Gospel," 55–60. See the quotation from this essay in n. 51 above.

78. The Gospel anticipates the evangelization of gentiles (13:10; 14:9), and since Jewish festivals need explanation (15:42), the Marcan community must include gentiles already. Members of the community need not observe the usual Torah regulations for the sabbath (2:23–28; 3:1–5), purification (7:1–8), and dietary matters (7:18–19).

79. Kingsbury, *The Christology of Mark's Gospel*, 115; cf. also Schweizer, *The Good News according to Mark*, 239–41.

80. The Lord's Supper is observed (14:22–25); sins are remitted (2:10); a fast day is kept (Fridays, 2:20); children are included in gatherings for worship (10:13–16); there are regulations on forgiving one another (11:25), on marriage and divorce (10:2–12), and on care for the poor (10:17–22); there are warnings against false prophets (13:5–6, 21–23); and there is a call for endurance (which would include group solidarity) in the face of persecution (13:9–13). Mark speaks of persons who are committed to Christ and his gospel (8:35; 10:29), and these persons have left normal familial ties and are bound together in discipleship to Christ (10:29–30).

81. Helmut Merklein, "Die Auferstehung Jesu und die Anfänge der Christologie (Messias bzw. Sohn Gottes und Menschensohn)," *ZNW* 72 (1981): 2.

82. Romans 10:9b; 1 Cor. 6:14; 15:15; 1 Thess. 1:10; Acts 2:32; 3:15; 4:10.

83. Cf. Dahl, "The Messiahship of Jesus in Paul," 41: "Paul represented a

strikingly advanced stage in the evolution that transformed *Christos* from a messianic designation to Jesus' second proper name."

84. In regard to the apostle Paul, the remark is appropriately made by Vincent Taylor, *The Atonement in New Testament Teaching*, 2d ed. (London: Epworth Press, 1945), 75: "It is God who forgives, justifies, reconciles, and sanctifies; it is with Him that man enters into peace, to Him that he has access, and from Him that he receives the gift of sonship."

85. See n. 80 above.

CHAPTER 6

1. Cf. Werner G. Kümmel, *Introduction to the New Testament,* rev. ed. (Nashville: Abingdon Press, 1975), 119–20; Reginald H. Fuller, *A Critical Introduction to the New Testament* (London: G. Duckworth, 1966), 114; Willi Marxsen, *Introduction to the New Testament* (Philadelphia: Fortress Press, 1968), 153; Helmut Koester, *Introduction to the New Testament,* 2 vols. (Philadelphia: Fortress Press; Berlin: Walter de Gruyter, 1982), 2:172; Georg Strecker, *Der Weg der Gerechtigkeit: Untersuchung zur Theologie des Matthäus,* FRLANT 82, 2d ed. (Göttingen: Vandenhoeck & Ruprecht, 1966), 35–37; Eduard Schweizer, *The Good News according to Matthew* (Atlanta: John Knox Press, 1975), 15–17; Jack D. Kingsbury, *Matthew,* PC (Philadelphia: Fortress Press, 1977), 93–94; John P. Meier, *The Vision of Matthew: Christ, Church, and Morality in the First Gospel* (New York: Paulist Press, 1979), 12–15; idem, "Locating Matthew's Church in Time and Space," in Raymond E. Brown and J. P. Meier, *Antioch and Rome: New Testament Cradles of Catholic Christianity* (New York: Paulist Press, 1983), 15–27; and Francis W. Beare, *The Gospel according to Matthew: A Commentary* (San Francisco: Harper & Row, 1981), 7–8. An earlier dating of A.D. 65–67 has been proposed by Robert H. Gundry, *Matthew: A Commentary on His Literary and Theological Art* (Grand Rapids: Wm. B. Eerdmans, 1982), 599–609, but his conclusions are not convincing; for example, he dismisses the evidence of Matt. 22:7 too easily.

2. W. D. Davies, *The Setting of the Sermon on the Mount* (Cambridge: Cambridge Univ. Press, 1964), 256–315 (esp. 300–315).

3. The author was not Matthew, one of the Twelve. The author (in the view of most critical scholars today) made use of Mark and Q as sources, which an eyewitness would not likely have done; he was fluent in literary Greek, which is not likely (though not impossible) for one of the Twelve; and he embellished stories in a way that would have been impossible for an eyewitness, e.g., in 21:1–11, the triumphal entry, Jesus is portrayed as riding on two animals (based on the author's reading of Zech. 9:9; see commentaries for details on how Matthew understood it), while all other accounts (Mark 11:1–10; Luke 19:28–38; John 12:12–18) have him on one, which is what one would expect—and expect from an eyewitness. On the question of authorship see further Kümmel, *Introduction,* 120–21.

4. Between the birth and infancy narrative (Matt. 1—2) and the passion, death, and resurrection narrative (Matt. 26—28) the material is ordered into five major blocks, each consisting of narrative and discourse, and ending with the Matthean

comment, "And when Jesus had finished these sayings, . . . " (or something similar, 7:28; 11:1; 13:53; 19:1; 26:1). Matthew has thus organized the material (particularly the teaching material) in a topical manner: the higher righteousness in the Sermon on the Mount (5:1—7:29); instruction for mission and exhortations to fearless confession and enduring persecution (9:35—11:1); parables of the kingdom (13:1–53); discourses on discipleship and discipline in the community (18:1—19:1); and an eschatological discourse (24:1—26:1). It has been suggested that Matthew ordered his Gospel into three sections (1:1—4:16; 4:17—16:20; and 16:21—28:20) by Jack D. Kingsbury, *Matthew: Structure, Christology, Kingdom* (Philadelphia: Fortress Press, 1975), 7–25; idem, *Matthew,* 21–29. This approach, however, seems to confuse the Matthean presentation of major turning points in Jesus' ministry with his literary ordering of the materials, as pointed out by Gundry, *Matthew,* 10; a criticism against Kingsbury's theory on other grounds is made by Reginald H. Fuller, "Christology in Matthew and Luke," in R. H. Fuller and Pheme Perkins, *Who Is This Christ? Gospel Christology and Contemporary Faith* (Philadelphia: Fortress Press, 1983), 81–82.

5. Cf. Howard C. Kee, *Jesus in History: An Approach to the Study of the Gospels,* 2d ed. (New York: Harcourt Brace Jovanovich, 1977), 171.

6. Cf. Kingsbury, *Matthew,* 93–106; and Meier, "Locating Matthew's Church," 22–23.

7. None of these comes from Q; three are taken from Mark (16:16; 22:42; 26:63); and eleven are distinctive to Matthew (1:1, 16, 17, 18; 2:4; 11:2; 16:20; 23:10; 26:68; 27:17, 22).

8. None is from Q; five are from Mark (12:8; 15:27a; 21:3; 22:44b, 45); and twenty-five are distinctive to Matthew (7:21, 22; 8:2, 6, 8, 21, 25; 9:28; 14:28, 30; 15:22, 25; 16:22; 17:4, 15; 18:21; 20:30, 31, 33; 22:43; 24:42; 25:11, 37, 44; 26:22). Four comments should be added: (1) at 7:21, 22; 25:11 "Lord, Lord" appears, but these instances are counted as three (not 6) instances of the term; (2) at 17:4 and 20:33 Matthew replaces Mark's "rabbi" with "Lord," and at 17:15 he replaces Mark's "teacher" with "Lord"; (3) the term "Lord" applies to God (rather than Christ) nineteen times in Matthew (often in Old Testament quotations); and (4) it applies also to earthly masters twenty-eight times.

9. Five are from Q (4:3, 6; 11:27 thrice); six are from Mark (3:17; 8:29; 17:5; 24:36; 26:63; 27:54); and six appear in Matthew's distinctive materials (2:15; 14:33; 16:16; 27:40, 43; 28:19).

10. These include sayings concerning (1) the future coming of the Son of Man (15 times)—two from Mark (24:30b; 26:64); six from Q (10:32; 12:40; 24:27, 37, 39, 44); and seven distinctive (10:23; 13:41; 16:27, 28; 19:28; 24:30a; 25:31)—(2) the suffering Son of Man (9 times)—none from Q; seven from Mark (17:9, 22–23; 20:18–19, 28; 26:24 twice, 45); and two distinctive (17:21; 26:2)— and (3) the present Son of Man (7 times)—two from Mark (9:6; 12:8); three from Q (8:20; 11:19; 12:32); and two distinctive (13:37; 16:13). The combined totals are nine sayings from Q, eleven from Mark, and eleven from Matthew's own traditions and/or composition. Three Son of Man sayings in Mark (8:31, 38; 9:12) are not reproduced by Matthew.

11. None is from Q; two are from Mark (20:30, 31); and six are distinctive to Matthew (1:1; 9:27; 12:23; 15:22; 21:9, 15).

12. Three are from Mark (27:11, 29, 37), and one is distinctive to Matthew (2:2).

13. The term "prophet" appears at 13:57 in an aphorism of Jesus, and at 21:11 and 46 as a general estimation of Jesus. Twice Jesus is addressed by Judas as "rabbi" (26:25, 49). The term "teacher" (*didaskalos*) is used by Jesus in aphorisms about himself twice (10:24, 25) and twice concerning his role (23:8; 26:18); otherwise he is spoken of as a teacher, or addressed as such, by scribes, Pharisees, Sadducees, and collectors of the temple tax (8:19; 9:11; 12:38; 17:24; 19:16; 22:16, 24, 36). That these terms (prophet, rabbi, and teacher) are not titles of majesty is also the judgment of Kingsbury, *Matthew: Structure, Christology, Kingdom*, 88, 92–93; idem, *Matthew*, 32, 43–44.

14. A summary of proposals on the importance attached to the various titles by modern interpreters has been provided by Kingsbury, *Matthew: Structure, Christology, Kingdom*, 40–42.

15. Edward P. Blair, *Jesus in the Gospel of Matthew* (Nashville: Abingdon Press, 1960), 83.

16. Willoughby C. Allen, *A Critical and Exegetical Commentary on the Gospel according to S. Matthew*, ICC, 3d ed. (Edinburgh: T. & T. Clark, 1912), lxvi–lxvii; and Floyd V. Filson, *A Commentary on the Gospel according to St. Matthew*, HNTC, 2d ed. (New York: Harper & Row, 1971), 27–28.

17. Wolfgang Trilling, *Das wahre Israel*, SANT 10, 3d ed. (Munich: Kösel Verlag, 1964), 21–51.

18. Kingsbury, *Matthew: Structure, Christology, Kingdom*, 40–83; and James D. G. Dunn, *Christology in the Making: A New Testament Inquiry into the Origins of the Doctrine of the Incarnation* (Philadelphia: Westminster Press, 1980), 48.

19. So Meier, *Vision of Matthew*, 217–19, who speaks of a "Son-Christology" consisting of "Son of God," "Son of Man," and "the Son." And Strecker, *Der Weg der Gerechtigkeit*, 118–20 and 123–26, claims that Matthew has brought about a unity of two titles: as "Lord," Jesus possesses an eschatological quality; "Son of David" designates his being sent to Israel in history.

20. See n. 10 above.

21. Cf. Meier, *Vision of Matthew*, 217–18.

22. See n. 8 above.

23. See n. 9 above.

24. Cf. Fuller, "Christology in Matthew and Luke," 83, who cites Günther Bornkamm, "End-Expectation and Church in Matthew," in G. Bornkamm, G. Barth, and H. J. Held, *Tradition and Interpretation in Matthew* (Philadelphia: Westminster Press, 1963), 15–51.

25. Cf. Horst R. Balz, *Methodische Probleme der neutestamentlichen Christologie*, WMANT 25 (Neukirchen-Vluyn: Neukirchener Verlag, 1967), 46.

26. These are introduced by the Matthean statement, "This took place to fulfill what the Lord spoke through the prophet," or a similar statement (1:22; 2:15, 17, 23; 4:14; 8:17; 12:17; 13:14, 35; 21:4; 27:9; cf. 2:5).

27. It has been said that in Matt. 5:21–48 (the "Antitheses") the Matthean Jesus does actually annul the law in three instances: concerning divorce, oaths, and retaliation (5:31–42). Such is the view of John P. Meier, *Law and History*

in Matthew's Gospel, AnBib 71 (Rome: Biblical Institute Press, 1976), 140–61; idem, *Vision of Matthew,* 248–62. But this is not accurate. Teaching that one should not divorce one's wife (except for unchastity) does not annul the law which prescribes the giving of a certificate of divorce (Deut 24:1–4; Matt. 5:31). Teaching that one must not swear at all does not annul the law against swearing falsely (Lev. 19:12; Num. 30:2; Deut. 23:21; Matt. 5:33), for the intent is that one speak the truth on all occasions, making oaths unnecessary. Teaching that one should refrain from retaliation entirely does not actually annul the *lex talionis* (Exod. 21:24; Lev. 24:20; Deut. 19:21; Matt. 5:38) but calls for the setting aside what the law permits for justice to be done (a modern parallel would be that, while litigation is possible to recover damages under the law, it need not be entered into). In these cases, as in others, the Matthean Jesus teaches the will of God. The law of Moses seeks to establish a just order in these three instances, and it is assumed to be just and good, but it can also be used to acquit oneself of doing the will of God. Jesus penetrates through the facade. If there is an annulment of the law in Matthew, that would be in regard to circumcision and laws regarding purification and diet. On the view that the Matthean Jesus does not annul the law, see B. L. Martin, "Matthew on Christ and the Law," *TS* 44 (1983): 53–70.

28. G. Barth, "Matthew's Understanding of the Law," in *Tradition and Interpretation in Matthew,* 77.

29. This point is amplified in Arland J. Hultgren, "The Double Commandment of Love in Mt. 22:34–40: Its Sources and Composition," *CBQ* 36 (1974): 373–78.

30. The major study here is M. Jack Suggs, *Wisdom, Christology, and Law in Matthew's Gospel* (Cambridge: Harvard Univ. Press, 1970). According to Suggs, the Matthean Jesus is the "incarnation of Wisdom" and "the embodiment of Torah" (130). Since, however, incarnation implies preexistence (a concept lacking in Matthew), it is better to say that "Jesus 'incarnated,' or 'embodied,' God's wisdom," as does Fuller, "Christology in Matthew and Luke," 85.

31. The verbal aspect of the name is highlighted by Werner Foerster, "Iēsous," *TDNT* 3:289.

32. Davies, *Setting of the Sermon on the Mount,* 428–31.

33. Cf. Strecker, *Der Weg der Gerechtigkeit,* 148–49.

34. Cf. Birger Gerhardsson, "Sacrificial Service and Atonement in the Gospel of Matthew," in *Reconciliation and Hope: New Testament Essays on Atonement and Eschatology Presented to L. L. Morris on His 60th Birthday,* ed. Robert Banks (Grand Rapids: Wm. B. Eerdmans, 1974), 30–31, who interprets the verse at the Matthean level as a saying about Jesus' sacrificial service as an act of unlimited obedience to God for the benefit of others.

35. This observation has been made by, among others, Martin Dibelius, *From Tradition to Gospel* (New York: Charles Scribner's Sons, 1934), 196–99; and Nils A. Dahl, "The Passion Narrative in Matthew," in *Jesus in the Memory of the Early Church* (Minneapolis: Augsburg Pub. House, 1976), 45–46. In regard to other places in his Gospel at which Matthew has heightened the christology, see G. M. Styler, "Stages in Christology in the Synoptic Gospels," *NTS* 10 (1963–64): 404–6.

36. Cf. Dibelius, *From Tradition to Gospel,* 197: In his passion narrative Mat-

thew portrays Jesus "even in suffering as the plenipotentiary Son of God who is master of His own fate."

37. Cf. Gundry, *Matthew,* 575.

38. On *hoi de edistasan* (28:17b) as rightly rendered "but some doubted" (RSV), see ibid., 594.

39. Cf. Gerhardsson, "Sacrificial Service and Atonement," 34.

40. Cf. Hans von Campenhausen, *Ecclesiastical Authority and Spiritual Power in the Church of the First Three Centuries* (Stanford: Stanford Univ. Press, 1969), 126; cf. also Herbert Braun, *Jesus: Der Mann aus Nazareth und seine Zeit,* Themen der Theologie 1, 2d ed. (Stuttgart: Kreuz Verlag, 1969), 145.

41. Cf. Rudolf Bultmann, *History of the Synoptic Tradition,* rev. ed. (New York: Harper & Row, 1968), 141; Günther Bornkamm, "The Authority to 'Bind' and 'Loose' in the Church in Matthew's Gospel," in *Jesus and Man's Hope,* ed. D. G. Buttrick, D. G. Miller, and D. Y. Hadidian, 2 vols. (Pittsburgh: Pittsburgh Theological Seminary, 1970–71), 1:40; Schweizer, *The Good News according to Matthew,* 371–72; and Gundry, *Matthew,* 368–69. The background and significance of this passage (as well as 16:19) are given detailed treatment by Richard H. Hiers, "'Binding' and 'Loosing': The Matthean Authorization," *JBL* 104 (1985): 233–50. He writes that "Matthew may have intended his authorization to encompass not only matters of doctrine but also excommunication, and even determination of the ultimate destiny of church members" (249).

42. Cf. the references and discussion in George F. Moore, *Judaism in the First Centuries of the Christian Era: The Age of the Tannaim,* 3 vols.(Cambridge: Harvard Univ. Press, 1927–30), 1:520–34.

43. For Matthew the history of salvation consists of two epochs: the time of prophecy which has come to an end, and the time of fulfillment, which has come. This has been discerned by Jack D. Kingsbury, "The Structure of Matthew's Gospel and His Concept of Salvation History," *CBQ* 35 (1973): 451–74; idem, *Matthew: Structure, Christology, Kingdom,* 25–37. This is also the view of Eduard Schweizer, *Matthäus und seine Gemeinde,* Stuttgarter Bibelstudien 71 (Stuttgart: Katholisches Bibelwerk, 1974), 154 n. 44; idem, *The Good News according to Matthew,* 26, 539–41. It has also been proposed that Matthew thinks in terms of three epochs (the time of prophecy in the Old Testament; the time of fulfillment by the early Jesus; and the time of the church); such is the view of Strecker, *Der Weg der Gerechtigkeit,* 184–88; and J. P. Meier, "The Antiochene Church of the Second Christian Generation (A.D. 70–100—Matthew)," in Brown and Meier, *Antioch and Rome,* 60. It must be said, however, that Matthew looks back upon the entire ministry of Jesus as a time of fulfillment and considers the so-called "time of the church" but an extension or subcategory of this time of fulfillment. The words of the risen Lord to his disciples about his authority and his commission (28:18–20) thus summarize major themes inaugurated in the gospel account of the earthly ministry of Jesus, as shown by Günther Bornkamm, "The Risen Lord and the Earthly Jesus: Matthew 28.16–20," in *The Future of Our Religious Past: Essays in Honour of Rudolf Bultmann,* ed. James M. Robinson (New York: Harper & Row, 1971), 203–29.

44. Interpreters are not agreed on this. It is agreed that the passage speaks of the final judgment of all humanity by Christ. But who are those who are saved/

condemned—and on what basis? The problem centers on the meaning of the phrase "one of the least of these" (25:40, 45; and 25:40 adds, "my brethren") to whom acts of kindness are to be done. Some have suggested that the phrase refers to Jesus' messengers, so that the criterion at the judgment of all humanity is how each person has treated Jesus' disciples. Such is the view of O. Lamar Cope, "Matthew xxv 31–46: 'The Sheep and the Goats' Reinterpreted," *NovT* 11 (1969): 39–41; Gundry, *Matthew*, 511–16; and J. M. Court, "Right and Left: The Implications for Matthew 25.31–46," *NTS* 31 (1985): 229–31. Yet the phrase does not imply such a limitation; it can refer to anyone in need. The Matthean Jesus (cf. also Mark 9:42; Luke 17:2) speaks of his disciples as "little ones" (10:42; cf. also 18:6, 10, 14, but referring to believing children) and uses the term *mikroteros* ("lesser" or, as in RSV, "least," 11:11) for a disciple, but he does not use the term used in 25:40, 45 (*elachistos*, "least") for a disciple. What is meant is that sacrificial service which regards the good of the person in need, by whomever it is performed, and which does not seek its own reward, characterizes life in the kingdom. Such service is therefore—if only indirectly—performed for the king (25:34, 40), who is the Son of Man and Lord, to whom all authority (including authority to judge) is given. It is certainly unlikely that Matthew would have thought that the criterion of judgment for all the nations of the world would depend on each person's treatment of Jesus' disciples under the conditions mentioned (hungering, thirsting, being sick, homeless, or imprisoned); it would be more fitting that judgment would be based on how persons respond to their message (cf. 10:14–15), not their condition. The conditions mentioned are the common and traditionally cited afflictions of the unfortunate (cf. Isa. 58:7, Job 22:7; Prov. 25:21), and the righteous person attends to such needs with kindness (Prov. 25:21; Ezek. 18:5, 7; Tob. 4:16; Sir. 7:32, 35). Interpreters who give a broader interpretation so that "the least of these" includes whoever is in need include A. H. McNeile, *The Gospel according to St. Matthew* (New York: St. Martin's Press, 1915), 368–71; Joachim Jeremias, *The Parables of Jesus,* rev. ed. (New York: Charles Scribner's Sons, 1963), 206–7; Floyd V. Filson, *A Commentary on the Gospel according to St. Matthew,* HNTC, 2d. ed. (New York: Harper & Row, 1971), 266–68; Schweizer, *The Good News according to Matthew,* 478–80; D. R. A. Hare and D. J. Harrington, "' Make Disciples of All the Gentiles' (Mt. 28.19)," *CBQ* 37 (1975): 365; Beare, *The Gospel according to Matthew,* 495–96; and Meier, *Vision of Matthew,* 177–78.

45. Cf. Bornkamm, "The Risen Lord and the Earthly Jesus," 222.

46. The early history of the community is treated by J. P. Meier, "The Antiochene Church of the First Christian Generation (A.D. 40–70—Galatians 2; Acts 11—15)," in Brown and Meier, *Antioch and Rome,* 32–44.

47. Cf. Kümmel, *Introduction,* 151, 186 (A.D. 70–90 for the Gospel; 80–100 for Acts); on the Gospel of Luke specifically, Joseph A. Fitzmyer, *The Gospel according to Luke (I–IX),* AB 28 (Garden City, N.Y.: Doubleday, 1981), 57 (who concludes A.D. 80–85); and Eduard Schweizer, *The Good News according to Luke* (Atlanta: John Knox Press, 1984), 6 ("around 80"). A later dating (the beginning of the second century for the Gospel of Luke and later, anywhere up to A.D. 135, for Acts) is proposed by Koester, *Introduction* 2:310, 312.

48. Various proposals, none judged to be certain, are reviewed by Kümmel,

Introduction, 151, 186–87; he excludes Palestine, however. Koester, *Introduction* 2:310, suggests Antioch, Ephesus, or Rome. Fitzmyer, *The Gospel according to Luke,* 57, excludes Palestine, and leaves the question open; Schweizer, *The Good News according to Luke,* 6, leaves the matter open but accepts Antioch as a "possibility."

49. Nor does exegesis of the prologues of Luke and Acts result in a decision about the purpose of Luke-Acts, as demonstrated by Schuyler Brown, "The Role of the Prologues in Determining the Purpose of Luke-Acts," in *Perspectives on Luke-Acts,* ed. Charles H. Talbert (Danville, Va.: Assoc. of Baptist Professors of Religion, 1978), 99–111.

50. Cf. BAGD, 358.

51. Koester, *Introduction* 2:308. He later modifies this statement: "Luke writes as if he was speaking primarily to the pagan world, yet he is always mindful of his Christian readers" (2:310).

52. The topic is treated by Hans Conzelmann, *The Theology of St. Luke* (Philadelphia: Fortress Press, 1980 [1960]), 138–44. Among other things, in Luke's Gospel the innocence of Jesus is attested by Pilate three times (23:4, 14–15, 22); his death was brought about by pressure from Jewish authorities (23:2, 5, 10, 13–14; Acts 2:23; 3:14; 4:10–11). Likewise in Acts, Paul, who was known to have been executed at Rome, is portrayed as one who never violated the laws of the Roman Empire (25:8).

53. Ibid., 209–13 (quotation from 212).

54. Jacob Jervell, "The Divided People of God: The Restoration of Israel and Salvation for the Gentiles" and "Paul: The Teacher of Israel: The Apologetic Speeches of Paul in Acts," in *Luke and the People of God: A New Look at Luke-Acts* (Minneapolis: Augsburg Pub. House, 1972), esp. 68, 175–77.

55. David L. Tiede, *Prophecy and History in Luke-Acts* (Philadelphia: Fortress Press, 1980), esp. 11–16, 127–32.

56. Donald Juel, *Luke-Acts: The Promise of History* (Atlanta: John Knox Press, 1984), 118–20.

57. Nils A. Dahl, "The Purpose of Luke-Acts," in *Jesus in the Memory of the Early Church,* 97, 93.

58. Fitzmyer, *The Gospel according to Luke,* 57–59 (quotation from 59).

59. Luke's use of Scripture, particularly his midrashic interpretation, is surveyed by John Drury, *Tradition and Design in Luke's Gospel: A Study in Early Christian Historiography* (Atlanta: John Knox Press, 1977), 46–81.

60. One of the first to make this point, demonstrate it in a masterful way, and provide a foundation for subsequent studies was Eduard Lohse, "Lukas als Theologe der Heilsgeschichte," *EvT* 14 (1954): 256–76; reprinted in *Die Einheit des Neuen Testaments: Exegetische Studien zur Theologie des Neuen Testaments* (Göttingen: Vandenhoeck & Ruprecht, 1973), 145–64.

61. Luke 2:49; 4:43; 9:22; 13:33; 17:25; 19:5; 22:37; 24:7, 26, 44; Acts 1:16; 3:21; 17:3.

62. Acts 1:21; 9:16; 19:21; 23:21; 27:24.

63. Among others, these include Ernst Haenchen, *The Acts of the Apostles: A Commentary* (Philadelphia: Westminster Press, 1971), 96; Siegfried Schulz, *Die Stunde der Botschaft: Einführung in die Theologie der vier Evangelisten*

(Hamburg: Furche Verlag, 1967), 237–38, 284; and Fitzmyer, *The Gospel according to Luke*, 18, 181–87.

64. Conzelmann, *Theology of St. Luke*, 12–17, 101, 107, 204.

65. Ibid., 22–27, 101, 112, 161.

66. Hans Conzelmann, *An Outline of the Theology of the New Testament* (New York: Harper & Row, 1969), 150. Cf. idem, *Theology of St. Luke*, 14.

67. Haenchen, *Acts of the Apostles*, 99 n. 1.

68. Included here are Helmut Flender, *St. Luke: Theologian of Redemptive History* (Philadelphia: Fortress Press, 1967), 124; Otto Betz, "The Kerygma of Luke," *Int* 22 (1968): 131–46; Werner G. Kümmel, "Current Theological Accusations against Luke," *Andover Newton Quarterly* 16/2 (1975): 137–38; Eric Franklin, *Christ the Lord: A Study in the Purpose and Theology of Luke-Acts* (London: SPCK, 1975), 45–47, 173–74; Schweizer, *The Good News according to Luke*, 92–96, 326–27; and Kee, *Jesus in History*, 189–90. Similarly, Fuller, "Christology in Matthew and Luke," 87, speaks of period one (promise) and period two with subcategories (what Jesus began and what Jesus continued).

69. Betz, "The Kerygma of Luke," 138.

70. The prophecy and fulfillment motif in Lucan theology has been emphasized by, among others, Lohse, "Lukas als Theologe der Heilsgeschichte," 265; Paul Schubert, "The Structure and Significance of Luke 24," in *Neutestamentliche Studien für Rudolf Bultmann*, ed. W. Eltester, BZNW 21 (Berlin: A. Töpelmann, 1957), 165–86; Paul S. Minear, "Luke's Use of the Birth Stories"; and Nils A. Dahl, "The Story of Abraham in Luke-Acts," in *Studies in Luke-Acts: Essays Presented in Honor of Paul Schubert*, ed. L. E. Keck and J. L. Martyn (Philadelphia: Fortress Press, 1980 [1966]), 111–30 and 139–58.

71. Referring to Conzelmann's work, Minear, "Luke's Use of the Birth Stories," 122, has made an oft-quoted remark: "Rarely has a scholar placed so much weight on so dubious an interpretation of so difficult a logion."

72. Cf. Walter Wink, *John the Baptist in the Gospel Tradition*, SNTSMS 7 (Cambridge: Cambridge Univ. Press, 1968), 51–57. He writes: "John's ministry is clearly distinguished both from the period of promise and from the period of Jesus. It can only be explained by a separate preparatory period within the time of fulfillment" (56). Cf. also Franklin, *Christ the Lord*, 86; Schweizer, *The Good News according to Luke*, 258; and Jack D. Kingsbury, *Jesus Christ in Matthew, Mark, and Luke*, PC (Philadelphia: Fortress Press, 1981), 98.

73. Cf. Paul S. Minear, *To Heal and To Reveal: The Prophetic Vocation according to Luke* (New York: Seabury Press, 1976), 122–47 (esp. 140–42). The functions of the Christian prophets in Acts have been surveyed by E. Earle Ellis, "The Role of the Christian Prophet in Acts," in *Apostolic History and the Gospel: Biblical and Historical Essays Presented to F. F. Bruce on His 60th Birthday*, ed. W. W. Gasque and R. P. Martin (Grand Rapids: Wm. B. Eerdmans, 1970), 55–67.

74. Cf. the preface to his book, *Luke and the People of God*, where Jervell remarks: "When reading current studies of Luke-Acts, I often get the feeling that the author was not a theologian writing in the second half of the first century, dealing with problems of his own time, but that he was a theologian of the Constantinian era" (14).

75. Contrast Luke 9:27 with Mark 9:1; and Luke 21:8 with Mark 13:6. See also Luke 17:20–21; 19:11; 21:9, 20–24; 22:69.

76. See Luke 12:38–40, 41–48, 54–56; 18:8; 21:32.

77. Conzelmann, *Outline*, 150.

78. These are, of course, features of the so-called "early catholicism," which have been attributed to Luke by various interpreters, such as Ernst Käsemann, "Ministry and Community in the New Testatment," in *Essays on New Testament Themes*, SBT 41 (London: SCM Press, 1964), 91: "It was Luke who was the first to propagate the theories of tradition and that legitimate succession which mark the advent of early Catholicism."

79. Of the 680 pages in the Nestle-Aland Greek text (twenty-sixth edition), Luke-Acts fills 186 (over 27 percent).

80. These include "Savior" (Luke 2:11; Acts 5:31; 13:23); "Son of David" (Luke 1:32; and from Mark at Luke 18:38, 39); "prophet" (once from Mark, Luke 4:24; then at 7:16; 13:33; 24:19; Acts 3:22, 23; 7:37);"master" (*epistatēs*, all distinctive: Luke 5:5; 8:24, 45; 9:33, 49; 17:13); "servant" (*pais*, Acts 2:13, 26; 4:27, 30); "author" or "leader" (*archēgos*, Acts 3:15; 5:31); the "holy one" (Luke 4:34; Acts 2:27; 3:14); the "righteous one" (Acts 3:14; 22:14); and "judge" (Acts 10:42; cf. the verbal use at 17:31). In the triumphal entry into Jerusalem, Jesus is hailed as "the King" (Luke 23:2) and then crucified as "King of the Jews" (23:3, 37, 38). Jesus is also addressed in the Gospel as "teacher" (*didaskale*, 7:40; 9:38; 10:25; etc.) but the term is not a christological title (it is also applied to John the Baptist, 3:12).

81. Twelve times in the Gospel: none from Q, four from Mark (9:20; 20:41; 22:67; 23:35), and eight distinctive (2:11, 26; 3:15; 4:41; 23:2, 39; 24:26, 46). Acts contains the title twenty-six times (2:31, 36, 38; 3:6, 18, 20; 4:10, 26; 5:42; 8:5, 12; 9:22, 34; 10:36, 48; 11:17; 15:26; 16:18; 17:3 twice; 18:5, 28; 20:21, 24; 26:23; 28:31). Some Greek witnesses include it also at Acts 4:33; 8:37. At Luke 4:41 the title is added to Marcan material (Mark 1:34).

82. It appears ten times in Luke—three from Q (4:3, 9; 10:22), four from Mark (3:22; 4:41; 8:28; 9:35), and three distinctive (1:32, 35; 22:70)—and twice in Acts (9:20; 13:33). Some Greek witnesses include it at Acts 8:37.

83. Besides the use of "Son of man" at Acts 7:56, the twenty-five instances in the Gospel of Luke include twelve instances of the coming Son of Man—six from Q (11:30; 12:8, 40; 17:24, 26, 30), three from Mark (9:26; 21:27; 22:69), and three distinctive (17:22; 18:8; 21:36)—five instances of the suffering Son of Man—none from Q, four from Mark (9:22, 44; 18:31; 22:22a), and one distinctive (24:7)—and eight instances of the present Son of Man—three from Q (7:34; 9:58; 12:10), two from Mark (5:24; 6:5), and three distinctive (6:22; 19:10; 22:48). The totals are nine from Q, nine from Mark, and seven distinctive. Luke 17:25 is not listed; it is a Son of Man saying, but its subject is "he," the antecedent to which is Son of Man in 17:24, which is listed. There are six suffering Son of Man sayings in Mark (9:9, 12; 10:33–34, 45; 14:21b, 41) which Luke does not incorporate.

84. Of these forty-one, none is from Q, four are from Mark (6:5; 19:31; 20:42, 44), and thirty-seven are distinctive (1:43; 2:11; 5:8, 12; 6:46; 7:6, 13, 19; 9:54,

59, 61; 10:1, 17, 39, 40, 41; 11:1, 39; 12:41, 42; 13:15, 23, 25; 17:5, 6, 37; 18:6, 41; 19:8 twice, 34; 22:33, 38, 49, 61 twice; 24:34).

85. In these instances it appears in the phrase "Lord Jesus Christ" four times (11:17; 15:26; 20:21; 28:31) and "Lord Jesus" fourteen times (1:21; 4:33; 7:59; 8:16; 9:17; 11:20; 15:11; 16:31; 19:5, 13, 17; 20:24, 35; 21:13).

86. Acts 1:6; 2:34, 36; 7:60; 9:1, 5, 10 twice, 11, 13, 15, 27, 29, 35, 42; 10:36; 13:2, 10, 11, 12; 14:3, 23; 15:35, 36, 40; 16:32; 18:8, 9, 25; 19:10, 20; 20:19; 21:14; 22:8, 10 twice, 19; 23:11; 26:15 twice.

87. Acts 1:24; 2:25, 47; 5:9, 14; 8:22, 24, 25, 39; 9:31; 11:8, 16, 21 twice, 23, 24; 13:49.

88. Besides Luke 7:13, at Luke 7:19; 10:1, 39, 41; 11:39; 12:42; 13:15; 17:5, 6; 18:6; 19:8; 22:61 twice; 24:3.

89. Cf. Flender, *St. Luke*, 42; and Fitzmyer, *The Gospel according to Luke*, 203.

90. Franklin, *Christ the Lord*, 49. A survey of the use of the title in Luke-Acts is provided by Franklin on 49–55. The implications of the title in Acts are drawn out by George W. MacRae, "Whom Heaven Must Receive until the Time: Reflections on the Christology of Acts," *Int* 27 (1973): 151–65.

91. Materials from other speeches in Acts are cited and connected with the Lucan portrayal of Jesus in his Gospel in Arland J. Hultgren, "Interpreting the Gospel of Luke," *Int* 30 (1976): 353–65 (esp. 354–56); reprinted in *Interpreting the Gospels*, ed. James L. Mays (Philadelphia: Fortress Press, 1981), 183–96.

92. This is a pronounced Lucan theme, which appears at Luke 2:22; 4:1, 14, 18, 36; 5:17; 6:19; 8:48; 9:1; 10:21, 38; Acts 10:38. Jesus is endowed with the Spirit at his baptism (Luke 3:22).

93. Cf. BAGD, 57; and Gerhard Delling, "Analambanō, Analēmpsis," *TDNT* 4:7–9.

94. The clause "and he was carried up into heaven" (Luke 24:51) is not found in Sinaiticus, but it appears in other important witnesses.

95. His innocence is attested three times by Pilate (23:4, 14–15, 22) and then by a fellow victim of crucifixion (23:41), the centurion (23:47), and (implicitly) Joseph of Arimathea (23:51). His suffering is spoken of frequently (Luke 9:22; 17:25; 22:15; 24:26, 46; Acts 3:18; 17:3).

96. Cf. Dibelius, *From Tradition to Gospel*, 201; Conzelmann, *Theology of St. Luke*, 201, who cites still other references (the works of C. H. Dodd, H. J. Cadbury, and A. Seeberg). To these can be added Philipp Vielhauer, "On the 'Paulinism' of Acts," in *Studies in Luke-Acts*, ed. Keck and Martyn, 44–45; Gerhard Voss, *Die Christologie der lukanischen Schriften in Grundzügen*, Studia neotestamentica 2 (Paris and Bruges: Desclée de Brouwer, 1965), 130; Kümmel, "Current Theological Accusations against Luke," 134 and 138; Franklin, *Christ the Lord*, 65; Goppelt, *Theology NT* 2:282; and Fitzmyer, *The Gospel according to Luke*, 219–20.

97. Cf. Dibelius, *From Tradition to Gospel*, 201; "Luke presents the Passion as a martyrdom." Cf. Lohse, "Lukas als Theologe der Heilsgeschichte," 273.

98. Goppelt, *Theology NT* 2:283.

99. Cf. Franklin, *Christ the Lord*, 66.

100. Cf. Flender, *St. Luke*, 158–59.

101. Cf. Richard Zehnle, "The Salvific Character of Jesus' Death in Lucan Soteriology," *TS* 30 (1969): 420–44.
102. Flender, *St. Luke*, 162.
103. Goppelt, *Theology NT* 2:231.
104. Cf. Jervell, "The Divided People of God," 68–69; and Franklin, *Christ the Lord*, 175.
105. See Acts 3:25 (citing Gen. 22:18); 13:47 (citing Isa. 49:6); and 15:17 (citing Amos 9:12). The issue is treated by Jervell, "The Divided People of God," 49–64; and Jacques Dupont, "Le salut des gentils et la signification théologique du livre des Actes," *NTS* 6 (1959–60): 132–55.
106. This is seen, for example, in the so-called "travel narrative" (Luke 9:51—19:44). Here Jesus gives instruction to his disciples to equip them as his witness after his departure (9:31, 51). Besides containing some twenty parables, it contains many sayings and discourses having to do with discipleship and church discipline (e.g., 9:60, 62; 11:2–4, 28; 12:8–12, 13–15, 22–34; 14:25–27; 16:10–13, 18; 17:1–6, 20–21; 18:15–17, 24–30). The section contains chiefly two types of material: instruction for Jesus' disciples as forerunners of the new community, and disputations with opponents. Cf. Bo Reicke, "Instruction and Discussion in the Travel Narrative," *Studia Evangelica I*, TU 73 (Berlin: Akademie Verlag, 1959), 206–16; E. Earle Ellis, *The Gospel of Luke*, NCB, rev. ed. (Grand Rapids: Wm. B. Eerdmans, 1974), 146–50; Fitzmyer, *The Gospel according to Luke*, 823–26; and Schweizer, *The Good News according to Luke*, 165–67.
107. Cf. Käsemann, "Ministry and Community in the New Testament," 92.

CHAPTER 7

1. Günther Bornkamm, *Paul* (New York: Harper & Row, 1971), 241–43; Willi Marxsen, *Introduction to the New Testament* (Philadelphia: Fortress Press, 1968), 184–98; Helmut Koester, *Introduction to the New Testament*, 2 vols. (Philadelphia: Fortress Press; Berlin: Walter de Gruyter, 1982), 2:261–72. Of course interpreters are not unanimous on this. Werner G. Kümmel, *Introduction to the New Testament*, rev. ed. (Nashville: Abingdon Press, 1975), 335–48, 350–66, concludes that Colossians was written by Paul, but that Ephesians is deutero-Pauline, incorporating materials from Colossians. The question of the authorship of Colossians is treated at length in two commentaries, weighing the evidence for and against, resulting in opposite conclusions. That the work is pseudonymous is concluded by Eduard Lohse, *Colossians and Philemon*, Hermeneia (Philadelphia: Fortress Press, 1971), 177–83; that it is genuinely Pauline, by Ralph P. Martin, *Colossians and Philemon*, NCB (London: Oliphants, 1974), 32–40. It has also been suggested that it was written by a coworker of Paul, but still within Paul's lifetime, by Eduard Schweizer, *The Letter to the Colossians* (Minneapolis: Augsburg Pub. House, 1982), 15–26. The evidence as a whole, considered cumulatively, appears in our judgment to favor considering it pseudonymous. Concerning Ephesians, the view that it is pseudonymous is held not only in the previously mentioned studies, but also by C. Leslie Mitton, *The Epistle to the Ephesians: Its Authorship, Origin and Purpose* (Oxford: Clarendon Press,

1951)—whose work is the most detailed on the subject, assigning the letter to A.D. 87–92—and John A. Allan, *The Epistle to the Ephesians,* TBC (London: SCM Press, 1959), 15–23. Its authenticity is held by Heinrich Schlier, *Der Brief an die Epheser,* 5th ed. (Düsseldorf: Patmos, 1965), 22–28; and Marcus Barth, *Ephesians,* AB 34–34A, 2 vols. (Garden City, N.Y.: Doubleday, 1974), 1:36–52. But the arguments for its pseudonymity (see esp. Kümmel, *Introduction*) are impressive.

2. These are at 1:1, 2, 3, 4, 7, 24, 27, 28; 2:2, 5, 6, 8, 11, 17, 20; 3:1 twice, 3, 4, 11, 15, 16, 24; 4:3, 12.

3. These instances are 1:3, 10; 2:6; 3:13, 17, 18, 20, 22, 23, 24; 4:1, 7, 17. In some of these instances (1:10; 3:13, 23, for example) it is not immediately clear whether the term "Lord" refers to Jesus or God. But the term is clearly applied to Jesus by the writer, as shown by its attachment to him frequently, as in 1:3; 2:6; 3:17, 24; 4:17.

4. These are at 1:1 twice, 2, 3, 4, 5, 10, 12, 17, 20; 2:5, 6, 7, 10, 12, 13 twice, 20; 3:1, 4, 6, 8, 11, 17, 19, 21; 4:7, 12, 13, 15, 20, 32; 5:2, 5, 14, 20, 21, 23, 24, 25, 29, 32; 6:5, 6, 23, 24.

5. This term appears at 1:2, 3, 15, 17; 2:21; 3:11; 4:1, 5, 17; 5:8, 10, 17, 19, 20, 22; 6:1, 4, 7, 8, 9, 10, 21, 23, 24.

6. A similar conception appears at Eph. 1:10: God's purpose though Christ was "to unite all things in him." The verb in this instance is *anakephalaioō;* see discussion in nn. 61 and 62 below.

7. A survey and analysis has been offered by G. H. MacGregor, "Principalities and Powers: The Cosmic Background of Paul's Thought," *NTS* 1 (1954): 17–28; and G. B. Caird, *Principalities and Powers: A Study in Pauline Theology* (Oxford: Clarendon Press, 1956). A more specialized study devoted to the manifestation of the cosmic powers in temporal rule, but also treating the topic in general, is that of Clinton D. Morrison, *The Powers That Be: Earthly Rulers and Demonic Powers in Romans 13.1–7,* SBT 29 (London: SCM Press, 1960).

8. A survey of texts in the New Testament and other ancient literature which speaks of the "principalities and powers" (by whatever names are used) is provided by Walter Wink, *Naming the Powers: The Language of Power in the New Testament* (Philadelphia: Fortress Press, 1984). A study of the general Hebrew and Semitic terminological background of the cosmic powers is provided by Matthew Black, "Pasai Exousiai Auto Hypotagesontai," in *Paul and Paulinism: Essays in Honour of C. K. Barrett,* ed. M. D. Hooker and S. G. Wilson (London: SPCK, 1982), 74–82. An attempt (unsuccessful, in our view) to refute the view that Paul and the deutero-Pauline writers believed in the existence of hostile cosmic powers has been made by Wesley Carr, *Angels and Principalities: The Background, Meaning and Development of the Pauline Phrase hai Archai kai hai Exousiai,* SNTSMS 42 (Cambridge: Cambridge Univ. Press, 1981). This study fails particularly in its treatment of Col. 1:15 (60–66) and in the fact that the author has to concede that at Eph. 6:12 the "principalities and powers" are considered "undoubtedly malevolent, hostile powers" and "no alternative view is possible" (104). But then the writer goes on to maintain that "the verse was interpolated into Ephesians" sometime "about the middle of the second century or just prior to it" (109). Such an assertion lacks foundation.

9. Empedocles *On Nature* (texts cited by G. Delling, "Stoicheion," *TDNT*
7:672–73); Plutarch *Moralia* 875c; *Diogenes Laertius* 7.137 (on Zeno the Stoic);
and *Orphic Hymns* 5 and 66, for which texts are provided in *The Orphic Hymns,*
trans. Apostolos N. Athanassakis, SBLTT 12 (Missoula, Mont.: Scholars Press,
1977), 10–11 and 88–89. See also the Orphic Derveni Papyrus 17.2 in Larry J.
Alderink, *Creation and Salvation in Ancient Orphism,* American Classical Studies
8 (Chico. Calif.: Scholars Press, 1981), 118.

10. *Sibylline Oracles* 2.206; 3.80; 8.337; Wisd. of Sol. 7:17; 19:18; Philo *De
aetern. mundi* 109–110; *Rer. div. her.* 134. Additional texts are cited, and treatment of the "powers" in the thought of Philo is given, by Harry A. Wolfson, *Philo,*
2 vols. (Cambridge: Harvard Univ. Press, 1947), 1:217–26.

11. *T. Levi* 3.8.

12. *1 Enoch* 61.10.

13. *T. Levi* 3.8; cf. *T. Solomon* 20.15.

14. Second Esdras 16:18; Prayer of Azariah 39; Philo *Conf. ling.* 171; *Mut.
nom.* 59; cf. 4 Macc. 5:13.

15. Cf. Wink, *Naming the Powers,* 9–11.

16. Plato *Apology* 26d. Cf. illustration from Hellenism (esp. the Stoics) in
Rudolf Bultmann, *Primitive Christianity in Its Contemporary Setting* (Philadelphia: Fortress Press, 1980 [1956]), 173–82.

17. *T. Solomon* 8.2: "We are heavenly bodies, rulers of the world of darkness";
and 18.2: "We are thirty-six heavenly bodies, the world-rulers *[stoicheia]* of the
darkness of this age." Quoted from the translation of D. C. Duling, "Testament
of Solomon," in *OTP* 1:969–70, 972.

18. *1 Enoch* 75.3. Quoted from the translation of E. Isaac, "1 (Ethiopic Apocalypse of) Enoch," in *OTP* 1:54–55.

19. *1 Enoch* 21.6. Quoted from *OTP* 1:24.

20. Cf. Lohse, *Colossians and Philemon,* 50–51; Schweizer, *The Letter to the
Colossians,* 69–71; and Martin, *Colossians and Philemon,* 56.

21. *1 Enoch* 6.1—10.16; 12.4–6; 15.3—16.3; 19.1–3; *2 Enoch* 18.3–6; *Jubilees*
4.22; 5.1–7; 10.1–2; *T. Reuben* 5.6; Josephus *Jewish Antiquities* 1.73 (in *Josephus* trans. H. St. J. Thackeray et al., LCL, 10 vols. [Cambridge: Harvard Univ.
Press, 1969–81], 4:34–35). For a discussion of passages in Philo, see Wolfson,
Philo 1:384–85; he cites *De gigantibus* 2.6 and 4.17.

22. Cf. Heinrich Schlier, *Principalities and Powers in the New Testament*
(Freiburg: Herder, 1961), 38–39; and Wink, *Naming the Powers,* 104.

23. Major essays on the identification of the so-called "Colossian heresy" are
reprinted in *Conflict at Colossae: A Problem in the Interpretation of Early Christianity Illustrated by Selected Modern Studies,* ed. Fred O. Francis and Wayne
A. Meeks, SBLSBS 4, rev. ed. (Missoula, Mont.: Scholars Press, 1975). The essays
(all in English from originals or in translation) included are by J. B. Lightfoot,
Martin Dibelius, Günther Bornkamm, Stanislas Lyonnet, and Fred O. Francis.
G. Bornkamm, "The Heresy of Colossians," 135, summarizes his view that the
heresy "originates in a gnosticized Judaism, in which Jewish and Iranian-Persian
elements, and surely also influences of Chaldean astrology, have . . . united with
Christianity." Another summary of the "philosophy" of the opponents is provided
by Lohse, *Colossians and Philemon,* 127–31, who considers it syncretistic (in-

cluding Jewish traditions), pre-Gnostic, and taking the form of a mystery religion. A detailed study of the opponents' terminology (as used in the letter itself, Col. 2:6–23) appears in Johannes Lähnemann, *Der Kolosserbrief: Komposition, Situation und Argumentation,* SNT 3 (Gütersloh: Gütersloher Verlagshaus Gerd Mohn, 1971), 110–52. It must be admitted that the data do not yield a great deal of information about the opponents and their views, as emphasized by Fred O. Francis, "The Christological Argument of Colossians," in *God's Christ and His People: Essays in Honour of Nils Alstrup Dahl,* ed. Jacob Jervell and Wayne A. Meeks (Oslo: Universitetsforlaget, 1977), 192–208. He writes: "Methodological simplicity requires that one acknowledge that Colossians provides no exact knowledge of the christology of the opponents, only the probability that they were Christians" (203).

24. Cf. Lohse, *Colossians and Philemon,* 118; and Schweizer, *The Letter to the Colossians,* 81. It has been suggested that the phrase "worship of angels" is to be taken as a subjective genitive, and so the opponents say that one must participate in an angelic liturgy; this is maintained by Fred O. Francis, "Humility and Angelic Worship in Col. 2:18," in *Conflict at Colossae,* ed. Francis and Meeks, 163–96. But this interpretation has not found favor, because when worship is spoken of again at 2:23 (alluding to 2:18) it clearly refers to a cult performed by human beings. So Lohse, *Colossians and Philemon,* 118–19 n. 36; Martin, *Colossians and Philemon,* 93–94; and Schweizer, *The Letter to the Colossians,* 159.

25. Cf. W. D. Davies, *Paul and Rabbinic Judaism: Some Rabbinic Elements in Pauline Theology,* 4th ed. (Philadelphia: Fortress Press, 1980), 170.

26. Ernst Käsemann, "A Primitive Christian Baptismal Liturgy," in *Essays on New Testament Themes,* SBT 41 (London: SCM Press, 1964), 150–54; Reinhard Deichgräber, *Gotteshymnus und Christushymnus in der frühen Christenheit: Untersuchungen zu Form, Sprache und Stil der früchristlichen Hymnen,* SUNT 5 (Göttingen: Vandenhoeck & Ruprecht, 1967), 148–49; Lohse, *Colossians and Philemon,* 42–43; and Schweizer, *The Letter to the Colossians,* 58–59.

27. Jack T. Sanders, *The New Testament Christological Hymns: Their Historical Religious Background,* SNTSMS 15 (Cambridge: Cambridge Univ. Press, 1971), 83, indicates that "the problem of reconciliation" in light of 1:15–18 is the "central problem" in attempts to discern the background of the whole unit (1:15–20).

28. Wayne G. Rollins, "Christological *Tendenz* in Colossians 1:15–20: A *Theologia Crucis,*" in *Christological Perspectives: Essays in Honor of Harvey K. McArthur,* ed. R. F. Berkey and S. A. Edwards (New York: Pilgrim Press, 1982), 132–36. The major objection to his view might rise in consequence of the claim that at 1:20 the phrase "through him" belongs to an extant hymn, to which "through the blood of his cross" has been added, as those in n. 24 have maintained. Rollins sees the phrase "through him" to be repetition for the sake of emphasis (135). Whether one takes the phrase "through the blood of his cross" as an insertion to a hymn or as part of a larger composition (1:18b–20), the juxtaposition of phrases is awkward. There is of course some question whether "through him" should appear in the text. It is lacking in certain majuscules (including B and D), but it is present in papyrus 46 and Sinaiticus.

29. Lohse, *Colossians and Philemon*, 111: "Because Christ was nailed to the cross in our stead, the debt is forgiven once and for all."

30. Moreover, writes Morna D. Hooker, "Were There False Teachers in Colossae?" in *Christ and Spirit in the New Testament: In Honour of Charles Francis Digby Moule*, ed. B. Lindars and S. S. Smalley (Cambridge: Cambridge Univ. Press, 1973), 330, the author maintains that Christ "has replaced the Jewish Torah; it is Christ, not the Torah, who is older than creation, the instrument of creation, the principle upon which creation itself depends and to which it coheres."

31. Translation from BAGD, 725.

32. Edward Schillebeeckx, *Christ: The Experience of Jesus as Lord* (New York: Crossroad, 1983), 193.

33. Cf. Nigel Turner, *Grammatical Insights into the New Testament* (Edinburgh: T. & T. Clark, 1965), 122–23; and Roy Yates, "Christ and the Powers of Evil in Colossians," in *Studia Biblica 1978: III. Papers on Paul and Other New Testament Authors*, ed. E. A. Livingstone, JSNTSup 3 (Sheffield, Eng.: JSOT Press, 1980), 464.

34. Cf. the comment on Colossians by Nils A. Dahl, "Christ, Creation and the Church," in *The Background of the New Testament and Its Eschatology: In Honour of Charles Harold Dodd*, ed. W. D. Davies and D. Daube (Cambridge: Cambridge Univ. Press., 1956), 434: "In the church the reconciliation and re-creation of the universe is already realized."

35. Lohse, *Colossians and Philemon*, 128: "The powers could be understood as representatives of the divine fulness or as dangerous principalities who block the way to the 'fulness' and allow free passage only after they have received their due reverence."

36. Cf. Wayne A. Meeks, "In One Body: The Unity of Humankind in Colossians and Ephesians," in *God's Christ and His People*, ed. Jervell and Meeks, 213.

37. Cf. Martin, *Colossians and Philemon*, 68.

38. Gerhard Friedrich, *Die Verkündigung des Todes Jesu im Neuen Testament*, BTS 6 (Neukirchen-Vluyn: Neukirchener Verlag, 1982), 110: "While for Paul (Rom. 5; 2 Cor. 5) God is the reconciler through Christ, Colossians 1:22 speaks directly of Christ as the one who reconciles"; translation mine.

39. Gerhard Delling, "Thriambeuō," *TDNT* 3:159–60, amplifies the term "triumphed" (RSV): "to triumph over, to lead in a triumphal procession." Cf. also Wink, *Naming the Powers*, 56–59.

40. Ralph P. Martin, "Reconciliation and Forgiveness in the Letter to the Colossians," in *Reconciliation and Hope: New Testament Essays on Atonement and Eschatology Presented to L. L. Morris on His 60th Birthday*, ed. R. Banks (Grand Rapids: Wm. B. Eerdmans, 1974), 115.

41. Käsemann, "A Primitive Christian Baptismal Liturgy," 168.

42. Paul S. Minear, *Images of the Church in the New Testament* (Philadelphia: Westminster Press, 1960), 206.

43. Examples are seen in comparing Eph. 1:1, 4, 7, 10, 13, 15; 2:1, 16, 20–21; 3:5; 4:16; 6:21–22, respectively, with Col. 1:1, 22b, 14, 20, 5–6, 4; 2:13; 1:22; 2:19; 1:26; 2:19; 4:7–8. These are only a few examples. The parallels are readily

seen when the texts are printed in parallel columns, as in Edgar J. Goodspeed, *The Key to Ephesians* (Chicago: Univ. of Chicago Press, 1956), 2–75.

44. The letter is associated with Ephesus as its destination, but the phrase "in Ephesus" is lacking at 1:1 in the earliest and generally regarded most reliable manuscripts, including papyrus 46 and the original (unaltered) Sinaiticus and Vaticanus. A thorough discussion of the problems is provided by Kümmel, *Introduction*, 352–56; and by Ernest Best, "Ephesians 1.1 Again," in *Paul and Paulinism*, ed. Hooker and Wilson, 273–79.

45. These are summarized by Barth, *Ephesians* 1:56–59.

46. Cf. Stig Hanson, *The Unity of the Church in the New Testament: Colossians and Ephesians*, ASNU 14 (Uppsala, Swed.: Almqvist & Wiksells, 1964), 126–41.

47. This is confirmed by other passages: Christ "preached peace to those who were near" as well as to "you who were far off" (2:17); "both have access in one Spirit to the Father" (2:18); both are "members of the household of God" built on apostolic foundation (2:19–20); and gentiles are "members of the same body, and partakers of the promise in Christ" (3:6). So Jewish Christians are in view. The theme of unity in Christ of Jew and gentile in Ephesians has been treated by E. Kenneth Lee, "Unity in Israel and Unity in Christ," in *Studies in Ephesians*, ed. F. L. Cross (London: Mowbray, 1956), 36–50; as well as by Ernst Käsemann, "Ephesians and Acts," in *Studies in Luke-Acts: Essays Presented in Honor of Paul Schubert*, ed. L. E. Keck and J. L. Martyn (Philadelphia: Fortress Press, 1980 [1966]), 295–97; and by Meeks, "In One Body," 214–17.

48. Both 2:20 and 3:5 presuppose that the apostles and prophets were of a former time now past, which situates the letter in the post-Pauline era. Cf., among others, R. Schnackenburg, "Die Kirche als Bau: Epheser 2.19–22 unter ökumenischem Aspekt," in *Paul and Paulinism*, ed. Hooker and Wilson, 261–62.

49. So it has been suggested (but not explained in what ways) that Ephesians treats the question of Jews and gentiles in view of Paul's statements in Romans. Cf. Koester, *Introduction* 2:269; and Schillebeeckx, *Christ*, 195.

50. For more on the designation of gentile Christians as belonging to a "third race," see Schillebeeckx, *Christ*, 201; and Ralph P. Martin, "Reconciliation and Unity in Ephesians," in *Reconciliation: A Study in Pauline Theology* (Atlanta: John Knox Press, 1981), 167.

51. Cf. Rudolf Bultmann, *Theology of the New Testament*, 2 vols. (New York: Charles Scribner's Sons, 1951–55), 2:151.

52. Ibid. 2:152.

53. Cf. Werner Foerster, "Aēr," *TDNT* 1:165.

54. Cf. Schlier, *Principalities and Powers*, 30–31.

55. Schillebeeckx, *Christ*, 212: "Ephesians sees Jesus Christ as being more active in the communication of salvation than Paul."

56. Cf. Schlier, *Der Brief an die Epheser*, 231–32; and C. Leslie Mitton, *Ephesians*, NCB (London: Oliphants, 1976), 176.

57. BAGD, 508, translates the phrase: "the barrier formed by the dividing wall."

58. Cf. *Aboth* 1.1, which contains the saying, "make a fence around the law." The text is in *The Mishnah*, ed. Herbert Danby (Oxford: Oxford Univ. Press, 1933), 446.

59. "Christ is active as the head *through the Spirit*," writes R. Schnackenburg, "Christus, Geist und Gemeinde (Eph. 4:1–16)," in *Christ and the Spirit in the NT*, ed. Lindars and Smalley, 283; translation mine.

60. Ernst Käsemann, "Das Interpretationsproblem des Epheserbriefes," in *Exegetische Versuche und Besinnungen*, 2d ed., 2 vols. (Göttingen: Vandenhoeck & Ruprecht, 1960–65), 2:261: "Where Christians act as Christians, Christ exercises his lordship on earth through them"; translation mine.

61. The various possibilities are discussed by Barth, *Ephesians* 1:89–92, who rejects "to renew" and finds merit in both "to unite" and "to make [Christ] the head" over all things, and finally proposes "to comprehend" as embracing both. Hanson, *The Unity of the Church in the NT*, 123–26, concludes that the verb "is an expression of the cosmic unity in Christ"; the original unity of the cosmos is restored in Christ's atonement. BAGD, 55–56, renders it: "to bring everything together in Christ." Cf. also Mitton, *Ephesians*, 55–56, who renders the verb as "to unite."

62. So Schlier, *Der Brief an die Epheser*, 65. Cf. also his treatment within the article, "Kephalē," *TDNT* 3:681–82. That ancient commentators on Eph. 1:10 interpreted the verb in the sense of uniting all things under Christ can be seen in the patristic passages cited by G. W. H. Lampe, *A Patristic Greek Lexicon* (Oxford: Clarendon Press, 1961), 106.

63. Cf. D. E. H. Whiteley, "Christology," in *Studies in Ephesians*, ed. Cross, 60–63.

64. This theme is explored by Heinrich Schlier, "Die Kirche als das Geheimnis Christi: Nach dem Epheserbrief," in *Die Zeit der Kirche: Exegetische Aufsätze und Vorträge*, 5th ed. (Freiburg: Herder, 1972), 299–307.

65. The pseudonymity of the Pastorals is affirmed by, among others, Fred D. Gealy, *The First and Second Epistles to Timothy and the Epistle to Titus*, Interpreter's Bible 11 (Nashville: Abingdon Press, 1955), 343–75; C. K. Barrett, *The Pastoral Epistles* (Oxford: Oxford Univ. Press, 1963), 4–12; Martin Dibelius and Hans Conzelmann, *The Pastoral Epistles*, Hermeneia (Philadelphia: Fortress Press, 1972), 1–5; Anthony T. Hanson, *The Pastoral Epistles*, NCB (Grand Rapids: Wm. B. Eerdmans, 1982), 2–11; Arland J. Hultgren, *1–2 Timothy, Titus*, ACNT (Minneapolis: Augsburg Pub. House, 1984), 12–19; Kümmel, *Introduction*, 370–87; Marxsen, *Introduction*, 212–15; Reginald H. Fuller, *A Critical Introduction to the New Testament* (London: G. Duckworth, 1966), 133–34; and Koester, *Introduction* 2:297–305. That the Pastorals were Paul's work drafted by a secretary is maintained by Joachim Jeremias, *Die Briefe an Timotheus und Titus*, NTD 9, 11th ed. (Göttingen: Vandenhoeck & Ruprecht, 1975), 1–11; Gottfried Holtz, *Die Pastoralbriefe*, THKNT 13 (Berlin: Evangelische Verlagsanstalt, 1965), 13–17; and J. N. D. Kelly, *A Commentary on the Pastoral Epistles*, HNTC (New York: Harper & Row, 1963), 30–34. That the Pastorals were written by Paul has been maintained in the commentaries of Donald Guthrie, *The Pastoral Epistles*, TNTC (Grand Rapids: Wm. B. Eerdmans, 1957), 11–53; and C. Spicq, *Saint Paul: Les Épîtres Pastorales*, EBib, 4th ed. (Paris: Gabalda, 1969), 157–204.

66. These are documented and developed in Hultgren, *1–2 Timothy, Titus*, 12–19.

67. This figure differs from that of the important work of P. N. Harrison, *The*

Problem of the Pastoral Epistles (London: Oxford Univ. Press, 1921), 20, 137–40; idem, *Paulines and Pastorals* (London: Villiers, 1964), 12. See the review of Harrison's work and the modification of his statistics in Hultgren, *1–2 Timothy, Titus,* 14–15, 181–82.

68. See the usage of "faith" in the Pastorals at 1 Tim. 1:2; 3:9, 13; 4:1; 2 Tim. 4:7; and Titus 1:13. This can be contrasted with Paul's usage in Rom. 1:17; 3:25, 30; 1 Cor. 13:2; 2 Cor. 5:7; Gal. 2:16; 3:26; Phil. 1:27; 3:9; etc. Paul can, however, also speak of "the faith" (Gal. 1:23; Phil. 1:25), meaning the Christian faith, and the writer of the Pastorals can speak of "faith in Christ Jesus" (2 Tim. 3:15). But the tendencies in Paul and the Pastorals for the most part differ.

69. For support of this view, see Hultgren, *1–2 Timothy, Titus,* 19–31.

70. Only once does "Christ" stand by itself (1 Tim. 5:11); otherwise it appears in the combination "Lord Jesus Christ," "Jesus Christ," or "Christ Jesus." The term appears thirty-two times: 1 Tim. 1:1 twice, 2, 12, 14, 15, 16; 2:5; 3:13; 4:6; 5:11, 21; 6:3, 13, 14; 2 Tim. 1:1 twice, 2, 9, 10, 13; 2:1, 3, 8, 10; 3:12, 15; 4:1; Titus 1:1, 4; 2:13; 3:6.

71. The term "Lord" *(kyrios)* applies to Jesus at 1 Tim. 1:2, 12, 14; 6:3, 14; 2 Tim. 1:2, 8, 16, 18a; 2:7, 22, 24; 3:11; 4:8, 14, 17, 18, 22. It also appears at 2 Tim. 2:14 in various ancient witnesses, which the RSV follows. Some of these are admittedly ambiguous (whether they refer to Jesus or God); the term is quite definitely a reference to God at 1 Tim. 6:15; 2 Tim. 1:18b; 2:19 twice.

72. It has been suggested, however, that the immediate background of the writer's usage is to be found in the mystery religions and the emperor cult; cf. Dibelius and Conzelmann, *The Pastoral Epistles,* 100–103.

73. This is a matter of dispute. Some interpreters deny that the Pastorals teach the preexistence of Christ, including Hans Windisch, "Zur Christologie der Pastoralbriefe," *ZNW* 34 (1935): 213–21; and Hanson, *The Pastoral Epistles,* 40. Those who affirm that they teach preexistence include Barrett, *The Pastoral Epistles,* 25; and Fuller, *A Critical Introduction,* 134.

74. Of course this statement is based on the conclusion that both "God" and "Savior" apply to Jesus in this verse. It is possible to translate the phrase "the great God and our Savior Jesus Christ" (cf. KJV and NAB), which *could* (although not necessarily) imply a distinction between God and Christ. Some interpreters take the verse to imply a distinction, including E. F. Scott, *The Pastoral Epistles,* MNTC (New York: Harper & Brothers, 1936), 169; Kelly, *Pastoral Epistles,* 246–47; Holtz, *Die Pastoralbriefe,* 227–28; Dibelius and Conzelmann, *The Pastoral Epistles,* 143; and Jeremias, *Die Briefe an Timotheus und Titus,* 73. Cf. also Vincent Taylor, *The Person of Christ in New Testament Teaching* (New York: St. Martin's Press, 1958), 131–32. One who translates the phrase so as to make a distinction but remains indecisive in his commentary on whether a distinction is implied is Norbert Brox, *Die Pastoralbriefe,* RNT 7 (Regensburg: Pustet, 1969), 297. But there are two reasons for holding that "our great God and Savior" is the better translation (cf. RSV, NEB, JB, TEV, and NIV) and that the entire phrase applies to Jesus. First, the pattern of the Greek, placing the word for "our" *(hēmōn)* after both "God and Savior," favors this rendering (contrast 2 Thess. 1:12 and 2 Pet. 1:1, which separate "our God" and "Savior"), as indicated by C. F. D. Moule, *An Idiom-Book of New Testament Greek,* 2d ed. (Cambridge:

Cambridge Univ. Press, 1959), 109–10; BDF, 145 (#276); and Ethelbert Stauffer, "Theos," *TDNT* 3:106. Second, the verse speaks of one appearing, that of Christ at his parousia, not two (God and Christ). Most commentators take the phrase to be inclusive, referring to Christ alone, including J. H. Bernard, *The Pastoral Epistles* (Cambridge: Cambridge Univ. Press, 1899), 172–73; Walter Lock, *A Critical and Exegetical Commentary on the Pastoral Epistles,* ICC (Edinburgh: T. & T. Clark, 1924), 145; Burton S. Easton, *The Pastoral Epistles* (New York: Charles Scribner's Sons, 1947), 95; Spicq, *Saint Paul,* 640; Gealy, *The First and Second Epistles to Timothy and the Epistle to Titus,* 540; Guthrie, *The Pastoral Epistles,* 200; Barrett, *The Pastoral Epistles,* 138; J. L. Houlden, *The Pastoral Epistles,* Pelican New Testament Commentaries (New York: Penguin Books, 1976), 150; Hanson, *The Pastoral Epistles,* 184–85; and Hultgren, *1–2 Timothy, Titus,* 164–65.

75. Cf. 1 Tim. 1:4–5; 2:10; 3:7; 4:12; 5:10, 23; 6:3, 6, 18; 2 Tim. 1:13; 2:22; 3:12, 16; Titus 1:18; 2:2–7, 12, 14; 3:2, 8.

76. Texts are cited in Str-B 4:467–70.

77. Stoic texts are cited in BAGD, 122.

78. Scott, *The Pastoral Epistles,* 50–51; Gealy, *The First and Second Epistles to Timothy and the Epistle to Titus,* 431.

79. Lock, *Pastoral Epistles,* 51–52; Jeremias, *Die Briefe an Timotheus und Titus,* 33; Guthrie, *The Pastoral Epistles,* 96; Barrett, *The Pastoral Epistles,* 70; Dibelius and Conzelmann, *The Pastoral Epistles,* 69; Brox, *Die Pastoralbriefe,* 178; and Hanson, *The Pastoral Epistles,* 92.

80. Spicq, *Saint Paul,* 145; Kelly, *The Pastoral Epistles,* 102; Holtz, *Die Pastoralbriefe,* 107; Houlden, *The Pastoral Epistles,* 89; and Hultgren, *1–2 Timothy, Titus,* 83–84.

81. Easton, *The Pastoral Epistles,* 146.

82. A survey of their teachings is provided in Hultgren, *1–2 Timothy, Titus,* 44–48. Cf. also Robert J. Karris, "The Background and Significance of the Polemic of the Pastoral Epistles," *JBL* 92 (1973): 549–64.

83. Cf. R. McL. Wilson, *Gnosis and the New Testament* (Philadelphia: Fortress Press, 1968), 41–44; and the comments of Frederik Wisse, "Prolegomena to the Study of the New Testament and Gnosis," in *The New Testament and Gnosis: Essays in Honour of Robert McL. Wilson,* ed. A. H. B. Logan and A. J. M. Wedderburn (Edinburgh: T. & T. Clark, 1983), 142–43.

84. Quoted from *The Nag Hammadi Library in English,* ed. James M. Robinson (San Francisco: Harper & Row, 1977), 53.

85. Cf. Kümmel, *Introduction,* 421–24; Marxsen, *Introduction,* 236–37; Gerhard Krodel, "The First Letter of Peter," in *Hebrews–James–1 and 2 Peter–Jude–Revelation,* PC (Philadelphia: Fortress Press, 1977), 53–59; and Koester, *Introduction* 2:292–93.

86. So A.D. 73–92 is proposed by John H. Elliott, *A Home for the Homeless: A Sociological Exegesis of 1 Peter, Its Situation and Strategy* (Philadelphia: Fortress Press, 1981), 84–89; idem, *1–2 Peter,* ACNT (Minneapolis: Augsburg Pub. House, 1982), 64–66; A.D. 80–100 by Ernest Best, *1 Peter,* NCB (Grand Rapids: Wm. B. Eerdmans, 1971), 63–64; and Raymond E. Brown, "The First Epistle of Peter," in R. E. Brown and J. P. Meier, *Antioch and Rome: New Testament Cradles*

of Catholic Christianity (New York: Paulist Press, 1983), 128–30; A.D. 90–95 by Kümmel, *Introduction,* 425; and A.D. 96 by B. H. Streeter, *The Primitive Church* (New York: Macmillan, 1929), 133–34. Krodel, "The First Epistle of Peter," 59, sets the outer limits as A.D. 80 and 111. An earlier date, between A.D. 65 and 80, is proposed by Leonhard Goppelt, *Der erste Petrusbrief,* MeyerK 12/1, 8th ed. (Göttingen: Vandenhoeck & Ruprecht, 1978), 64–65; and a date shortly after Peter's death (ca. A.D. 65) is proposed by Bo Reicke, *The Epistles of James, Peter, and Jude,* AB 37 (Garden City, N.Y.: Doubleday, 1964), 71–72.

87. The date proposed by these interpreters is usually about the time of Pliny's *Letter to Trajan,* A.D. 112. Such is proposed by John Knox, "Pliny and I Peter: A Note on I Pet 4:14 and 3:15," *JBL* 72 (1953): 187–89; Francis W. Beare, *The First Epistle of Peter,* 3d ed. (Oxford: Basil Blackwell, 1970), 28–38; and Koester, *Introduction* 2:293.

88. On such terminology, see Raymond E. Brown, *The Churches the Apostles Left Behind* (New York: Paulist Press, 1984), 15–16.

89. These appear at 1:1, 2, 3 twice, 7, 11 twice, 13, 19; 2:5, 21; 3:15, 16, 18, 21; 4:1, 11, 13, 14; 5:1, 10, 14.

90. These instances are at 1:1, 2, 3 twice, 7, 13; 2:5; 3:21; 4:11.

91. At 2:3, 13 it is not clear whether the term refers to Christ or God. The title "Lord" *(kyrios)* is applied to God at 1:25 and 3:12 twice. It is curious that J. N. D. Kelly has written that the writer "restricts the title 'Lord' " to God, *A Commentary on the Epistles of Peter and Jude,* HNTC (New York: Harper & Row, 1969), 15— a point he contradicts in his commentary on 1:3 and 3:15 (47, 142).

92. Other similarities to Pauline thought (particularly in Romans) on various topics are summarized by Brown, "The First Epistle of Peter," 134–39.

93. Interpreters have said that the thought of the writer is theocentric, not christocentric; cf. Edward G. Selwyn, *The First Epistle of Peter,* 12th ed. (New York: St. Martin's Press, 1947), 76; Eva Kraft, "Christologie und Anthropologie im ersten Petrusbrief," *EvT* 10 (1950/51): 120–26; J. P. Love, "The First Epistle of Peter," *Int* 8 (1954): 63–87; Beare, *The First Epistle of Peter,* 52; and John H. Elliott, *The Elect and the Holy: An Exegetical Examination of I Peter 2:4–10 and the Phrase Basileion Hierateuma,* NovTSup 12 (Leiden: E. J. Brill, 1966), 172. It is of course correct to say that the letter is theocentric; it emphasizes God as creator (4:19), as the one who cares (5:7), has shown mercy (2:10), and to whom the redeemed are finally brought (3:18). There is also a repeated emphasis on doing the will of God (2:15; 3:17; 4:2, 19; cf. 2:20; 3:4). Redemption itself is the work of God in the final analysis, since it is God who destined, revealed, and raised Christ (1:3, 20–21; 3:18b). Yet in terms of the redemptive action, the focus is upon Christ, as indicated in our survey above.

94. But 1 Pet. 3:18 recalls the Pauline statements, "the death he died he died to sin, once for all" (Rom. 6:10) and "[Christ] gave himself for our sins" (Gal. 1:14).

95. The verbal parallels show probable dependence: *"hamartias . . . autos anēnegken"* (1 Pet. 3:18) and *"autos hamartias . . . anēnegken"* (Isa. 53:12).

96. A lengthy treatment, reviewing the history of exegesis and the positions taken, is provided by Selwyn, *The First Epistle of Peter,* 313–62.

97. Cf. *Sanhedrin* 10.3, "The generation of the Flood have no share in the

world to come, nor shall they stand in the judgment." Quoted from *The Mishnah*, ed. Danby, 397.

98. Beare, *The First Epistle of Peter*, 170–73; C. E. B. Cranfield, *I & II Peter and Jude*, TBC (London: SCM Press, 1960), 102–4, 109–10; Leonhard Goppelt, *Theology of the New Testament*, 2 vols. (Grand Rapids: Wm. B. Eerdmans, 1981–82), 2:177–78; and Schillebeeckx, *Christ*, 229–34. That 4:6 can be interpreted in this way (but not 3:19) is held by Reicke, *The Epistles of James, Peter, and Jude*, 109–12, 119; and Best, *I Peter*, 140–45, 155–57.

99. Goppelt, *Theology NT* 2:178. Cf. also idem, *Der erste Petrusbrief*, 246–50, 275.

100. Creedal and liturgical christological traditions can be detected within 1:20; 2:24; 3:18–19, 22; and perhaps elsewhere. Regarding 3:18–19, 22 in particular, see Rudolf Bultmann, "Bekenntnis- und Liedfragmente im ersten Petrusbrief," in *Exegetica: Aufsätze zur Erforschung des Neuen Testaments*, ed. E. Dinkler (Tübingen: J. C. B. Mohr [Paul Siebeck], 1967), 285–97. For a discussion of still other texts, see Krodel, "The First Letter of Peter," 66–72.

101. On the relationship of the community to the larger social setting and on its group consciousness, cf. Elliott, *A Home for the Homeless*, 101–64.

102. At 1:17 it is God the Father who judges. At 4:5, however, the phrase is traditional, as illustrated in Acts 10:42 and 2 Tim. 4:1, where Christ is explicitly named as the one who will judge "the living and the dead."

103. The title appears in papyrus 46, commonly judged to date from ca. A.D. 200, and it is used by Clement of Alexandria, as cited by Eusebius *Ecclesiastical History* 6.14.4.

104. Ibid.

105. Ibid.

106. Ibid. 6.25.11. For other considerations against Pauline authorship and on the history of the question, see Kümmel, *Introduction*, 392–94.

107. At 10:5–7, for example, the author quotes from LXX Ps. 40:6–8 and then at 10:10 picks up the term "body" from 40:5 (LXX Ps. 40:6), which is not found in the Hebrew text. Other cases are cited by George W. Buchanan, *To the Hebrews*, AB 36 (Garden City, N.Y.: Doubleday, 1972), xxviii. One should not conclude, however, that the writer was always dependent on the LXX. A statistical survey on the writer's usage is provided by George Howard, "Hebrews and the Old Testament Quotations," *NovT* 10 (1968): 208–16.

108. These instances are at *1 Clement* 17.1 (from Heb. 11:37) and 32.2–5 (from Heb. 1:3–5; 7:13). Comparisons are shown by B. F. Westcott, *The Epistle to the Hebrews*, 2d ed. (London: Macmillan, 1892), lxii–lxiii; and James Moffatt, *A Critical and Exegetical Commentary on the Epistle to the Hebrews*, ICC (Edinburgh: T. & T. Clark, 1924), xiii–xv.

109. At both 2:3 and 13:7 the readers are reminded of predecessors in the faith, and in 13:7 these predecessors are referred to as having already died.

110. Among others, Erich Grässer, "Der Hebräerbrief, 1938–63," *TRu*, n.s. 30 (1964–65): 152; Kümmel, *Introduction*, 403; Marxsen, *Introduction*, 221–22; Fuller, *A Critical Introduction*, 144–45; and Goppelt, *Theology NT* 2:238. Some interpreters have maintained an earlier date (prior to A.D. 70), including Hugh Montefiore, *A Commentary on the Epistle to the Hebrews*, HNTC (New York:

Harper & Row, 1964), 11–12; F. F. Bruce, *The Epistle to the Hebrews*, NICNT
(Grand Rapids: Wm. B. Eerdmans, 1964), xlii–xliv; Jean Héring, *The Epistle to
the Hebrews* (London: Epworth Press, 1970), xv; and Buchanan, *To the Hebrews*,
256–63. But the arguments for dating the letter so early are refuted by Reginald
H. Fuller, "The Letter to the Hebrews," in *Hebrews–James–1 and 2
Peter–Jude–Revelation*, 3–4; and Raymond E. Brown, "The Epistle to the He-
brews," in Brown and Meier, *Antioch and Rome*, 149–51. Commentators of the
past were also divided over the issue of dating the epistle. Thus, for example,
Westcott, *The Epistle to the Hebrews*, xlii–xliii, placed it prior to A.D. 70, while
Moffatt, *Epistle to the Hebrews*, xxii, placed it in the era A.D. 70–85.

111. The scribal subscription to Codex Alexandrinus (5th century) reads:
"Written to Hebrews from Rome." Various Byzantine texts read: "Written from
Italy."

112. Cf. Kümmel, *Introduction*, 401, who cites various interpreters. To these
can be added Goppelt, *Theology NT* 2:238–39; and Brown, "The Epistle to the
Hebrews," 142–49.

113. The combination "Jesus Christ" appears three times (10:10; 13:8, 21)
and "Christ" twelve times (3:6, 14; 5:5; 6:1; 8:6; 9:11, 14, 24, 28; 10:5, 12;
11:26).

114. Once "Lord" is in an Old Testament quotation but applied to Jesus (1:10);
there are four other instances of the title applied to him (2:3; 7:14; 12:14; 13:20).

115. This occurs at 4:14; 6:6; 7:3; 10:29.

116. In four cases the term is in Old Testament quotations applied to Jesus
(1:5 twice; 2:6; 5:5); there are five other instances (1:2, 8; 3:6; 5:8; 7:28).

117. This appears at 2:17; 3:1; 4:14, 15; 5:5, 10; 6:20; 7:26; 8:1; 9:11.

118. In three cases the term is in Old Testament quotations applied to Jesus
(5:6; 7:17, 21); there are four other instances (7:11, 15, 16; 10:21).

119. Cf. Oscar Cullmann, *The Christology of the New Testament*, rev. ed.
(Philadelphia: Westminster Press, 1963), 94: "Hebrews understands the hu-
manity of Jesus in a more comprehensive way than the Gospels or any other early
Christian writing."

120. Cf. ibid., 98: "We find precisely in Hebrews the boldest of all assertions
of Christ's deity: it could not be asserted more strongly than in Heb. 1:10, in
which the Son is addressed directly as Creator of heaven and earth."

121. Cf. Goppelt, *Theology NT* 2:255. A review of scholarship on the question
of when Christ becomes high priest in the perspective of Hebrews, leading to
the conclusion that he was consecrated as such through his act of offering himself,
is provided by David Peterson, *Hebrews and Perfection: an Examination of the
Concept of Perfection in the 'Epistle to the Hebrews,'* SNTSMS 47 (Cambridge:
Cambridge Univ. Press, 1982), 191–95.

122. The theme of the perfecting of Christ is elucidated well in Peterson,
Hebrews and Perfection, 49–125. According to Peterson, the perfecting of Christ
in Hebrews is a process related to Christ's vocation. He is "perfected" by God
through his life of obedience, sacrificial death, and exaltation to heaven.

123. Cf. the work of James Swetnam, *Jesus and Isaac: A Study of the Epistle
to the Hebrews in the Light of the Aqedah*, AnBib 94 (Rome: Biblical Institute

Press, 1981), 166, 187–88. Swetnam writes that in Hebrews Jesus is the "originator" of salvation.

124. Commentators struggle over 7:27, and no clear resolution seems forthcoming. Cf. Héring, *The Epistle to the Hebrews*, 63–64; and Buchanan, *To the Hebrews*, 130–31.

125. These, of course, are not the only passages which portray Christ as intercessor. A treatment of all such passages, leading to the conclusion that it was a traditional concept, has been made by William R. G. Loader, *Sohn und Hoherpriester: Eine traditionsgeschichtliche Untersuchung zur Christologie des Hebräerbriefes*, WMANT 53 (Neukirchen-Vluyn: Neukirchener Verlag, 1981), 151–60. Cf. also Ferdinand Hahn, *The Titles of Jesus in Christology: Their History in Early Christianity* (Cleveland: World Pub. Co., 1969), 229–39.

126. Cf. Graham Hughes, *Hebrews and Hermeneutics: The Epistle to the Hebrews as a New Testament Example of Biblical Interpretation*, SNTSMS 36 (Cambridge: Cambridge Univ. Press, 1979), 150 n. 50.

127. Cf. ibid., 47, 50–51, 57. Buchanan, *To the Hebrews*, xix, suggests that Hebrews as a whole is a midrash on Psalm 110. But as Hughes points out (144 n. 11), only Ps. 110:1 and 4 are actually cited by Hebrews.

128. Cf. Fred L. Horton, Jr., *The Melchizedek Tradition: A Critical Examination of the Sources to the Fifth Century A.D. and in the Epistle to the Hebrews*, SNTSMS 30 (Cambridge: Cambridge Univ. Press, 1976), 163. But Horton goes too far to say summarily that "Melchizedek . . . has no successor. Rather, Christ's priesthood is of another order, a heavenly order" (164). There is a confusion of categories (successor and order) here. Although not a successor, Christ's priesthood is of the same "order" according to the quotations from Ps. 110:4. "Order" *(taxis)* has to do with the "nature" or "quality" of his priesthood; cf. BAGD, 804. That is, it is established by divine oath (rather than derived from hereditary succession) and eternal (rather than temporal).

129. Ibid., 164: "The author of Hebrews has little interest in Melchizedek *per se.*"

130. Cf. Loader, *Sohn und Hoherpriester*, 212–15.

131. Buchanan, *To the Hebrews*, 128–31, 254, chiefly on the basis of 7:27, concludes that, for the writer of Hebrews, Jesus made an offering for his own sins, as well as for those of others. But this is not possible. First, the author affirms that Jesus was without sin (4:15). Second, the author's point in 7:27 is to make a contrast: The priests of the old covenant made sacrifices *daily* (for their own sins, and then for the sins of others), but Christ made a sacrifice *"once for all" (ephapax)*. Buchanan refers also to the passages in which Christ is spoken of as "perfected" (2:10; 5:8–9; 7:28). But the "perfection" of the Son has to do with his having been consecrated a priest by God through his suffering and return to God, as maintained by Loader, *Sohn und Hoherpriester*, 39–49; and Peterson, *Hebrews and Perfection*, 49–125. The debate over the questions whether the writer of Hebrews thought of Christ as sinless and at what point in Christ's life that would have been so has been extended. Competing positions are found in the essay of Ronald Williamson, "Hebrews 4:15 and the Sinlessness of Jesus," *ExpTim* 86 (1974–75): 4–8; and in an appendix on "The Sinlessness of Christ and His Perfection," to Peterson, *Hebrews and Perfection*, 188–90.

132. Cf. BAGD, 417; Héring, *The Epistle to the Hebrews,* 20; Buchanan, *To the Hebrews,* 35. The NEB renders the verb "breaking the power" of the devil. The verb is also found in *The Epistle of Barnabas* 15.5, where it is said that Christ "put an end to the time of the lawless one." A different verb is used—which does mean "to annihilate" (in this case, the devil's works)—at 1 John 3:8: "the reason the Son of God appeared was to destroy the works of the devil." The verb is *luein.*

133. Cf. Ernst Käsemann, *The Wandering People of God: An Investigation of the Letter to the Hebrews* (Minneapolis: Augsburg Pub. House, 1984), 166–67.

134. Cf. Vincent Taylor, *The Atonement in New Testament Teaching,* 2d ed. (London: Epworth Press, 1945), 103–4.

135. Contra W. E. Brooks, "The Perpetuity of Christ's Sacrifice in the Epistle to the Hebrews," *JBL* 89 (1970): 205–14. A solid refutation of this position is made by V. C. Pfitzner, *Hebrews,* Chi Rho Commentary (Adelaide: Lutheran Pub. House, 1979), 148–49.

136. Cf. Käsemann, *The Wandering People of God,* 231.

137. See the discussion of Paul's use of the *hyper*-formula in chapter 5 (pp. 48–49).

138. Cf. Loader, *Sohn und Hoherpriester,* 254.

139. Cf. C. K. Barrett, "Eschatology in the Epistle to the Hebrews," in *Background of the New Testament,* ed. Davies and Daube, 391.

140. Cf. Hughes, *Hebrews and Hermeneutics,* 66–74.

141. Cf. Bultmann, *Theology NT* 1:168; and Hans Conzelmann, *An Outline of the Theology of the New Testament* (New York: Harper & Row, 1969), 312.

142. Cf. Käsemann, *The Wandering People of God,* 37–48; Bultmann, *Theology NT* 2:167; and Erich Grässer, *Der Glaube im Hebräerbrief,* Marburger Theologische Studien 2 (Marburg: Elwert Verlag, 1965), 35, 39, 62–63, 70, 117–25.

143. The statement in 2:9 (that Christ tasted death "for every one") is the closest the author comes to the concept of Christ's work as effective for all people, but in the context of the whole letter it has potential significance only.

144. Cf., for example, Conzelmann, *Outline,* 306.

145. It has been said that Hebrews presents an "argued christology," a christology not of "address" but of "argumentation." So Herbert Braun, "Die Gewinnung der Gewissheit im Hebräerbrief," *TLZ* 96 (1971): 325.

146. This remains so even if one rightly stresses the eschatological "today" (4:7) and the sense of presence of the grace of God as the basis for salvation, as does Erich Grässer, "Zur Christologie des Hebräerbriefes: Eine Auseinandersetzung mit Herbert Braun," in *Neues Testament und christliche Existenz: Festschrift für Herbert Braun zum 70. Geburtstag am 4. Mai 1973,* ed. Hans Dieter Betz and Luise Schottroff (Tübingen: J. C. B. Mohr [Paul Siebeck], 1973), 205–6.

147. Bultmann, *Theology NT* 2:168.

148. Interpreters who share these points generally include R. H. Charles, *A Critical and Exegetical Commentary on the Revelation of St. John,* ICC, 2 vols. (Edinburgh: T. & T. Clark, 1920), 1:xxii; G. B. Caird, *A Commentary on the Revelation of St. John the Divine,* HNTC (New York: Harper & Row, 1966), 3–6; G. R. Beasley-Murray, *The Book of Revelation,* NCB (London: Oliphants, 1974), 32–38; Kümmel, *Introduction,* 466–72; Marxsen, *Introduction,* 277–78; Fuller,

A *Critical Introduction*, 187–88; and Koester, *Introduction* 2:250–51. A date of A.D. 90–100 and composition by John the Elder is proposed by Austin Farrer, *The Revelation of St. John the Divine* (Oxford: Clarendon Press, 1964), 32–50. A bold proposal that the book was composed in stages up to A.D. 70 (a core document containing a message of John the Baptist recorded by a disciple, supplemented by an interpretation, and then a final redaction) has been proposed by J. Massyngberde Ford, *Revelation*, AB 38 (Garden City, N.Y.: Doubleday, 1975), 28–57. This proposal is highly speculative, and it is asserted rather than maintained through a discussion of relevant factors brought to light by other investigators.

149. The most extensive study of the christological titles in the book is that of Traugott Holtz, *Die Christologie der Apokalypse des Johannes*, TU 85 (Berlin: Akademie Verlag, 1962), 5–26. It has been proposed that christological titles and perspectives differ even within Revelation itself, and that the differences can be attributed to the use of a source (a non-Christian Jewish apocalypse, 4:1—22:7) and a Christian framework (1:1—3:22; 22:8–21), by Sarah A. Edwards, "Christological Perspectives in the Book of Revelation," in *Christological Perspectives*, ed. Berkey and Edwards, 139–54. Actually the alleged differences cited by Edwards are used to make a case that such a source and framework exist. The points made, however, appear to be overdrawn. To take one example, the term *kyrios* ("Lord") at 14:13 must not, in her account, refer to Jesus as the Christ; this view is most improbable.

150. The term "Christ" or "Jesus Christ" (never "Christ Jesus") appears at 1:1, 2, 5; 11:15; 12:10; 20:4, 6; 22:21.

151. Although the term is applied to God fourteen times (1:8; 4:8, 11; 11:4, 15, 17; 15:3, 4; 16:7; 18:8; 19:6; 21:22; 22:5, 6), it applies to Christ at 11:8; 14:13; 17:14; 19:16; 22:20, 21. Cf. also 1:10 where the adjective "dominical" is used in reference to Christ ("the Lord's day").

152. Once (at 21:27) there is an alternative reading, but we include this verse, since the term is strongly attested in the witnesses. The instances are at 5:6, 8, 12, 13; 6:1, 16; 7:9, 10, 14, 17; 12:11; 13:8; 14:1, 4 twice, 10; 15:3; 17:14 twice; 19:7, 9; 21:9, 14, 22, 23, 27; 22:1, 3.

153. The term "lamb" (*amnos*) appears in reference to Christ at Acts 8:32 and 1 Pet. 1:19 as well. Paul speaks also of Christ as the paschal lamb having been sacrificed (1 Cor. 5:7), but does not actually use the term *amnos;* he uses *pascha.*

154. Cf. Charles, *Revelation of St. John* 1:137–38; and Caird, *Revelation of St. John the Divine*, 70–72. Caird reviews four possible meanings of what the scroll represents and concludes that this is the most fitting.

155. Charles, *Revelation of St. John* 1:lxv–lxxxiii, lists scores of allusions to the Old Testament. He writes: "Our author never definitely makes a quotation, though he continually incorporates phrases and clauses of the O.T." (lxvi).

156. This seems more probable than the suggestion that the passage alludes to regulations for holy war, as suggested by Caird, *Revelation of St. John the Divine,* 179.

157. This is in agreement with ibid.

158. The theme of priesthood as a gift bestowed on all of the redeemed is treated by Elisabeth Schüssler Fiorenza, *Priester für Gott: Studien zum Herr-*

schafts- und Priestermotiv in der Apokalypse, NTAbh, n.s. 7 (Münster: Verlag Aschendorf, 1972).

159. So Goppelt, *Theology NT* 2:186–88; cf. Kümmel, *Introduction,* 462.

160. It is not clear whether it is Michael or God who throws Satan down in 12:9. The passive voice ("he was thrown down"), however, suggests that God is the actor. Other reasons are proposed by Beasley-Murray, *The Book of Revelation,* 203.

161. For a crisp survey of the various possible meanings of 666, concluding that it most likely represents Nero, see ibid., 219–21.

162. On the future ("not yet") perspective of redemption in Revelation, see Elisabeth Schüssler Fiorenza, *The Book of Revelation: Justice and Judgment* (Philadelphia: Fortress Press, 1985), 4, 48–51.

163. Cf. Goppelt, *Theology NT* 2:194.

164. Matthias Rissi, *The Future of the World: An Exegetical Study of Revelation 19:11—22:15,* SBT 23 (London: SCM Press, 1972), 80.

165. Ibid., 81–82.

166. Ibid., 83.

167. Cf. Caird, "The Theology of the Book of Revelation," in *Revelation of St. John the Divine,* 300.

168. Schüssler Fiorenza, *The Book of Revelation,* 52; for more on the universal scope of redemption, see her comments on 55–56, 68, 74, 76. Cf. also Holtz, *Die Christologie der Apokalypse des Johannes,* 204, 212.

169. Cf. Bultmann, *Theology NT* 2:174.

170. Schillebeeckx, *Christ,* 461.

171. Suetonius *Domitian* 13. The text is provided by C. K. Barrett, *The New Testament Background: Selected Documents* (London: SPCK, 1956; New York: Harper & Row, 1961), 19.

172. Cf. Col. 1:12–13; Eph. 1:11, 20–23; 3:11; 1 Tim. 2:4; Titus 2:11; 3:5; 1 Pet. 1:2–3; Heb. 2:9; Rev. 5:1–8.

173. On the preexistence of Christ in the documents, see Col. 1:15–17; Eph. 1:4; 4:9–10; 1 Tim. 3:16; Titus 3:4; 1 Pet. 1:20; Heb. 1:2; 2:10; Rev. 22:13. That all of these passages affirm preexistence is disputed by James D. G. Dunn, *Christology in the Making: A New Testament Inquiry into the Origins of the Doctrine of the Incarnation* (Philadelphia: Westminster Press, 1980). He grants that Revelation assumes the preexistence of Christ (247), but he denies that such a concept can be found in the passages cited for Ephesians (186–87, 238), the Pastorals (237), 1 Peter (236–37), and even for Col. 1:15–20 (187–94) and the Epistle to the Hebrews (54, 237)! As indicated in chap. 1 (pp. 6–8) of this book, Dunn also claims that the writings of the apostle Paul lack the concept as well. The criticism that I made on those pages and the accompanying notes applies to Dunn's judgment about these other passages as well.

174. The theme is explored above all in the work of Gustaf Aulén, *Christus Victor: An Historical Study of the Three Main Types of the Idea of the Atonement* (London: SPCK, 1931). He treats the fathers on 32–76 and New Testament writers on 77–96.

175. Quoted from *Prayers We Have in Common: Agreed Liturgical Texts Pre-*

pared by the International Consultation on English Texts, 2d ed. (Philadelphia: Fortress Press, 1975), 22.

176. Cf. the use of "sins" *(hamartiai)* at Col. 1:14; Eph. 2:1; 1 Tim. 5:22, 24; 2 Tim. 3:6; Heb. 1:3; 9:28; 10:12; 1 Pet. 2:24; 3:18; Rev. 1:5; "trespasses" at Col. 2:14; Eph. 2:1; and "iniquity" at Titus 2:14.

177. Cf. the use of the noun *apolytrōsis* at Col. 1:14; Eph. 1:7; the verb *lytroō* at Titus 2:14; 1 Pet. 1:18; the noun *lytrōsis* at Heb. 9:12; and the verb *agorazō* at Rev 5:9.

178. The *hyper*-formula is used concerning persons at Eph. 5:2, 25; 1 Tim. 2:6; Titus 2:14; Heb. 2:9; and 1 Pet. 2:21; it is used concerning sins at Heb. 10:12; 1 Pet. 3:18.

179. The term "sin" in the singular also appears at Heb. 9:26, 28. Yet Christ was offered "to bear the sins of many" (9:28).

180. Cf. Col. 1:13; 2:13; 3:4; Eph. 1:7; 2:1, 5–6, 8; 2 Tim. 1:9; Titus 3:5; 1 Pet. 1:3, 23; Heb. 6:4–5; 9:26; 12:22–24; Rev. 1:5; 5:9–10.

181. That Christ gave himself for all, or for humanity, in his death is affirmed in 1 Tim. 2:6 (cf. 2:4; 4:10); 1 Pet. 3:18 (cf. 2:24); Heb. 2:9; Rev. 5:13. That Christ has reconciled all things to God or to himself is affirmed in Col. 1:20; Eph. 1:10.

182. Such views and others were held by critics of Christianity from the second to the fourth centuries; they are described and documentd by Robert L. Wilken, *The Christians as the Romans Saw Them* (New Haven: Yale Univ. Press, 1984).

183. Cf. C. F. D. Moule, "The Influence of Circumstances on the Use of Christological Terms," in *Essays in New Testament Interpretation* (Cambridge: Cambridge Univ. Press, 1982), 179–83. The essay is reprinted from *JTS*, n.s. 10 (1959): 247–63. Cf. also Reginald H. Fuller, *The Foundations of New Testament Christology* (New York: Charles Scribner's Sons, 1965), 87–89, for a survey of terminology related to the emperor cult and the conclusion (89): "There is little or no direct introduction of vocabulary from that source."

184. Cf. Col. 1:15–18a; Eph. 2:14–16; 1 Tim. 3:16; 2 Tim. 2:11–13; 1 Pet. 2:22, 24; 3:18, 22; Heb. 1:3; Rev. 5:9–10.

CHAPTER 8

1. Interpreters are generally agreed and confident about the time of composition, but they are less certain about the place. Those who either tend toward or are fairly certain about Syria at the close of the first century include Werner G. Kümmel, *Introduction to the New Testament,* rev. ed. (Nashville: Abingdon Press, 1975), 246–47; and Helmut Koester, *Introduction to the New Testament,* 2 vols. (Philadelphia: Fortress Press; Berlin: Walter de Gruyter, 1982), 2:185. Those who tend toward or are fairly certain about Ephesus at the close of the first century include Raymond E. Brown, *The Gospel according to John,* AB 29–29A, 2 vols. (Garden City, N.Y.: Doubleday, 1966–70), 1:lxxx–lxxxvi, ciii–civ; and C. K. Barrett, *The Gospel according to St. John,* 2d ed. (Philadelphia: Westminster Press, 1978), 123–34. Two scholars who do not suggest a date (but by implication place it late in the first century) and yet propose Ephesus as the place of composition are C. H. Dodd, *The Interpretation of the Fourth Gospel* (Cam-

bridge: Cambridge Univ. Press, 1953), 3–9, 444–53; and Rudolf Schnackenburg, *The Gospel according to St. John,* 3 vols. (New York: Herder & Herder; Seabury; Crossroad, 1968–82), 1:149–52. Either Ephesus or Syria is said to be possible by Barnabas Lindars, *The Gospel of John,* NCB (London: Oliphants, 1972), 42–44; and Reginald H. Fuller, *A Critical Introduction to the New Testament* (London: G. Duckworth, 1966), 176–77. The close of the first century, but uncertainty of place of composition, is also held by Oscar Cullmann, *The Johannine Circle* (Philadelphia: Westminster Press, 1976), 95–99. A survey and assessment of research on the rise of the Gospel of John, covering studies up to the mid-1970s, is provided by Robert Kysar, *The Fourth Evangelist and His Gospel: An Examination of Contemporary Scholarship* (Minneapolis: Augsburg Pub. House, 1975), 86–101, 166–72. A theory of the rise of the Fourth Gospel through five stages (oral tradition, development of the tradition into Johannine patterns of thought, the writing of a gospel, its revision, and its redaction) has been proposed by Brown, *The Gospel according to John* 1:xxxiv–xl.

2. Twice the term is linked with Jesus (so "Jesus Christ," 1:17; 17:3); otherwise "Christ" appears at 1:20, 25, 41; 3:28; 4:25, 29; 7:26, 27, 31, 41 twice, 42; 9:22; 10:24; 11:27; 12:34; 20:13.

3. "Son of man" appears at 1:51; 3:13, 14; 5:27; 6:27, 53, 62; 8:28; 9:35; 12:23, 34 twice; 13:31.

4. "Lord" *(kyrios)* is a designation for God at 1:23; 12:13, 38 twice, and it probably means no more than "sir" or "master" eight times (4:11, 15, 19, 49; 5:7; 9:36; 12:21; 13:16). The term is applied as a christological title at 4:1; 6:23, 34, 68; 9:38; 11:2, 3, 12, 21, 27, 32, 34, 39; 13:6, 9, 13, 14, 25, 36, 37; 14:5, 8, 22; 20:2, 13, 18, 20, 25, 28; 21:7 twice, 12, 15, 16, 17, 20, 21. To these thirty-seven instances another might be added (8:11), although it is in a pericope not attested in the earliest witnesses. If it is included (as in the twenty-sixth edition of the Nestle-Aland Greek New Testament and in the RSV), the total is then thirty-eight instances.

5. "Son of God" appears at 1:34, 49; 3:18; 5:25; 10:36; 11:4, 27; 19:7; 20:31.

6. These are at 1:18; 3:16, 17, 35, 36 twice; 5:19 twice, 20, 21, 22, 23 twice; 5:26; 6:40; 8:36; 14:13; 17:1 twice.

7. Cf. Ferdinand Hahn, *The Titles of Jesus in Christology: Their History in Early Christianity* (Cleveland: World Pub. Co., 1969), 314; and Schnackenburg, *The Gospel according to St. John* 2:172–86.

8. At 1:1 three times and at 1:14.

9. Jesus is also designated a "prophet" at 4:19, 44; 7:52; 9:17, but in these instances "*the* prophet" as the meaning is not indicated.

10. Surveys are made by Oscar Cullmann, *The Christology of the New Testament,* rev. ed. (Philadelphia: Westminster Press, 1963), 30–38; Hahn, *Titles of Jesus,* 372–88; and Reginald H. Fuller, *The Foundations of New Testament Christology* (New York: Charles Scribner's Sons, 1965), 167–73. Both Cullmann (37) and Hahn (383) indicate that for John the title is not regarded simply as a "popular" one, but is of significance for the Fourth Evangelist himself. The background of the concept in Jewish sources is surveyed in brief by J. Louis Martyn, *History and Theology in the Fourth Gospel,* rev. ed. (Nashville: Abingdon Press, 1979), 106–11. A major treatment is by H. M. Teeple, *The Mosaic Escha-*

tological Prophet, SBLMS 10 (Philadelphia: Society of Biblical Literature, 1957). The most significant work, surveying Jewish traditions and the Johannine usage, is by Wayne A. Meeks, *The Prophet-King: Moses Traditions and the Johannine Christology,* NovTSup 14 (Leiden: E. J. Brill, 1967).

11. The use of the language of kingship in John is surveyed by Marinus de Jonge, "Jesus as Prophet and King in the Fourth Gospel," in *Jesus: Stranger from Heaven and Son of God: Jesus Christ and the Christians in Johannine Perspective,* SBLSBS 11 (Missoula, Mont.: Scholars Press, 1977), 49–76 (esp. 58–69).

12. Yet it has been correctly observed that the function of the Son of Man as judge at his parousia in the Synoptics has its counterpart in John 5:27–29, at which it is said that he will function as judge at the resurrection. This observation has been made by Robert Maddox, "The Function of the Son of Man in the Gospel of John," in *Reconciliation and Hope: New Testament Essays on Atonement and Eschatology Presented to L. L. Morris on His 60th Birthday,* ed. Robert Banks (Grand Rapids: Wm. B. Eerdmans, 1974), 203–4.

13. Cf. Martyn, *History and Theology in the Fourth Gospel,* 139; Barnabas Lindars, "The Son of Man in the Johannine Christology," in *Christ and the Spirit in the New Testament: In Honour of Charles Francis Digby Moule,* ed. B. Lindars and S. S. Smalley (Cambridge: Cambridge Univ. Press, 1973), 57; idem, *Jesus Son of Man: A Fresh Examination of the Son of Man Sayings in the Gospels in the Light of Recent Research* (London: SPCK, 1983; Grand Rapids: Wm. B. Eerdmans, 1984), 153–54. The theme of descent/ascent is treated specifically in the work of Godfrey C. Nicholson, *Death as Departure: The Johannine Descent-Ascent Schema,* SBLDS 63 (Chico, Calif.: Scholars Press, 1983).

14. Cf. Ernst Haenchen, *John,* Hermeneia, 2 vols. (Philadelphia: Fortress Press, 1984), 1:96. A slight difference in nuance is posited by Johannes Reidl, *Das Heilswerk Jesu nach Johannes,* Freiburger Theologische Studien 93 (Freiburg: Herder, 1973), 50–58. According to him, *pempō* is used to designate the "inner" or supratemporal side of the Father's sending of the Son, and *apostellō* is used to designate the "outer" or temporal side.

15. The verb *apostellō* is used seventeen times: 3:17, 34; 5:36, 38; 6:29, 57; 7:29; 8:42; 10:36; 11:42; 17:3, 8, 18, 21, 23, 25; 20:31. The verb *pempō* is used twenty-four times: 4:34; 5:23, 24, 30, 37; 6:38, 39, 44; 7:16, 18, 28, 33; 8:16, 18, 26, 29; 9:4; 12:44, 45, 49; 13:20; 14:24; 15:21; 16:5.

16. The verb *hypagō* is used fourteen times: 7:33; 8:14, 21, 22; 13:3, 33, 36 twice; 14:4, 5; 16:5 twice, 10, 17. The verb *poreuomai* is used six times: 14:2, 3, 12, 28; 16:7, 28.

17. Haenchen, *John* 1:96.

18. "Life" appears at 1:4; 5:24b, 26, 29, 40; 6:33, 35, 48, 51, 53, 63; 8:12; 10:10; 11:25; 14:6; 20:31.

19. "Eternal life" appears at 3:15, 16, 36; 4:14, 36; 5:24, 39; 6:27, 40, 47, 54, 68; 10:28; 12:25, 50; 17:2, 3.

20. "Life" appears at Mark 9:43, 45//Matt. 18:8; Matt. 7:14; 18:9; 19:17; and "eternal life" appears at Mark 10:17//Matt. 19:16//Luke 10:25 and 18:18; Mark 10:30//Luke 18:30; Matt. 19:9, 29; 25:46.

21. These interpreters include Dodd, *The Interpretation of the Fourth Gospel,* 148; Rudolf Bultmann, *The Gospel of John* (Philadelphia: Westminster Press,

1971), 257–62; Brown, *The Gospel according to John* 1:cxx; idem, *The Community of the Beloved Disciple* (New York: Paulist Press, 1979), 50; Schnackenburg, *The Gospel according to St. John* 2:426–37; and Josef Blank, *Krisis: Untersuchungen zur johanneischen Christologie und Eschatologie* (Freiburg: Lambertus, 1964), 343–46.

22. Cf. J. Terence Forestall, *The Word of the Cross: Salvation as Revelation in the Fourth Gospel*, AnBib 57 (Rome: Biblical Institute Press, 1974), 74–82.

23. Ibid., 157–66. Cf. also W. R. G. Loader, "The Central Structure of Johannine Christology," *NTS* 30 (1984): 199.

24. Cf., among others, Rudolf Bultmann, *Theology of the New Testament*, 2 vols. (New York: Charles Scribner's Sons, 1951–55), 2:53–55; Barrett, *The Gospel according to St. John*, 81; and M. de Jonge, "Variety and Development in Johannine Christology," in *Jesus: Stranger from Heaven and Son of God*, 210.

25. Cf. Blank, *Krisis*, 83–84; Barrett, *The Gospel according to St. John*, 72; Hans Conzelmann, *An Outline of the Theology of the New Testament* (New York: Harper & Row, 1969), 348; and Ernst Käsemann, *The Testament of Jesus: A Study of the Gospel of John in the Light of Chapter 17* (Philadelphia: Fortress Press, 1968), 10, 18–19.

26. Loader, "The Central Structure of Johannine Christology," 198.

27. The term "to judge" can have the meaning "to condemn" in the Fourth Gospel, as most certainly here and also at 3:17, 18; 12:47; 16:11. Cf. BAGD, 451–52.

28. Cf. Käsemann, *The Testament of Jesus*, 40, 47, 53, 63; and Forestall, *The Word of the Cross*, 101–2, 190–93.

29. Cf. Bultmann, *Theology NT* 2:74; Conzelmann, *Outline*, 339; Werner G. Kümmel, *The Theology of the New Testament: According to Its Main Witnesses, Jesus-Paul-John* (Nashville: Abingdon Press, 1973), 304–6; and Käsemann, *The Testament of Jesus*, 25: "Faith means one thing only: to know who Jesus is."

30. Particularly by Bultmann, *Theology NT* 2:10–14. He describes the so-called gnostic redeemer myth at 1:66–67. The existence of such a myth so early has been challenged by Carsten Colpe, *Die religionsgeschichtliche Schule: Darstellung und Kritik ihres Bildes vom gnostischen Erlösermythos*, FRLANT 78 (Göttingen: Vandenhoeck & Ruprecht, 1961); and more recently by Kurt Rudolph, *Gnosis: The Nature and History of Gnosticism* (San Francisco: Harper & Row, 1983), 121–31.

31. This statement hardly does justice to the energies expended by scholars and to the nuances of the various positions, but to say more would involve entry into a field of study that is beyond the scope of our discussion. The major works are those of Martyn, *History and Theology in the Fourth Gospel;* idem, "Glimpses into the History of the Johannine Community," in *The Gospel of John in Christian History: Essays for Interpreters* (New York: Paulist Press, 1979), 90–121; and Brown, *The Community of the Beloved Disciple*. Drawing upon the works of Martyn, Brown, and others, and making its own contribution, is the monograph by Rodney A. Whitacre, *Johannine Polemic: The Role of Tradition and Theology*, SBLDS 67 (Chico, Calif.: Scholars Press, 1982).

32. Brown, *The Community of the Beloved Disciple*, 67.

33. Cf. Martyn, *History and Theology in the Fourth Gospel,* 72, 78–81; idem, "Glimpses into the History of the Johannine Community," 104–5.

34. C. K. Barrett, "Christocentric or Theocentric? Observations on the Theological Method of the Fourth Gospel," in *Essays on John* (Philadelphia: Westminster Press, 1982), 8. Cf. also Schnackenburg *The Gospel according to St. John* 2:185.

35. Barrett, *The Gospel according to St. John,* 72–73.

36. Cf. the work of Philip B. Harner, *The "I Am" of the Fourth Gospel: A Study in Johannine Usage and Thought,* FBBS 26 (Philadelphia: Fortress Press, 1970), 6–26; and Schnackenburg, *The Gospel according to St. John* 2:83–86.

37. Cf. Schnackenburg, *The Gospel according to St. John,* 2:42, who provides a saying from the midrash on Eccl. 1:9, "As the first redeemer brought down manna, Ex 16:4, so will the last redeemer bring down manna—see Ps 72:16." On the imagery of the messianic shepherd-king, see Isa. 40:11; Ezek. 34:11–24; 37:24.

38. Cf. Brown, *The Gospel according to John* 1:534; and Schnackenburg, *The Gospel according to St. John* 2:88.

39. Nils A. Dahl, "The Johannine Church and History," in *Jesus in the Memory of the Early Church* (Minneapolis: Augsburg Pub. House, 1976), 115, has written: "What John sees already latent in pre-Christian mankind is simply the duality which appears in the attitude taken to Christ. The whole outlook of the Fourth Gospel is characterized by its consistent christocentricity. The sin of the world is its self-assertion against the Word by which it was created, the Word who was in the beginning with God and who became flesh and dwelt among us. The conflict between light and darkness, between Christ and the world, is the one essential theme of history. The incarnation of Christ brought the conflict into the open."

40. This is said in spite of John 20:31. The heavy concentration on churchly concerns (christology, sacraments, unity, the role of the Spirit, etc.) and the polemical tone (against unbelief, the world, and the Jews) do not commend the book for missionary purposes. Even 20:31 may attest its purpose as other than a missionary one: to strengthen faith so that the believer continues in it. Cf. Barrett, *The Gospel according to St. John,* 134–41; Brown, *The Gospel according to John* 1:lxxvii–lxxxix; Cullmann, *The Johannine Circle,* 12–14; M. de Jonge, "The Fourth Gospel: The Book of the Disciples," in *Jesus: Stranger from Heaven and Son of God,* 1–2; and Conzelmann, *Outline,* 331–32. Another view, that the purpose of John was in fact to win a people (specifically, Greek-speaking diaspora Judaism) to the faith, has been suggested by J. A. T. Robinson, "The Destination and Purpose of St. John's Gospel," in *Twelve New Testament Studies,* SBT 34 (London: SCM Press, 1962), 107–125.

41. Kümmel, *The Theology NT,* 262–63.

42. Cf. Brown, *The Community of the Beloved Disciple,* 43, who speaks of "the antagonistic overtones of Johannine christology."

43. Cf. Maurice F. Wiles, *The Spiritual Gospel: The Interpretation of the Fourth Gospel in the Early Church* (Cambridge: Cambridge Univ. Press, 1960); and T. E. Pollard, *Johannine Christology and the Early Church,* SNTSMS 13 (Cambridge: Cambridge Univ. Press, 1970).

44. That all three epistles were written by the same author is affirmed by Kümmel, *Introduction*, 449–51; Fuller, *A Critical Introduction*, 179; and Raymond E. Brown, *The Epistles of John*, AB 30 (Garden City, N.Y.: Doubleday, 1982), 14–19; idem, *The Community of the Beloved Disciple*, 94. The question is left undecided (and considered not capable of a certain answer) by Rudolf Bultmann, *The Johannine Epistles*, Hermeneia (Philadelphia: Fortress Press, 1973), 1; Willi Marxsen, *Introduction to the New Testament* (Philadelphia: Fortress Press, 1968), 269; and Koester, *Introduction* 2:195–96.

45. That the letters share a common authorship with the Gospel is affirmed by Kümmel, *Introduction*, 442–45, 449–51; and J. A. T. Robinson, "The Destination and Purpose of the Johannine Epistles," in *Twelve New Testament Studies*, 126. That none of the letters was written by the Fourth Evangelist is the view of Bultmann, *The Johannine Epistles*, 1; Marxsen, *Introduction*, 264, 269; Brown, *The Community of the Beloved Disciple*, 95; idem, *The Epistles of John*, 19–30.

46. Brown, *The Community of the Beloved Disciple*, 94–97; idem, *The Epistles of John*, 14–30.

47. This is delineated well by de Jonge, "Variety and Development in Johannine Christology," 200–206.

48. This is summarized by Brown, *The Community of the Beloved Disciple*, 109–35.

49. Cf. Bultmann, *The Johannine Epistles*, 1; and Brown, *The Community of the Beloved Disciple*, 97.

50. The term "the Son" appears at 1 John 1:3, 7; 2:22, 23 twice, 24; 3:23; 4:9, 10, 14; 5:9, 10, 11, 12, 20; 2 John 9.

51. The full phrase "the Son of God" appears at 1 John 3:8; 4:15; 5:5, 10, 12, 13, 20.

52. "Christ" appears at 1 John 1:3; 2:1, 22; 3:23; 4:2; 5:1, 6, 20; 2 John 3, 7, 9. In one Greek witness (codex B) it also appears at 4:15.

53. The term "the Holy One" could refer to either God or Jesus at 1 John 2:20, but it most likely refers to Jesus, as various interpreters have concluded. A survey of opinions and conclusions is made by Brown, *The Epistles of John*, 347–48.

54. While the Gospel of John uses two verbs, *apostellō* and *pempō*, for the "sending" of the Son, the letters use only the former.

55. Cf. Brown, *The Community of the Beloved Disciple*, 116–20; idem, *The Epistles of John*, 76–79.

56. Cf. J. A. T. Robinson, "The Destination and Purpose of the Johannine Epistles," 133–34. He writes that since the teaching of the opponents "denies the reality of sin it denies that anything has to be done about sin which takes sin seriously; it denies the necessity of expiation through the blood of Christ as the only way to become pure as he is pure; and hence it denies the need for the Incarnation."

57. Cf. Brown, *The Epistles of John*, 612–19.

58. Cf. Koester, *Introduction* 2:194.

CHAPTER 9

1. Cf. Rudolf Bultmann, *The History of the Synoptic Tradition*, 2d ed. (New York: Harper & Row, 1968), 349; Vincent Taylor, *The Person of Christ in New*

Testament Teaching (New York: St. Martin's Press, 1958), 8; Philipp Vielhauer, "Erwägungen zur Christologie des Markusevangeliums," in *Zeit und Geschichte: Dankesgabe an Rudolf Bultmann zum 80. Geburtstag,* ed. Erich Dinkler (Tübingen: J. C. B. Mohr [Paul Siebeck], 1964), 156; Hans Conzelmann, *An Outline of the Theology of the New Testament* (New York: Harper & Row, 1969), 144; and James D. G. Dunn, *Christology in the Making: A New Testament Inquiry into the Origins of the Doctrine of the Incarnation* (Philadelphia: Westminster Press, 1980), 46–48. An attempt (unsuccessful, in our view) to maintain that Mark did have a concept of preexistence has been made by Johannes Schreiber, "Die Christologie des Markusevangeliums: Beobachtungen zur Theologie und Komposition des zweiten Evangeliums," *ZTK* 58 (1961): 166–67.

2. Cf. Oscar Cullmann, *The Earliest Christian Confessions* (London: Lutterworth Press, 1949).

3. The influence of liturgy on the selection and use of christological terms is surveyed by C. F. D. Moule, "The Influence of Circumstances on the Use of Christological Terms," *JTS,* n.s. 10 (1959): 247–63; reprinted in *Essays in New Testament Interpretation* (Cambridge: Cambridge Univ. Press, 1982), 165–83. The relevant pages are 166–73 in the latter.

4. Pliny the Younger *Epistles* 10.96.7.

5. A survey of Jewish sources which ascribe divine attributes and functions to intermediaries is contained in Maurice Casey, "Chronology and Development of Pauline Christology," in *Paul and Paulinism: Essays in Honour of C. K. Barrett,* ed. M. D. Hooker and S. G. Wilson (London: SPCK, 1982), 124–34. Casey seems to go too far, however, in his assertion that within gentile Christianity the restraint of monotheism (secure in Paul) was removed, allowing for the development of "higher" forms of christology (130, 133). A survey of wisdom traditions which bear upon New Testament christology and the expression of wisdom motifs in christology is provided by Dunn, *Christology in the Making,* 163–212.

6. Cf. Martin Dibelius and Hans Conzelmann, *The Pastoral Epistles,* Hermeneia (Philadelphia: Fortress Press, 1972), 100–103.

7. See the survey of Kurt Rudolph, *Gnosis: The Nature and the History of Gnosticism* (San Francisco: Harper & Row, 1983), 299–308.

8. The major challenge to its existence so early has been made by Carsten Colpe, *Die religionsgeschichtliche Schule: Darstellung und Kritik ihres Bildes vom gnostischen Erlösermythos,* FRLANT 78 (Göttingen: Vandenhoeck & Ruprecht, 1961); and another has been made by Rudolph, *Gnosis,* 121–31. Cf. also the surveys of the myth and assessments of it in regard to the New Testament by Reginald H. Fuller, *The Foundations of New Testament Christology* (New York: Charles Scribner's Sons, 1965), 93–97; Larry W. Hurtado, "The Study of New Testament Christology: Notes for the Agenda," in *Society of Biblical Literature 1981 Seminar Papers,* ed. Kent H. Richards, SBLSPS 20 (Chico, Calif.: Scholars Press, 1981), 188–91; and Kurt Rudolph, "Gnosis and Gnosticism—the Problems of Their Definition and Their Relation to the Writings of the New Testament," in *The New Testament and Gnosis: Essays in Honour of Robert McL. Wilson,* ed. A. H. B. Logan and A. J. M. Wedderburn (Edinburgh: T. & T. Clark, 1983), 21–37 (esp. 28–30).

Notes

CHAPTER 10

1. Cf. Ignatius *To the Ephesians* 19.3; *To the Smyrnaens* 1.1—2.1; *2 Clement* 1.7; Justin Martyr *First Apology* 63; and Irenaeus *Against Heresies* 3.18.7; 5.1.1; 5.19.1–5.21.1.

2. John Knox, *The Humanity and Divinity of Christ: A Study of Pattern in Christology* (Cambridge: Cambridge Univ. Press, 1967), 24.

3. Ignatius *To the Trallians* 9.1. Quoted from *Early Christian Fathers*, trans. and ed. Cyril C. Richardson, LCC 1 (Philadelphia: Westminster Press, 1953), 100.

4. Gregory of Nazianzus *Epistle* 101: "For that which he has not assumed he has not healed." Text in *Christology of the Later Fathers*, trans. and ed. Edward R. Hardy, LCC 3 (Philadelphia: Westminster Press, 1954), 218.

5. Those who deny success in this include Vincent Taylor, *The Person of Christ in New Testament Teaching* (New York: St. Martin's Press, 1958), 96; and E. F. Scott, *The Epistle to the Hebrews* (Edinburgh: T. & T. Clark, 1922), 152. Scott writes that in Hebrews the earthly life of Jesus is "nothing but an interlude in a larger, heavenly life." Those who grant success to the writer include Oscar Cullmann, *The Christology of the New Testament*, rev. ed. (Philadelphia: Westminster Press, 1963), 94; and Knox, *The Humanity and Divinity of Christ*, 42. Going even further, G. B. Caird, "Son by Appointment," in *The New Testament Age: Essays in Honour of Bo Reicke*, ed. William C. Weinrich (Macon, Ga.: Mercer University Press, 1984), 81, has written: "The author of Hebrews has no place in his theology for preexistence as an ontological concept. His essentially human Jesus attains to perfection, to preeminence, and even to eternity."

6. Ernst Käsemann, *The Testament of Jesus: A Study of the Gospel of John in the Light of Chapter 17* (Philadelphia: Fortress Press, 1968), 27; cf. 8–9 and 75.

7. Ibid., 20.

8. James D. G. Dunn, *Christology in the Making: A New Testament Inquiry into the Origins of the Doctrine of the Incarnation* (Philadelphia: Westminster Press, 1980), 59.

9. This theme has been explored by many, including Günther Bornkamm, *Jesus of Nazareth* (New York: Harper & Brothers, 1960), 82–84; Herbert Braun, *Jesus of Nazareth: The Man and His Time* (Philadelphia: Fortress Press, 1979), 105–15; John Riches, *Jesus and the Transformation of Judaism* (New York: Seabury Press, 1981), 98–111; and Leonhard Goppelt, *Theology of the New Testament*, 2 vols. (Grand Rapids: Wm. B. Eerdmans, 1981–82), 1:127–34.

10. Insufficient attention has been given to the deeds of Jesus in this regard. A study which summarizes work up to the time of its writing and also makes its own contribution is that of Norman A. Beck, "Efficacious Symbolic Acts of Jesus Christ during His Public Ministry" (Ph.D. diss., Princeton Theological Seminary, Princeton, N.J., 1967). A book which takes the deeds of Jesus seriously (particularly his act of Temple cleansing) in regard to Jesus' apparent self-understanding and the interpretation of others is that of E. P. Sanders, *Jesus and Judaism* (Philadelphia: Fortress Press, 1985), esp. 294–318, 334–35.

11. See chapter 3 for a discussion of the points made in this paragraph.

CHAPTER 11

1. Three interpreters who have shown ways to interpret such imagery for today are Amos N. Wilder, "Kerygma, Eschatology and Social Ethics," in *The Background of the New Testament and Its Eschatology: In Honour of Charles Harold Dodd*, ed. W. D. Davies and D. Daube (Cambridge: Cambridge Univ. Press, 1956), 527–36; Heinrich Schlier, *Principalities and Powers in the New Testament* (Freiburg: Herder, 1961), 21–39, 56–57 n. 54; and Walter Wink, *Naming the Powers: The Language of Power in the New Testament* (Philadelphia: Fortress Press, 1984), 99–148. The proposal of Wink is to understand the "principalities and powers" in a more down-to-earth manner, essentially as the dynamic (or "spiritual dimension," 103) of institutions. He denies that the "powers" have a "separate, spiritual existence" (105), i.e., separate from institutions. While it must be granted that there are instances in the New Testament where institutions are in view when "the powers" are being spoken of (e.g., at 1 Cor. 2:8), that is not always the case (e.g., at Col.1:16). Wink has said that he has sought in his descriptive work to respect the New Testament "data in all their alienness" (102). But his proposal for interpreting the language of the powers seems to suggest that while the "data" are alien, the "real meaning" of the data is not.

2. John Hick, "Jesus and the World Religions," in *The Myth of God Incarnate*, ed. J. Hick (Philadelphia: Westminster Press, 1977), 180.

3. Ibid., 181.

4. Cf. Patrick Keifert, "Labor Room or Morgue: The Power and Limits of Pluralism and Christology," *Word & World* 5 (1985): 80.

5. These, of course, are lines from the hymn of Martin Luther, "A Mighty Fortress."

6. Michael Goulder, "Jesus the Man of Universal Destiny," in *The Myth of God Incarnate*, ed. Hick, 58.

7. In modern times this approach can be found, for example, in Francis Pieper, *Christian Dogmatics*, 4 vols. (St. Louis: Concordia Pub. House, 1950–57), 3:548–59.

8. Irenaeus *Against Heresies* 3.18.1. Quoted from *The Ante-Nicene Fathers*, ed. Alexander Roberts and James Donaldson, 9 vols. (New York: Christian Literature Co., 1890), 1:446. On the theme of "recapitulation" in Irenaeus, particularly in regard to the consummation, see Gustaf Wingren, *Man and the Incarnation: A Study of the Biblical Theology of Irenaeus* (Philadelphia: Muhlenberg Press, 1959), 192–201.

9. Irenaeus *Against Heresies* 5.21.1. Quoted from *The Ante-Nicene Fathers* 1:549.

10. Athanasius *On the Incarnation* 9. Quoted from *Christology of the Later Fathers*, trans. and ed. Edward R. Hardy, LCC 3 (Philadelphia: Westminster Press, 1954), 63.

11. Quoted from *Prayers of the Eucharist: Early and Reformed*, trans. and ed. R. C. D. Jasper and G. J. Cuming, 2d ed. (New York: Oxford Univ. Press, 1980), 170.

12. Quoted from *The Alternative Service Book 1980: Services Authorized for Use in the Church of England in Conjunction with The Book of Common Prayer* (Cambridge: Cambridge Univ. Press, 1980), 148–49.

13. Quoted from the *Lutheran Book of Worship: Ministers Desk Edition* (Minneapolis: Augsburg Pub. House; Philadelphia: Board of Publication, Lutheran Church in America, 1978), 212.

14. Carl E. Braaten, "The Christian Doctrine of Salvation," *Int* 35 (1981): 131. Cf. also his discussion in "The Uniqueness and Universality of Jesus Christ," in *Christian Dogmatics*, ed. Carl E. Braaten and Robert W. Jenson, 2 vols. (Philadelphia: Fortress Press, 1984), 1:557–69.

15. Quoted from the *Lutheran Book of Worship*, 206.

16. An exception is the section entitled "Christology and Soteriology" in Rudolf Bultmann, *Theology of the New Testament*, 2 vols. (New York: Charles Scribner's Sons, 1951–55), 2:155–202. A limited treatment (devoted only to Paul, Hebrews, and John) is made in the section "Christology and the Work of Christ" of Vincent Taylor's *The Person of Christ in New Testament Teaching* (New York: St. Martin's Press, 1958), 224–32.

Index of Ancient Sources

16:5—60
16:6—62, 63, 73, 169
16:8—60, 62, 169, 226 n. 72

Luke
1:3—77
1:6—80
1:9—80
1:32—235 nn. 80, 82
1:35—235 n. 82
1:41—80
1:43—236 n. 84
1:67—80
1:68—210 n. 26
1:73—210 n. 29
1:76—80
2:11—107, 235 nn. 80, 81; 236 n. 84
2:21—80
2:22-24—80
2:22—236 n. 92
2:26-27—80
2:26—235 n. 81
2:38—210 n. 26
2:39—80
2:49—233 n. 61
3:12—235 n. 80
3:15—235 n. 81
3:22—235 n. 82, 236 n. 92
4:1—236 n. 92
4:3—235 n. 82
4:5-8—204
4:9—235 n. 82
4:14—236 n. 92
4:18—219 n. 9, 236 n. 92
4:24—235 n. 80
4:34—235 n. 80
4:36—236 n. 92
4:41—235 nn. 81, 82
4:43—233 n. 61
5:5—235 n. 80
5:8—236 n. 84
5:12—236 n. 84
5:17—236 n. 92
5:20—84, 170
5:24—84, 170, 235 n. 83
6:5—235 nn. 83, 84
6:19—236 n. 92
6:22—235 n. 83
6:46—236 n. 84
7:6—236 n. 84
7:13—82, 236 nn. 84, 88
7:16—80, 235 n. 80
7:19—70, 236 nn. 84, 88
7:26—80
7:27—80

7:28—14
7:34—235 n. 83
7:40—235 n. 80
7:47-49—84
7:47-48—170
8:24—235 n. 80
8:28—235 n. 82
8:45—235 n. 80
8:48—236 n. 92
9:1—236 n. 92
9:20—235 n. 81
9:22—83, 233 n. 61, 235 n. 83, 236 n. 95
9:26—83, 235 n. 83
9:27—235 n. 75
9:31—83, 84, 237 n. 106
9:33—235 n. 80
9:35—235 n. 82
9:38—235 n. 80
9:44—83, 235 n. 83
9:49—235 n. 80
9:51–19:44—83, 237 n. 106
9:51—83, 237 n. 106
9:54—236 n. 84
9:58—21, 235 n. 83
9:59—236 n. 84
9:60—237 n. 106
9:61—236 n. 84
9:62—237 n. 106
10:1—236 nn. 84, 88
10:9—14
10:16—14
10:17—236 n. 84
10:21-22—14
10:21—236 n. 92
10:22—235 n. 82
10:25—235 n. 80, 255 n. 20
10:38—236 n. 92
10:39—236 nn. 84, 88
10:40—236 n. 84
10:41—236 nn. 84, 88
11:1—236 n. 84
11:2-4—172, 237 n. 106
11:4—184, 210 n. 29
11:28—237 n. 106
11:30—235 n. 83
11:39—236 nn. 84, 88
11:49-51—20
12:2-3—14
12:8-12—237 n. 106
12:8-9—14, 21, 155
12:8—83, 235 n. 83
12:10—21, 235 n. 83
12:13-15—237 n. 106
12:22-34—237 n. 106

12:38-40—235 n. 76
12:39-40—14
12:40—21, 81, 235 n. 83
12:41-48—235 n. 76
12:41-46—14
12:41—236 n. 84
12:42—236 n. 88
12:46—81
12:54-56—235 n. 76
13:15—236 nn. 84, 88
13:23—236 n. 84
13:25—236 n. 84
13:28-30—14
13:33—233 n. 61, 235 n. 80
13:34—20
14:25-27—237 n. 106
14:27—21
16:10-13—237 n. 106
16:16—14, 79-80
16:18—237 n. 106
17:1-6—237 n. 106
17:2—232 n. 44
17:5—236 nn. 84, 88
17:6—236 nn. 84, 88
17:13—235 n. 80
17:20-21—235 n. 75, 237 n. 106
17:20—79
17:21—84
17:22-25—14
17:22—235 n. 83
17:24—235 n. 83
17:25—233 n. 61, 236 n. 95
17:26-30—14, 21, 83
17:26—235 n. 83
17:30—235 n. 83
17:37—236 n. 84
18:6—236 nn. 84, 88
18:8—81, 83, 235 nn. 76, 83
18:15-17—237 n. 106
18:18—255 n. 20
18:24-30—237 n. 106
18:30—255 n. 20
18:31-33—83
18:31—79, 235 n. 83
18:38—235 n. 80
18:39—235 n. 80
18:41—236 n. 84
19:5—233 n. 61
19:7-10—84
19:8—236 nn. 84, 88
19:10—235 n. 83
19:11—81, 235 n. 75
19:12—21

11:8—236 n. 87
11:15–18—19
11:16—236 n. 87
11:17—235 n. 81, 236 n. 85
11:18—81
11:19–20—76
11:20—236 n. 85
11:21—236 n. 87
11:23—236 n. 87
11:24—236 n. 87
13:2—236 n. 86
13:10—236 n. 86
13:11—236 n. 86
13:12—236 n. 86
13:23—107, 235 n. 80
13:26—85
13:27—18
13:33—37, 235 n. 82
13:38—84
13:47—237 n. 105
13:49—236 n. 87
14:3—85, 236 n. 86
14:23—236 n. 86
15:11—236 n. 85
15:17—237 n. 105
15:26—235 n. 81, 236 n. 85
15:35—236 n. 86
15:36—236 n. 86
15:40—236 n. 86
16:18—18, 235 n. 81
16:31—236 n. 85
16:32—236 n. 86
17:3—18, 84, 233 n. 61, 235 n. 81, 236 n. 95
17:30–31—87
17:31—87, 88, 171, 235 n. 80
18:5—235 n. 81
18:8—236 n. 86
18:9—236 n. 86
18:25—80, 236 n. 86
18:28—235 n. 81
19:5—236 n. 85
19:6—80
19:10—236 n. 86
19:13–18, 236 n. 85
19:17—236 n. 85
19:20—236 n. 86
19:21—80, 233 n. 62
20:7—80
20:19—236 n. 86
20:21—81, 235 n. 81, 236 n. 85
20:22—80

20:24—235 n. 81, 236 n. 85
20:28—84
20:32—85
20:35—236 n. 85
21:4—80
21:9—80
21:13—236 n. 85
21:14—236 n. 86
22:8—236 n. 86
22:10—236 n. 86
22:14—235 n. 80
22:19—236 n. 86
23:11—236 n. 86
23:21—233 n. 62
25:8—233 n. 52
26:15—236 n. 86
26:18—84
26:20—87
26:23—18, 84, 235 n. 81
27:24—233 n. 62
28:31—235 n. 81, 236 n. 85

Romans
1:3–4—37, 218 n. 48
1:3—47
1:4—37
1:16—57
1:17—244 n. 68
1:18–2:16—55
3:9—52, 108
3:20—72
3:21–26—52–53
3:21–25—57
3:21—52
3:24—53, 210 n. 26
3:25–26—53
3:25—53, 104, 220 n. 21, 244 n. 68
3:28—57
3:30—244 n. 68
4:17—203
4:25—29, 38, 49, 73, 104
5:1—55, 56
5:6—49, 50, 114, 168
5:8—49, 50, 104, 114, 155, 175
5:9–10—93, 140
5:9—175
5:10—92
5:12–21—53–55, 221 n. 25
5:12–14—54
5:12—92, 108
5:15—53, 54, 220 nn. 24, 25
5:16–17—122

5:16—93
5:17—53, 54, 55, 220 n. 25
5:18–19—54, 93, 110
5:18—53, 54, 200, 220 n. 24
5:19—54, 65, 220 n. 24
5:20–21—50
5:20—54
5:21—92, 108, 221 n. 25
6:1—51
6:2—51
6:4—35, 51, 186
6:5—51
6:6—51
6:8—51
6:10—51, 125, 246 n. 94
6:11—51
6:12–13—92
6:16—55
6:18—50
6:21–23—55
6:23—122
7:13–14—92
7:14—108
7:24—210 n. 29
8:1—55, 56
8:2—92
8:3—7, 49, 50, 93, 114, 175
8:11—35, 186
8:17—178
8:21—57, 200, 221 n. 33
8:23—210 n. 26
8:32—49, 50, 104, 114
8:34—114, 119
8:38–39—56
8:38—93
8:39—75
10:9—112, 186, 226 n. 82
10:17—51
11:3—56
11:16—56
11:17–24—102
11:25–36—102
11:25–32—110, 200
11:25–31—55
11:26—57, 210 nn. 28, 29
11:32—57
12:1—104
13:1–7—204
13:11—112, 140
15:16—56, 221 n. 30
15:18—56
15:31—210 n. 29
16:5—56
16:25–27—218 n. 1

1:8—108, 118, 137, 248
n. 115
1:10—118, 248 nn. 114,
120
1:13—118
1:14—126
2:3—247 n. 109, 248 n.
114
2:5—117, 118, 127
2:6—248 n. 116
2:8—118
2:9—118, 119, 122, 123,
125, 219 n. 7, 250 n.
143, 252 n. 172, 253
nn. 178, 181
2:10—117, 118, 122, 137,
249 n. 131, 252 n. 173
2:14–15—121, 138
2:14—118, 186
2:15—119
2:17—119, 123, 124, 186,
248 n. 117
2:18—121
3:1—118, 126, 140, 248
n. 117
3:6—141, 248 nn. 113,
116
3:8—121
3:13—138
3:14—126, 248 n. 113
4:7—250 n. 146
4:9—119
4:11—125, 140
4:14—118, 122, 141, 248
nn. 115, 117
4:15—121, 122, 186, 248
n. 117, 249 n. 131
5:5–6—175
5:5—37, 118, 119, 248
nn. 113, 116, 117
5:6—119–20, 248 n. 118
5:8–9—118, 249 n. 131
5:8—118, 248 n. 116
5:10—119, 248 n. 117
5:11—117
6:1—127, 248 n. 113
6:4–6—126
6:4–5—126, 127, 139,
253 n. 180
6:4—35, 126, 127
6:5—127
6:6—127, 248 n. 115
6:8—126
6:12—126, 139
6:20—118, 119, 122, 125,
248 n. 117
7:2—120

7:3—120, 121, 248 n. 115
7:4—120
7:6–7—120
7:9–10—120
7:11—119, 121, 248 n.
118
7:13—119, 247 n. 108
7:14—248 n. 114
7:15–16—120
7:15—119, 121, 248 n.
118
7:16—118, 248 n. 118
7:17—119, 120, 248 n.
118
7:20–21—120
7:21—119, 120, 248 n.
118
7:22—118, 124
7:23—120
7:24—120
7:25—119, 125
7:26—118, 122, 248 n.
117
7:27—118, 119, 123, 125,
175, 249 nn. 124, 131
7:28—120, 248 n. 116,
249 n. 131
8:1–2—122
8:1—117, 118, 248 n. 117
8:6—124, 248 n. 113
8:8–12—124
9:5—117
9:7—119
9:11—124, 248 nn. 113,
117
9:12—118, 119, 121, 123,
124, 125, 136, 175, 210
n. 26, 253 n. 177
9:14—4, 119, 121, 123,
124, 248 n. 113
9:15—117, 123, 124, 139,
210 n. 26
9:18–22—124
9:23–26—104
9:24—118, 119, 122, 123,
125, 248 n. 113
9:25—119
9:26—121, 124, 125, 126,
136, 177, 253 nn. 179,
180
9:28—118, 123, 125, 138,
248 n. 113, 253 nn.
176, 179
10:1—119, 124
10:2—121
10:3—119
10:4—121, 124

10:5–7—247 n. 107
10:5—248 n. 113
10:9–10—119
10:9—124
10:10—125, 247 n. 107,
248 n. 113
10:11—121, 124
10:12—104, 118, 121,
123, 125, 248 n. 113,
253 nn. 176, 178
10:13—124
10:14—121
10:17—125
10:19–20—122
10:21—248 n. 118
10:26–31—126
10:26—127
10:29—127, 248 n. 115
10:32—126
10:36—126, 127, 140
11:13—124
11:26—248 n. 113
11:32—117
11:37—247 n. 108
11:39–40—126
12:1—128
12:2—117, 118, 122
12:4—138
12:12—128
12:14—248 n. 114
12:16–17—127
12:22–24—126, 253 n.
180
12:24—117, 124
12:25–26—126
13:7—247 n. 109
13:8—248 n. 113
13:12—118, 124
13:14—127
13:15–16—104
13:20—118, 125, 136,
248 n. 114
13:21—141, 248 n. 13
13:22–26—116
13:22—128
13:24—116, 117

1 Peter
1:1—115, 246 nn. 89, 90
1:2–3—252 n. 172
1:2—35, 141, 246 nn. 89,
90
1:3—35, 113, 114, 139,
246 nn. 89, 90, 91, 93;
253 n. 180
1:4—139, 140, 177, 184
1:7—116, 246 nn. 89, 90
1:8—115

Index of Modern Authors

281